Not For Tourists™ Guide to **WASHINGTON DC**

2005

Not For Tourists Inc New York

published and designed by
Not For Tourists Inc
NFT$_{TM}$—Not For Tourists$_{TM}$ Guide to WASHINGTON DC 2005
www.notfortourists.com

Publisher
Jane Pirone

Information Design
Jane Pirone
Rob Tallia
Scot Covey
Diana Pizzari

Editor
Jane Pirone

Managing Editors
Rob Tallia
Diana Pizzari

City Editor
Janice Darcy

Writing and Editing
Cathleen Cueto
Janice Darcy
Brendan Lynch
Jane Pirone
Diana Pizzari
Rob Tallia

Research
Alli Hirschman
Annie Holt
Erin Kreindler
Sherry Wasserman

Editorial Interns
Jessica Cepelak
Christina Nicholls
Jennifer Spelkoman

Research Interns
Kamilah Jones
Beverley Langevine
Orsiola Mehmeti

Database Design
Scot Covey

Graphic Design/Production
Alexandra Anderson
Scot Covey
Sana Hong
Lisa Lee
Ran Lee
Christopher Salyers
Galina Rybatsky
Danielle Young

Contributors
Kriston Capps
Matthew Gilmore

Printed in China
350 pages
ISBN# 0-9740131-9-6 $16.95
Copyright © 2004 by Not For Tourists, Inc.

Every effort has been made to ensure that the information in this book is as up-to-date as possible at press time. However, many details are liable to change—as we have learned. The publishers cannot accept responsibility for any consequences arising from use of this book.

Dear **NFT**_{TM} User:

The relentless real estate boom is transforming this place thick and fast. So it's about time we had our own guide. The book in your hands isn't one of those tour tomes that care only for The Mall and Georgetown. It's a guide that would actually take note if, say, Tenleytown burned to the ground. It's also a guide with tips and suggestions and maps for us townies. A guide that points out all the interesting newbies we think are worth checking out and, of course, visits the longtime neighborhood favorites.

NFT is landing in DC just as us locals are having trouble keeping up with all the changes. Last week H Street NE was scary, now it's got a theater and farmers market. Could other yuppie accoutrements be far behind? If you haven't been to 8th Street SE in a while, you won't recognize it. And forget trying to pick up hookers along 14th Street NW. The fun there now is all about interior design.

We update annually and we'll need your help to stay current. By this time next year, we could have a new president, a major league baseball team and, more importantly, a newly cool neighborhood. So help us out by sending us your suggestions through wwww.notfortourists.com. Together, we'll keep up.

Here's hoping you find what you need,

Jane, Rob, Diana & Janice

Table of Contents

Map 1 • National Mall

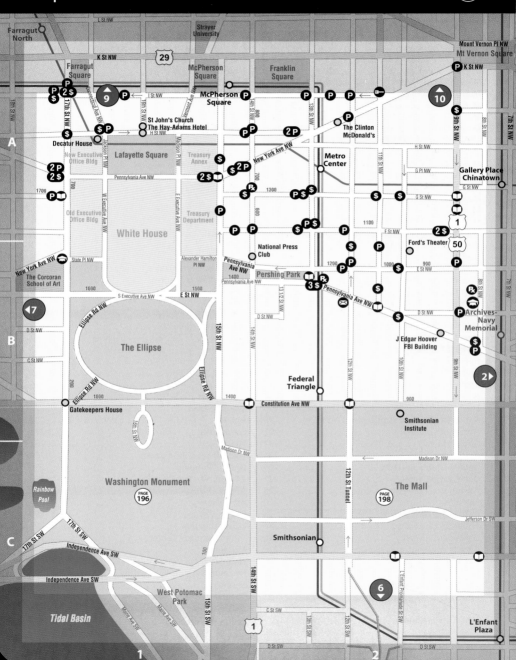

Here are many of the reasons the city's a top tourist destination. The White House, Washington Monument, The Smithsonian—it's a must visit. But it does get old. Tip: Photocopy this map and give it to visiting relatives, then promise to meet them for a drink later along U Street.

$ Banks

- **Bank of America** · 1001 Pennsylvania Ave NW
- **Bank of America** · 1501 Pennsylvania Ave NW
- **Bank of America** · 700 13th St NW
- **Bank of America** · 888 17th St NW
- **BB&T** · 601 13th St NW
- **BB&T** · 815 Connecticut Ave NW
- **Chevy Chase** · 1299 Pennsylvania Ave NW
- **Chevy Chase** · 1717 Pennsylvania Ave NW
- **Citibank** · 1400 G St NW
- **Citibank** · 435 11th St NW
- **Independence Federal Savings** · 1006 E St NW
- **Industrial Bank** · 1317 F St NW
- **Industrial Bank** · 906 9th St NW
- **M&T Bank** · 555 12th St NW
- **National Cooperative** · 1725 I St
- **Riggs** · 1503 Pennsylvania Ave NW
- **Riggs** · 800 17th St NW
- **Sun Trust** · 1100 G St NW
- **Sun Trust** · 1445 New York Ave NW
- **Sun Trust** · 900 17th St NW
- **United Bank** · 1001 G St NW
- **United Bank** · 1275 Pennsylvania Ave NW
- **Wachovia** · 1301 Pennsylvania Ave NW
- **Wachovia** · 1310 G St NW
- **Wachovia** · 1700 Pennsylvania Ave NW
- **Wachovia** · 740 15th St NW
- **Wachovia** · 801 Pennsylvania Ave NW

 Car Rental

- **Hertz** · 901 11th St NW

o Landmarks

- **The Clinton McDonald's** · 1229 New York Ave NW
- **Decatur House** · 748 Jackson Place NW
- **Ford's Theater** · 511 10th St NW
- **Gatekeepers House** · 17th St NW & Constitution Ave NW
- **The Hay-Adams Hotel** · 16th St & H St NW
- **J Edgar Hoover FBI Building** · 935 Pennsylvania Ave NW
- **National Press Club** · 529 14th St NW, 13th Fl
- **Smithsonian Institute** · On the National Mall
- **St John's Church** · 16th St NW & H St NW

Libraries

- **Dibner Library** · 12th St & Constitution Ave NW
- **Federal Aviation Administration Libraries** · 800 Independence Ave SW #930
- **Information Resources** · 1300 Pennsylvania Ave NW #7-5
- **Martin Luther King Jr Memorial Library** · 901 G St NW
- **National Clearinghouse Library** · 624 9th St NW #600
- **National Endowment for the Humanities Library** · 1100 Pennsylvania Ave NW #217
- **Office of Thrift Supervision Library** · 1700 G St NW
- **Treasury Library** · 1500 Pennsylvania Ave NW #142
- **US Department of Commerce Library** · 1401 Constitution Ave NW
- **US Department of Energy Library** · 1000 Independence Ave SW

P Parking

Pharmacies

- **CVS** · 1275 Pennsylvania Ave NW
- **CVS** · 435 8th St NW
- **CVS** · 717 14th St NW

Post Offices

- **Benjamin Franklin** · 1200 Pennsylvania Ave NW

Schools

- **Corcoran College of Art & Design (Downtown Campus)** · 17th St NW & New York Ave NW
- **Marriott Hospitality Public Charter** · 410 8th St NW

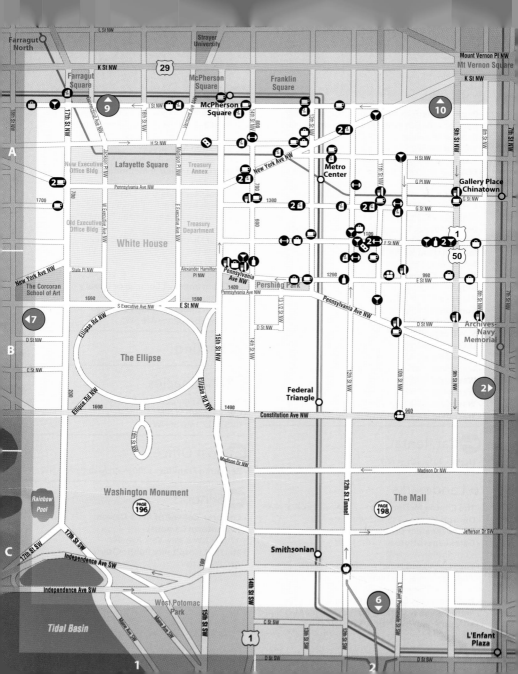

This neighborhood caters mainly to tourists and office workers. Lunch spots (such as the ubiquitous Cosi) and happy hours abound. At night, look harder to avoid tourist and expense account traps and you'll find treasures like soaring architecture and belly dancers at Zaytinya. Not hungry? Catch an indie flick at the Landmark E Street Theater to build up an appetite.

Coffee
- **Caribou Coffee** · 1701 Pennsylvania Ave NW
- **Caribou Coffee** · 601 13th Street NW
- **Coffee Espress** · 1250 H St NW
- **Cosi** · 1001 Pennsylvania Ave NW
- **Cosi** · 1333 H St NW
- **Cosi** · 1700 Pennsylvania Ave NW
- **Cosi** · 700 11th St NW
- **JX Coffee** · 1400 I St NW
- **ME Swing** · 1702 G St NW
- **Starbucks** · 1301 Pennsylvania Ave NW
- **Starbucks** · 1401 New York Ave NW
- **Starbucks** · 555 11th St NW
- **Starbucks** · 700 14th St NW
- **Starbucks** · 701 9th St NW
- **Starbucks** · 901 15th St NW
- **Teresa's Coffee** · 1300 I St NW
- **Wally's World Coffee** · 1225 I St NW

Copy Shops
- **Ace Press** · 910 17th St NW
- **Advanced Printing** · 1201 New York Ave NW
- **Alpha Graphics Printshop** · 1325 G St NW
- **Docimaging.com** · 1001 G St NW
- **Ikon Office Solutions** · 1120 G St NW
- **Judicial Copy** · 1620 I St NW
- **Lex Reprographics** · 1225 New York Ave NW
- **Metro Press** · 1444 I St NW
- **Minuteman Press** · 1308 G St NW
- **Nightrider Overnite** · 1120 G St NW
- **Partners Legal Copy** · 1401 New York Ave NW
- **Penn Press II** · 1350 New York Ave NW
- **Reliable Copy** · 555 12th St NW
- **Reprodoc** · 1300 I St NW
- **Sir Speedy Printing** · 1212 G St NW
- **Sir Speedy Printing** · 1429 H St NW
- **Staples** · 1250 H St NW
- **Superior Group** · 1401 New York Ave NW

Farmer's Markets
- **US Dept of Agriculture Farmers Market** · 12th St & Independence Ave SW

Gyms

- **Astoria Arms** · 809 14th St NW
- **Club Fitness at Washington Center** · 1001 G St NW
- **Downtown Boxing Club** · 1101 F St NW
- **Fitness Co** · 555 12th St NW
- **One To One Fitness** · 555 13th St NW
- **Pure Joe Studios** · 1101 F St NW
- **Washington Sports Clubs** · 1345 F St NW
- **Washington Sports Clubs** · 730 12th St NW

Liquor Stores
- **Central Liquor Store** · 917 F St NW
- **Press Liquors** · 527 14th St NW
- **Washington Wine & Liquor** · 1200 E St NW

Movie Theaters
- **Johnson IMAX Theater** · Constitution Ave NW & 10th St NW
- **Landmark E St Cinema** · 555 11th St NW

Nightlife
- **Capitol City Brewing Company** · 1100 New York Ave NW
- **Eyebar** · 1716 I St NW
- **Gordon Biersch Brewery** · 900 F St NW
- **Grand Slam Sports Bar** · 1000 H St NW
- **Harry's Saloon** · 436 11th St NW
- **Home** · 911 F St NW
- **Platinum** · 915 F St NW
- **Polly Esther's** · 605 12th St NW
- **Poste Brasserie Bar** · 555 8th St NW
- **Round Robin Bar** · 1401 Pennsylvania Ave NW
- **Tequila Beach** · 1115 F St NW

Restaurants
- **Bistro D'Oc** · 518 10th St NW
- **Cafe Atlantico** · 405 8th St NW
- **Caucus Room** · 401 9th St NW
- **Ceiba** · 701 14th St NW
- **Occidental** · 1475 Pennsylvania Ave NW
- **Ortanique** · 730 11th St NW
- **Ten Penh** · 1001 Pennsylvania Ave NW
- **Willard Room** · 1401 Pennsylvania Ave NW
- **Zaytinya** · 701 9th St NW

Shopping
- **ADC Map & Travel Center** · 1636 I St NW
- **Blink** · 1776 I St NW
- **Café Mozart** · 1331 H St NW
- **Chanel Boutique** · 1455 Pennsylvania Ave NW
- **Caledon Spa** · 1180 F St NW
- **Fahrney's** · 1317 F St NW
- **International Spy Musuem Gift Shop** · 800 F St NW
- **Penn Camera** · 840 E St NW
- **Political Americana** · 1331 Pennsylvania Ave NW
- **Utrecht Art & Drafting Supplies** · 1250 I St NW
- **Weschler's** · 909 E St NW

Video Rental
- **Kung-Fu Video** · 1105 F St NW
- **White House Video** · 1510 H St NW

Map 2 · **Chinatown / Union Station** N

L St NW

New York Ave NW

Mount Vernon Pl NW
Mt Vernon Square
K St NW

L St NW
First Ter
Temple Ct NW

L St NW

Pierce St NE

1st St NE

2nd St NE

10

Massachusetts Ave NW

K St NW

Prather Ct NW

I St NW

500

800

H St NW

11

T St NW

Chinatown Gate

Gallery Place
Chinatown

G Pl NW

700

300

200

100

2nd St NW

1st St NW

900

G Pl NE

G St NW

G St NE

G St NE

P

MCI Center

PAGE
228

Union
Station

PAGE
258
Union Station

1
50

Judiciary
Square

F St NW

F St NW

McCullough Ct NW

N Capitol St NW

Union Station Dr

Columbus Monument Dr

600

500

E St NW

Madison Al NW

Chews Ct NW
Chews Al NW

E St NE

Rx

2

7th St NW

2 P

5th St NW

400

300

4th St NW

3rd St NW

2nd St NW

00

New Jersey Ave NW

Louisiana Ave NE

Massachusetts Ave NE

Archives–
Navy
Memorial

D St NW

Indiana Ave NW

D St NW

100

1

C St NW

Indiana Ave NW

C St NW

100

Union Station
Plaza

Delaware Ave NE

C St NE

1st St NE

3

B

11

Newseum
Front Pages

John
Marshall
Park

395

200

Louisiana Ave NW

SCOTUS

Constitution Ave NW

Pennsylvania Ave NW

Constitution Ave NW

200

Constitution Ave NE

Maryland Ave NE

East Capitol Cir

Capitol Cir NE

Madison Dr NW

9th St SW

The Mall

PAGE
198

4th St NW

3rd St NW

600

300

Capitol
Reflecting
Pool

East Capitol Cir

United States
Capitol Building

East Capitol Cir

Capitol Driveway NE

Supreme
Court

East Capitol St

Jefferson
Building

Jefferson Dr SW

US Botanical
Garden

PAGE
192

South Capitol Cir SW

Capitol Driveway SE

Library of
Congress

PAGE
201

C

Maryland Ave SW

4th St SW

6

Federal
Triangle SW

5

Independence Ave SE

South Capitol St

Madison
Building

L'Enfant
Plaza

C St SW

D St SW

D St SW

Virginia Ave SW

School St SW

D St SW

2nd St SW

Washington Ave SW

C St SE

D St SE

Capitol
South

New Jersey Ave SE

2nd St SE

1st St SE

Capitol Cir SE

Folger
Park

North Carolina Ave SE

E St SW

1

2

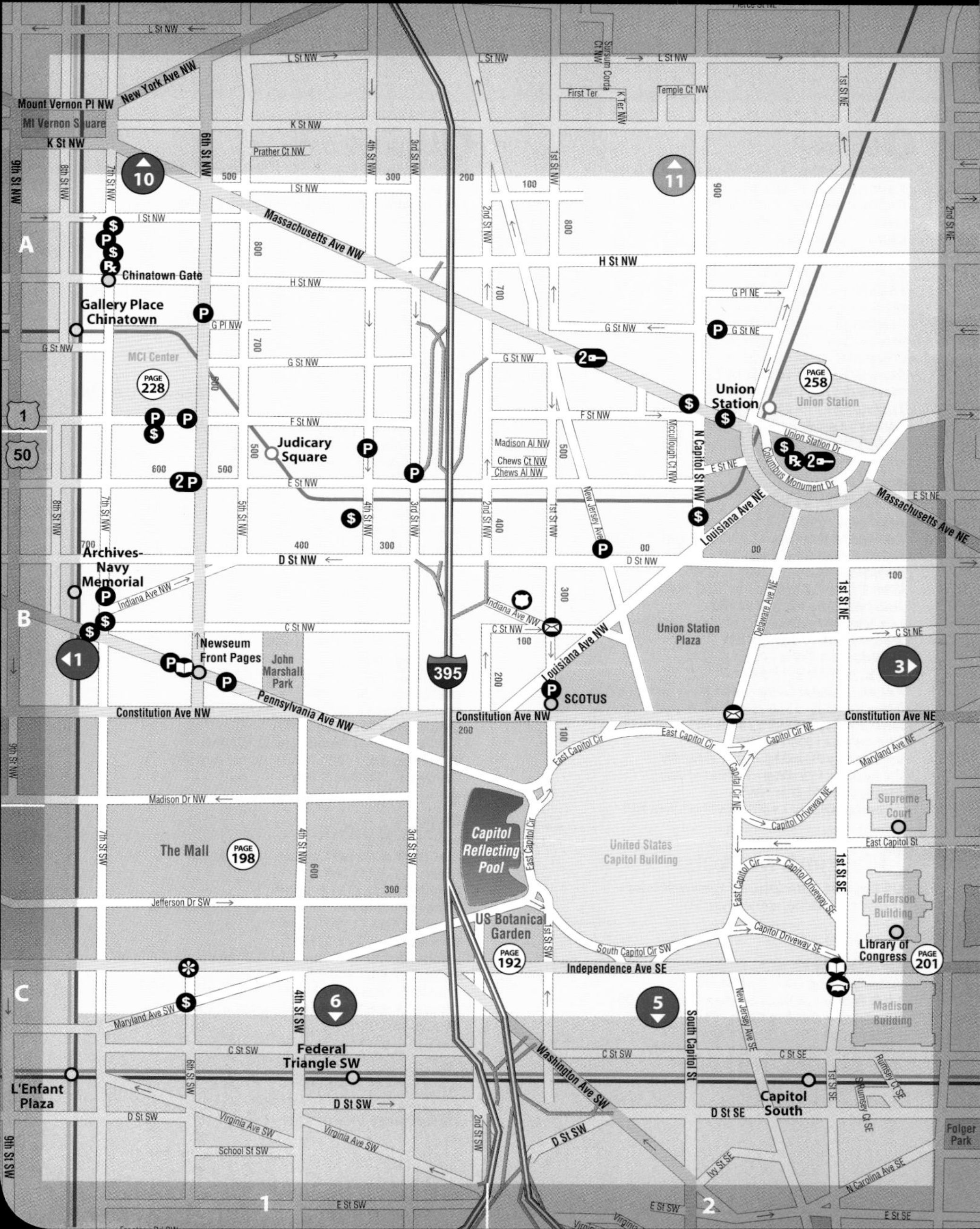

These blocks are roiling with change and competing interests. Upscale new condos overlook vacant lots, and young professionals mingle with students and the homeless. Openings and closings make it tough to keep up, but also make it one of the most dynamic neighborhoods in the city.

$ Banks

- **Adams National** · 50 Massachusetts Ave NE
- **Adams National** · 802 7th St NW
- **Chevy Chase** · 650 F St NW
- **Chevy Chase** · 701 Pennsylvania Ave NW
- **Industrial Bank** · 441 4th St NW
- **Riggs** · 301 7th St NW
- **Riggs** · 833 7th St NW
- **Sun Trust** · 2 Massachusetts Ave NW
- **Wachovia** · 444 N Capitol St NW
- **Wachovia** · 600 Maryland Ave SW

Car Rental

- **Alamo** · 50 Massachusetts Ave NE
- **Budget** · 50 Massachusetts Ave NW
- **Hertz** · 50 Massachusetts Ave NW
- **National** · 50 Massachusetts Ave NE

Community Gardens

o Landmarks

- **Chinatown Gate** · H St NW & 7th St NW
- **Library of Congress** · 101 Independence Ave SE
- **Newseum Front Pages** · 6th St NW & Pennsylvania Ave NW
- **Supreme Court of the United States** · 1st St NE

Libraries

- **Federal Trade Commission Library** · 600 Pennsylvania Ave NW #630
- **US Library of Congress** · 101 Independence Ave SE
- **US Senate Library** · Russell Senate Office Bldg, B15

P Parking

Rx Pharmacies

- **CVS** · 801 7th St NW
- **Tschiffely Pharmacy** · 50 Massachusetts Ave NE

Police

- **MPDC Headquarters** · 300 Indiana Ave NW

Post Offices

- **National Capitol Station** · 2 Massachusetts Ave NE

Schools

- **House of Representatives Page School** · 101 Independence Ave SE

Residential amenities and shopping are gradually taking root, but it was restaurateurs who first realized the potential here. Some of the city's most daring entrepreneurs are also damn good cooks. Jaleos has the best tapas anywhere this side of Madrid, and Matchbox wedges in crowds for its pizzas. If all you're after is a beer, skip the Capital City Brewing Company and head to Fados Irish Pub.

Coffee

- **Bucks County Coffee** · 50 Massachusetts Ave NE
- **Cafe Renee** · 50 Massachusetts Ave NE
- **Cosi** · 601 Pennsylvania Ave NW
- **Starbucks** · 325 7th St NW
- **Starbucks** · 800 7th St NW

Copy Shops

- **Copy General** · 701 Pennsylvania Ave NW
- **Document Technology Centre** · 50 F St NW
- **Kinko's** · 325 7th St NW
- **Minuteman Press** · 555 New Jersey Ave NW
- **Silver Lining** · 630 I St NW
- **UPS Store** · 220 Pennsylvania Ave NW

Farmer's Markets

- **Freshfarm Market** · 8th St NW & E St NW

Liquor Stores

- **Corner Store** · 800 N Capitol St NW
- **G&G Beverages** · 706 6th St NW
- **Kogod Liquors** · 441 New Jersey Ave NW
- **Union Wine & Liquors Store** ·
  50 Massachusetts Ave NE

Movie Theaters

- **AMC Union Station 9** · 50 Massachusetts Ave NE
- **Lockheed Martin IMAX Theater** ·
  601 Independence Ave SW
- **Mary Pickford Theater** · Library of Congress,
  James Madison Memorial Bldg, Independence Ave
  SE b/w 1st St SE & 2nd St SE

Nightlife

- **Capitol City Brewing Company** ·
  2 Massachusetts Ave NE
- **Coyote Ugly** · 717 6th St NW
- **Fado Irish Pub** · 808 7th St NW
- **Insomnia** · 714 6th St NW
- **Juste Lounge** · 1015 1/2 7th St NW
- **RFD Washington** · 810 7th St NW

Restaurants

- **701** · 701 Pennsylvania Ave NW
- **B Smith's** · 50 Massachusetts Ave NE
- **Bistro Bis** · 15 E St NW
- **Burma** · 740 6th St NW
- **Capital Q** · 707 H St NW
- **Capitol City Brewing Company** ·
  2 Massachusetts Ave NE
- **Fado Irish Pub** · 808 7th St NW
- **Flying Scotsman** · 233 2nd St NW
- **Jaleo** · 480 7th St NW
- **Matchbox** · 713 H St NW
- **Rosa Mexicano** · 575 7th St NW

Shopping

- **Alamo Flags** · Union Station
- **Apartment Zero** · 406 7th St NW
- **Comfort One Shoes** · 50 Massachusetts Ave NE
- **Godiva Chocolatier** · 50 Massachusetts Ave NE
- **Marvelous Market** · 730 7th St NW
- **Olsson's Books** · 418 7th St NW
- **Political Americana-Memorabilia** ·
  Union Station
- **Washington Redskins Official Store** ·
  50 Massachusetts Ave NE

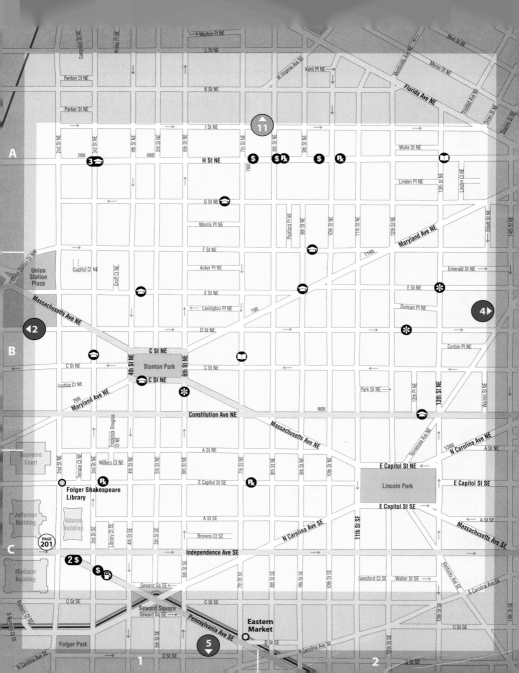

Map 3

Blocks that used to be Congressional member and staff domain are now stuck in stroller gridlock. Urban homesteaders have bought row house after row house and turned the neighborhood into one that is highly coveted by young families.

Banks

- **Bank of America** · 201 Pennsylvania Ave SE
- **Bank of America** · 722 H St NE
- **Bank of America** · 961 H St NE
- **Riggs** · 800 H St NE
- **Sun Trust** · 300 Pennsylvania Ave SE
- **Wachovia** · 215 Pennsylvania Ave SE

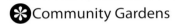 Community Gardens

 Gas Stations

- **Exxon** · 339 Pennsylvania Ave SE

o Landmarks

- **Folger Shakespeare Library** · 201 E Capitol St SE

Libraries

- **Northeast Library** · 330 7th St NE
- **RL Christian Community Library** · 1300 H St NE

Pharmacies

- **Grubb's Care Pharmacy & Medical Supply** · 326 E Capitol St NE
- **Morton's Care Pharmacy** · 724 E Capitol St NE
- **Rite Aid** · 801 H St NE
- **Super Pharmacy** · 1019 H St NE

Schools

- **Brent Elementary** · 330 3rd St NE
- **Cornerstone Community School** · 907 Maryland Ave NE
- **Ludlow-Taylor Elementary** · 659 G St NE
- **Maury Elementary** · 1250 Constitution Ave NE
- **Options Middle** · 800 3rd St NE
- **Peabody Elementary** · 425 C St NE
- **Prospect Learning Center** · 920 F St NE
- **Stuart-Hobson Middle** · 410 E St NE
- **Tree of Life Community Elementary** · 800 3rd St NE
- **Washington Jesuit Academy** · 800 3rd St NE

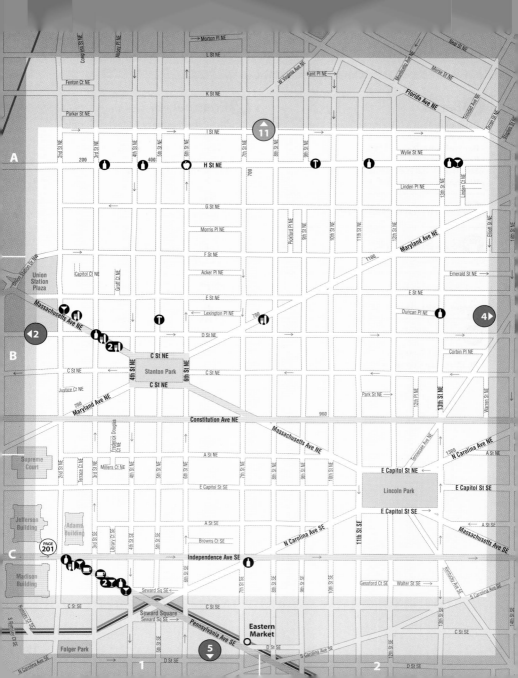

Map 3

The nightlife is heavy on drunken Hill staffers bar-crawling their way home after a grueling day of sucking up. Hey gang, happy hour at Hawk and Dove! If the barely post-college atmosphere isn't your scene, retreat south a few blocks and find cooler environs below Eastern Market.

Coffee
- **Cosi** · 301 Pennsylvania Ave SE
- **Starbucks** · 237 Pennsylvania Ave SE

Farmer's Markets
- **Freshfarm Market** · 600 H St NE

Hardware Stores
- **Park's Hardware** · 920 H St NE

Liquor Stores
- **Capitol Hill Liquor & Deli** · 323 Pennsylvania Ave SE
- **Excello Liquor & Grocery** · 419 13th St NE
- **Gandel's Liquors** · 211 Pennsylvania Ave SE
- **H Street Liquor Store** · 303 H St NE
- **Hayden's Liquor Store** · 700 North Carolina Ave SE
- **Jumbo Liquors** · 1122 H St NE
- **Kelly's Liquor Store** · 415 H St NE
- **Northeast Beverage** · 1344 H St NE
- **Schneider's of Capitol Hill** · 300 Massachusetts Ave NE

Nightlife
- **Capitol Lounge** · 229 Pennsylvania Ave SE
- **DC Sanctuary** · 1355 H St NE
- **Hawk and Dove** · 329 Pennsylvania Ave SE
- **Lounge 201** · 201 Massachusetts Ave NE
- **Politiki** · 319 Pennsylvania Ave SE
- **Top of the Hill** · 319 Pennsylvania Ave SE

Restaurants
- **Café Berlin** · 322 Massachusetts Ave NE
- **Il Radicchio** · 223 Pennsylvania Ave SE
- **Kenny's Smokehouse** · 732 Maryland Ave NE
- **La Brasserie** · 239 Massachusetts Ave NE
- **Two Quail** · 320 Massachusetts Ave NE
- **White Tiger** · 301 Massachusetts Ave NE

Essentials

The baby boom to the west has unleashed rampant gentrification that is marching toward the stadium. Crime and newcomer backlash are holding off the pampering amenities that are expected to follow the soaring home prices. Until the pet shops and coffeehouses move in, just be happy that you can walk to DC United games.

$ Banks

• **Bank of America** • 1330 Maryland Ave NE

⛽ Gas Stations

• **Amoco** • 1396 Florida Ave NE
• **Amoco** • 1950 Benning Rd NE
• **Exxon** • 2651 Benning Rd NE

📖 Libraries

• **Langston Community Library** •
  2600 Benning Rd NE

℞ Pharmacies

• **Sterling Care Pharmacy** • 1647 Benning Rd NE

✉ Post Offices

• **Northeast Station** • 1563 Maryland Ave NE

🏫 Schools

• **Eliot Junior High** • 1830 Constitution Ave NE
• **Friendship-Edison-Blow-Pierce Campus** •
  725 19th St NE
• **Gibbs Elementary** • 500 19th St NE
• **Holy Comforter-St Cyprian** • 1503 E Capitol St SE
• **Miner Elementary** • 601 15th St NE
• **Payne Elementary** • 305 15th St NE
• **Phelps Career High** • 704 26th St NE
• **Sasha Bruce Middle** • 1375 E St NE
• **Spingham Center** • 2500 Benning Rd NE
• **St Benedict of the Moor** • 320 21st St NE
• **Two Rivers Elementary** • 1830 Constitution Ave
• **Village Learning Center Elementary** •
  702 15th St NE

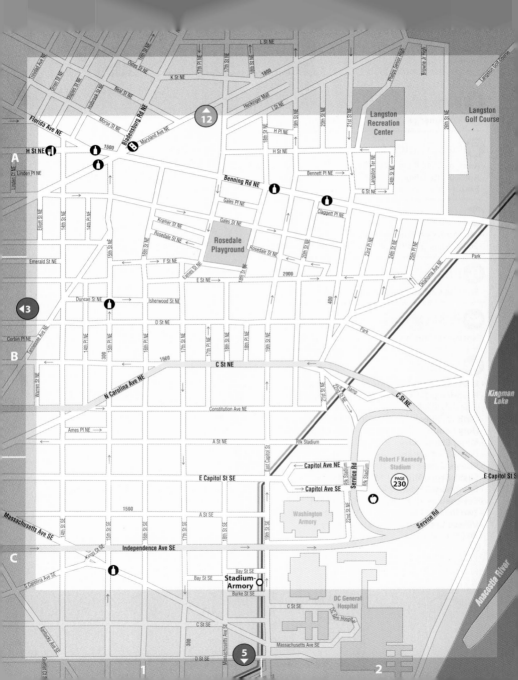

A few entrepreneurs like those behind the Phish Tea Café are making a go of it to cater to a flagging theater crowd along H Street. Otherwise, this is not the area for a moonlit stroll. Better to visit one of the many liquor stores in the daylight hours and plan to gather indoors in the evening.

Farmer's Markets

- **DC Open Air Farmers Market** · RFK Stadium parking lot 6, Independence Ave & 22nd St SE

Liquor Stores

- **Friends Liquors** · 1406 H St NE
- **New York Liquor Store** · 1447 Maryland Ave NE
- **S&J Liquor Store** · 1500 Massachusetts Ave SE
- **Silverman's Liquor** · 2033 Benning Rd NE
- **Sylvia's Liquor Store** · 1818 Benning Rd NE
- **Viggy's Liquors** · 409 15th St NE

Restaurants

- **Phish Tea Café** · 1335 H St NE

Video Rental

- **Blockbuster Video** · 1555 Maryland Ave NE

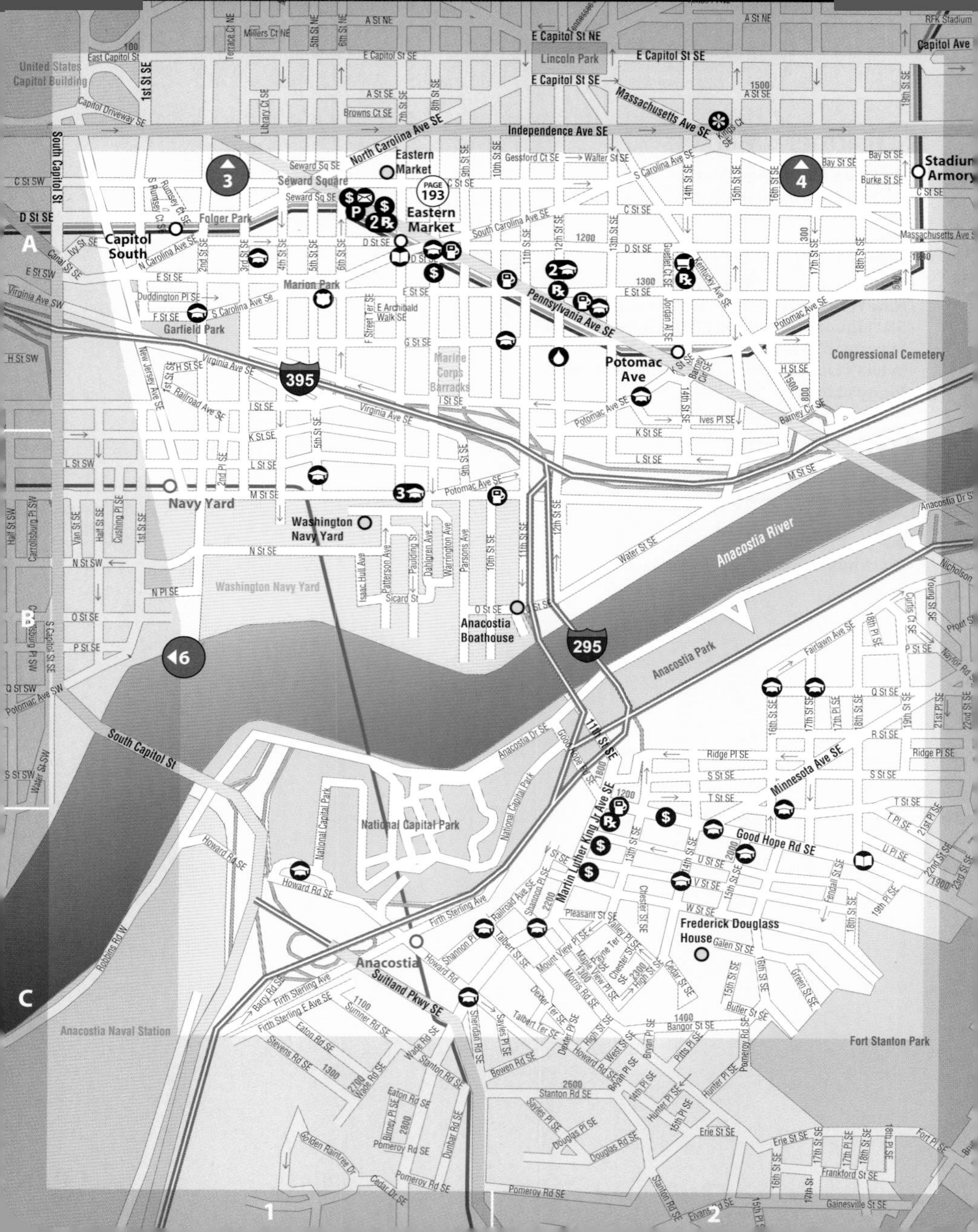

United States
Capitol Building

Capitol
South

Folger Park

Seward Square

Eastern
Market

Eastern Market
PAGE 193

Marion Park

Garfield Park

Duddington Pl SE

Marine
Corps
Barracks

Pennsylvania Ave SE

Potomac
Ave

Congressional Cemetery

Stadium
Armory

Navy Yard

Washington
Navy Yard

Washington Navy Yard

Anacostia
Boathouse

National Capital Park

Anacostia River

Anacostia Park

Ridge Pl SE

Minnesota Ave SE

Good Hope Rd SE

Anacostia

Frederick Douglass
House

Anacostia Naval Station

Fort Stanton Park

Eighth Street is the center of a funky revitalization, drawing risk-taking residents and retailers. Wandering too far off the main drag can lead you to some dismal stretches because, unlike other whip-fast developer-fueled neighborhood turnarounds in the city, the process here seems to be a bit more organic.

Banks

- **Bank of America** •
  2100 Martin Luther King Jr Ave SE
- **Bank of America** • 401 8th St SE
- **Citibank** • 600 Pennsylvania Ave SE
- **Riggs** • 2000 Martin Luther King Jr Ave SE
- **Riggs** • 650 Pennsylvania Ave SE
- **Sun Trust** • 1340 Good Hope Rd SE

Car Washes

- **Capitol Car Cleaning** • 709 12th St SE

Community Gardens

Gas Stations

- **Amoco** • 1234 Good Hope Rd SE
- **Amoco** • 823 Good Hope Rd SE
- **Exxon** • 1022 M St SE
- **Exxon** • 1201 Pennsylvania Ave SE
- **Sunoco** • 1248 Pennsylvania Ave SE
- **Texaco** • 1022 Pennsylvania Ave SE

Landmarks

- **Anacostia Boathouse** • 1105 O St NE
- **Eastern Market** • 225 7th St SE
- **Frederick Douglass House** • 1411 W St SE
- **Washington Navy Yard** • 805 Kidder Breese SE

Libraries

- **Anacostia Library** • 1800 Good Hope Rd SE
- **Southeast Library** • 403 7th St SE

Parking

Pharmacies

- **Capitol Hill Care Pharmacy** •
  650 Pennsylvania Ave SE
- **CVS** • 500 12th St SE
- **CVS** • 661 Pennsylvania Ave SE
- **Neighborhood Pharmacy** •
  1932 Martin Luther King Jr Ave SE
- **Safeway** • 415 14th St SE

Police

- **MPDC 1st District Substation** • 500 E St SE

Post Offices

- **Southeast Station** • 600 Pennsylvania Ave SE

Schools

- **Ambassador Baptist Church Christian Academy**
  • 1412 Minnesota Ave SE
- **Anaconsita** • 1601 16th St
- **Anacostia Bible Church Christian** • 1610 T St SE
- **Birney Elementary** • 2501 Martin Luther King Jr Ave SE
- **Capitol Hill Day School** • 210 South Carolina Ave SE
- **Clara Muhammad School** •
  2313 Martin Luther King Jr Av
- **Eagle Academy** • 770 M St SE
- **Friendship-Edison-Chamberlain Campus** •
  1345 Potomac Ave SE
- **Hine Junior High** • 335 8th St SE
- **Holy Temple Christian Academy** • 439 12th St SE
- **Howard Road Academy** • 701 Howard Rd SE
- **Ketcham Elementary** • 1919 15th St SE
- **Kipp DC/Key Academy** • 770 M St SE
- **Kramer Middle** • 1700 Q St SE
- **Our Lady of Perpetual Help, V Street Unit** •
  1409 V St SE
- **Savoy Elementary** • 2400 Shannon Pl SE
- **St Peters Interparish** • 422 3rd St SE
- **Tyler Elementary** • 1001 G St SE
- **Van Ness Elementary** • 1150 5th St SE
- **Washington Math Science and Technology High**
  • 770 M St SE
- **Watkins Elementary** • 420 12th St SE

Supermarkets

- **Safeway** • 415 14th St SE

Map 5 · **Southeast / Anacostia**

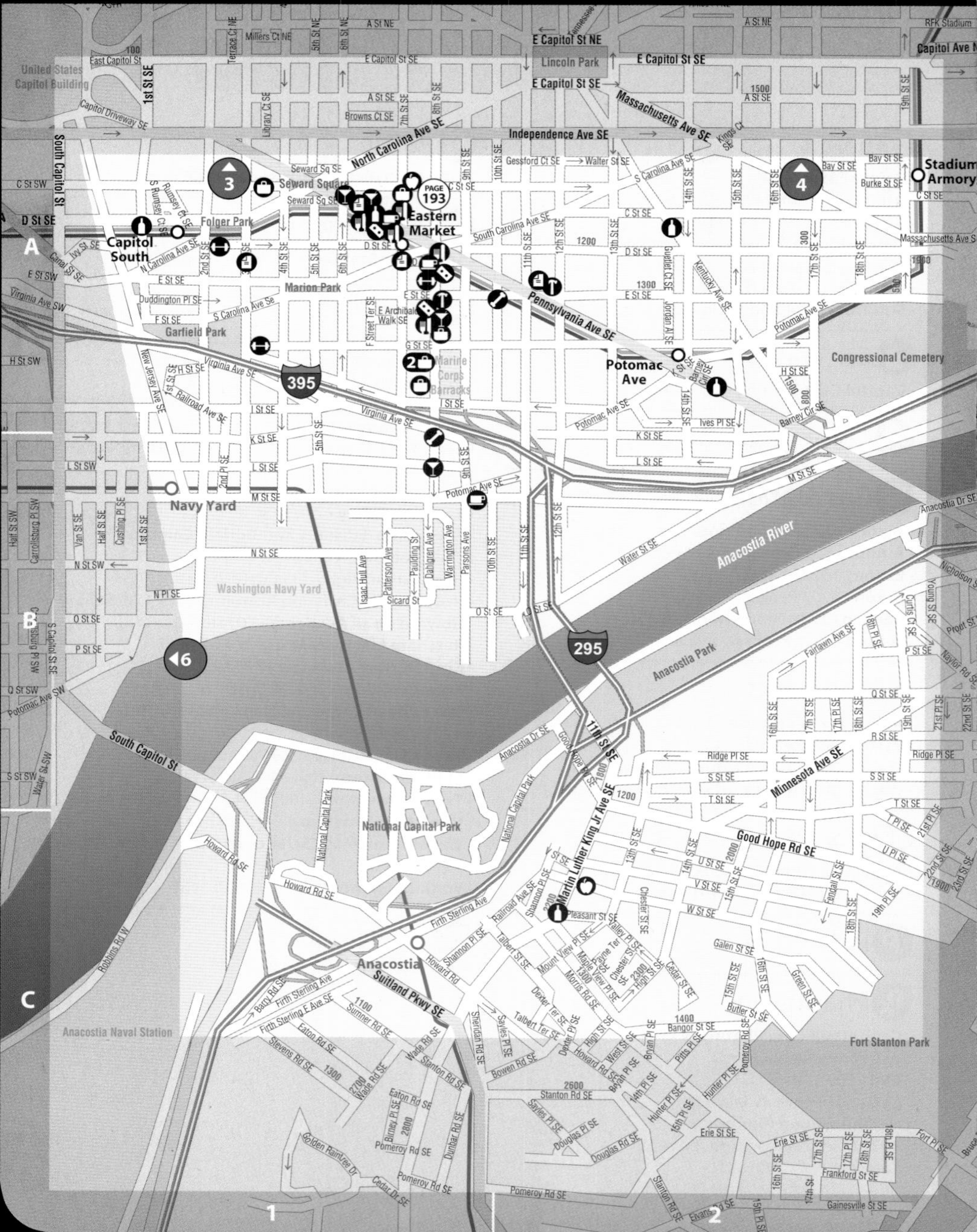

Ⓝ

United States
Capitol Building

RFK Stadium

100
East Capitol St

Miller's Ct NE

A St NE

A St NE

Terrace Ct NE

5th St NE

E Capitol St NE

Lincoln Park

E Capitol St SE

Capitol Ave NE

Capitol Driveway

Capitol St SE

E Capitol St SE

E Capitol St SE

Massachusetts Ave SE

1500

A St SE

Library Ct SE

A St SE

Browns Ct SE

Independence Ave SE

Gessford Ct SE

Walter St SE

S Carolina Ave SE

14th St SE

Bay St SE

Stadium
Armory

3

Seward Sq NE

Seward Square

Seward Sq SE

PAGE
193

**Eastern
Market**

S Carolina Ave SE

12th St SE

1200

C St SE

15th St SE

Burke St SE

4

Bay St SE

Massachusetts Ave SE

1400

**Capitol
South**

Folger Park

N Carolina Ave SE

S Rumsey

C St SW

D St SE

E St SW

Virginia Ave SW

F St SW

Duddington Pl SE

S Carolina Ave SE

Marion Park

Garfield Park

E St SE

4th St SE

D St SE

S Carolina Ave SE

11th St SE

D St SE

E St SE

1300

Kentucky Ave SE

Potomac Ave SE

300

Massachusetts Ave SE

1600

F Terr SE

E Archibald
Walk SE

Pennsylvania Ave SE

Jordan St SE

Potomac Ave SE

Congressional Cemetery

H St SW

New Jersey Ave SE

Virginia Ave SE

395

1st St SE

2nd St SE

Virginia Ave SE

2

Marine
Corps
Barracks

**Potomac
Ave**

Ives Pl SE

13th St SE

Barney Circle

L St SE

H St SE

1100

F St SE

S Railroad Ave SE

K St SE

J St SE

3rd St SE

M St SE

I St SE

Potomac Ave SE

L St SE

K St SE

11th St SE

12th St SE

Navy Yard

M St SE

N St SE

Water St SE

M St SE

Anacostia Dr SE

Half St SE

Carrollsburg Pl SW

Cushing Pl SE

1st St SE

2nd St SE

Isaac Hull Ave

Patterson St

Paulding Ave

Dahlgren Ave

Warrington Ave

Parsons Ave

Sicard St

O St SE

N St SE

N Pl SE

Washington Navy Yard

Anacostia River

295

B

P St SW

O St SW

P St SW

Half St SW

S Capitol St SW

◄6

South Capitol St

Anacostia Park

Nicholson St

16th St SE

17th St SE

18th St SE

19th St SE

20th St SE

21st St SE

22nd St SE

Fairlawn Ave SE

Q St SE

R St SE

Minnesota Ave SE

Ridge Pl SE

R St SW

S St SW

T St SW

S Capitol St

Potomac Ave SW

S Capitol St

Anacostia Dr SE

Good Hope Rd SE

National Capital Park

Anacostia Dr SE

11th St SE

1200

Ridge Pl SE

S St SE

T St SE

Good Hope Rd SE

T St SE

T Pl SE

U St SE

U Pl SE

16th St SE

17th St SE

18th St SE

19th St SE

20th St SE

21st St SE

Howard Rd SE

Firth Sterling Ave

Howard Rd SE

National Capital Park

Martin Luther King Jr Ave SE

Shannon Pl SE

Sumner Rd SE

Mount View Pl SE

Maple View Pl SE

Morris Rd SE

U St SE

V St SE

W St SE

Galen St SE

16th St SE

17th St SE

18th St SE

19th St SE

20th St SE

Bangor St SE

Butler St SE

**Anacostia
Suitland Pkwy SE**

Bells Rd SE

Firth Sterling Ave

1100

Sumner Rd SE

Mellon St SE

Pleasant St SE

Chicago St SE

Talbert St SE

W St SE

Butler St SE

Pomeroy Rd SE

C

Anacostia Naval Station

Firth Sterling Ave

Stevens Rd SE

1300

Eaton Rd SE

Wade Rd SE

Stanton Rd SE

Bowen Rd SE

Howard Rd SE

Talbert Ter SE

Bangor St SE

Hunter Pl SE

Fort Stanton Park

Bolling AFB

Howard Rd SE

Barry Rd SE

1100

Eaton Rd SE

Wahler Pl SE

2600
Stanton Rd SE

Sumner Rd SE

Douglas Pl SE

Bangor St SE

Pitts Pl SE

Hunter Pl SE

16th St SE

17th St SE

Fort Pl SE

Golden Rain Ter SE

Pomeroy Rd SE

Dunbar Rd SE

2000

Blaine Pl SE

Pomeroy Rd SE

Center Dr SE

Pomeroy Rd SE

Douglas Rd SE

Erie St SE

Erie St SE

Frankford St SE

Gainesville St SE

1   **2**

Better and better amenities are pushing out storefront Chinese take-outs along Eighth Street. Banana Café and the more upscale Starfish are owned by the same neighborhood devotee who is doing his bit to remake the neighborhood into a citywide draw. Cross Pennsylvania Ave and you'll find yourself in an already polished 'hood where Montmarte calls for special occasions and Bread & Chocolate for a sidewalk brunch.

Coffee

- **Murky Coffee** · 660 Pennsylvania Ave SE
- **Starbucks** · 401 8th St SE
- **William III Gourmet Coffee** · 901 M St SE

Copy Shops

- **Image Delivery Systems** ·
  1101 Pennsylvania Ave SE
- **Kinko's** · 715 D St SE
- **UPS Store** · 611 Pennsylvania Ave SE

Farmer's Markets

- **Anacostia Farmers Market** · 1225 W St SE
- **Angora Farms** · 7th & C Sts SE
- **Eastern Market** · 225 7th St SE

Gyms

- **Curves** · 407 8th St SE
- **Results the Gym** · 315 G St SE
- **Washington Sports Clubs** · 214 D St SE

Hardware Stores

- **District Lock & Hardware** · 505 8th St SE
- **Frager's Hardware** · 1115 Pennsylvania Ave SE

Liquor Stores

- **Albert's Liquor Store** · 328 Kentucky Ave SE
- **Big K Liquors** · 2252 Martin Luther King Jr Ave SE
- **Congressional Liquors** · 404 1st St SE
- **JJ Mutts Wine & Spirits** · 643 Pennsylvania Ave SE
- **World Liquors** · 1453 Pennsylvania Ave SE

Nightlife

- **Bachelor's Mill** · 1106 8th St SE
- **Mr Henry's Capitol Hill** · 601 Pennsylvania Ave SE
- **Phase One** · 525 8th St SE
- **Remington's** · 639 Pennsylvania Ave SE
- **Tunnicliff's Tavern** · 222 7th St SE

Pet Shops

- **Dog-ma** · 821 Virginia Ave SE
- **Doolittles** · 224 7th St SE
- **Zoolatry** · 520 10th St SE

Restaurants

- **Banana Cafe & Piano Bar** · 500 8th St SE
- **Bread & Chocolate** · 666 Pennsylvania Ave SE
- **Meyhane** · 633 Pennsylvania Ave SE
- **Montmartre** · 327 7th St SE
- **Starfish** · 539 8th St SE
- **Tortilla Coast** · 400 1st St SE

Shopping

- **American Rescue Workers' Thrift Store** ·
  745 8th St SE
- **Backstage** · 545 8th St SE
- **Capitol Hill Bikes** · 709 8th St SE
- **Capitol Hill Books** · 657 C St SE
- **Eastern Market** · 225 7th St SE
- **Plaid** · 715 8th St SE
- **Wooven History & Silk Road** · 315 7th St SE

Video Rental

- **Blockbuster Video** · 400 8th St SE
- **Capitol Video Sales** · 514 8th St SE
- **Penn Video** · 645 Pennsylvania Ave SE

Large-scale Sixties' redevelopment turned this prime geography into a village of concrete. District officials are now taking another crack at a publicly financed overhaul that pledges shops and waterfront cafes. Let's hope they make good, and that their solutions age better than those of previous generations.

 Banks
- **Bank of America** · 401 M St SW
- **M&T Bank** · 500 C St SW
- **Riggs** · 935 L'Enfant Plz SW
- **Sun Trust** · 965 L'Enfant Plz SW

Car Rental
- **Enterprise** · 970 D St SW
- **Rent-A-Wreck** · 1252 Half St SE

 **Car Washes**
- **Splash the Car Wash** · 10 I St SE

Community Gardens

Gas Stations
- **Amoco** · 1244 S Capitol St SE
- **Exxon** · 1001 S Capitol St SW
- **Exxon** · 950 S Capitol St SE
- **Sunoco** · 50 M St SE

Landmarks
- **Arena Stage** · 1101 6th St SW
- **Ft Lesley J McNair** · 4th St and P St
- **Thomas Law House** · 1252 6th St SW
- **Tiber Island** · 4th St SW b/w N St & M St
- **USS Sequoia** · 6th St SW & Maine Ave SW

Libraries
- **Comptroller of Currency Library** · 250 E St SW
- **DOT Law Library, Coast Guard Branch** · 2100 2nd St SW #B726
- **International Trade Commission Library** · 500 E St SW
- **NASA Headquarters Library** · 300 E St SW #1J20
- **Southwest Library** · 900 Wesley Pl SW
- **US Housing & Urban Development Library** · 451 7th St SW #8141

Parking

Pharmacies
- **CVS** · 401 M St SW
- **CVS** · 433 L'Enfant Plz SW

Police
- **MPDC 1st District Station** · 415 4th St SW

Post Offices
- **For McNair Station** · 300A St SW
- **L'Enfant Plaza Station** · 437 L'Enfant Plz SW
- **Southwest Station** · 45 L St SW

Schools
- **Amidon Elementary** · 401 I St SW
- **Bowen Elementary** · 101 M St SW
- **Jefferson Junior High** · 801 7th St SW
- **National Defense University** · Fort Lesley J McNair
- **Southeastern University** · 501 I St SW

Supermarkets
- **Safeway** · 401 M St SW

Map 6

Once the car's been parked by the valet at one of the big box destinations, expect to hunker down for the night. There's little opportunity to roam between your mediocre Mexican at the Cantina Marina and Zanzibar's dance floor. The waterfront promenade, especially at night, is best when you're in the mood for an eerie sense of desolation.

Coffee
- **Olympic Espresso** · 475 L'Enfant Plz SW
- **Olympic Espresso** · 955 L'Enfant Plz SW

Farmer's Markets
- **US Dept of Transportation Farmers Market** · 400 7th St SW

Gyms
- **Gold's Gym** · 409 3rd St SW
- **Metro Fitness** · 480 L'Enfant Plz SW
- **Waterside Fitness & Swim Club** · 901 6th St SW

Liquor Stores
- **Harry's Liquor Wine & Cheese** · 401 M St SW
- **L'Enfant Wine & Beverage** · 459 L'Enfant Plz SW
- **Normandie Liquors** · 83 M St SE
- **Shulman's Southwest Liquor** · 1550 1st St SW

Nightlife
- **Abyss** · 1824 Half St SW
- **Edge** · 52 L St SE
- **Nation** · 1015 Half St SE
- **Secrets** · 1345 Half St SE
- **Zanzibar on the Waterfront** · 700 Water St SW
- **Ziegfields** · 1345 Half St SE

Restaurants
- **Cantina Marina** · 600 Water St SW
- **H2O at Hogate's** · 800 Water St SW
- **Pier 7** · 650 Water St SW

Shopping
- **Maine Avenue Fish Market** · Maine Ave & Potomac River

Video Rental
- **In & Out Video** · 61 K St SE

Foggy

Whitehurst Frwy NW

K St NW

Washington Circle Park

Farrag

25th St NW

Queen Annes Ln

Hughes Mews St NW

Snows Ct NW

Foggy Bottom - GWU

George Washington University

Pennsylvania Ave NW

Farragut West

I St NW

19th St NW

Edward R Murrow Park

H St NW

18th St NW

Rock Creek and Potomac Pkwy NW

Watergate Hotel

New Hampshire Ave NW

I St NW

Colonial Ln NW

'Crossfire' Taping

H St NW

PAGE 218

24th St NW

22nd St NW

21st St NW

20th St NW

G St NW

F St NW

23rd St NW

F St NW

JFK Center for Performing Arts

PAGE 298

Virginia Ave NW

E St NW

E Street Exwy

E St NW

The Octagon

Rawlings Sq NW

New York Ave NW

The Corcoran School of Art

E St NW

D St NW

D St NW

Edward J Kelly Park

C St NW

C St NW

Constitution Ave NW

22nd St NW

21st St NW

20th St NW

50

66

Einstein Statue

2300

Constitution Ave NW

2000

Independence Ave SW

Constitution Ave NW

Potomac River

Lincoln Memorial Circle

Lincoln Memorial Park

Reflecting Pool

Rainbow Pool

Henry Bacon Dr NW

PAGE 196

Constitution Gardens

17th St N

Ohio Dr SW

Daniel French Dr SW

Arlington Memorial Bridge

Independence Ave SW

George Washington Memorial Pkwy

West Potomac Park

17th St S

Tidal Basin

Ohio Dr SW

West Basin Dr SW

The serious tone and immovable hairdos are hard to miss here, in the neighborhood that the State Department, the Kennedy Center and the Watergate all call home. Thankfully, George Washington University students introduce some levity and the occasional set of flip-flops.

$ Banks

- **Bank of America** · 2001 Pennsylvania Ave NW
- **Bank of America** · 801 22nd St NW
- **Citibank** · 1775 Pennsylvania Ave NW
- **Riggs** · 1919 Pennsylvania Ave NW
- **Riggs** · 2600 Virginia Ave NW
- **Sun Trust** · 1750 New York Ave NW
- **United Bank** · 1875 I St NW
- **Wachovia** · 502 23rd St NW

Gas Stations

- **Chevron** · 2643 Virginia Ave NW
- **Exxon** · 2708 Virginia Ave NW

Hospitals

- **George Washington University** ·
  901 23rd St NW

o Landmarks

- **"Crossfire" Taping** · 805 21st St NW
- **Einstein Statue** · Constitution Ave NW &
  23rd St NW
- **Kennedy Center** · 2700 F St NW
- **The Octagon** · 1799 New York Ave NW
- **Watergate Hotel** · 2650 Virginia Ave NW

Libraries

- **Federal Reserve Board Research & Law Libraries** ·
  20th St & Constitution Ave NW
- **General Services Adm Library** ·
  1800 F St NW #1033
- **National Research Council Library** ·
  2101 Constitution Ave NW
- **US Department of the Interior Library** ·
  1849 C St NW
- **US State Library** · 2201 C St NW

P Parking

Pharmacies

- **CVS** · 1901 Pennsylvania Ave NW
- **CVS** · 2125 E St NW
- **CVS** · 2530 Virginia Ave NW
- **Foer's Pharmacy** · 818 18th St NW

Post Offices

- **McPherson Station** · 1750 Pennsylvania Ave NW
- **Watergate Station** · 2512 Virginia Ave NW

Schools

- **George Washington University** · 2121 I St NW
- **School Without Walls** · 2130 G St NW

Supermarkets

- **Safeway** · 2550 Virginia Ave NW

The mix of upscale and college dive is obvious. Aquarelle and Kinkead's are reserved for the power crowd and their hangers-on. If you forgot your jacket, duck into a gyro joint and then head for the nearest neon window to mingle with the college crowd.

Coffee

- **Cup'a Cup'a** · 600 New Hampshire Ave NW
- **Starbucks** · 1730 Pennsylvania Ave NW
- **Starbucks** · 1825 I St NW
- **Starbucks** · 1919 Pennsylvania Ave NW
- **Starbucks** · 800 21st St NW
- **Starbucks** · 801 18th St NW

Copy Shops

- **B&B Duplicators** · 818 18th St NW
- **Discovery Copy** · 2001 Pennsylvania Ave NW
- **Fast Copying & Printing** · 1745 Pennsylvania Ave NW
- **Merrill Corp** · 1776 I St NW
- **U Nik Press** · 900 19th St NW
- **Watergate Photo & Copy** · 2560 Virginia Ave NW

Gyms

- **Fitness Co** · 1875 I St NW

Liquor Stores

- **McReynold's Liquors** · 1776 G St NW
- **Pan Mar Wine & Liquors** · 1926 I St NW
- **Riverside Liquors** · 2123 E St NW
- **S&R Liquors** · 1800 I St NW
- **Tokay Liquors** · 506 23rd St NW
- **Watergate Wine & Beverage** · 2544 Virginia Ave NW

Movie Theaters

- **AFI Theater-Kennedy Center for the Performing Arts** · 2700 F St NW

Nightlife

- **Potomac Lounge** · 2650 Virginia Ave NW

Restaurants

- **Aquarelle** · 2650 Virginia Ave NW
- **Brasserie at the Watergate** · 600 New Hampshire Ave NW
- **Dish** · 924 25th St NW
- **Karma** · 1919 I St NW
- **Kinkead's** · 2000 Pennsylvania Ave NW
- **Nectar** · 824 New Hampshire Ave NW
- **Primi Piatti** · 2013 I St NW

Shopping

- **Motophoto** · 1819 H St NW
- **Saks Jandel** · 2522 Virginia Ave NW
- **Tower Records** · 2000 Pennsylvania Ave NW

Map 8 · **Georgetown**

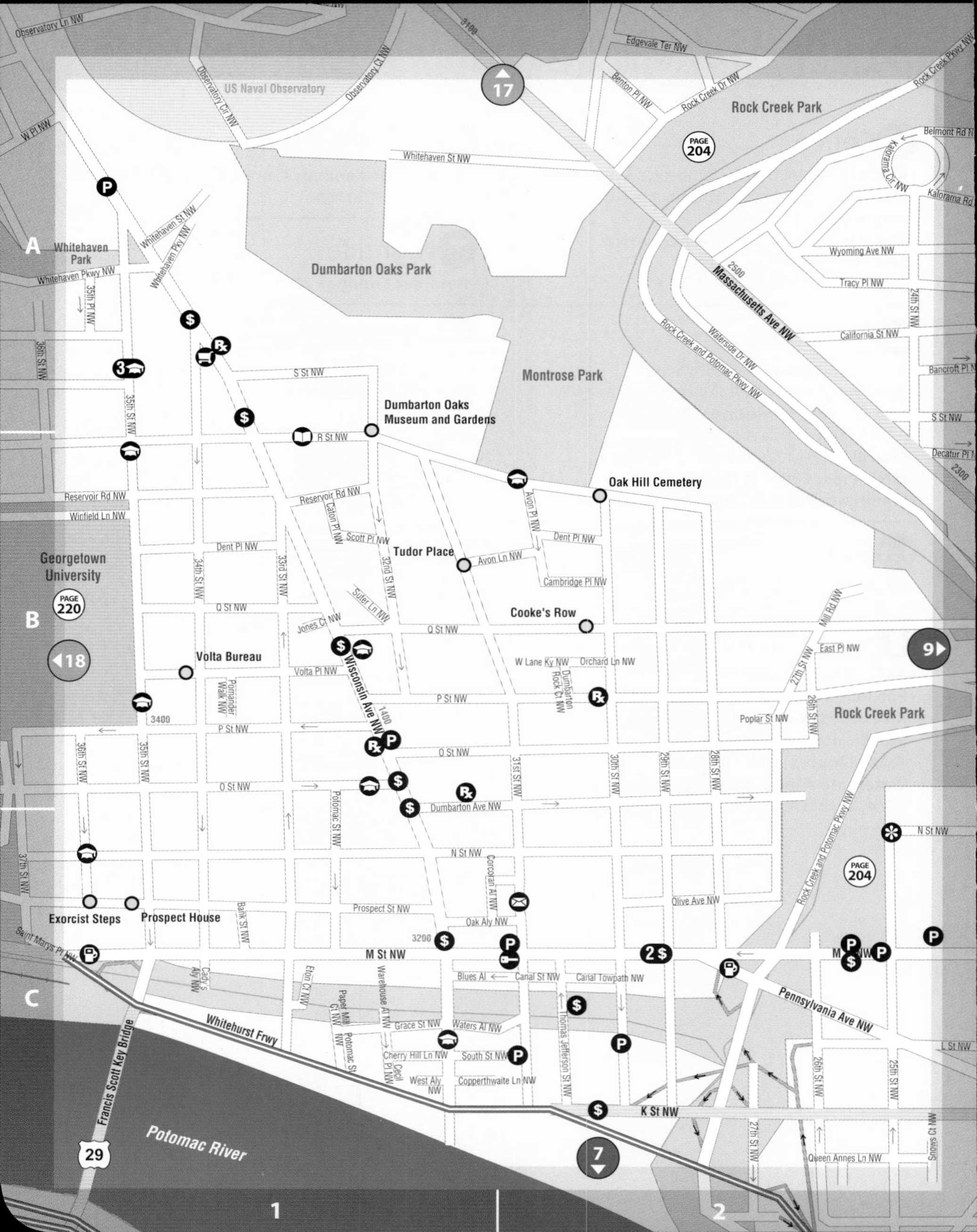

N

US Naval Observatory

Observatory Ln NW

Observatory Ct NW

31st

Edgevale Ter NW

Rock Creek Dr NW

Rock Creek Pkwy NW

Rock Creek Park

Belmont Rd NW

Whitehaven St NW

PAGE 204

W Pl NW

Benton Pl NW

Kalorama Rd NW

A

Whitehaven St NW

Dumbarton Oaks Park

Whitehaven Pkwy NW

Whitehaven Park

Whitehaven Pkwy NW

35th Pl NW

P

2500

Wyoming Ave NW

Tracy Pl NW

24th St NW

California St NW

Massachusetts Ave NW

Rock Creek and Potomac Pkwy NW

Waterside Dr NW

Bancroft Pl NW

S

36th St NW

R

Montrose Park

S St NW

Decatur St NW

2600

S St NW

35th St NW

3

S St NW

$

R St NW

Dumbarton Oaks Museum and Gardens

Reservoir Rd NW

Reservoir Rd NW

Oak Hill Cemetery

Wirfield Ln NW

Calvert St NW

Scott Pl NW

Dent Pl NW

Avon Pl NW

Dent Pl NW

B

Georgetown University

PAGE 220

34th St NW

33rd St NW

Q St NW

Cambridge Pl NW

Tudor Place

Avon Ln NW

Cooke's Row

◄18

Volta Bureau

Jones Ct NW

Pomander Walk NW

Volta Pl NW

3400

P St NW

Q St NW

28th St NW

27th St NW

Mill Rd NW

East Pl NW

9►

Wisconsin Ave NW

$

$

Snow Ct NW

W Lane Ky NW

Orchard Ln NW

P St NW

Dumbarton Rock Ct NW

Rock Creek Park

36th St NW

35th St NW

O St NW

R

Poplar St NW

O St NW

P

R

Potomac St NW

31st St NW

29th St NW

28th St NW

N St NW

37th St NW

Prospect St NW

$

R

$

Dumbarton Ave NW

N St NW

PAGE 204

✳

N St NW

Exorcist Steps

Bank St NW

Prospect House

Prospect St NW

Olive Ave NW

P

P

P

Oak Aly NW

Corcoran Aly NW

✉

M St NW

P

P

3200

$

2 **$**

P

26th St NW

25th St NW

Pennsylvania Ave NW

C

Whitehurst Frwy

Blues Aly

Canal St NW

Canal Towpath NW

Potomac St NW

Cherry Hill Ln NW

South St NW

Copperthwaite Ln NW

Grace St NW

Waters Al NW

West Aly NW

Cecil Pl NW

Thomas Jefferson St NW

$

P

P

L St NW

Potomac River

29

Francis Scott Key Bridge

St Mary's Pl NW

Cady's Aly NW

Pearl Aly NW

Warehouse Al NW

Potomac Aly NW

Ebbit St NW

$

K St NW

7

Queen Annes Ln NW

Sausalito St NW

Queen Annes Ct NW

1

2

Precious townhouses and stately manses. Cobblestone streets and garden tours. Yes, darling, this is a beautiful neighborhood. Society matrons have good reason to cluck. The main drags of K and Wisconsin are another matter altogether. Jammed by car and foot traffic day and night, no one worries that the upper-crust class on the side streets is rubbing off.

 $ Banks
- **Adams National** · 1729 Wisconsin Ave NW
- **Bank of America** · 1339 Wisconsin Ave NW
- **BB&T** · 1365 Wisconsin Ave NW
- **Chevy Chase** · 1545 Wisconsin Ave NW
- **Citibank** · 1901 Wisconsin Ave NW
- **Provident** · 1055 Thomas Jefferson St NW
- **Riggs** · 1201 Wisconsin Ave NW
- **Riggs** · 2550 M St NW
- **Riggs** · 3050 K St NW
- **Sun Trust** · 2929 M St NW
- **Wachovia** · 2901 M St NW

Car Rental
- **Enterprise** · 3307 M St NW

Community Gardens

Gas Stations
- **Exxon** · 3607 M St NW
- **Getty** · 2715 Pennsylvania Ave NW

o Landmarks
- **Cooke's Row** · 3009 - 3029 Q St NW
- **Dumbarton Oaks Museum and Gardens** · 1703 32nd St NW
- **Exorcist Steps** · 3600 Prospect St NW
- **Oak Hill Cemetery** · 3000 R St NW
- **Prospect House** · 3508 Prospect St NW
- **Tudor Place** · 1644 31st St NW
- **Volta Bureau** · 3417 Volta Pl NW

 Libraries
- **Georgetown Library** · 3260 R St NW

P Parking

 Pharmacies
- **CVS** · 1403 Wisconsin Ave NW
- **Dumbarton Pharmacy** · 3146 Dumbarton Ave NW
- **Morgan Care Pharmacy** · 3001 P St NW
- **Safeway** · 1855 Wisconsin Ave NW

Post Offices
- **Georgetown Station** · 1215 31st St NW

Schools
- **Corcoran School of Art & Design (Georgetown Campus)** · 1801 35th St NW
- **Devereux Children's Center of Washington, DC** · 3050 R St NW
- **Ellington School of the Arts** · 1698 35th St NW
- **Fillmore Arts Center Elementary** · 1819 35 St NW
- **Georgetown Montessori** · 1041 Wisconsin Ave NW
- **Georgetown Visitation Preparatory** · 1524 35th St NW
- **Hardy Middle** · 1819 35th St NW
- **Holy Trinity** · 1325 36th St NW
- **Hyde Elementary** · 3219 O St NW
- **Montessori School of Washington** · 1556 Wisconsin Ave NW

Supermarkets
- **Safeway** · 1855 Wisconsin Ave NW

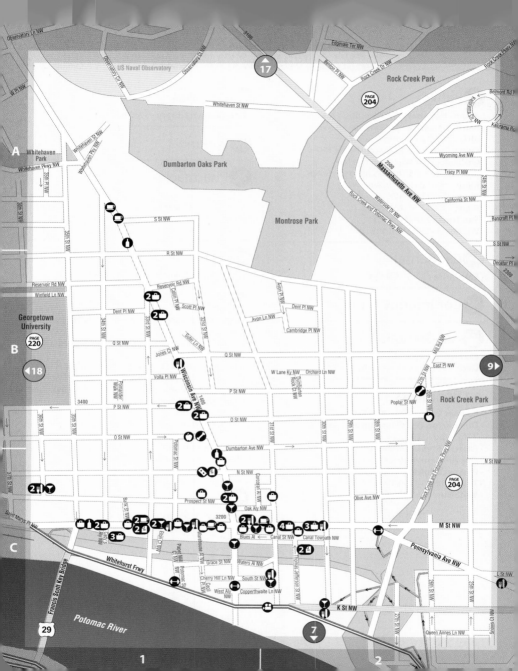

Map 8

Hands down the most comprehensive shopping strips in the city are here, which is why everybody packs onto its skinny sidewalks. At night, the human traffic jams don't disperse because there's also a raging nightlife. The bars and restaurants roughly fall into three categories: The Tombs and the like for the college crowd, a few joints like Pizza Paradiso for regular folks, and Nathan's and Farenheit for those annoying few who like to see themselves referred to in print as "glitterati."

Coffee
- **Cafe Europa** · 3222 M St NW
- **Starbucks** · 1810 Wisconsin Ave NW
- **Starbucks** · 1855 Wisconsin Ave NW
- **Starbucks** · 3122 M St NW

Copy Shops
- **Copy General** · 1055 Thomas Jefferson St NW
- **Kinko's** · 3329 M St NW
- **Staples** · 3307 M St NW
- **UPS Store** · 3220 N St NW
- **Zap Copies & Communications** · 1052 Thomas Jefferson St NW

Farmer's Markets
- **Freshfarm Market** · 3219 O St NW
- **Georgetown Farm Stand in Rose Park** · 26th & O Sts NW

Gyms
- **Fitness Co** · 1010 Wisconsin Ave NW
- **Four Seasons Fitness Club** · 2800 Pennsylvania Ave NW
- **Rich Bodies Gym** · 1000 Potomac St NW

Liquor Stores
- **Dixie Wine & Spirits** · 3429 M St NW
- **Towne Wine & Liquors** · 1326 Wisconsin Ave NW
- **Wagner's Liquor Shop** · 1717 Wisconsin Ave NW

Movie Theaters
- **Loews Georgetown 14** · 3111 K St NW

Nightlife
- **Blues Alley** · 1073 Wisconsin Ave NW
- **Degrees** · 3100 South St NW
- **Martin's Tavern** · 1264 Wisconsin Ave NW
- **Mie N Yu** · 3125 M St NW
- **Modern** · 3287 M St NW
- **Rino-Bar Pump House** · 3295 M St NW
- **Saloun** · 3239 M St NW
- **Sequoia** · 3000 K St NW
- **The Third Edition - Bar** · 1218 Wisconsin Ave NW
- **Tombs** · 1226 36th St NW

Pet Shops
- **Chichie's Canine Design** · 2614 P St NW
- **Georgetown Pet Gallery** · 3204 O St NW

Restaurants
- **1789** · 1226 36th St NW
- **Cafe Bonaparte** · 1522 Wisconsin Ave NW
- **Citronelle** · 3000 M St NW
- **Clyde's** · 3236 M St NW
- **Fahrenheit Restaurant** · 3100 South St NW
- **The Landmark** · 2430 Pennsylvania Ave NW
- **Nathan's** · 3150 M St NW
- **Old Glory All-American BBQ** · 3139 M St NW
- **Pizzeria Paradiso** · 3282 M St NW
- **Sequoia** · 3000 K St NW
- **The Tombs** · 1226 36th St NW

Shopping
- **Ann Saks** · 3328 M St NW
- **The Art Store** · 3019 M St NW
- **Baker Georgetown** · 3330 M ST NW
- **BCBG** · 3210 M St NW
- **Betsey Johnson** · 1319 Wisconsin Ave NW
- **Beyond Comics 2** · 1419-B Wisconsin Ave NW
- **Blink** · 3029 M St NW
- **Blue Mercury** · 3059 M St NW
- **Bo Concepts** · 3342 M St
- **Commander Salamander** · 1420 Wisconsin Ave NW
- **Dean and DeLuca** · 3276 M St NW
- **Deja Blue** · 3005 M St NW
- **Design Within Reach** · 3307 Cady's Alley NW
- **Georgetown Running Company** · 3401 M St NW
- **Georgetown Tobacco** · 3144 M St NW
- **Illuminations** · 3323 Cady's Alley NW
- **Jaryam** · 1631 Wisconsin Ave NW
- **Kate Spade** · 3061 M St NW
- **Kenneth Cole** · 1259 Wisconsin Ave NW
- **Ligne Roset** · 3306 M St NW
- **Marvelous Market** · 3217 P St NW
- **Movie Madness** · 1083 Thomas Jefferson St NW
- **Old Print Gallery** · 1220 31st St NW
- **Pottery Barn** · 3077 M St NW
- **Proper Topper** · 3213 P St NW
- **Relish** · 3312 Cady's Alley NW
- **Revolution Cycles** · 3411 M St NW
- **Sassanova** · 1641 Wisconsin Ave NW
- **Sherman Pickey** · 1647 Wisconsin Ave NW
- **Smith & Hawken** · 3077 M St NW
- **Sugar** · 1633 Wisconsin Ave NW
- **Toka Salon** · 3251 Prospect St NW
- **Urban Outfitters** · 3111 M St NW
- **Zara** · 1234 Wisconsin Ave NW

Video Rental
- **Video Plus** · 3222 N St NW

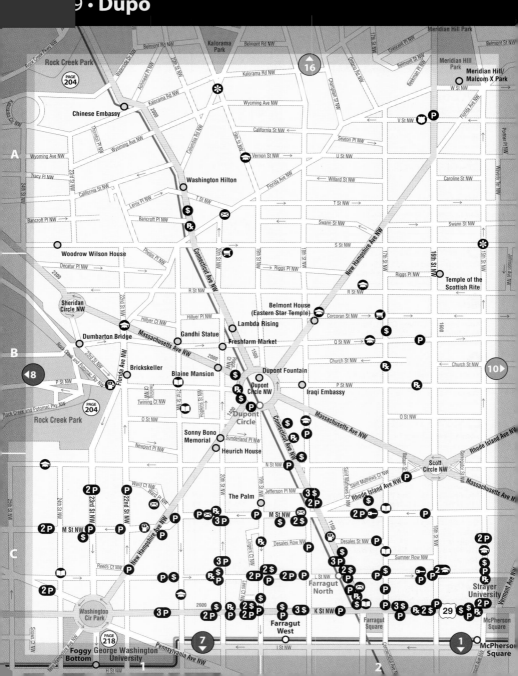

Meridian Hill Park

Meridian HIll Park
Malcom X Square

Rock Creek Park

PAGE 204

Chinese Embassy

Kalorama Park

Belmont Rd NW

Kalorama Rd NW

Wyoming Ave NW

California St NW

Vernon St NW

U St NW

Willard St NW

Caroline St NW

Washington Hilton

T St NW

Swann St NW

Swann St NW

S St NW

Woodrow Wilson House

Riggs Pl NW

Riggs Pl NW

Temple of the Scottish Rite

R St NW

R St NW

Sheridan Circle NW

Belmont House (Eastern Star Temple)

Corcoran St NW

Dumbarton Bridge

Lambda Rising

Q St NW

Gandhi Statue

Freshfarm Market

Brickskeller

Church St NW

Church St NW

PAGE 204

Blaine Mansion

Dupont Fountain

Dupont Circle NW

P St NW

Dupont Circle

Iraqi Embassy

O St NW

Rock Creek Park

Sonny Bono Memorial

Massachusetts Ave NW

Heurich House

Scott Circle NW

Massachusetts Ave NW

The Palm

M St NW

Farragut North

Strayer University

Washington Cir Park

Farragut West

Farragut Square

McPherson Square

PAGE 218

29

Foggy Bottom

George Washington University

Pennsylvania Ave NW

McPherson Square

Essentials

This is an urban mix of mostly single (gay or straight) young professionals living in an urban mix of row houses and apartments and milling among an urban mix of residential, office towers, and retail. Everybody's very proud of the urban mix. They even carry around bags from Kramerbooks with the cringe-inducing slogan "city living." Evenings and weekend afternoons, the neighborhood mobs up with newcomers. They all stroll through the restaurants and boutiques and sit around the fountain lawn at the neighborhood's center to watch the locals preen.

$ Banks
- **Adams National** · 1130 Connecticut Ave NW
- **Adams National** · 1501 K St NW
- **Adams National** · 1604 17th St NW
- **Bank of America** · 1612 K St NW
- **Bank of America** · 1801 K St NW
- **Bank of America** · 2102 L St NW
- **Bank of America** · 3 Dupont Cir NW
- **BB&T** · 1730 Rhode Island Ave NW
- **BB&T** · 1909 K St NW
- **Chevy Chase** · 1100 17th St NW
- **Chevy Chase** · 1800 M St NW
- **Chevy Chase** · 1850 K St NW
- **Citibank** · 1000 Connecticut Ave NW
- **Citibank** · 1225 Connecticut Ave NW
- **Eagle Bank** · 1228 Connecticut Ave NW
- **Eagle Bank** · 2001 K St NW
- **Independence Federal Savings** · 1020 19th St NW
- **Independence Federal Savings** · 1229 Connecticut Ave NW
- **M&T Bank** · 1680 K St NW
- **M&T Bank** · 1899 L St NW
- **Mellon Bank** · 1801 K St NW
- **Potomac Valley Bank** · 1629 K St NW
- **Presidential Savings** · 1660 K St NW
- **Riggs** · 1101 15th St NW
- **Riggs** · 1800 M St NW
- **Riggs** · 1875 Connecticut Ave NW
- **Riggs** · 1913 Massachusetts Ave NW
- **Riggs** · 1920 L St NW
- **Sun Trust** · 1111 Connecticut Ave NW
- **Sun Trust** · 1369 Connecticut Ave NW
- **Sun Trust** · 1925 K St NW
- **United Bank** · 1667 K St NW
- **United Bank** · 2301 M St NW
- **Wachovia** · 1100 Connecticut Ave NW
- **Wachovia** · 1300 Connecticut Ave NW
- **Wachovia** · 1510 K St NW
- **Wachovia** · 1800 K St NW
- **Wachovia** · 1850 M St NW
- **Wachovia** · 2000 L St NW

Car Rental
- **Avis** · 1722 M St NW
- **Budget** · 1620 L St NW

Community Gardens

Gas Stations
- **Exxon** · 2150 M St NW
- **Mobil** · 2200 P St NW
- **Unocal** · 1150 Connecticut Ave NW

Landmarks
- **Belmont House (Eastern Star Temple)** · 1618 New Hampshire Ave NW
- **Blaine Mansion** · 2000 Massachusetts Ave NW
- **Brickskeller** · 1523 22nd St NW
- **Chinese Embassy** · 2300 Connecticut Ave NW
- **Dumbarton Bridge** · 23rd St NW and Q St NW
- **Dupont Fountain** · Dupont Cir
- **Freshfarm Market** · 20th St NW near Q St
- **Gandhi Statue** · Massachusetts Ave & 21st St
- **Heurich House** · 1307 New Hampshire Ave NW

- **Iraqi Embassy** · 1801 P St NW
- **Lambda Rising** · 1625 Connecticut Ave NW
- **Meridian Hill/Malcolm X Park** · 15th & 16th St and W St NW
- **The Palm** · 1225 19th St NW
- **Sonny Bono Memorial** · 20th St NW & New Hampshire Ave NW
- **Temple of the Scottish Rite** · 1733 16th St NW
- **Washington Hilton** · 1919 Connecticut Ave NW
- **Woodrow Wilson House** · 2340 S St NW

Libraries
- **Arthur R Ashe Jr Foreign Policy Library** · 1426 21st St NW
- **Foundation Center** · 1001 Connecticut Ave NW
- **National Geographic Society Library** · 1145 17th St NW
- **Polish Library in Washington** · 1503 21st St NW
- **US Institute of Peace** · 1200 17th St NW # 200
- **West End Library** · 1101 24th St NW

P Parking

R Pharmacies
- **CVS** · 1025 Connecticut Ave NW
- **CVS** · 1500 K St NW
- **CVS** · 1517 17th St NW
- **CVS** · 1637 P St NW
- **CVS** · 1990 K St NW
- **CVS** · 2000 L St NW
- **CVS** · 2000 M St NW
- **CVS** · 6 Dupont Cir NW
- **Rite Aid** · 1034 15th St NW
- **Rite Aid** · 1815 Connecticut Ave NW
- **Stat Script Pharmacy** · 1638 K St NW
- **Tschiffely Pharmacy** · 1145 19th St NW
- **Tschiffely Pharmacy** · 1330 Connecticut Ave NW

Police
- **MPDC 3rd District Station** · 1620 V St NW

Post Offices
- **Farragut Station** · 1800 M St NW
- **Temple Heights Station** · 1921 Florida Ave NW
- **Twentieth St Station** · 2001 M St NW
- **Ward Place Station** · 2121 Ward Pl NW
- **Washington Square Station** · 1050 Connecticut Ave NW

Schools
- **Adams Elementary** · 2020 19th St NW
- **Arts Explorer Performing Conservatory** · 2209 Massachusetts Ave NW
- **Auto Arts Academy** · 1100 16th St NW
- **Emerson Preparatory** · 1324 18th St NW
- **Francis Junior High** · 2425 N St NW
- **Rock Creek International Upper School** · 1621 New Hampshire Ave NW
- **Ross Elementary** · 1730 R St NW
- **School for Arts in Learning** · 1100 16th St NW
- **Stevens Elementary** · 1050 21st St NW
- **Strayer University (Washington Campus)** · 1133 15th St NW

Supermarkets
- **Safeway** · 1701 Corcoran St NW
- **Safeway** · 1800 20th St NW

Map 9

Dupont serves a crowd a bit older than the potential *Elimidate* contestants that jam Adams Morgan's 18th Street. Connecticut Avenue is a dining destination with some of the city's best restaurants, such as Galileo, and some of the city's most popular, like the always packed Lauriol Plaza. Afterward, Firefly is a good place to witness Duponters' self-image as sophisticated drinkers. Local 16 and Chi-Cha Lounge, both on U Street, are good antidotes to the more frenetic meat markets in lower Adams Morgan.

Coffee
- **Andalus Coffee Shop** · 2118 18th St NW
- **Caribou Coffee** · 1101 17th St NW
- **Casey's Coffee** · 2000 L St NW
- **Coffee Espress** · 2001 L St NW
- **Coffee Express** · 1101 Connecticut Ave NW
- **Coffee & the Works** · 1627 Connecticut Ave NW
- **Cosi:** · 1350 Connecticut Ave NW
  - · 1501 K St NW · 1647 20th St NW
  - · 1875 K St NW · 1919 M St NW
- **Donna's Coffee Bar** · 2033 M St NW
- **Java Green** · 1020 19th St NW
- **Jolt'n Bolt Coffee & Tea House** · 1918 18th St NW
- **Love Café** · 1506 U Street NW
- **Net Cafe** · 2400 N St NW
- **Puccini's Espresso** · 1620 L St NW
- **Seattle's Best Coffee** · 2055 L St NW
- **Soho Tea & Coffee** · 2150 P St NW
- **Starbucks:**
  - · 1600 K St NW · 1001 Connecticut Ave NW
  - · 1205 19th St NW · 1301 Connecticut Ave NW
  - · 1600 U St NW · 1501 Connecticut Ave NW
  - · 1734 L St NW · 1700 Connecticut Ave NW
  - · 1900 K St NW · 2101 P St NW

Copy Shops
- **ABC Imaging** · 1133 20th St NW
- **ABS Complete Printing** · 1150 Connecticut Ave NW
- **Color Imaging Center** · 1725 Desales St NW
- **Commercial Duplicating Service** · 1920 L St NW
- **Cop Cats** · 1140 17th St NW
- **Copy General** · 2000 L St NW
- **Courthouse Copy** · 2029 K St NW
- **Da 2 Da Legal** · 1925 K St NW
- **Deadline Press** · 1020 19th St NW
- **Document Technology** · 2000 M St NW
- **Dupont Circle Copy** · 11 Dupont Cir NW
- **Eagle Printing** · 1156 15th St NW
- **Hot-Line Duplicating** · 1718 20th St NW
- **Ikon Office Solutions** · 1120 20th St NW
- **Kinko's:** · 1612 K St NW · 2020 K St NW
- **Minuteman Press** · 2000 K St NW
- **Office Depot** · 2000 K St NW
- **Omni Dox** · 2101 L St NW
- **Panic Press** · 2055 L St NW
- **Park Press** · 1518 K St NW
- **Press Express Copy & Printing** · 1015 18th St NW
- **Printer** · 1803 Florida Ave NW
- **Reprographic Technologies** · 2000 L St NW
- **RLS Legal Solutions** · 1233 20th St NW
- **Sequential** · 1615 L St NW
- **Sir Speedy Printing:**
  - · 1025 17th St NW · 1300 Connecticut Ave NW
  - · 1660 L St NW · 2134 L St NW
- **Spee-Dee-Que Duplicating** · 1417 22nd St NW
- **Staples** · 1901 L St NW
- **UPS Store:** · 1718 M St NW · 2100 M St NW
- **US Printing & Copying** · 1725 M St NW

Farmer's Markets
- **Freshfarm Market** · 20th St NW & Q St NW

Gyms
- **Bally Total Fitness** · 2000 L St NW
- **Curves** · 1710 Rhode Island Ave NW
- **Fitness First** · 1075 19th St
- **Gold's Gym** · 1120 20th St NW
- **One To One Fitness** · 1770 K St NW
- **Results the Gym** · 1612 U St NW
- **Sports Club/LA** · 1170 22nd St NW
- **Third Power Fitness** · 2007 18th St NW
- **Train Like a Pro** · 1050 Connecticut Ave NW
- **Training for Results** · 1612 U St NW
- **Washington Hilton Sport Club** ·
  1919 Connecticut Ave NW
- **Washington Sports Clubs** · 1211 Connecticut Ave NW
- **Washington Sports Clubs** · 1990 M St NW
- **Washington Sports Health Club** · 1835
  Connecticut Ave NW

Hardware Stores
- **Adams Morgan Hardware** · 2200 18th St NW
- **Candey Hardware** · 1210 18th St NW
- **District True Value Hardware** · 2003 P St NW
- **True Value Hardware** · 1623 17th St NW

Liquor Stores
- **Barmy Wine & Liquor** · 1912 L St NW
- **Bell Liquor & Wine Shoppe** · 1821 M St NW
- **Benmoll Liquors** · 1700 U St NW
- **Cairo Wine & Liquor Store** · 1618 17th St NW
- **Downtown Spirits & Deli** · 1522 K St NW
- **Imperial Liquor** · 1050 17th St NW
- **State Liquors** · 2159 P St NW
- **Wine Specialists** · 2115 M St NW

Movie Theaters
- **Loews Dupont Circle 5** · 1350 19th St NW
- **Visions Cinema Bistro Lounge** · 1927 Florida Ave NW

Nightlife
- **17th St Bar & Grill** · 1615 Rhode Island Ave NW
- **Acropolis** · 1337 Connecticut Ave NW
- **Aroma** · 2401 Pennsylvania Ave NW
- **Bar Rouge** · 1315 16th St NW
- **Biddy Mulligan's** · 1500 New Hampshire Ave NW
- **Big Hunt** · 1345 Connecticut Ave NW
- **Bravo Bravo** · 1001 Connecticut Ave NW
- **Brickskeller** · 1523 22nd St NW
- **Buffalo Billiards** · 1330 19th St NW
- **Café Japone** · 2032 P St NW
- **Chaos** · 1603 17th St NW
- **Chi-Cha Lounge** · 1624 U St NW
- **Common Share** · 2003 18th St NW
- **Dragonfly** · 1215 Connecticut Ave NW
- **Eighteenth Street Lounge** · 1212 18th St NW
- **Firefly** · 1310 New Hampshire Ave NW
- **Fireplace** · 2161 P St NW
- **Gazuza** · 1629 Connecticut Ave NW
- **Improv** · 1140 Connecticut Ave NW
- **La Frontera Cantina** · 1633 17th St NW
- **Local 16** · 1604 U St NW
- **Lucky** · 1221 Connecticut Ave NW
- **Lulu's** · 1217 22nd St NW
- **McClellan's** · 1919 Connecticut Ave NW
- **Omega** · 2122 P St NW
- **Ozio** · 1813 M St NW
- **Recessions** · 1823 L St NW
- **Red** · 1802 Jefferson Pl NW
- **Rendezvous** · 2226 18th St NW
- **Rumors** · 1900 M St NW
- **Russia House Restaurant and Lounge** ·
  1800 Connecticut Ave NW
- **Sign of the Whale** · 1825 M St NW
- **Soussi** · 2228 18th St NW
- **Staccato** · 2006 18th St NW
- **Stetson's Famous Bar & Restaurant** · 1610 U St NW
- **Tabard Inn - Bar** · 1739 N St NW
- **Topaz Bar** · 1733 N St NW
- **Townhouse Tavern** · 1637 R St NW
- **Trio's Fox & Hounds** · 1537 17th St NW
- **Wave** · 1731 New Hampshire Ave NW
- **Zebra Bar and Lounge** · 1170 22nd St NW

Pet Shops
- **Companions Pet Shop** · 1626 U St NW

Restaurants
- **Chi-Cha Lounge** · 1624 U St NW
- **Galileo** · 1110 21st St NW
- **Kramerbooks & Afterwards Cafe** ·
  1517 Connecticut Ave NW
- **Lauriol Plaza** · 1835 18th St NW
- **Local 16** · 1602 U St NW
- **Love Cafe** · 1501 U St NW
- **Luna Grill & Diner** · 1301 Connecticut Ave NW
- **Marcel's** · 2401 Pennsylvania Ave NW
- **Olives** · 1600 K St NW
- **Pizzeria Paradiso** · 2029 P St NW
- **Tabard Inn** · 1739 N St NW
- **Thaiphoon** · 2011 S St NW
- **Vidalia** · 1990 M St NW

Shopping
- **Andre Chreky, the Salon Spa** · 1604 K St NW
- **Bang Salon** · 1612 U St NW
- **Bedazzled** · 1507 Connecticut Ave NW
- **Best Cellars** · 1643 Connecticut Ave NW
- **Betsy Fisher** · 1224 Connecticut Ave NW
- **Blue Mercury** · 1745 Connecticut Ave NW
- **Brooks Brothers** · 1201 Connecticut Ave NW
- **Burberry** · 1155 Connecticut Ave NW
- **Cake Love** · 1506 U St NW
- **Chapters Literary Bookstore** · 1512 K St NW
- **Comfort One Shoes** · 1621 Connecticut Ave NW
- **Comfort One Shoes** · 1630 Connecticut Ave NW
- **Custom Shop Clothiers** · 1033 Connecticut Ave NW
- **Doggie Style** · 1825 18th St NW
- **Downs Engravers & Stationers** · 1746 L St NW
- **Drilling Tennis & Golf** · 1040 17th St NW
- **Fufua** · 1642 R St NW
- **Ginza** · 1721 Connecticut Ave NW
- **Godiva Chocolatier** · 1143 Connecticut Ave NW
- **The Guitar Shop** · 1216 Connecticut Ave NW
- **Human Rights Campaign** · 1629 Connecticut Ave NW
- **J Press** · 1801 L St NW
- **The Kid's Closet** · 1226 Connecticut Ave NW
- **Kramerbooks** · 1517 Connecticut Ave NW
- **Kulturas** · 1706 Connecticut Ave NW
- **Lambda Rising Bookstore** · 1625 Connecticut Ave NW
- **Marvelous Market** · 1511 Connecticut Ave NW
- **Meeps and Aunt Neensy's** · 1520 U St NW
- **Melody Records** · 1623 Connecticut Ave NW
- **Millenium Decorative Arts** · 1528 U St NW
- **Nana** · 1534 U St NW
- **National Geographic Shop** · 17 & M St NW
- **Newsroom** · 1754 Connecticut Ave NW
- **Pasargad Antique and Fine Persian** ·
  1217 Connecticut Ave NW
- **Pleasure Palace** · 1710 Connecticut Ave NW
- **Proper Topper** · 1350 Connecticut Ave NW
- **Rizik's** · 1100 Connecticut Ave NW
- **Rock Creek** · 2029 P St NW
- **Second Story** · 2000 P St NW
- **Secondi** · 1702 Connecticut Ave NW
- **Skynear and Co** · 2122 18th St NW
- **Sticky Fingers Bakery** · 1904 18th St NW
- **Tabletop** · 1608 20th St NW
- **Taxation Without Representation** · 1500 U St NW
- **The Third Day** · 2001 P St NW
- **Thomas Pink** · 1127 Connecticut Ave NW
- **Tiny Jewel Box** · 1147 Connecticut Ave NW
- **Wild Women Wear Red** · 1512 U St NW
- **Wine Specialists** · 2115 M St NW
- **The Written Word** · 1365 Connecticut Ave NW

Video Rental
- **Blockbuster Video** · 1639 P St NW
- **Capitol Video Sales** · 1729 Connecticut Ave NW
- **Capitol Video Sales** · 2028 P St NW
- **Empire Video** · 1511 17th St NW
- **Tapeheadz Video** · 1709 17th St NW
- **Video American of Dupont** ·
  2104 18th St NW

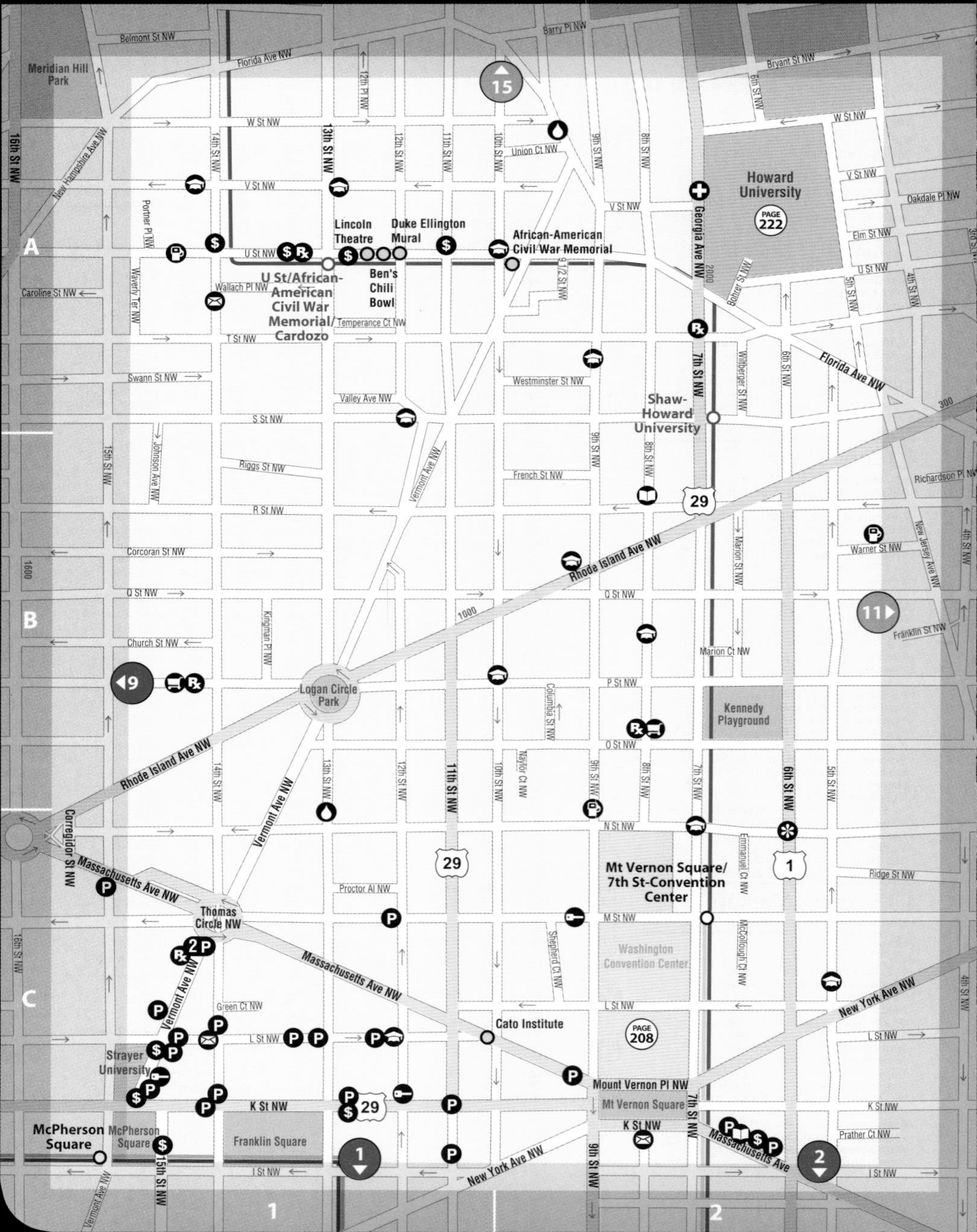

Map 10 · **Logan Circle / U Street**

N

Meridian Hill
Park

Belmont St NW

Florida Ave NW

Barry Pl NW

Bryant St NW

16th St NW

New Hampshire Ave NW

W St NW

13th St NW

12th Pl NW

11th St NW

9th St NW

8th St NW

6th St NW

W St NW

V St NW

V St NW

14th St NW

Union Ct NW

V St NW

**Howard
University**

PAGE
222

Oakdale Pl NW

Portner Pl NW

Waverly Ter NW

Caroline St NW

U St NW

Lincoln
Theatre

Duke Ellington
Mural

9 1/2 St NW

African-American
Civil War Memorial

Georgia Ave NW

Bohrer St NW

Elm St NW

5th St NW

A

Ben's
Chili
Bowl

Wallach Pl NW

U St/African-
American
Civil War
Memorial/
Cardozo

Temperance Ct NW

Florida Ave NW

300

T St NW

Swann St NW

Valley Ave NW

Westminster St NW

**Shaw-
Howard
University**

7th St NW

Wiltberger St NW

6th St NW

Richardson Pl NW

Johnson Ave NW

Riggs St NW

Vermont Ave NW

S St NW

French St NW

9th St NW

8th St NW

Warner St NW

New Jersey Ave NW

R St NW

29

Corcoran St NW

1600

Q St NW

Rhode Island Ave NW

Q St NW

11

Kingman Pl NW

1000

Columbia St NW

Marion St NW

Franklin St NW

Church St NW

9

P St NW

P St NW

Marion Ct NW

**Kennedy
Playground**

B

Logan Circle
Park

13th St NW

12th St NW

11th St NW

10th St NW

9th St NW

8th St NW

7th St NW

6th St NW

5th St NW

O St NW

Rhode Island Ave NW

14th St NW

Vermont Ave NW

N St NW

Mt Vernon Square/
7th St-Convention
Center

Emmanuel Ct NW

N St NW

Ridge St NW

29

Najdof Ct NW

McCullough St NW

1

Corregidor St NW

Massachusetts Ave NW

P

Thomas
Circle NW

Proctor Al NW

**Washington
Convention Center**

New York Ave NW

15th St NW

P

2 P

Vermont Ave NW

Massachusetts Ave NW

Shepherd Ct NW

PAGE
208

C

Green Ct NW

P

Cato Institute

L St NW

**Strayer
University**

P P

L St NW

P P

P

Mount Vernon Pl NW

Mt Vernon Square

7th St NW

S

K St NW

K St NW

P

P

New York Ave NW

2

**McPherson
Square**

McPherson
Square

S

15th St NW

Franklin Square

P

K St NW

29

S

1

9th St NW

New York Ave NW

Massachusetts Ave

Prather Ct NW

I St NW

I St NW

1

2

Map 10

Watch the young, hip crowd transform these former drug-and-crime infested blocks into ever more creative, and expensive, retail. Just make sure to get here before the march of gentrification tramples the independent shops, eclectic music scene, and loungey nightlife.

$ Banks
- **Bank of America** · 1090 Vermont Ave NW
- **Bank of America** · 635 Massachusetts Ave NW
- **BB&T** · 1316 U St NW
- **Chevy Chase** · 925 15th St NW
- **Citibank** · 1000 Vermont Ave NW
- **Industrial Bank** · 2000 11th St NW
- **Industrial Bank** · 2000 14th St NW
- **Sun Trust** · 1250 U St NW
- **Sun Trust** · 1275 K St NW

Car Rental
- **Enterprise** · 1029 Vermont Ave NW #1
- **Rent-A-Wreck** · 910 M St NW
- **Thrifty** · 1001 12th St NW

Car Washes
- **Mr Wash** · 1311 13th St NW
- **Sparkle Car Wash** · 933 Florida Ave NW

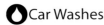 Community Gardens

Gas Stations
- **Amoco** · 1317 9th St NW
- **Chevron** · 4200 Burroughs Ave NE
- **Mobil** · 1442 U St NW

Hospitals
- **Howard University** · 2112 Georgia Ave NW

o Landmarks
- **African-American Civil War Memorial** · 1000 U St NW
- **Ben's Chili Bowl** · 1213 U St NW
- **Cato Institute** · 1000 Massachusetts Ave NW
- **Duke Ellington Mural** · 1200 U St NW
- **Lincoln Theatre** · 1215 U St NW

Libraries
- **Bureau of Alcohol & Tobacco Library** · 650 Massachusetts Ave NW
- **Watha T Daniel Branch Library** · 1701 8th St NW

P Parking

Pharmacies
- **CVS** · 1199 Vermont Ave NW
- **CVS** · 1418 P St NW
- **CVS** · 1900 7th St NW
- **Giant Food Pharmacy** · 1414 8th St NW
- **Rite Aid** · 1306 U St NW

Post Offices
- **Martin Luther King Jr Station** · 1400 L St NW
- **Mid City Station** · 1915 14th St NW
- **Techworld Station** · 800 K St NW

Schools
- **Children's Studio School** · 1301 V St NW
- **Garnet-Patterson Middle** · 2001 10th St NW
- **Garrison Elementary** · 1200 S St NW
- **Immaculate Conception** · 711 N St NW
- **Maya Angelou Public Charter** · 1851 9th St NW
- **Seaton Elementary** · 1503 10th St NW
- **Shaw Junior High** · 925 Rhode Island Ave NW
- **St Augustine** · 1421 V St NW
- **Sunrise Academy** · 1130 6th St NW
- **Thomson Elementary** · 1200 L St NW
- **Ujima Ya Ujamaa School** · 1554 8th St NW

 Supermarkets
- **Giant Food** · 1414 8th St NW
- **Whole Foods Market** · 1440 P St NW

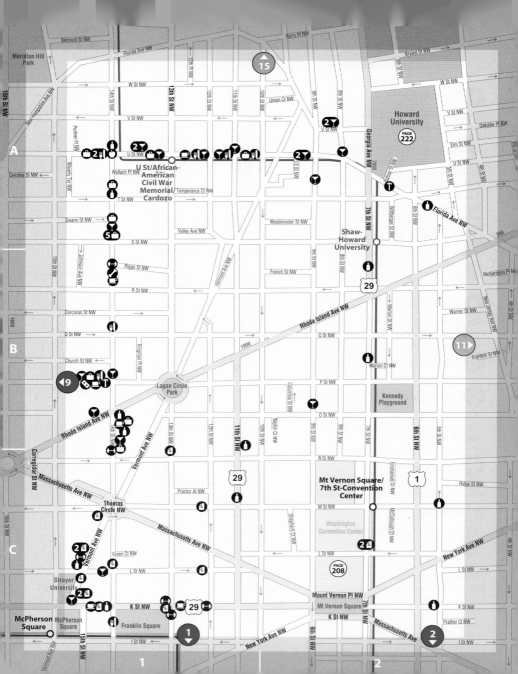

A 14th Street makeover has turned a former prostitutes' catwalk into an interior design haven. At the same time, U Street has raised from the riot ashes to become boutique-ville. At night, both have some of the best martinis and relaxed bars in the city. Score one of Cafe Saint-Ex's outdoor tables on a summer night and you're set. Otherwise, check out the jazz at Bohemian Caverns or the bands at the 9:30 Club or Black Cat.

Coffee
- **Caribou Coffee** • 1400 14th St NW
- **Cosi** • 1275 K St NW
- **Sparky's Expresso Cafe** • 1720 14th St NW
- **Starbucks** • 1250 U St NW
- **Starbucks** • 1429 P St NW
- **Starbucks** • 1455 K St NW

Copy Shops
- **Bar Legal Copy** • 1224 M St NW
- **Bar Legal Copy** • 1312 13th St NW
- **Barrister Copy Solutions** • 1090 Vermont Ave NW
- **Capitol Press** • 1101 Vermont Ave NW
- **Clicks Professional Copy** • 1424 K St NW
- **CPN Technology** • 1111 7th St NW
- **Global Printing** • 1301 K St NW
- **Imagenet** • 1110 Vermont Ave NW
- **Instant Copies & Print** • 1010 Vermont Ave NW
- **KCR Copy** • 1 Thomas Cir NW
- **Miller Copying Service** • 1111 7th St NW
- **Print Express** • 1101 14th St NW
- **Sir Speedy Printing** • 1029 Vermont Ave NW
- **UPS Store** • 1220 L St NW

Farmer's Markets
- **14th & U Farmers Market** • 14th & U Sts NW

Gyms
- **Crew Club** • 1321 14th St NW
- **Franklin Plaza Health Club** • 1200 K St NW
- **Franklin Square Athletic Club** • 1301 K St NW
- **Nautilus Fitness Center** • 1101 Vermont Ave NW
- **One World Fitness** • 1738 14th St NW
- **Renaissance Swim & Fitness** • 999 9th St NW

Hardware Stores
- **Best Price Hardware** • 636 Florida Ave NW
- **Logan Hardware** • 1416 P St NW

Liquor Stores
- **A-1 Wine & Liquor** • 1420 K St NW
- **Barrel House** • 1341 14th St NW
- **Best in Liquors** • 1450 P St NW
- **Bestway Liquors** • 2011 14th St NW
- **Continental Liquors** • 1100 Vermont Ave NW
- **District Liquors** • 1211 11th St NW
- **Log Cabin Liquors** • 1748 7th St NW
- **Longs Liquors** • 520 Florida Ave NW
- **Market Liquor** • 1337 11th St NW
- **NNN Liquors** • 1549 7th St NW
- **Paradise Liquor** • 1900 14th St NW
- **S&W Liquors** • 1428 9th St NW
- **Sav-On-Liquors** • 1414 14th St NW
- **Subway Liquors II** • 500 K St NW
- **Weiman's Liquor** • 1201 5th St NW

Nightlife
- **2-K9** • 2008 8th St NW
- **9:30** • 815 V St NW
- **Bar Nun** • 1326 U St NW
- **Between Friends** • 1115 U St NW
- **Black Cat** • 1811 14th St NW
- **Bohemian Caverns** • 2003 11th St NW
- **Cafe Saint-Ex** • 1847 14th St NW
- **Daedalus** • 1010 Vermont Ave NW
- **DC9** • 1940 9th St NW
- **Helix Lounge** • 1430 Rhode Island Ave NW
- **Kingpin** • 917 U St NW
- **Republic Gardens** • 1355 U St NW
- **The Saint** • 1520 14th St NW
- **The Saloon** • 1205 U St NW
- **So Much More** • 1428 L St NW
- **Titan** • 1337 14th St NW
- **Twins Jazz** • 1344 U St NW
- **Velvet Lounge** • 915 U St NW

Pet Shops
- **Pet Essentials** • 1722 14th St NW

Restaurants
- **Ben's Chili Bowl** • 1213 U St NW
- **Coppi's** • 1414 U St NW
- **DC Coast** • 1401 K St NW
- **Dukem** • 1114 U St NW
- **Georgia Brown's** • 950 15th St NW
- **Logan Tavern** • 1423 P St NW
- **Oohhs and Aahhs** • 1005 U St NW
- **Rice** • 1608 14th St NW
- **U-topia** • 1418 U St NW

Shopping
- **Blink** • 1431 P ST NW
- **Capitol Records** • 1020 U St NW
- **Garden District** • 1801 14th St NW
- **Go Mama Go!** • 1809 14th St NW
- **Good Wood** • 1428 U St NW
- **Home Rule** • 1807 14th St NW
- **Maison 14** • 1325 14th St NW
- **Muleh** • 1831 14th St NW
- **Pop** • 1803 14th St NW
- **Pulp** • 1803 14th St NW
- **Reincarnation Furnishings** • 1401 14th St NW
- **Ruff and Ready** • 1908 14th St NW
- **Urban Essentials** • 1330 U St NW

## Video Rental
- **Empire Video** • 1435 P St NW

This is one of the rougher neighborhoods still not fully recovered from the '60s riots. Developers and newcomers are venturing in while a redevelopment plan is in full swing along H Street. A new New York Avenue metro stop promises a brighter future.

 Banks
- **Bank of America** · 340 Florida Ave NE
- **Riggs** · 1348 4th St NE
- **Riggs** · 800 Florida Ave NE
- **Sun Trust** · 410 Rhode Island Ave NE

Car Washes
- **NY Avenue Car Wash** · 39 New York Ave NE

Gas Stations
- **Amoco** · 1231 New York Ave NE
- **Amoco** · 306 Rhode Island Ave NW
- **Amoco** · 400 Rhode Island Ave NE
- **Amoco** · 45 Florida Ave NE
- **Exxon** · 1 Florida Ave NE
- **Hess** · 1739 New Jersey Ave NW

Libraries
- **Sursum Corda Community Library** · 135 New York Ave NW

Parking

Pharmacies
- **CVS** · 660 Rhode Island Ave NE
- **Ennis Pharmacy** · 1904 4th St NE
- **Giant Food Pharmacy** · 1050 Brentwood Rd
- **Safeway** · 514 Rhode Island Ave NE

Post Offices
- **Washington Main Office** · 900 Brentwood Rd NE

 Schools
- **Calvary Christian Academy** · 616 Rhode Island Ave NE
- **City Lights** · 62 T St NE
- **Cleaveland Elementary** · 300 Bryant St NW
- **Cook Elementary** · 30 P St NW
- **DC Preparatory Academy** · 701 Edgewood St NE
- **Dunbar High** · 1301 New Jersey Ave NW
- **Emery Elementary** · 1720 1st St NE
- **Gage Eckington Elementary** · 2025 3rd St NW
- **Gallaudet University** · 800 Florida Ave NE
- **Gonzaga College** · 19 I St NW
- **Hamilton Special Education Center** · 1401 Brentwood Pkwy NE
- **Holy Name** · 1217 West Virginia Ave NE
- **Holy Redeemer** · 1135 New Jersey Ave NW
- **Hyde Leadership** · 101 T St NE
- **Kendall Demonstration Elementary/Model Secondary School** · 800 Florida Ave NE
- **Kennedy Institute Upper School** · 680 Rhode Island Ave NE
- **McKinley Technology Senior High** · 151 T St NE
- **MM Washington Career Senior High** · 27 O St NW
- **Montgomery Elementary** · 421 P St NW
- **Noyes Elementary** · 1401 Brentwood Rd NE
- **Pre-Engineering Senior High** · 1301 New Jersey Ave NW
- **Shaed Elementary** · 301 Douglas St NE
- **Terrell Center** · 1000 1st St NE
- **Walker-Jones Elementary** · 100 L St NW
- **Washington Center** · 27 O St NW
- **William E Doar Jr Elementary** · 705 Edgewood St
- **Wilson** · 660 K St NE

Supermarkets
- **Giant Food** · 1050 Brentwood Rd
- **Safeway** · 514 Rhode Island Ave NE

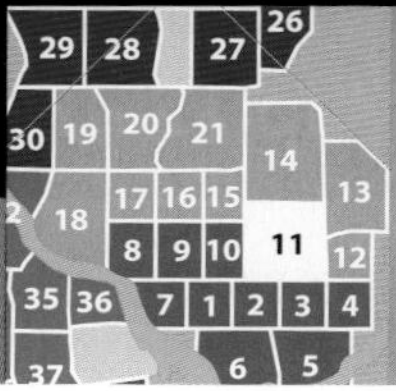

Waiting for revitalization to kick in means traveling to another neighborhood for amenities.

Map 11

Farmer's Markets

- **DC Farmer's Market** · 1309 5th St NE
- **North Capitol Neighborhood Farmer's Market** · 1626 N Capitol St NE
- **Rhode Island Flea Market & Farmer's Market** · 4th St & Rhode Island Ave NE

Gyms

- **Aerobodies Fitness** · 147 Rhode Island Ave NW

Hardware Stores

- **Home Depot** · 901 Rhode Island Ave

Liquor Stores

- **Big Ben Liquor Store** · 1300 N Capitol St NW
- **Bloomingdale Liquor** · 1836 1st St NW
- **Coast-In Liquors** · 301 Florida Ave NE
- **Edgewood Liquor Store** · 2303 4th St NE
- **J&J Liquor Store** · 1211 Brentwood Rd NE
- **JB Liquorette** · 1000 Florida Ave NE
- **Mac's Wine & Liquor** · 401 Rhode Island Ave NE
- **Northeast Liquors** · 1300 5th St NE
- **Oasis Liquors** · 1179 3rd St NE
- **Rhode Island Subway Liquor** · 914 Rhode Island Ave NE
- **Sosnik's Liquor Store** · 2318 4th St NE
- **Star Wine & Liquor Store** · 1824 N Capitol St NW
- **Sunset Liquors** · 1627 1st St NW
- **Walter Johnson's Liquor Store** · 1542 N Capitol St NW

Nightlife

- **Bud's** · 501 Morse St NE

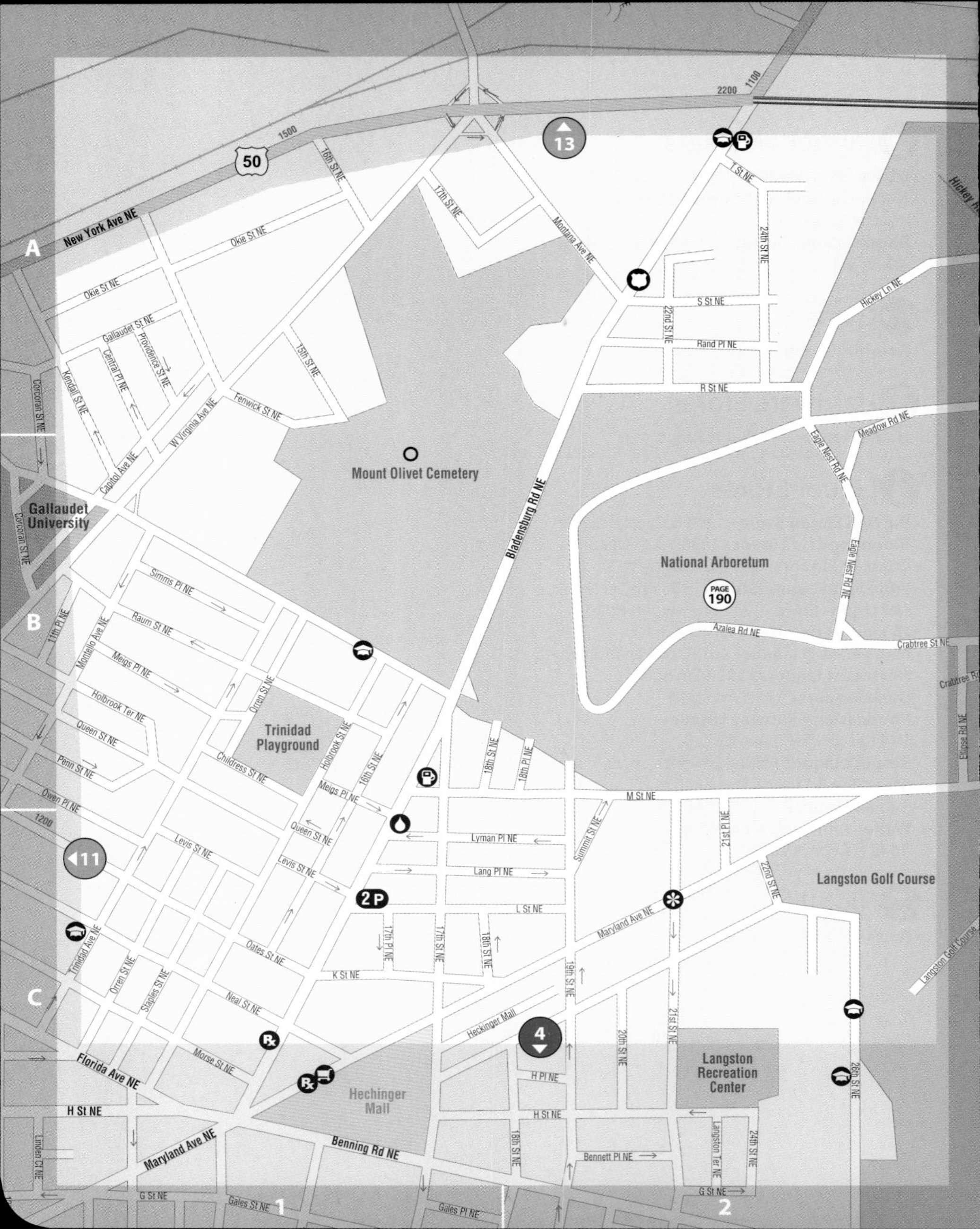

Map 12 · **Trinidad**

Ⓝ

New York Ave NE

50

1500

2200

1700

T St NE

A

Okie St NE

17th St NE

18th St NE

Montana Ave NE

24th St NE

Hickey Ln NE

Hickey R

13

S St NE

22nd St NE

Gallaudet St NE

Prospect St NE

Central Pl NE

19th St NE

Fenwick St NE

W Virginia Ave NE

Rand Pl NE

R St NE

Eagle Nest Rd NE

Meadow Rd NE

Kendall St NE

Corcoran St NE

Capitol Ave NE

Mount Olivet Cemetery

National Arboretum

PAGE
190

Eagle Nest Rd NE

**Gallaudet
University**

Corcoran St NE

Azalea Rd NE

Crabtree St NE

Crabtree

B

15th St NE

Montana Ave NE

Simms Pl NE

Baum St NE

Meigs Pl NE

Holbrook Ter NE

Queen St NE

Penn St NE

Childress St NE

**Trinidad
Playground**

Levis St NE

Owen Pl NE

1200

Holbrook St NE

Meigs Pl NE

Queen St NE

Levis St NE

18th St NE

18th St NE

Simms St NE

M St NE

21st St NE

26th St NE

Ellicott Rd NE

Langston Golf Course

Langston Golf Course

11

Lyman Pl NE

Lang Pl NE

L St NE

Trinidad Ave NE

Orren St NE

Staples St NE

Neal St NE

17th Pl NE

17th St NE

18th St NE

Maryland Ave NE

19th St NE

2 P

❋

K St NE

C

Florida Ave NE

Morse St NE

Rx

Rx

Heckinger Mall

4

Heckinger Mall

20th St NE

21st St NE

**Langston
Recreation
Center**

24th St NE

26th St NE

**Hechinger
Mall**

H St NE

18th Pl NE

H St NE

Langston Golf Course

H St NE

Maryland Ave NE

Benning Rd NE

18th St NE

Bennett Pl NE

Langston Ter NE

24th St NE

Linden Ct NE

G St NE

Gales Pl NE

Gales Pl NE

G St NE

1

2

A neglected rabbit's warren of dead-end streets, this neighborhood has only pockets of stability. For the rest of the city residents, these parts are seen from the window of a car en route to the Beltway or the Arboretum.

Map

⬤ Car Washes

· **Smoke Detail Hand Carwash** ·
  1161 Bladensburg Rd NE

✳ Community Gardens

⛽ Gas Stations

· **Amoco** · 1201 Bladensburg Rd NE
· **Exxon** · 1925 Bladensburg Rd NE

○ Landmarks

· **Mount Olivet Cemetery** ·
  1300 Bladensberg Rd NW

Ⓟ Parking

℞ Pharmacies

· **CVS** · 845 Bladensburg Rd
· **Safeway** · 1601 Maryland Ave NE

✪ Police

· **MPDC 5th District Station** ·
  1805 Bladensburg Rd NE

🏫 Schools

· **Browne Junior High** · 850 26th St NE
· **New School for Enterprise and Development** ·
  1920 Bladensburg Rd NE
· **Webb Elementary** · 1375 Mount Olive Rd NE
· **Wheatley Elementary** · 1299 Neal St NE
· **Young Elementary** · 820 26th St NE

🛒 Supermarkets

· **Safeway** · 1601 Maryland Ave NE

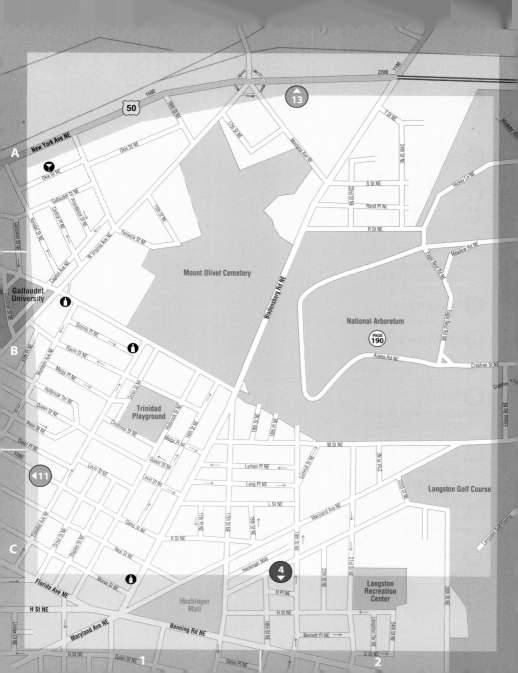

Beyond the drivable destination nightclubs, like Dream, there ain't much here to slow down for.

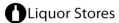Liquor Stores

- **Acme Liquors** · 1730 Trinidad Ave
- **Kovaks Liquors** · 1237 Mount Olivet Rd NE
- **Rose's Liquor** · 830 Bladensburg Rd NE

Nightlife

- **Dream** · 1350 Okie St NE

Here's an architecturally diverse little slice of the suburbs within city limits. It's a traditionally African-American middle-class enclave that is diversifying with newcomers from downtown who want more room and yard work.

Banks
- **Wachovia** · 2119 Bladensburg Rd NE

Car Rental
- **A&D Auto Rental** · 2712 Bladensburg Rd NE
- **Enterprise** · 1502 Franklin St NE
- **Thrifty** · 3210 Rhode Island Ave

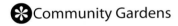**Car Washes**
- **Montana Double Car Wash** · 2327 18th St NE

Community Gardens

**Gas Stations**
- **Amoco** · 2210 Bladensburg Rd NE
- **Hess** · 1801 New York Ave NE
- **Shell** · 1830 Rhode Island Ave NE
- **Texaco** · 1765 New York Ave NE

 Landmarks
- **Franciscan Monastery** · 1400 Quincy St NE

Libraries
- **Woodridge Library** · 1801 Hamlin St NE

Pharmacies
- **Rite Aid** · 1401 Rhode Island Ave

Post Offices
- **Woodridge Station** · 2211 Rhode Island Ave NE

Schools
- **Bunker Hill Elementary** · 1401 Michigan Ave NE
- **Burroughs Elementary** · 1820 Monroe St NE
- **Friendship-Edison-Woodridge Campus** · 2959 Carlton Ave NE
- **Langdon Elementary** · 1900 Evarts St SE
- **Latin American Montessori Bilingual** · 1725 Michigan Ave NE
- **Rhema Christian Center** · 1825 Michigan Ave NE
- **Slowe Elementary** · 1404 Jackson St NE
- **St Anselm's Abbey** · 4501 South Dakota Ave NE
- **St Francis de Sales** · 2019 Rhode Island Ave NE
- **Taft** · 1800 Perry St NE

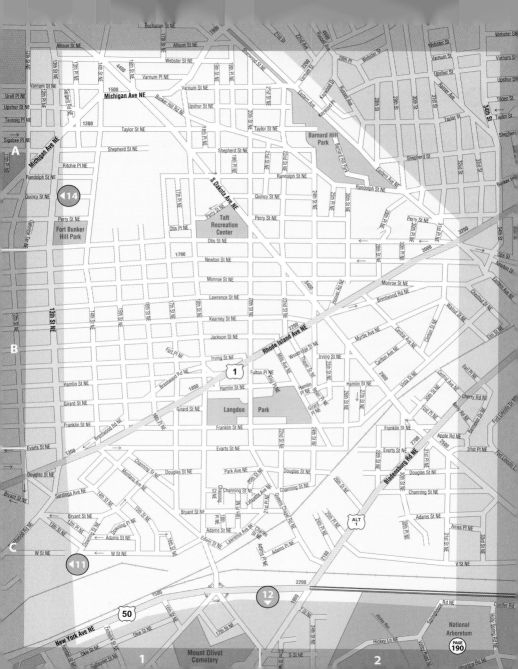

People here came to get away from the urban hubbub. And they did.

Map

Coffee
- **Dunkin' Donuts** · 2420 New York Ave NE

Gyms
- **Mini Health Club** · 1818 New York Ave NE

Liquor Stores
- **Good Ole Reliable Liquor** ·
  1513 Rhode Island Ave NE
- **Montana Liquors** · 1805 Montana Ave NE
- **National Wine & Liquors** ·
  2310 Rhode Island Ave NE
- **Pal Liquors** · 1905 Brentwood Rd NE
- **Peacock Liquors** · 1625 New York Ave NE
- **Sammy's Liquor** · 2725 Bladensburg Rd NE
- **Stop & Shop Liquors** · 3011 Rhode Island Ave NE
- **Syd's Drive-In Liquor Store** ·
  2325 Bladensburg Rd NE
- **Woodridge Vet's Liquors** · 1358 Brentwood Rd NE

Nightlife
- **Aqua** · 1818 New York Ave NE
- **Breeze Metro** · 2335 Bladensburg Rd NE
- **DC Tunnel** · 2135 Queens Chapel Rd NE

Restaurants
- **Bamboo Joint Café** · 2062 Rhode Island Ave NE

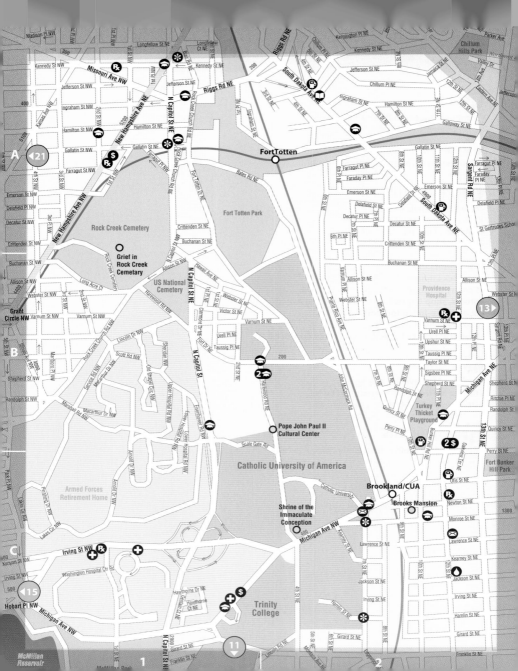

The name says it all. Devoted Catholics have their pick of prayer space here as the university's pastoral campus rolls into the Basilica of the National Shrine grounds that rolls into the Pope John Paul II Cultural Center's sprawling lawn. Amen.

Banks
• **Chevy Chase** • 210 Michigan Ave NE
• **Citibank** • 3800 12th St NE
• **Riggs** • 3806 12th St NE
• **Wachovia** • 5005 New Hampshire Ave NW

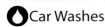 Car Washes
• **McDonald Custom Car Care** • 3221 12th St NE

✱ Community Gardens

Ⓟ Gas Stations
• **Amoco** • 3701 12th St NE
• **Amoco** • 4925 South Dakota Ave NE
• **Exxon** • 1020 Michigan Ave NE
• **Exxon** • 5501 South Dakota Ave NE

✚ Hospitals
• **Children's National Medical** •
  111 Michigan Ave NW
• **Providence** • 1150 Varnum St NE
• **US Veterans Medical Center** • 50 Irving St NW
• **Washington Hospital Center** • 110 Irving St NW

⚬ Landmarks
• **Brooks Mansion** • 901 Newton St NE
• **Grief in Rock Creek Cemetery** •
  Rock Creek Church Rd NW
• **Pope John Paul II Cultural Center** •
  3900 Harewood Road NE
• **Shrine of the Immaculate Conception** •
  400 Michigan Ave NE

Libraries
• **Lamond-Riggs Library** •
  5401 South Dakota Ave NE

℞ Pharmacies
• **CVS** • 128 Kennedy St NW
• **CVS** • 3601 12th St NE
• **New Hampshire Pharmacy** •
  5001 New Hampshire Ave NW
• **Physicans Office Building Pharmacy** •
  106 Irving St NW
• **Wellington Pharmacy** • 1160 Varnum St NE

✉ Post Offices
• **Brookland Station** • 3401 12 St NE
• **Catholic University Cardinal Station** •
  620 Michigan Ave NE

🎓 Schools
• **Archbishop Carroll** • 4300 Harewood Rd NE
• **Backus Middle** • 5171 South Dakota Ave NE
• **Brookland Elementary** • 1150 Michigan Ave NE
• **Catholic University of America** •
  620 Michigan Ave NE
• **JOS-ARZ Academy** • 220 Taylor St NE
• **Luke Moore Academy** • 1000 Monroe St NE
• **Maime Lee Elementary** • 100 Gallatin St NE
• **Roots Public Charter** • 15 Kennedy St NW
• **Rudolph Elementary** • 5200 2nd St NW
• **St Anthony** • 12th St NE & Lawrence St NE
• **Tri-Community Elementary** • 3700 N Capitol St NW
• **Trinity College** • 125 Michigan Ave NE
• **Universal Ballet Academy** • 4301 Harewood Rd NE
• **Village Learning Center Middle & High** • 3
  3 Riggs Rd NE

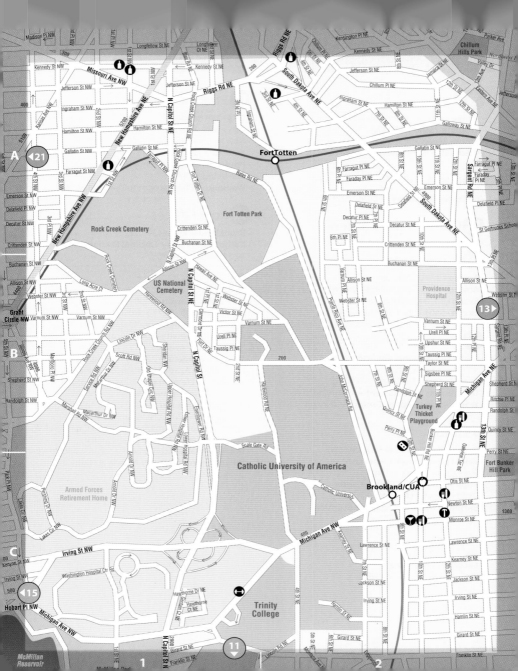

A few neighborhood taverns and neighborhood restaurants serve the locals. But if you live elsewhere, there's no secular reason to make a pilgrimage here.

Farmer's Markets
- **Historic Brookland Farmer's Market** ·
  10th St NE & Otis St NE

Gyms
- **Curves** · 212 Michigan Ave NE

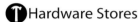
Hardware Stores
- **Brookland True Value** · 3501 12th St NE

Liquor Stores
- **Dakota Liquors** · 5510 3rd St NE
- **Fair Liquors** · 5008 1st St NW
- **Kennedy Liquors** · 5501 1st St NW
- **Northwest Liquors** · 300 Kennedy St NW
- **Riggs Wine & Liquors** · 5581 South Dakota Ave NE
- **Whelan's Liquors** · 3903 12th St NE

Nightlife
- **Colonel Brooks' Tavern** · 901 Monroe St NE

Restaurants
- **Colonel Brooks' Tavern** · 901 Monroe St NE
- **Java Head Café** · 3629 12th St NE
- **Kelly's Ellis Island** · 3908 12th St NE

Video Rental
- **Stage One Video** · 3748 10th St NE

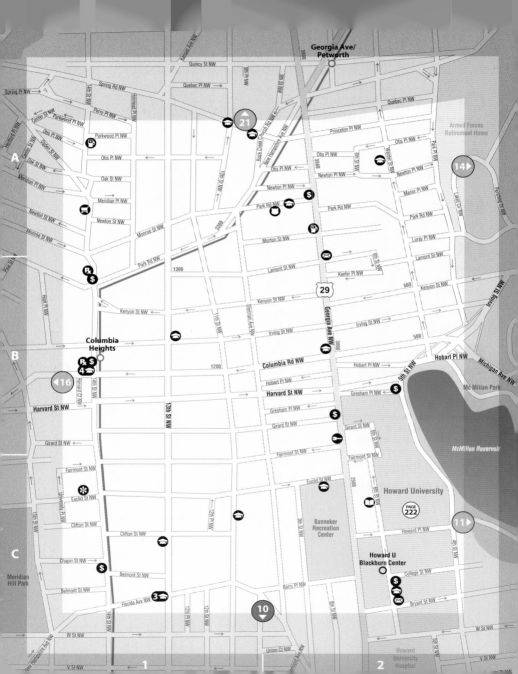

Transitional with a capital T. These blocks have, for years, been caught between the entrenched families who live here, gangs who sporadically rage through here, and developers who want to gentrify here.

Banks

- **Bank of America** · 2397 6th St NW
- **Bank of America** · 2400 14th St NW
- **Bank of America** · 3031 14th St NW
- **Bank of America** · 3500 Georgia Ave NW
- **Bank of America** · 511 Gresham Pl NW
- **Riggs** · 3300 14th St NW
- **Wachovia** · 2801 Georgia Ave NW

Car Rental

- **Enterprise** · 2730 Georgia Ave NW

Community Gardens

Gas Stations

- **Amoco** · 3426 Georgia Ave NW
- **Exxon** · 3540 14th St NW

o Landmarks

- **Howard U Blackburn Center** · 2400 6th St NW

Libraries

- **Howard University School of Business Library** · 2600 6th St NW

Pharmacies

- **Columbia Heights Pharmacy** · 3316 14th St NW
- **CVS** · 3031 14th St NW

Police

- **MPDC 3rd District Substation** · 750 Park Rd NW

Post Offices

- **Columbia Heights Finance** · 3321 Georgia Ave NW
- **Howard University** · 2400 6th St NW

Schools

- **Banneker High** · 800 Euclid St NW
- **Booker T Washington Public Charter School For Technical** · 1346 Florida Ave NW
- **Bruce-Monroe Elementary** · 3012 Georgia Ave NW
- **Capital City Public Charter Elementary** · 3029 14th St NW
- **Cardozo High** · 1300 Clifton St NW
- **Cesar Chavez Public Charter School for Public Policy** · 1346 Florida Ave NW
- **DC Bilingual Public Charter** · 1420 Columbia Rd NW
- **EL Haynes Elementary** · 3029 14th St NW
- **Howard University** · 2400 6th St NW
- **Meridian Public Charter** · 1328 Florida Ave NW
- **Meyer Elementary** · 2501 11th St NW
- **Nation House Watoto Shule/Sankofa Fie** · 770 Park Rd NW
- **Next Step/El Proximo Paso** · 1419 Columbia Rd NW
- **Park View Elementary** · 3560 Warder St NW
- **Paul Robeson Center Elementary** · 3700 10th St NW
- **Raymond Elementary** · 915 Spring Rd NW
- **Tubman Elementary** · 3101 13th St NW

Supermarkets

- **Giant Food** · 3460 14th St NW

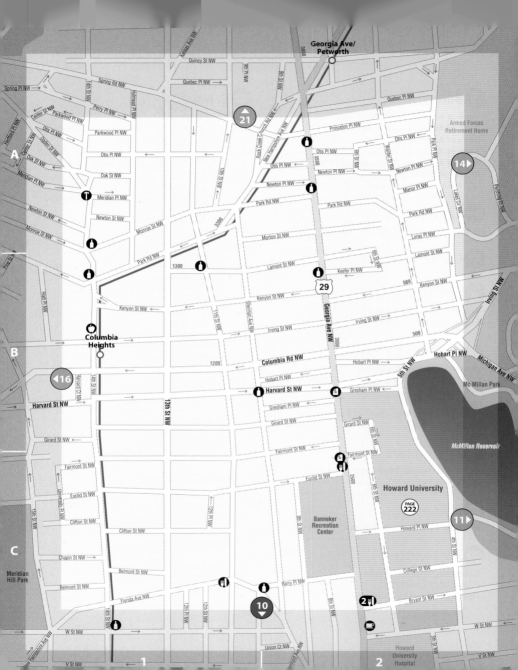

A handful of restaurants are local favorites, like the greasy spoon Florida Avenue Grill and the laid-back Soul Vegetarian and Exodus Café. But, for now, the after-meal nightlife is less dicey in other neighborhoods.

Coffee
• **Starbucks** • 2225 Georgia Ave NW

Copy Shops
• **Howard Copy** • 2618 Georgia Ave NW
• **Uptown Offices** • 2851 Georgia Ave NW

Farmer's Markets
• **Columbia Heights Community Marketplace** • 14th & Irving Sts NW

Hardware Stores
• **Cooper Hardware Inc** • 3459 14th St NW

Liquor Stores
• **CC Liquor** • 3401 14th St NW
• **Florida Liquors** • 2222 14th St NW
• **Gayle Enterprises** • 3313 11th St NW
• **Giant Liquors** • 3504 Georgia Ave NW
• **Harvard Wine & Liquor Store** • 2901 Sherman Ave NW
• **Petworth Liquors** • 3210 Georgia Ave NW
• **Robin's Liquor Store** • 997 Florida Ave NW
• **Speedy Liquors** • 3328 14th St NW
• **Young Hee-Kim Liquors** • 3614 Georgia Ave NW

Restaurants
• **Five Guys** • 2301 Georgia Ave NW
• **Florida Grill** • 1100 Florida Ave NW
• **Negril** • 2301 Georgia Ave NW
• **Soul Vegetarian and Exodus Café** • 2606 Georgia Ave NW

From the Salvadorian community garden to the glut of Ethiopian eats to the frat house scene along 18th street, these two neighborhoods are where different races and ethnicities mix most in DC. Adams Morgan is the nightlife destination, especially for those who may or may not be of drinking age. Mt. Pleasant has fewer offerings, but those that are there are laid-back sanctuaries from the rowdiness to the south.

Banks

- **Bank of America** · 1835 Columbia Rd NW
- **Bank of America** · 3131 Mount Pleasant St NW
- **Citibank** · 1749 1/2 Columbia Rd NW
- **Riggs** · 1779 Columbia Rd NW
- **Sun Trust** · 1800 Columbia Rd NW

 Community Gardens

Gas Stations

- **Exxon** · 1827 Adams Mill Rd NW

o Landmarks

- **Marilyn Monroe Mural** · Connecticut Ave NW & Calvert St NW
- **Meridian International Center** · 1630 Crescent Place NW
- **Mexican Cultural Institute** · 2829 16th St NW
- **White-Meyer House** · 1624 Crescent Place NW

Libraries

- **Mt Pleasant Library** · 3160 16th St NW

 Parking

Pharmacies

- **CVS** · 1700 Columbia Rd NW
- **Mt Pleasant Care Pharmacy** · 3169 Mount Pleasant St NW
- **Safeway** · 1747 Columbia Rd NW

Post Offices

- **Kalorama Station** · 2300 18th St NW

 Schools

- **Bancroft Elementary** · 1755 Newton St NW
- **Bell Multicultural High** · 3145 Hiatt Pl NW
- **Carlos Rosario High** · 16th St NW & Irving St NW
- **Cooke Elementary** · 2525 17th St NW
- **Elsie Whitlow Stokes Community Freedom** · 3220 16th St NW
- **Lincoln Middle** · 3101 16th St NW
- **Marie Reed Elementary** · 2200 Champlain St NW
- **Sacred Heart** · 1625 Park Rd NW
- **San Miguel** · 1525 Newton St NW

Supermarkets

- **Safeway** · 1747 Columbia Rd NW

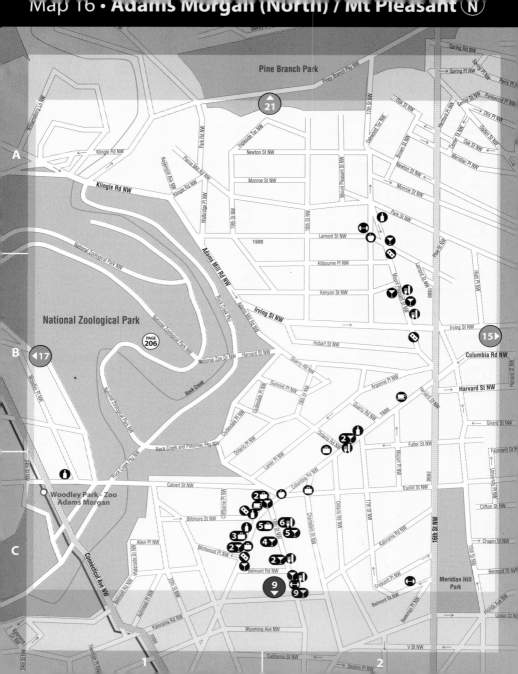

Map 16 • Adams Morgan (North) / Mt Pleasant Ⓝ

These neighborhoods cater to the drinking crowd. A good day would start with nursing a hangover at the beloved Mt. Pleasant institution Dos Gringos. Then, stumble down to wait for a window seat at Tryst, where you can linger over a sandwich. Or save the appetite for a perfectly seasoned steak at Rumba Café. By then you'll be ready for a bar crawl that will, inevitably, end with you shimmying to "Little Red Corvette" at Chief Ike's Mambo Room.

Coffee
- **Cafe Park Plaza** · 1629 Columbia Rd NW
- **Starbucks** · 1801 Columbia Rd NW

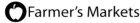Farmer's Markets
- **Adams Morgan** · 18th St & Columbia Rd NW
- **Mt Pleasant Farmers Market** ·
  17th & Lamont Sts NW

Gyms
- **Curves** · 3220 17th St NW
- **Gold's Gym** · 2318 18th St NW
- **One on One Fitness** · 1616 Belmont St NW

Liquor Stores
- **AB Liquor** · 1803 Columbia Rd NW
- **Comet Liquors** · 1815 Columbia Rd NW
- **Metro Liquors** · 1726 Columbia Rd NW
- **Sherry's Wine & Liquor** · 2315 Calvert St NW
- **Sportsman's Wine & Liquors** ·
  3249 Mount Pleasant St NW

Nightlife
- **Adams Mill Bar and Grill** ·
  1813 Adams Mill Rd NW
- **Angles** · 2339 18th St NW
- **Angry Inch Saloon** · 2450 18th St NW
- **Asylum** · 2471 18th St NW
- **Bedrock Billiards** · 1841 Columbia Rd NW
- **Blue Room Lounge** · 2321 18th St NW
- **Bossa** · 2463 18th St NW
- **Brass Monkey** · 2317 18th St NW
- **Café Toulouse** · 2431 18th St NW
- **Chief Ike's Mambo Room** · 1725 Columbia Rd NW
- **Columbia Station** · 2325 18th St NW
- **Cosmo Lounge** · 1725 Columbia Rd NW
- **Crush** · 2323 18th St NW
- **Dan's** · 2315 18th St NW
- **Felix Lounge** · 2406 18th St NW
- **Kokopooli's Pool Hall** · 2305 18th St NW
- **Madam's Organ** · 2461 18th St NW
- **Mantis** · 1847 Columbia Rd NW
- **Marx Café** · 3203 Mt Pleasant St NW
- **Pharmacy Bar** · 2337 18th St NW

- **The Raven** · 3125 Mt Pleasant Ave NW
- **The Reef** · 2446 18th St NW
- **Rumba Cafe** · 2443 18th St NW
- **Saki** · 2477 18th St NW
- **Spy Lounge** · 2406 18th St NW
- **Timehri International** · 2439 18th St NW
- **Tom Tom** · 2333 18th St NW
- **Tonic Bar** · 3155 Mt Pleasant St NW
- **Zucchabar** · 1841 Columbia Rd NW

Restaurants
- **Bardia's New Orleans Café** · 2412 18th St NW
- **The Diner** · 2453 18th St NW
- **Dos Gringos** · 3116 Mt Pleasant St NW
- **La Fourchette** · 2429 18th St NW
- **Leftbank** · 2424 18th St NW
- **The Little Fountain Café** · 2339 18th St NW
- **Meskerem** · 2434 18th St NW
- **Pasta Mia** · 1790 Columbia Rd NW
- **Rumba Café** · 2443 18th St NW
- **Tonic** · 3155 Mt Pleasant St NW
- **Tryst** · 2459 18th St NW

Shopping
- **All About Jane** · 2438 1/2 18th St NW
- **Betty** · 2439 18th St NW
- **City Bikes** · 2501 Champlain St NW
- **Daisy** · 1814 Adams Mill Rd
- **Fleet Feet** · 1841 Columbia Rd NW
- **Idle Times Books** · 2467 18th St NW
- **Kobos African Clothiers** · 2444 18th St NW
- **Little Shop of Flowers** · 1812 Adams Mill Rd NW
- **Miss Pixie's Furnishing and What-Not** ·
  1810 Adams Mill Rd NW
- **Shake Your Booty** · 2439 18th St NW
- **So's Your Mom** · 1831 Columbia Road NW
- **Trim** · 2700 Ontario Rd NW 2nd Flr
- **Yes! Natural Gourmet** · 1825 Columbia Rd NW

Video Rental
- **Blockbuster Video** · 1805 Columbia Rd NW
- **Lamont Video** · 3171 Mount Pleasant St NW
- **Luna & Children Video** ·
  3064 Mount Pleasant St NW
- **Video King** · 1845 Columbia Rd NW

Map 9 • **Woodley Park / Cleveland Park**

Melvin C Hazen Park

Quebec Pl NW

Porter St NW

35th St NW

35th St NW

34th Pl NW

33rd St NW

Ordway St NW

Quebec St NW

Quebec St NW

Cleveland Park

Porter St NW

Williamsburg Ln NW

Highland Pl NW

20

Ashley Ter NW

30th St NW

29th St NW

36th St NW

Newark St NW

34th St NW

Ross Pl NW

34th St NW

27th St NW

A

Macomb St NW

34th St NW

2700

Klingle Rd NW

National Zoological Park

PAGE 206

35th St NW

Lowell St NW

33rd St NW

34th Pl NW

33rd Pl NW

Devonshire Pl NW

30th St NW

National Zoological Park NW

Washington National Cathedral

32nd St NW

Cortland Pl NW

28th St NW

Hawthorne St NW

16 ►

◄ 18

33rd Pl NW

Cleveland Ave NW 3200

Woodley Rd NW

Cathedral Ave NW

29th St NW

Connecticut Ave NW

Hawthorne St NW

B

Garfield St NW

Hawthorne St NW

27th St NW

Woodley Pl NW

3500

35th Pl NW

35th St NW

34th Pl NW

Fulton St NW

31st St NW

Garfield Ter NW

Garfield St NW

Woodley Rd NW

36th St NW

35th Pl NW

Massachusetts Ave NW

31st Pl NW

Thompson Cir NW

Woodland Dr NW

29th St NW

2600

Edmunds St NW

31st St NW

Normanstone Dr NW

Normanstone Ter NW

30th St NW

28th St NW

Davis St NW

Observatory Cir NW

US Naval Observatory

2500

Calvert St NW

2 $

W Pl NW

US Naval Observatory

Normanstone Park

McGill Ter NW

30th St NW

Woodley Park - Zoo Adams Morgan

Observatory Pl NW

3100

Normanstone Ln NW

24th St NW

C

Observatory Ln NW

8

Edgevale Ter NW

Montrose Park

Wisconsin Ave NW

Observatory Pl NW

Benton Pl NW

Rock Creek Pkwy

Whitehaven St NW

Rock Creek Dr NW

Wake me when we get to Dupont. Oh, it's not *that* boring. Certainly, it's not a snoozer like the faux suburbs to the north, but it could use some jazzing up. When the Connecticut Avenue restaurants shutter for the night, the young professionals who rent here have to walk to Adams Morgan or jump the metro to keep the buzz on.

 Banks

- **Bank of America** · 2631 Connecticut Ave NW
- **Bank of America** · 3401 Connecticut Ave NW
- **M&T Bank** · 2620 Connecticut Ave NW

 **Car Rental**

- **Enterprise** · 2601 Calvert St NW #M

 **Community Gardens**

 Landmarks

- **US Naval Observatory** · Massachusetts Ave NW

 **Libraries**

- **Cleveland Park Library** ·
  3310 Connecticut Ave NW
- **James Melville Gilliss Library** ·
  3450 Massachusetts Ave NW

 Pharmacies

- **Cathedral Pharmacy** · 3000 Connecticut Ave NW
- **CVS** · 3327 Connecticut Ave NW

Post Offices

- **Cleveland Park Station** ·
  3430 Connecticut Ave NW

Schools

- **Aidan Montessori** · 2700 27th St NW
- **Beauvoir-The National Cathedral Elementary** ·
  3500 Woodley Rd NW
- **Eaton Elementary** · 3301 Lowell St NW
- **Maret School** · 3000 Cathedral Ave NW
- **National Child Research Center** ·
  3209 Highland Pl NW
- **Oyster Elementary** · 2801 Calvert St NW
- **Washington International Upper School** ·
  3100 Macomb St NW

Melvin C Hazen Park

Quebec Pl NW

Porter St NW

35th St NW

Quebec St NW

Ordway St NW

Quebec St NW

Highland Pl NW

34th Pl NW

33rd St NW

Ashley Ter NW

Cleveland Park

Porter St NW

29th St NW

Williamsburg Ln NW

Newark St NW

20

A

Ross Pl NW

34th St NW

35th St NW

Macomb St NW

2700

33rd St NW

National Zoological Park

Lowell St NW

Klingle Rd NW

34th St NW

27th St NW

PAGE
206

National Zoological Park NW

Washington National Cathedral

Cortland Pl NW

Devonshire Pl NW

28th St NW

◀18

32nd St NW

Woodley Rd NW

Cathedral Ave NW

33rd Pl NW

Cleveland Ave NW 3200

Hawthorne St NW

Connecticut Ave NW

Hawthorne St NW

16▶

B

Garfield St NW

35th St NW

34th Pl NW

Fulton St NW

31st NW

29th St NW

28th St NW

27th St NW

Garfield St NW

Woodley Rd NW

Woodley Rd NW

Woodley Rd NW

3500

Massachusetts Ave NW

35th Pl NW

31st Pl NW

Garfield Ter NW

Thompson Cir NW

Woodland Dr NW

29th Pl NW

Edmunds St NW

4▶

29th St NW

Davis St NW

Observatory Cir NW

31st St NW

Normanstone Dr NW

Normanstone Ter NW

2900

Calvert St NW

36th Pl NW

W Pl NW

US Naval Observatory

30th St NW

2500

Woodley Park - Zoo
Adams Morgan

C

US Naval Observatory

3100

Normanstone Park

Mcgill Ter NW

28th St NW

Montrose Park

Observatory Ln NW

Observatory Cir NW

Normanstone Ln NW

30th St NW

Edgevale Ter NW

Rock Creek Pkwy

8

Wisconsin Ave NW

Observatory Cir NW

Rock Creek Dr NW

Benton Pl NW

Whitehaven St NW

Connecticut Avenue is the lifeline for these blocks. It is lined with some destination restaurants, like the group-friendly Lebanese Taverna, the upscale Yanyu, and the interesting storefront ethnic eats. 4P's is an especially good Irish bar with live music to entertain the ruddy-faced crowd.

Map 17

Coffee

- **Starbucks** · 2660 Woodley Rd NW
- **Starbucks** · 3000 Connecticut Ave NW
- **Starbucks** · 3420 Connecticut Ave NW

Farmer's Markets

- **All Souls Episcopal Church Farmer's Market** · Woodley Rd & Cathedral Ave NW

Liquor Stores

- **Cathedral Liquors** · 3000 Connecticut Ave NW
- **Cleveland Park Liquor & Wines** · 3423 Connecticut Ave NW

Movie Theaters

- **Cineplex Odeon Uptown** · 3426 Connecticut Ave NW

Nightlife

- **Aroma** · 3417 Connecticut Ave NW
- **Ireland's Four Provinces (4Ps)** · 3412 Connecticut Ave NW
- **Nanny O'Brien's** · 3319 Connecticut Ave NW
- **Oxford Tavern Zoo Bar** · 3000 Connecticut Ave NW

Restaurants

- **Café Paradiso** · 2649 Connecticut Ave NW
- **Lavandou** · 3321 Connecticut Ave NW
- **Lebanese Taverna** · 2641 Connecticut Ave NW
- **Petits Plats** · 2653 Connecticut Ave NW
- **Sake Club** · 2635 Connecticut Ave NW
- **Sorriso** · 3518 Connecticut Ave NW
- **Spices** · 3333A Connecticut Ave NW
- **Yanyu** · 3433 Connecticut Ave NW

Shopping

- **Vace** · 3315 Connecticut Ave NW

Video Rental

- **Potomac Video** · 3418 Connecticut Ave NW

Map 18 • **Glover Park / Foxhall**

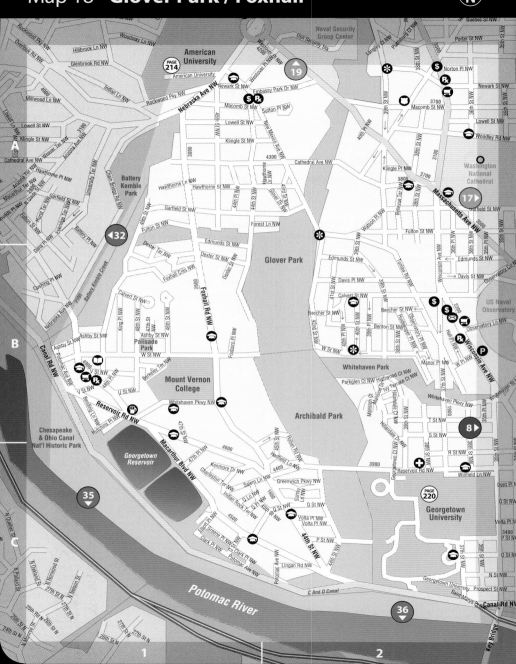

With homes from basic to bodacious, this residential stretch has ample green space and hometown pride. When the city tried to build a mayoral mansion here last year, residents rose up in a successful not-our-kind protest.

Banks
- **M&T Bank** · 2440 Wisconsin Ave NW
- **Sun Trust** · 3301 New Mexico Ave NW
- **Sun Trust** · 3440 Wisconsin Ave NW
- **Wachovia** · 3700 Calvert St NW

Community Gardens

Gas Stations
- **Exxon** · 4812 MacArthur Blvd NW

Hospitals
- **Georgetown University** · 3800 Reservoir Rd NW

Landmarks
- **National Cathedral** · Massachusetts Ave NW & Wisconsin Ave NW

Libraries
- **Palisades Library** · 4901 V St NW

Parking

Pharmacies
- **CVS** · 2226 Wisconsin Ave NW
- **CVS** · 4859 Macarthur Blvd
- **Giant Food Pharmacy** · 3406 Wisconsin Ave NW
- **Rite Aid** · 3301 New Mexico Ave NW

Police
- **MPDC 2nd District Station** · 3320 Idaho Ave NW

Post Offices
- **Calvert Station** · 2336 Wisconsin Ave NW

Schools
- **Annunciation** · 3825 Klingle Pl NW
- **Georgetown Day Lower School** · 4530 MacArthur Blvd NW
- **Georgetown University** · 37th St NW & O St NW
- **Lab School of Washington** · 4759 Reservoir Rd NW
- **Mann Elementary** · 4430 Newark St NW
- **National Cathedral School** · 3612 Woodley Rd NW
- **Our Lady of Victory** · 4755 Whitehaven Pkwy
- **River School** · 4880 MacArthur Blvd NW
- **Rock Creek International Lower School** · 1550 Foxhall Rd NW
- **St Albans School** · 3665 Massachusetts Ave NW
- **St Patrick's Episcopal Day School** · 4700 Whitehaven Pkwy NW
- **Stoddert Elementary** · 4001 Calvert St NW
- **The Field School** · 2301 Foxhall Rd NW
- **Washington International Lower School** · 1609 36th St NW

Supermarkets
- **Giant Food** · 3336 Wisconsin Ave NW
- **Safeway** · 4865 MacArthur Blvd NW
- **Whole Foods Market** · 2323 Wisconsin Ave NW

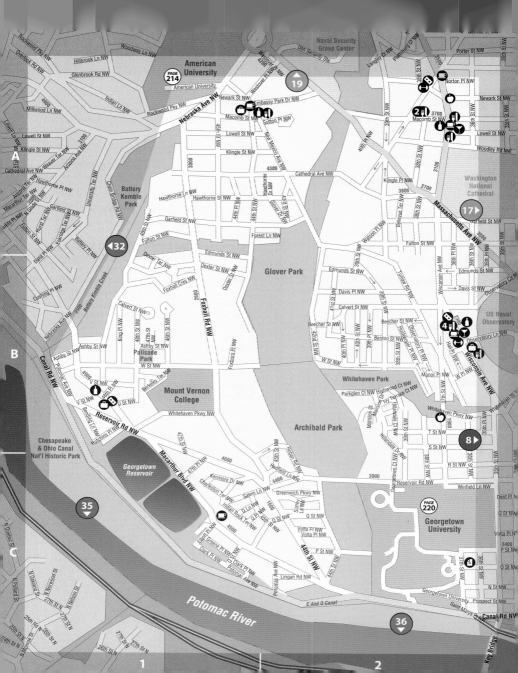

The bit of Wisconsin Avenue that runs through this northeast section provides the most vibrancy here. You could die happy eating only 2 Amys' pizza for all eternity. But if your friends insist on some variety, the best sushi place in town, Sushi-Ko, is down the block. If you can find Bourbon, which apparently adheres to the notion that no signage is cooler than any signage, it's the best spot around for a drink.

Coffee

- **Foster Brothers Coffee** · 3238 Wisconsin Ave NW
- **Foxhall Gourmet** · 4418 MacArthur Blvd NW
- **Starbucks** · 2302 Wisconsin Ave NW
- **Starbucks** · 3301 New Mexico Ave NW
- **Starbucks** · 3430 Wisconsin Ave NW

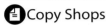Copy Shops

- **UPS Store** · 1419 37th St NW

Farmer's Markets

- **New Morning Farm Market** · 37th St NW & Newark St NW
- **New Morning Farm Market** · 37th St NW & Whitehaven Pwy NW

Gyms

- **Curves** · 3414 Idaho Ave NW
- **Washington Sports Clubs** · 2251 Wisconsin Ave NW

Liquor Stores

- **Ace Beverage** · 3301 New Mexico Ave NW
- **MacArthur Liquors** · 4877 Macarthur Blvd NW
- **Papa's Liquor** · 3703 Macomb St NW
- **Pearson's Liquor & Wine Annex** · 2436 Wisconsin Ave NW

Nightlife

- **Bourbon** · 2348 Wisconsin Ave NW
- **Zebra Lounge** · 3238 Wisconsin Ave NW

Restaurants

- **2 Amys** · 3715 Macomb St NW
- **Cactus Cantina** · 3300 Wisconsin Ave NW
- **Cafe Deluxe** · 3228 Wisconsin Ave NW
- **Faccia Luna Trattoria** · 2400 Wisconsin Ave NW
- **Heritage India** · 2400 Wisconsin Ave NW
- **Rocklands** · 2418 Wisconsin Ave NW
- **Saveur** · 2218 Wisconsin Ave NW
- **Sushi Sushi** · 3714 Macomb St NW
- **Sushi-Ko** · 2309 Wisconsin Ave NW

Shopping

- **Inga's Once Is Not Enough** · 4830 MacArthur Blvd NW
- **Skynear and Co** · 3301 New Mexico Ave NW
- **Theodore's** · 2233 Wisconsin Ave NW
- **Treetop Toys** · 3301 New Mexico Ave NW

Video Rental

- **Blockbuster Video** · 2332 Wisconsin Ave NW
- **Potomac Video** · 3408 Idaho Ave NW
- **Potomac Video** · 4828 Macarthur Blvd NW

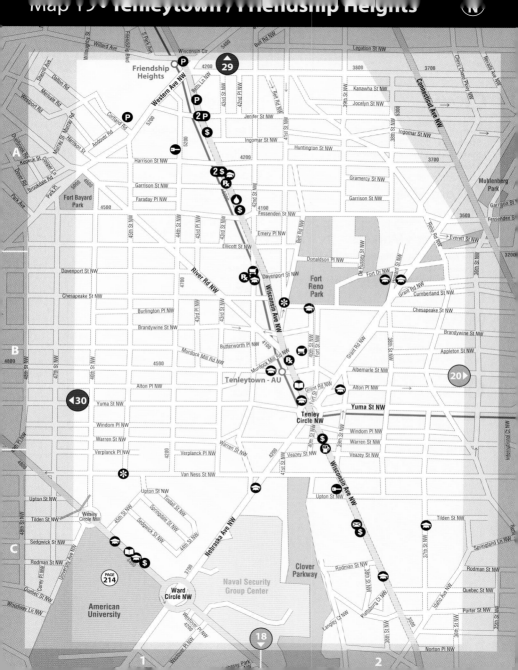

So you want to live in the city, but you really really like the 'burbs? You've found your home! This is a perfectly pleasant area with a feel-good mix of residential, retail, and non-offensive entertainment. It's a good bet you could spend your life in this section of DC and never, ever see a crack pipe.

Map

Banks

- **Bank of America** · 5201 Wisconsin Ave NW
- **BB&T** · 5200 Wisconsin Ave NW
- **Chevy Chase** · 4000 Wisconsin Ave NW
- **Chevy Chase** · 4400 Massachusetts Ave
- **Citibank** · 5001 Wisconsin Ave NW
- **Riggs** · 4249 Wisconsin Ave NW
- **Riggs** · 5252 Wisconsin Ave

 Car Rental

- **Alamoot Rent A Car** · 4123 Wisconsin Ave NW
- **Enterprise** · 5220 44th St NW

Car Washes

- **Wash & Shine** · 5020 Wisconsin Ave NW

Community Gardens

Gas Stations

- **Exxon** · 4244 Wisconsin Ave NW

Libraries

- **American University Library** ·
  4400 Massachusetts Ave NW
- **Tenley-Friendship Library** ·
  4450 Wisconsin Ave NW

 Parking

Pharmacies

- **CVS** · 4555 Wisconsin Ave
- **Rodman's Pharmacy** · 5100 Wisconsin Ave NW
- **Safeway** · 4203 Davenport St NW

Post Offices

- **Friendship Station** · 4005 Wisconsin Ave NW

Schools

- **American University** · 4400 Massachusetts Ave NW
- **DC Alternative Learning Academy** ·
  3920 Alton Pl NW
- **Deal Junior High** · 3815 Fort Dr NW
- **Georgetown Day Upper School** ·
  4200 Davenport St NW
- **Hearst Elementary** · 3950 37th St NW
- **Janney Elementary** · 4130 Albermarle St NW
- **National Presbyterian School** ·
  4121 Nebraska Ave NW
- **Potomac College** · 4000 Chesapeake St NW
- **Rose Elementary** · 4820 Howard St NW
- **Sidwell Friends** · 3825 Wisconsin Ave NW
- **St Ann's Academy** · 4404 Wisconsin Ave NW
- **St Johns Community Services** ·
  5151 Wisconsin Ave NW
- **Wesley Theological Seminary** ·
  4500 Massachusetts Ave NW

Supermarkets

- **Safeway** · 4203 Davenport St NW
- **Whole Foods Market** · 4530 40th St NW

Map 19 • Tenleytown / Friendship Heights

Easy, if bland, living here. There are lots of bright, friendly restaurants with menus heavy on the portobello mushrooms and herbs D'provence. Krupin's, one of the city's only full-scale Jewish delis, is a rare exception.

 # Coffee

- **Cafe Cafe** · 4224 Fessenden St NW
- **Cosi** · 5252 Wisconsin Ave NW
- **Starbucks** · 4513 Wisconsin Ave NW
- **Starbucks** · 5335 Wisconsin Ave NW

 # Copy Shops

- **Kinko's** · 5225 Wisconsin Ave NW
- **Kwik Kopy Printing** · 4000 Wisconsin Ave NW
- **UPS Store** · 4200 Wisconsin Ave NW
- **UPS Store** · 4410 Massachusetts Ave NW

 # Gyms

- **Body College** · 4708 Wisconsin Ave NW
- **Forever Fit Personal Training** · 4631 41st St NW
- **H&H Spa** · 4652 Wisconsin Ave NW
- **Sport & Health Clubs** · 4001 Brandywine St NW
- **Washington Sports Clubs** ·
  5345 Wisconsin Ave NW

 # Liquor Stores

- **Tenley Wine & Liquors** · 4525 Wisconsin Ave NW

Movie Theaters

- **AMC Mazza Gallerie 7** · 5300 Wisconsin Ave NW
- **Cineplex Odeon Cinema** ·
  5100 Wisconsin Ave NW
- **Cineplex Odeon Wisconsin Avenue Cinemas** ·
  4000 Wisconsin Ave NW

 # Nightlife

- **Chadwick's** · 5247 Wisconsin Ave NW

Pet Shops

- **Animal Hut** · 4620 Wisconsin Ave NW

Restaurants

- **Cafe Ole** · 4000 Wisconsin Ave NW
- **Krupin's** · 4620 Wisconsin Ave NW
- **Maggiano's Little Italy** · 5333 Wisconsin Ave NW
- **Matisse** · 4934 Wisconsin Ave NW
- **Murasaki** · 4620 Wisconsin Ave NW
- **Steak 'n Egg Kitchen** · 4700 Wisconsin Ave NW

Shopping

- **The Container Store** · 4500 Wisconsin Ave
- **Elizabeth Arden Red Door Salon & Spa** ·
  5225 Wisconsin Ave NW
- **Georgette Klinger** · 5345 Wisconsin Ave NW
- **Hudson Trail Outfitters** · 4530 Wisconsin Ave NW
- **Johnson's Florist & Garden Centers** ·
  4200 Wisconsin Ave NW
- **Neiman Marcus** · 5300 Wisconsin Ave NW
- **Pottery Barn** · 5335 Wisconsin Ave NW
- **Roche Bobois** · 5301 Wisconsin Ave NW
- **Serenity Day Spa** · 4000 Wisconsin Ave NW

Video Rental

- **Graffiti Audio-Video** · 4914 Wisconsin Ave NW
- **Hollywood Video** · 4520 40th St NW

Map 20 • **Cleveland Park / Upper Connecticut** N

Self-satisfied liberals unite! These blocks are dominated by well-meaning professionals who carry their own bags to the organic market, shun fancy restaurants for Vietnamese, and endure one-sided leftist debates at Politics & Prose. But don't get too radical; they like their coffeehouses grunge-free.

$ Banks

• **Bank of America** · 4201 Connecticut Ave NW
• **Chevy Chase** · 3519 Connecticut Ave NW
• **Chevy Chase** · 4455 Connecticut Ave NW
• **Riggs** · 4000 Connecticut Ave NW
• **Sun Trust** · 5000 Connecticut Ave NW
• **United Bank** · 3050 Military Rd NW
• **Wachovia** · 4340 Connecticut Ave NW

Car Rental

• **Avis** · 4400 Connecticut Ave NW

 Car Washes

• **Connecticut Avenue Brushless** ·
  4432 Connecticut Ave NW

 Gas Stations

• **Amoco** · 5001 Connecticut Ave NW
• **Sunoco** · 4940 Connecticut Ave NW

Pharmacies

• **CVS** · 4309 Connecticut Ave NW
• **CVS** · 5013 Connecticut Ave

Schools

• **Auguste Montessori** · 3600 Ellicott St NW
• **Edmund Burke School** · 2955 Upton St NW
• **Franklin Montessori School Forest Hills**
  Campus · 4473 Connecticut Ave NW
• **Montessori School of Chevy Chase** ·
  5312 Connecticut Ave NW
• **Murch Elementary** · 4810 36th St NW
• **Sheridan School** · 4400 36th St NW
• **University of the District of Columbia** ·
  4200 Connecticut Ave NW

 Supermarkets

• **Giant Food** · 4303 Connecticut Ave NW

Map 20 · **Cleveland Park / Upper Connecticut** Ⓝ

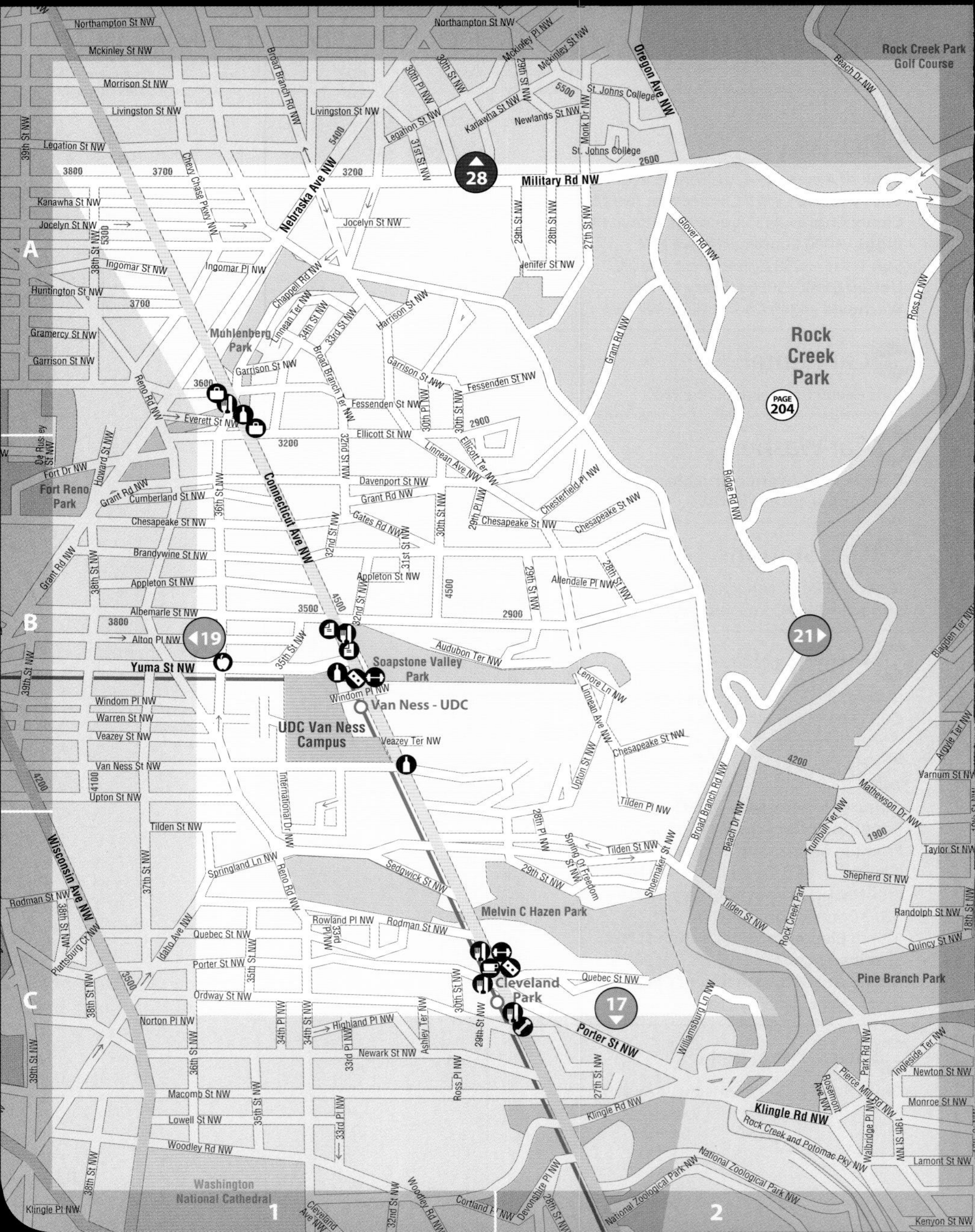

Northampton St NW

Mckinley St NW

Morrison St NW

Livingston St NW

Legation St NW

3800   3700

Kanawha St NW

Jocelyn St NW

Ingomar St NW

Huntington St NW

3700

Gramercy St NW

Garrison St NW

A

3500

Rock Creek Park Golf Course

Beach Dr NW

Northampton St NW

Mckinley Pl NW

Livingston St NW

Kanawha St NW

5500   St. Johns College

Newlands St NW

St. Johns College   2600

Military Rd NW

28

Jocelyn St NW

Ingomar Pl NW

Harrison St NW

Garrison St NW   Fessenden St NW

Fessenden St NW   2900

Ellicott St NW

Linnean Ave NW

Davenport St NW

Grant Rd NW

Chesterfield Pl NW

Gates Rd NW   Chesapeake St NW

Appleton St NW   4500

Allendale Pl NW

2900

Oregon Ave NW

Glover Rd NW

Grant Rd NW

Ross Dr NW

Rock Creek Park

PAGE 204

Ridge Rd NW

Nebraska Ave NW

Chappell Rd NW

Broad Branch Ter NW

Broad Branch Rd NW

Broad Branch Rd NW

Muhlenberg Park

Garrison St NW

3600

Everett St NW

3200

Reno Rd NW

Grant Rd NW

Cumberland St NW

Chesapeake St NW

Brandywine St NW

Appleton St NW

Albemarle St NW

3800   Alton Pl NW

◄19

Yuma St NW

Windom Pl NW

Warren St NW

Veazey St NW

Van Ness St NW

Upton St NW

Fort Reno Park

Grant Rd NW

3800

4100

B

Audubon Ter NW

Soapstone Valley Park

Windom Pl NW

Van Ness - UDC

UDC Van Ness Campus

Veazey Ter NW

Tilden Pl NW

Chesapeake St NW

Upton St NW

Linnean Ave NW

Tenure Ln NW

Spring of Freedom

28th Pl NW

21►

4200

Bladen Ter NW

Kanawha St NW

Varnum St NW

1900

Taylor St NW

Shepherd St NW

Randolph St NW

Quincy St NW

Matthewson Dr NW

Turnhill Ter NW

Pine Branch Park

International Dr NW

Tilden St NW

Springland Ln NW

Reno Rd NW

Sedgwick St NW

Rowland Pl NW

Quebec St NW

Porter St NW

Ordway St NW

Norton Pl NW

Highland Pl NW

Newark St NW

Macomb St NW

Lowell St NW

Woodley Rd NW

Klingle Pl NW

Rodman St NW

Idaho Ave NW

33rd Pl NW

Rodman St NW

Melvin C Hazen Park

Cleveland Park

Quebec St NW

17

Porter St NW

29th Pl NW

Sherrill Dr NW

Tilden St NW

Tilden St NW

Williamsburg Ln NW

Broad Branch Rd NW

Beach Dr NW

Rock Creek Dr NW

Klingle Rd NW

Klingle Rd NW

Rock Creek and Potomac Pkwy NW

National Zoological Park NW

Porter St NW

Ingleside Ter NW

Newton St NW

Monroe St NW

Lamont St NW

Kenyon St NW

Park Rd NW

Piney Branch Pkwy NW

Rosemont Ave NW

Walbridge Pl NW

MT US 14B

Pierce Mill Rd NW

Wisconsin Ave NW

Plattsburg Ct NW

Rodman St NW

38th St NW

C

4200

Washington National Cathedral

Cleveland Ave NW

Cortland Pl NW

Devonshire Pl NW

Woodley Rd NW

Connecticut Ave NW

34th St NW

33rd Pl NW

National Zoo NW

1   **2**

Map 2

Luckily, liberals tend to have adventuresome palates. Outside of Virginia's immigrant neighborhoods, this area has the best sampling of worldly menus. Delhi Dhaba, Indique, and Sala Thai are all worth the trek.

Coffee
· **L Lounge** · 3515 Connecticut Ave NW

Copy Shops
· **Office Depot** · 4455 Connecticut Ave NW
· **UPS Store** · 4401 Connecticut Ave NW

Farmer's Markets
· **New Morning Farm Market** · 4400 36th St NW

Gyms
· **City Fitness Gym** · 3525 Connecticut Ave NW
· **Gold's Gym** · 4310 Connecticut Ave NW

Liquor Stores
· **Calvert Woodley Liquors** ·
  4339 Connecticut Ave NW
· **Sheffield Wine & Liquor Shoppe** ·
  5019 Connecticut Ave NW
· **Van Ness Liquors** · 4201 Connecticut Ave NW

Pet Shops
· **Petco** · 3505 Connecticut Ave NW

Restaurants
· **Buck's Fishing & Camping** ·
  5031 Connecticut Ave NW
· **Delhi Dhaba** · 4455 Connecticut Ave NW
· **Indique** · 3512 Connecticut Ave NW
· **Palena** · 3529 Connecticut Ave NW
· **Sala Thai** · 3507 Connecticut Ave NW

Shopping
· **Marvelous Market** · 5035 Connecticut Ave NW
· **Politics & Prose** · 5015 Connecticut Ave NW

Video Rental
· **Blockbuster Video** · 3519 Connecticut Ave NW
· **Video Warehouse** · 4300 Connecticut Ave NW

Rock Creek Park
Golf Course

Military Rd NW

Rock Creek Park

PAGE 204

Rock Creek
Park

Beach Dr NW

Joyce Rd NW

Morrow Dr NW

Nicholson St NW

Kennedy Pl NW

Ross Dr NW

Rock Creek

Ridge Rd NW

Glover Rd NW

A

B

C

Rock Creek

Williamson
Ln NW

Pine Branch Park

Klingle Rd NW

Rock Creek and Potomac Pkwy

Adams Mill Rd NW

Rosemont Ave NW

Park Rd NW

Walbridge Pl NW

Ashbury Pl NW

Ontario Rd NW

Hillside Ln NW

Newton St NW

Monroe St NW

Lamont St NW
1800

Kilbourne Pl NW

Ingleside Ter NW

Mount Pleasant St NW

Brown St NW

Oakwood Ter NW

Crestwood Dr NW

Tilden St NW

Mathewson Dr NW

Trumbull Ter NW

Archie Ter NW

16th St

5900

5200

4700

4200

1900

1700

4000

Piney Branch Rd NW

Blagden Ter NW

Blagden Ave NW

12th St NW

13th St NW

14th St

15th St NW

16th St

18th St NW

17th St NW

Iowa Ave NW

Arkansas Ave NW

Colorado Ave NW

Missouri Ave NW

Oglethorpe St NW

Manchester Ln NW

Nicholson St NW

Montague St NW

Madison St NW

Farragut St NW

Delafield Pl NW

Crittenden St NW

Allison St NW

Webster St NW

Varnum St NW

Upshur St NW

Taylor St NW

Shepherd St NW

Randolph St NW

Quincy St NW

Spring Rd NW

Spring Pl NW

Spring Pl NW

Perry Pl NW

Parkwood Pl NW

Otis Pl NW

Oak St NW

Meridian Pl NW

Newton St NW

Monroe St NW

Lamont St NW

Manchester St NW

Quebec Pl NW

Quebec Pl NW

Princeton Pl NW

Otis Pl NW

Newton St NW

Park Rd NW

Somerset Pl NW

Sheridan St NW

Rittenhouse St NW

Fort Stevens Dr NW

Rock Creek Ford Rd NW

Missouri Ave NW
900

Nicholson St NW

Marietta Pl NW

Shepherd Rd NW

Longfellow St NW
500

Kennedy St NW

Jefferson St NW

Ingraham St NW
400

Hamilton St NW

Gallatin St NW

Farragut St NW

Emerson St NW

Decatur St NW

Crittenden St NW

Buchanan St NW

Allison St NW

Webster St NW

Varnum St NW

Taylor St NW

Shepherd St NW

Randolph St NW

Quincy St NW

Georgia Ave
Petworth

Quebec Pl NW

Otis Pl NW

Newton St NW

Park Rd NW

Morton St NW

Luray Pl NW

Keefer Pl NW

Kenyon St NW

Somerset Pl NW

Roxboro Pl NW

Rittenhouse St NW

Quintana Pl NW

Quackenbos St NW

Powhatan St NW

Oneida Pl NW

Oglethorpe St NW

Marietta Pl NW

Madison St NW

Piney Branch Rd NW

Illinois Ave NW

Georgia Ave NW

Kansas Ave NW

New Hampshire Ave NW

Grant Circle NW

Illinois Ave NW

5th St NW

7th St NW

8th St NW

9th St NW

10th St NW

3rd St NW

4th St NW

New Hampshire Ave NW

Varnum Pl NW

Marlboro Pl NW

Manor Pl NW

Lamont St NW

N Dakota Ave NW

US Soldiers' &
Airmen's Home

4300

4500

4100

4000

3800

Special Ed. Ctr.

27

20

14

16

15

High-rise apartment buildings give way to single-family bungalows and primly cut lawns. The only real community gathering spots are for your car along 16th, 13th, and Georgia at rush hour.

Banks

- **Industrial Bank** · 4812 Georgia Ave NW

Car Rental

- **Enterprise** · 927 Missouri Ave NW

 Car Washes

- **Car Wash Express** · 5758 Georgia Ave NW

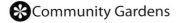 Community Gardens

 Gas Stations

- **Exxon** · 4501 14th St NW
- **Shell** · 4140 Georgia Ave NW

Libraries

- **Petworth Library** · 4200 Kansas Ave NW

Pharmacies

- **CVS** · 5227 Georgia Ave NW
- **Rite Aid** · 5600 Georgia Ave NW
- **Safeway** · 3830 Georgia Ave NW

Post Offices

- **Petworth Station** · 4211 9th St NW

Schools

- **Barnard Elementary** · 430 Decatur St NW
- **Brightwood Elementary** · 1300 Nicholson St NW
- **British School of Washington** · 4715 16th St NW
- **Clark Elementary** · 4501 7th St NW
- **Community Academy** · 1300 Allison St NW
- **Kennedy Institute Lower School** · 801 Buchanan St NW
- **Macfarland Middle** · 4400 Iowa Ave NW
- **Metropolitan Day School** · 1240 Randolph St NW
- **Parkmont School** · 4842 16th St
- **Paul Junior High** · 5800 8th St NW
- **Powell Elementary** · 1350 Upshur St NW
- **Roosevelt High** · 4301 13th St NW
- **Sharpe Health** · 4300 13th St NW
- **St Gabriel** · 510 Webster St NW
- **The Academy for Ideal Education Lower School** · 1501 Gallatin St NW
- **Truesdell Elementary** · 800 Ingraham St NW
- **West Elementary** · 1338 Farragut St NW

 Supermarkets

- **Safeway** · 3830 Georgia Ave NW

Map 2

Colorado Kitchen is worth a trip, or many trips, even if you live in Alaska. Otherwise, the offerings here are few and far between and a car is essential to get to them or, better yet, to drive elsewhere.

Coffee
- **Mocha Hut** · 4706 14th St NW

Farmer's Markets
- **14th St Heights Community Market** ·
14th & Crittenden Sts NW

Hardware Stores
- **Capitol Locksmith** · 3655 Georgia Ave NW

Liquor Stores
- **Colony Liquor & Groceries** · 4901 Georgia Ave NW
- **Colorado Liquor Store** · 5514 Colorado Ave NW
- **Hamilton Wine & Liquor Store** ·
5205 Georgia Ave NW
- **Jefferson Liquor Store** · 5307 Georgia Ave NW
- **La Casa Morata** · 5421 Georgia Ave NW
- **Target Liquor** · 500 Kennedy St NW
- **Twins Liquor** · 5117 Georgia Ave NW

Nightlife
- **Twins Lounge** · 5516 Colorado Ave NW

Restaurants
- **Colorado Kitchen** · 5515 Colorado Ave NW

Video Rental
- **Woodner Video** · 3636 16th St NW

Kingswood Rd
Broad St
Kingswood Rd
Edward Rd
Fleming Rd
Thornwood Rd
Glenrose St
Franklin

Jarvis Ln
5800
Ipswich Rd
Raleigh Rd
Tilden Tavern Dr
Tiffany Hill Ct
Whitley Park Pl
Wisconsin Ave
Bellevue Dr
Parkmont Dr
Edgemont Rd
Glenridge St
Roxbury Dr

495

Maplewood Park Dr
Montgomery Dr
Barrister Ct
Whitley Park Ter
Pooks Hill Rd
Dudley Ct
Bristol Square Ln
Asbury Ln
Broad Brook Ct
Broad Brook Dr
Delmont Rd
4500
Conifer Ln
Amherst Ln
4600
Culver Dr
Carriage Ct
Bramber Ct

Maplewood Park Pl
Maplewood Park Ct
Edgely Rd
Barrister Ct
Page Blvd
Nelson Rd
Forest Pl
Linden Ct
Dudley Ter
Dudley Ln
Alta Vista Rd
Elsmere Ave
Enfield Rd
Locust Hill Ct
Rock Creek Regional Park
Culver St

A
Ryland Dr
Old Georgetown Rd
Wyngate Dr
Forest Rd
Forest Pl
Widgeon Dr
Linden Ave
Alta Vista Rd
Viking Rd
5100
Wicket Ter
Holland Ave
Corsica Dr
Elsmere Ave
Elmhirst Dr
W Fairhill Dr
Rockville Pike
495

5800
Walton Rd
Beech Ave
Phoenix Ln
Forest Rd
Spruce Tree Ave
Balfour Dr
Elsmere Ct
Balfour Ave
Holliday Ave
Jason Dr
Danbury Rd
Danbury Ct
Elmhirst Dr
E Fairhill Dr
Gretna St
Aramere Ct
Traymore St

Anniston Rd
5700
Comanche Rd
Longford Ct
Lundigan Dr
Shields Dr
Charles St
Spruce Tree Ct
Elsmere Ave
Fordyce Pl
Chandler St
Benton Ave
Acacia Ave
Cedar Walk
4000
Palmer Road North

Rolston Rd
Johnson Ave
Camberley Ave
W Cedar Ln
West Cedar Ln
5200
National Institutes of Health

B
Folkstone Rd
Oakmont Dr
Oak Pl
West Dr
North Dr
Wilson Ln
Wood Rd
R B Brown Dr
University Rd
University Rd

Johnson Ave
Sonoma Rd
5800
Oneida Ln
Mohawk Ln
Grant St
Seneca Ln
Convent Dr
Memorial Rd
Center Dr
East Palmer Rd
East Riley
South Palmer Rd

Garfield St
Southwick St
Madison St
South Dr
South Dr
Srv Rd South
Palmer Road South
Bethesda National Naval Medical Center
Medical Center
Jones Bridge Rd

Lincoln St
Hoover St
Lincoln Dr
Convent Dr
Srv Rd West
Srv Rd South
Meldar Dr
Glenbrook Pkwy
Bywood Ct
Gladwyne Ct
Fairfield Dr
Columbia Country Club

McKinley St
Roosevelt St
5400
Glenwood Rd
N Chelsea Ln
S Chelsea Ln
Windsor Ln
23

C
Bradley Blvd
Northfield Rd
Charlotte Rd
Custer Rd
Rayland Dr
Chestnut St
Rosedale Ave
Maple Ave
Highland Ave
Kentucky Ave
Lynbrook Rd

Aberdeen Rd
Huntington Pkwy
5400
Lambeth Rd
Maple Ridge Rd
Lucas Ln
N Brook Ln
Keystone Ave
Rugby Ave
Wisconsin Ave
Tilbury St
Chase Ave
Harling Ln
Lynbrook Dr

York Ln
English Ct
Westover Rd
Overhill Rd
Harwood Rd
York Ln
Goddard Rd
Battery Pl
Del Ray Ave
Norfolk Ave
Rugby Ave
W Virginia Ave
Cheltenham Dr
Sleaford Rd

Midwood Rd
Stratford Rd
Marion St
Maple Ridge Rd
Park Ln
Auburn Ave
Cordell Ave
St Elmo Ave
Fairmont Ave
Middleton Ln
Lynbrook Dr

Wilson Ln
5400
5200
Clarendon Rd
29
Avondale St
Commerce Ln
Bethesda

McLean Dr
5600
Fairfax Rd
Moorland Ln
Waverly St
Montgomery Ave
Elm St
4th St

Durbin Rd
5600
Hampden Ln
Edgemoor Ln
North Ln
Montgomery Ln

1
2

Downtown Bethesda is really its own city more than a neighborhood. It's got enough hotels, shopping, business life, and traffic to make it feel urban—well, urban for upper-middle-class folks who don't like the hassle of a real city.

$ Banks

- **Chevy Chase** · 4825 Cordell Ave
- **Chevy Chase** · 7700 Old Georgetown Rd
- **Citibank** · 8001 Wisconsin Ave
- **Eagle Bank** · 7815 Woodmont Ave
- **Sun Trust** · 9000 Rockville Pike
- **Wachovia** · 7901 Wisconsin Ave

 Car Rental

- **Budget** · 8400 Wisconsin Ave · 301-816-6000
- **Enterprise** · 7725 Wisconsin Ave · 301-907-7780
- **Sears Rent A Car & Truck** · 8400 Wisconsin Ave · 301-816-6050

Gas Stations

- **Amoco** · 8101 Wisconsin Ave
- **Mobil** · 7975 Old Georgetown Rd
- **Shell** · 8240 Wisconsin Ave

Hospitals

- **National Naval Medical Center** · 8901 Wisconsin Ave
- **Suburban** · 8600 Old Georgetown Rd

o Landmarks

- **National Institutes of Health** · 9000 Rockville Pike

P Parking

 Pharmacies

- **CVS** · 7809 Wisconsin Ave
- **Foer's Pharmacy** · 8218 Wisconsin Ave
- **Village Green** · 5415 W Cedar Ln

Post Offices

- **National Naval Medical Center** · 8901 Rockville Pike

Schools

- **Bethesda-Chevy Chase High** · 4301 East West Hwy
- **Bradley Hills Elementary** · 8701 Hartsdale Ave
- **French International** · 9600 Forest Rd
- **Stone Ridge** · 9101 Rockville Pike
- **Uniformed Services University** · 4301 Jones Bridge Rd

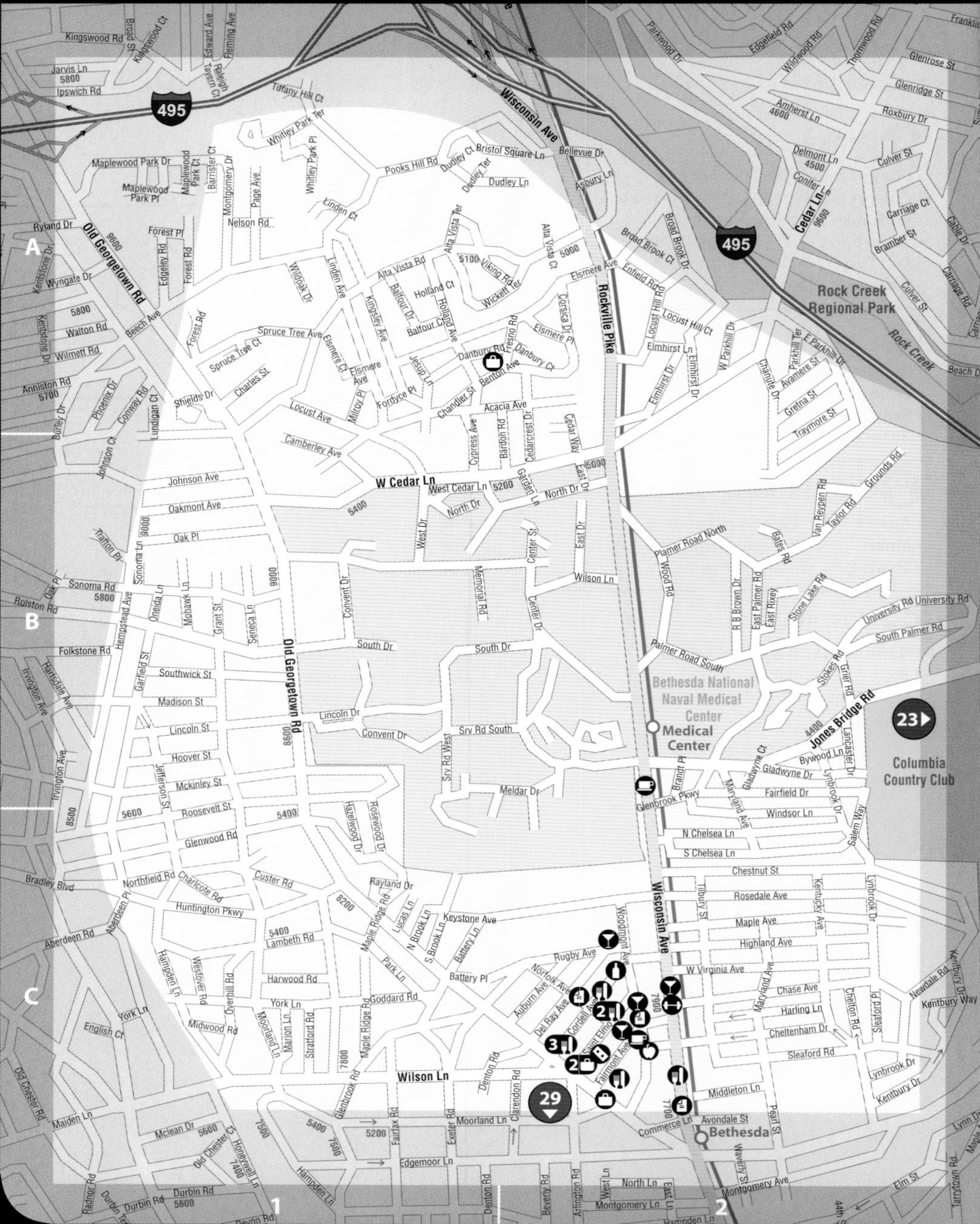

Map 22 • **Downtown Bethesda**

N

495
495

Wisconsin Ave

Rock Creek
Regional Park

Rock Creek

Rockville Pike

A

Kingswood Rd
Kingswood Ct
Edward Ct
Fleming Ave
Jarvis Ln
5800
Ipswich Rd
Tiffany Hill Ct
Whitley Park Ter
Bristol Square Ln
Bellevue Dr
Park Overlook Dr
Edgefield Rd
Thornwood Rd
Glenrose Rd
Franklin

Maplewood Park Dr
Whitley Park Ter
Pooks Hill Rd
Dudley Ct
Dudley Ter
Dudley Ln
Asbury Ln
Amherst Ave
4600
Delmont Ln
4500
Conifer Ln
Culver St
Glenridge St
Roxbury Dr
Carriage Ct
Bramber St
Cedar Ln

Maplewood Park Pl
Barrister Ct
Montgomery Ave
Page Ave
Linden Ct
Alta Vista Ter
Alta Vista Rd
5000

Ryland Dr
Old Georgetown Rd
Forest Pl
Nelson Rd
Linden Ave
5100
Viking Rd
Wickett Ter
Elsmere Ave
Broad Brook Dr
Broad Brook Dr
Locust Hill Ct
E Parkhill Dr
W Parkhill Dr
Parkhill Ter
Avamere St
Gretna St
Tramores Ave
Grounds Rd

Wyngate Dr
5800
Edgeley Rd
Forest Rd
Tilton Dr
Alta Vista Ct
Holland Ct
Holland Ave
Balfour Dr
Sonata Dr
Elsmere Dr
Enfield Rd
Enfield Rd
Elmhirst Ln
Elmhirst Dr
Charlotte Dr

Walton Rd
Beach Dr
Spruce Tree Ave
Bonnet Ct
Elsmere Ave
Danbury Rd
Danbury Ct
Acacia Ave
Cedar Way

Wilmett Rd
Spruce Tree Ave
Elsmere Ave
Fordice Pl
Chandler Rd
Cedarcrest Dr

Anniston Rd
5700
Phoenix Ct
Lundigan Ct
Shields Dr
Charles St
Locust Ave
Milford Pl
Bardon Rd
Cedarcrest Dr
-5000
Taylor Rd
Van Reagon Dr

Burley Dr
Kentsdale Dr
Conway Rd
Camberley Ave
Cypress Ave
North Dr Ct
Palmer Road North
Wood Rd
Stone Lake Rd

Johnson Ave
W Cedar Ln
West Cedar Ln
5200
North Dr
North Dr Ct
East Dr
Wilson Ln

B
Ralston Rd
Folkstone Rd
Traftan Ln
Sonoma Rd
5800
Sonoma Ln
Oneida Ln
Mohawk Ln
Seneca Ln
Grant St
Oakmont Ave
5400
Oak Pl
West Dr
Memorial Rd
Center St
Palmer Road North
R.B. Brown Dr
East Palmer Rd
East Rixey
University Rd University Rd
South Palmer Rd

Garfield St
Southwick St
Madison St
Lincoln St
Hoover St
McKinley St
Roosevelt St
5600
Convent St
South Dr
South Dr
Lincoln Dr
Convent Dr
Srv Rd South
Palmer Road South
Meldar Dr
Bethesda National
Naval Medical
Center
Medical Center
Jones Bridge Rd
23▶
Columbia
Country Club

Irvington Ave
8500
Jefferson St
Glenwood Rd
5400
Rosswood Rd
Fairfield Dr
Windsor Ln
N Chelsea Ln
S Chelsea Ln
Chestnut St

Bradley Blvd
Northfield Rd
Charlotte Rd
Custer Rd
Rayland Dr
Glenbrook Pkwy
Rosedale Ave
Maple Ave
Highland Ave
Chase Ave
Harling Ln
Cheltenham Dr
Sleaford Rd

Aberdeen Rd
Huntington Pkwy
Hempstead Ave
Maple Ridge Rd
5400
Lambeth Rd
Keystone Ave
N Brook Ln
S Brook Ln
Battery Pl
Rugby Ave
Woodmont Ave
W Virginia Ave
Maryland Ave

C
English Ch
York Ln
Midwood Rd
7000
Stratford Rd
Marion St
Harwood Rd
York Ln
Goddard Rd
Auburn Ave
Del Ray Ave
Cordell Ave
Norfolk Ave
Fairmont Ave
2
3
2
Montgomery Ln
Middleton Ln
Kentbury Way
Newdale Rd

Old Chester Rd
Maiden Ln
McLean Dr
5600
Old Chester Rd
Durbin Rd
5800
Radnor Rd
Overhill Rd
Glenwood Rd
Fairfax Rd
Clarendon Rd
Moorland Ln
Edgemoor Ln
Wilson Ln
29▼
Commerce Ln
Avondale St
◎ Bethesda
Waverly St
Montgomery Ave
Elm St

5400
5200
7600
Beverly Rd
Arlington Rd
North Ln
Montgomery Ln
Hampden Ln
4th

1
2

Lots of good clean fun here, just what the residents of, say, Stepford would enjoy.

Coffee
- **Dunkin' Donuts** · 8901 Wisconsin Ave
- **Starbucks** · 7700 Norfolk Ave

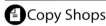Copy Shops
- **Metprint** · 8007 Norfolk Ave
- **Reprographic Technologies** ·
  7902 Woodmont Ave
- **Spectrum Printing** · 7700 Wisconsin Ave

Farmer's Markets
- **Bethesda Farmer's Market** · Norfolk &
  Woodmont Aves

Gyms
- **Fitness First** · 7900 Wisconsin Ave NW

Liquor Stores
- **Montgomery County Liquor** · 4800 Auburn Ave

Nightlife
- **Rock Bottom Brewery** · 7900 Norfolk Ave
- **Saphire** · 7940 Wisconsin Ave
- **South Beach Cafe - Bar** · 7904 Woodmont Ave
- **Yacht Club of Bethesda** · 8111 Woodmont Ave

Restaurants
- **Bacchus** · 7945 Norfolk Ave
- **Faryab** · 4917 Cordell Ave
- **Grapeseed** · 4865 Cordell Ave
- **Haandi** · 4904 Fairmont Ave
- **Matuba** · 4918 Cordell Ave
- **Olazzo** · 7921 Norfolk Ave
- **Tako Grill** · 7756 Wisconsin Ave
- **Tragara** · 4935 Cordell Ave

Shopping
- **Crate & Barrel** · Montgomery Mall, Benton Ave &
  Fresno Rd
- **Daisy Too** · 4940 Saint Elmo Ave
- **Mystery Bookshop** · 7700 Old Georgetown Rd
- **Zelaya** · 4940 Saint Elmo Ave

Video Rental
- **Version Francaise** · 4930 Saint Elmo Ave

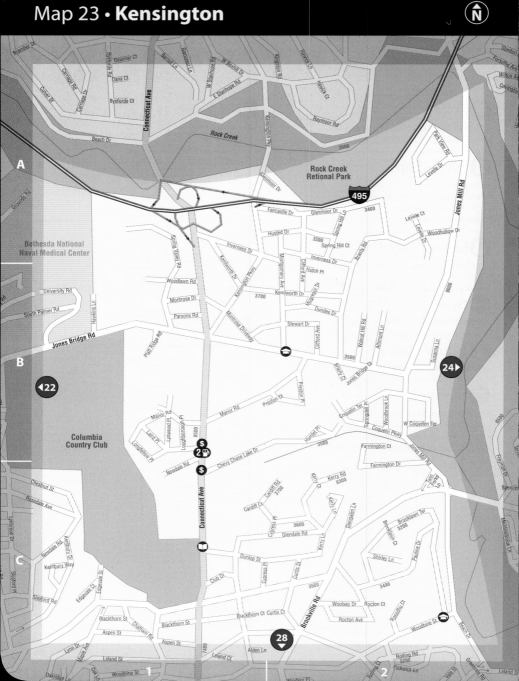

Map 23 · **Kensington**

You are on location at a Smith & Hawken catalog shoot. The fussy homes and landscaping here make it a sought-after suburb for those who don't mind driving everywhere and not possessing the more prestigious Chevy Chase address.

Banks

- **Chevy Chase** · 8401 Connecticut Ave
- **Sun Trust** · 8510 Connecticut Ave

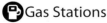Gas Stations

- **Citgo** · 8505 Connecticut Ave
- **Sunoco** · 8500 Connecticut Ave

Libraries

- **Chevy Chase Library** · 8005 Connecticut Ave

Schools

- **Lycee Rochambeau** · 3200 Woodbine St
- **North Chevy Chase Elementary** ·
  3700 Jones Bridge Rd

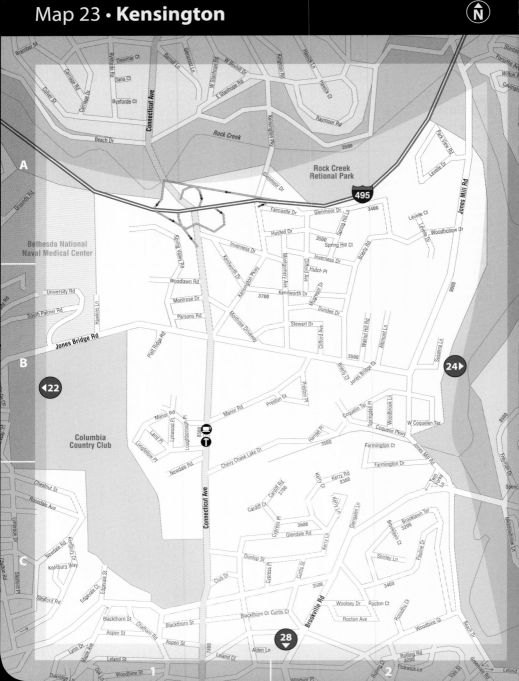

Map 23 · **Kensington**

N

Stanton

Forsythe Av

Wilton

Bramber St

Byford Rd

Dewmar Ct

Carriage Rd

Barrall Ln

Bestrest Ln

W Stanhope Rd

W Bexhill Dr

Havock Ln

Kingston Rd

Havock Ln

Govington

Colver St

Dana Ct

Carriage Dr

Byeforde Ct

S Stanhope Rd

Raymoor Rd

Connecticut Ave

Beach Dr

Rock Creek

Kensington Pkwy

3500

Park View Rd

Jones Mill Rd

A

Rock Creek
Retional Park

Grounds Rd

495

Levelle Ct

Levelle Dr

Woodhollow Dr

Glenmoor Dr

Faircastle Dr

Glenmoor Dr

3400

Spring Hill Ln

Bethesda National
Naval Medical Center

Spring Glen Rd

Husted Dr

3500

Spring Hill Ct

Brieny Rd

9000

Inverness Dr

Kenilworth Dr

Montgomery Pkwy

Montgomery Ave

Clifford Ave

Hutch Pl

Inverness Dr

Manmoor Dr

Dundee Dr

Woodlawn Rd

University Rd

Montrose Dr

3700

Kenilworth Dr

Walnut Hill Rd

Altmont Ln

Susanna Ln

South Palmer Rd

Parsons Rd

Montrose Driveway

Stewart Dr

Hawkins Ln

Clifford Ave

Jones Bridge Rd

Brieny Ct

3500

B

Jones Bridge Rd

Platt Ridge Rd

Brieny Ln

Preston Pl

Jones Bridge Rd

24

◄22

Manor Rd

Preston Ct

Coquelin Ter

Springdale Pl

Woodbrook Ln

W Coquelen Ter

Jones Mill Rd

Columbia
Country Club

Manor Rd

Lynwood Pl

Loughborough Pl

Manor Rd

Hamlet Pl

Coquelin Pkwy

Laird Pl

3500

Farmington Ct

Longfellow Pl

T

Farmington Ct

Newdale Rd

Chevy Chase Lake Dr

Farmington Dr

Chestnut St

Cardiff Rd

3700

Kerry Rd

Kerry Rd 8300

Twin Fork Ln

Spenc

Rosedale Ave

Cardiff Ct

Kerry Ln

Brooklawn Ter

Meadowbrook Ln

Freyman Dr

C

Livingston Dr

Newdale Rd

Kentbury Dr

Cypress Pl

3500

Glendale Rd

Kerry Ln

Glengalen Ln

Brooklawn Ct 3200

Brooklawn Dr

Pauline Dr

Chalfen Rd

Stanford Pl

Kentbury Way

Dunlop St

Cypress St

Curtis St

Shirley Ln

Connecticut Ave

Edgvale St

Edgvale St

Club Dr

3500

3400

Sleaford Rd

Rosedale Ct

Woodbine St

Lynn St

Maple Ave

Blackthorn St

Chatham Rd

Blackthorn St

Aspen St

Aspen St

Blackthorn Ct Curtis St

Brookville Rd

Woolsey Dr

Rocton Ct

Rocton Ave

Rolling Rd 3200

Beach Dr

Greenhill Rd

Oakridge Ln

Oak Ln

Leland St

Woodbine Ln

7400

Leland Ct

Alden Ln

28

Pickwick Ln

Vale St

Leland

Windsor Rd

Rolling Rd

1

2

Good thing there's HBO.

Coffee

· **Starbucks** · 8542 Connecticut Ave

Hardware Stores

· **Thomas W Perry** · 8513 Connecticut Ave

Map 24 · **Upper Rock Creek Park**

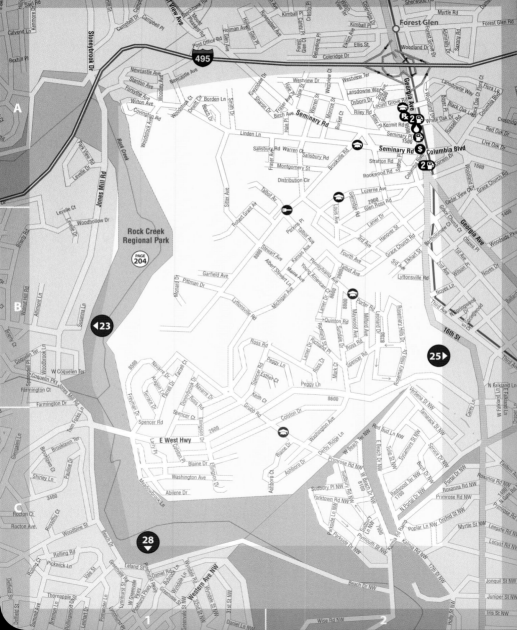

Mix of residential, schools, and industrial with zero attraction for outsiders.

 Banks
· **Citibank** · 9400 Georgia Ave

 Car Rental
· **Enterprise** · 9151 Brookville Rd · 301-565-4000

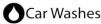 Car Washes
· **Montgomery Hills Car Wash** · 9500 Georgia Ave

 Gas Stations
· **Amoco** · 9475 Georgia Ave
· **Exxon** · 9331 Georgia Ave
· **Exxon** · 9336 Georgia Ave
· **G&G Service Center** · 9501 Georgia Ave
· **Shell** · 9510 Georgia Ave

 Pharmacies
· **CVS** · 9520 Georgia Ave

Schools
· **Calvary Lutheran** · 9545 Georgia Ave
· **Jewish Primary Day** · 2010 Linden Ln
· **Rock Creek Forest Elementary** · 8330 Grubb Rd
· **Rosemary Hills Elementary** · 2111 Porter Rd
· **Woodlin Elementary** · 2101 Luzerne Ave

Map 24 · **Upper Rock Creek Park**

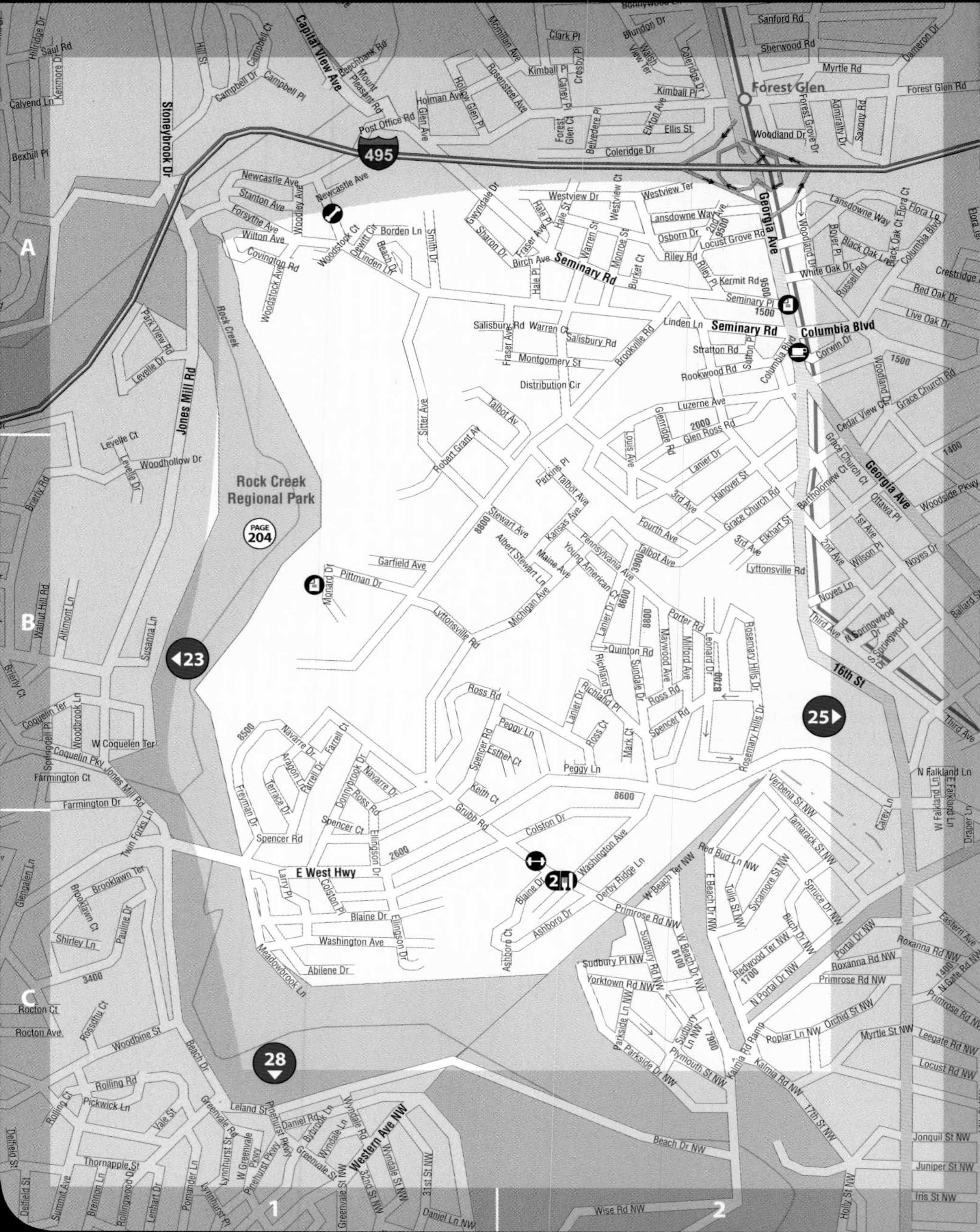

N

Forest Glen

Rock Creek
Regional Park

PAGE
204

◄23

25►

28

Seminary Rd

Columbia Blvd

Georgia Ave

16th St

E West Hwy

Western Ave NW

A

B

C

1

2

If you're in the mood for excitement, just hope your car doesn't stall.

Map

Coffee
- **Dunkin' Donuts** · 9328 Georgia Ave

 Copy Shops
- **Allied Printing** · 8844 Monard Dr
- **Staples** · 9440 Georgia Ave

Gyms
- **Rock Creek Sport Club** · 8325 Grubb Rd

Pet Shops
- **Cat Practice** · 2816 Linden Ln

Restaurants
- **Parkway Deli** · 8317 Grubb Rd
- **Red Dog Cafe** · 8301A Grubb Rd

This is Maryland's urban suburb that's getting more urbane all the time. It's a partially realized redevelopment that has made it a "let's check out Silver Spring" option for city folks, and puffed up the chest of area residents. Don't let them become braggarts; their downtown still has a long way to go before it becomes a consistent draw.

$ Banks

- **Adams National** · 8121 Georgia Ave
- **Bank of America** · 8788 Georgia Ave
- **BB&T** · 1100 Wayne Ave
- **Chevy Chase** · 8315 Georgia Ave
- **Chevy Chase** · 8676 Georgia Ave
- **Eagle Bank** · 8677 Georgia Ave
- **M&T Bank** · 8737 Colesville Rd
- **Provident** · 1411 East West Hwy
- **Provident** · 8730 Georgia Ave
- **Sun Trust** · 1286 East West Hwy
- **Sun Trust** · 8700 Georgia Ave
- **United Bank** · 8630 Fenton St
- **Wachovia** · 8701 Georgia Ave

Car Rental

- **Enterprise** · 8208 Georgia Ave · 301-563-6500
- **Enterprise** · 8401 Colesville Rd · 301-495-4120
- **Hertz** · 8203 Georgia Ave · 301-588-0608

Car Washes

- **Mr Wash** · 7996 Georgia Ave

Gas Stations

- **Citgo** · 8333 Fenton St
- **Crown** · 8600 Georgia Ave
- **Exxon** · 8301 Fenton St
- **Exxon** · 8384 Colesville Rd

o Landmarks

- **AFI Theater** · 8633 Colesville Rd

Libraries

- **NOAA Central Library** · 1315 East West Hwy
- **Silver Spring Library** · 8901 Colesville Rd

P Parking

Pharmacies

- **CVS** · 1290 East West Hwy
- **Giant Food Pharmacy** · 1280 East West Hwy
- **Rite Aid** · 1411 East West Hwy
- **Safeway** · 909 Thayer Ave

Post Offices

- **Silver Spring Finance Centre** · 8455 Colesville Rd
- **Silver Spring Main Office** · 8616 2nd Ave

Schools

- **Chelsea** · 711 Pershing Dr
- **East Silver Spring Elementary** · 631 Silver Spring Ave
- **Grace Episcopal Day** · 9115 Georgia Ave
- **Quality Time Early Learning** · 8122 Georgia Ave
- **Sligo Creek Elementary** · 500 Schuyler Rd
- **St Michael's Elementary** · 824 Wayne Ave
- **The Nora** · 955 Sligo Ave

Supermarkets

- **Giant Food** · 1280 East West Hwy
- **Safeway** · 909 Thayer Ave
- **Whole Foods Market** · 833 Wayne Ave

Map 2

The American Film Institute Theater is the reason to come to Silver Spring. After catching an obscure film treasure here, don't pass up a spot that has the guts to call itself Eggspectation. You have to give it up for anyplace that promises an all-day "eggsperience."

Coffee

- **Caribou Coffee** · 1316 East West Hwy
- **Java Works** · 1 Discovery Pl
- **Mayorga Coffee Factory** · 8040 Georgia Ave
- **Starbucks** · 8399 Colesville Rd
- **Starbucks** · 915 Ellsworth Dr

Copy Shops

- **ABC Imaging** · 1300 Spring St
- **Copy Connection** · 8252 Georgia Ave
- **Kinko's** · 1407 East West Hwy
- **Perfect Copy** · 8209 Fenton St
- **UPS Store** · 8639 16th St

Farmer's Markets

- **Silver Spring Farmer's Market** · Fenton St & Wayne Ave

Gyms

- **Curves** · 1320 Fenwick Ln
- **Gold's Gym** · 8661 Colesville Rd

Hardware Stores

- **Strosnider's Hardware Stores** · 815 Wayne Ave

Liquor Stores

- **Silver Spring Liquor Store** · 8715 Colesville Rd

Movie Theaters

- **AFI Silver Theater** · 8633 Colesville Rd
- **AMC City Place 10** · 8661 Colesville Rd
- **The Majestic 20** · 900 Ellsworth Dr

Nightlife

- **Mayorga** · 8040 Georgia Ave
- **Quarry House Tavern** · 8401 Georgia Ave

Restaurants

- **Cubano's** · 1201 Fidler Ln
- **Eggspectation** · 923 Ellsworth Dr
- **El Aguila** · 8649 16th St
- **Mi Rancho** · 8701 Ramsey Ave
- **Roger Miller Restaurant** · 941 Bonifant St

Shopping

- **Kingsbury Chocolates** · 1017 King St

Video Rental

- **Blockbuster Video** · 8601 16th St
- **Hollywood Video** · 825 Wayne Ave

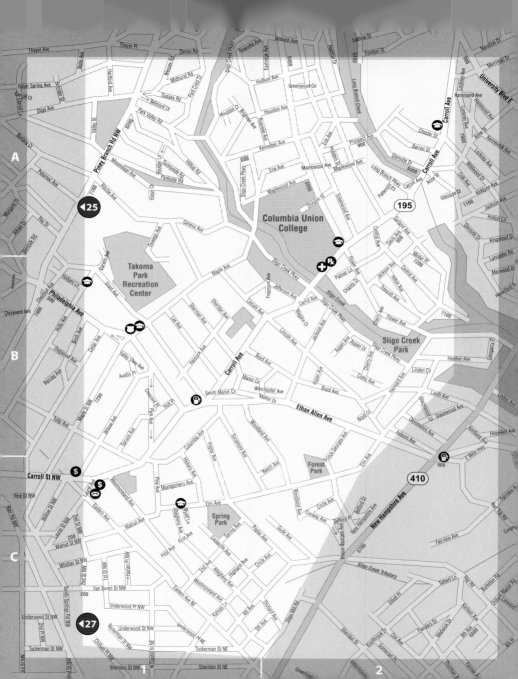

Everybody here likes to call themselves residents of "The People's Republic of Takoma Park," thanks to their liberal ways—it's a designated nuclear-free zone. They are, for the most part, sincere left-wingers. But these well-off suburbanites do have bigger houses and more video stores than most proletariats.

Banks
- **Bank of America** · 6950 Carroll Ave
- **Sun Trust** · 6931 Laurel Ave

Gas Stations
- **Amoco** · 920 East West Hwy
- **Citgo** · 7224 Carroll Ave

Hospitals
- **Washington Adventist** · 7600 Carroll Ave

Pharmacies
- **Takoma Park Family Pharmacy** ·
  7610 Carroll Ave

Police
- **Takoma Park Police Dept** · 7500 Maple Ave

Post Offices
- **Takoma Park** · 6909 Laurel Ave

Schools
- **Columbia Union College** · 7600 Flower Ave
- **John Nevins Andrews** · 117 Elm Ave
- **Piney Branch Elementary** · 7510 Maple Ave
- **Takoma Academy** · 8120 Carroll Ave
- **Takoma Park Elementary** · 7511 Holly Ave

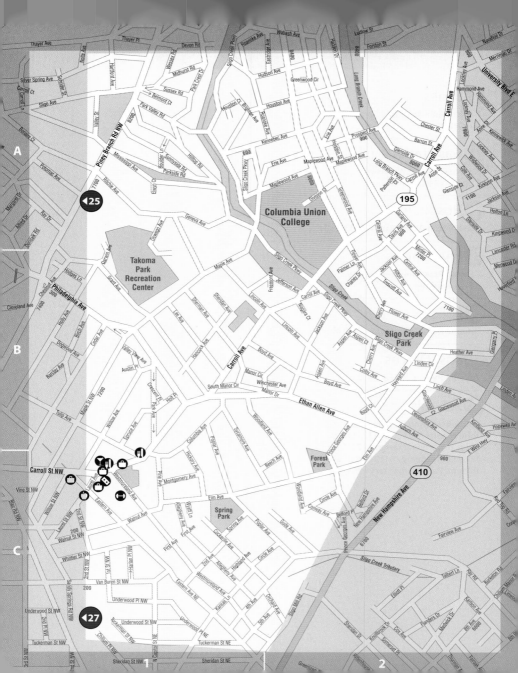

If you're into organic markets and independent shops that sell homemade crafts and tie-dye, endure the long metro ride to spend a few hours here. Once the sun starts setting, catch a train back. It is, after all, a suburb…

Map

Farmer's Markets
· **Takoma Park Farmer's Market** ·
  Laurel & Eastern Aves

Gyms
· **Curves** · 7008 Westmoreland Ave

Nightlife
· **Taliano's** · 7001 Carroll Ave

Restaurants
· **Mark's Kitchen** · 7006 Carroll Ave
· **Savory** · 7071 Carroll Ave

Shopping
· **Chuck & Dave's Books** · 7001 Carroll Ave
· **Dan the Music Man** · 6855 Eastern Ave
· **Polly Sue's** · 6915 Laurel Ave
· **Takoma Underground** · 7030 Carroll Ave

Video Rental
· **Video American Takoma Park** · 6937 Laurel Ave

This is a residential strip that surrounds the idyllic campus of the hospital where broken soldiers come to get fixed. Don't think you'll get a peek at what war wreaks, though; Walter Reed is under lock and key.

💲Banks

- **Independence Federal Savings** ·
  7901 Eastern Ave
- **M&T Bank** · 6434 Georgia Ave NW
- **Riggs** · 7601 Georgia Ave NW
- **Sun Trust** · 6422 Georgia Ave NW

🌢Car Washes

- **Mr Gee's Car Wash** · 6315 Georgia Ave NW

✳Community Gardens

⛽Gas Stations

- **Amoco** · 6300 Georgia Ave NW
- **Amoco** · 6401 Georgia Ave NW
- **Amoco** · 7000 Blair Rd NW
- **Amoco** · 7605 Georgia Ave NW
- **Eastern Auto Repair** · 7949 Eastern Ave
- **Exxon** · 7401 Georgia Ave NW
- **Shell** · 6419 Georgia Ave NW
- **Texaco** · 2300 Columbia Pike

➕Hospitals

- **Walter Reed Army Medical Center** ·
  6900 Georgia Ave NW

⭘ Landmarks

- **Battleground National Military Cemetery** ·
  6625 Georgia Ave NW
- **Walter Reed Army Medical Center** ·
  6900 Georgia Ave NW

📖Libraries

- **Shepherd Park Library** · 7420 Georgia Ave NW
- **Takoma Park Library** · 416 Cedar St NW

℞ Pharmacies

- **CVS** · 110 Carroll Ave NW
- **CVS** · 6217 Georgia Ave NW
- **Medicine Shoppe** · 7814 Eastern Ave NW
- **Phamily Pharmacy** · 6323 Georgia Ave NW
- **Safeway** · 6500 Piney Branch Rd NW

🚔Police

- **MPDC 4th District Station** ·
  6001 Georgia Ave NW

✉Post Offices

- **Brightwood Station** · 6323 Georgia Ave NW
- **Walter Reed Station** · 6800 Georgia Ave NW

🎓Schools

- **A-T Seban Mesut** · 5924 Georgia Ave NW
- **Academia de la Recta Porta** ·
  7614 Georgia Ave NW
- **Coolidge High** · 6315 5th St NW
- **Jewish Primary Day School of the Nation's Capital** · 6045 16th St NW
- **Lowell School** · 1460 Kalmia Rd NW
- **Montgomery College (Takoma Park Campus)** ·
  7600 Takoma Ave
- **Nativity** · 6008 Georgia Ave NW
- **New Testament Church School** ·
  400 Butternut St NW
- **Shepherd Elementary** · 7800 14th St NW
- **Strayer University (Takoma Park Campus)** ·
  6830 Laurel St NW
- **Takoma** · 7010 Piney Branch Rd NW
- **The Bridges Academy** · 6119 Georgia Ave NW
- **Washington Theological Union** ·
  6896 Laurel St NW
- **Whittier Elementary** · 6201 5th St NW

🛒Supermarkets

- **Safeway** · 6500 Piney Branch Rd NW

Map 2

The back roads are pleasantly sleepy for the families who live here, while the major road that cuts through caters to commuters, who use it as a speedway from the beltway to downtown. If you like your food fast and your banks drive-through, then by all means spend an afternoon here.

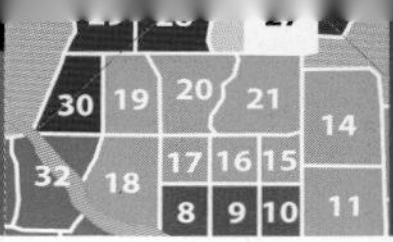

Coffee
- **Electric Maid Community Exchange** ·
  268 Carroll St NW
- **Starbucks** · 6500 Piney Branch Rd NW

Copy Shops
- **Akashic Copiers** · 5920 Georgia Ave NW
- **Boby Express** · 835 Juniper St NW
- **Community Printing** · 6979 Maple St NW

Gyms
- **A-1 Karate & Health** · 7616 Georgia Ave NW

Liquor Stores
- **Brightwood Liquor Store** ·
  5916 Georgia Ave NW
- **Mayfair Liquor** · 7312 Georgia Ave NW
- **Morris Miller Liquors** · 7804 Georgia Ave NW
- **S&S Liquors** · 6925 4th St NW

Nightlife
- **Charlie's** · 7307 Georgia Ave NW
- **Takoma Station Tavern** · 6914 4th St NW

Shopping
- **KB News Emporium** · 7898 Georgia Ave

Video Rental
- **Blockbuster Video** · 6428 Georgia Ave NW

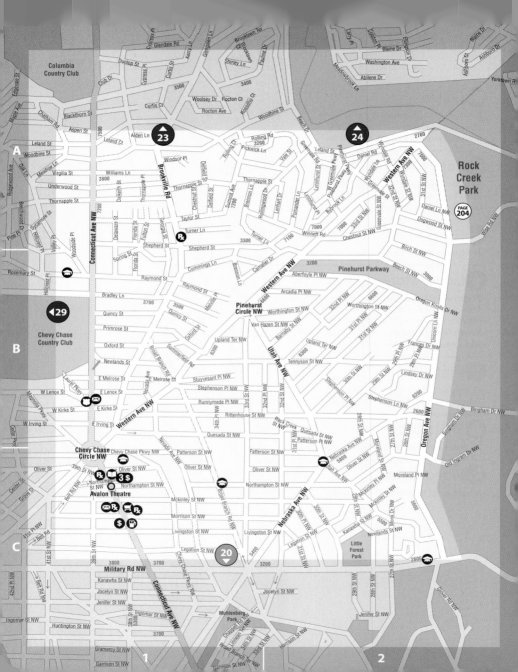

You'll have to have a bank account on par with the comedian of the same name if you want to settle here. It's the poshest of the city's Maryland suburbs. (Don't bother debating the point with Bethesda folks.)

Banks

- **Citibank** · 5700 Connecticut Ave NW
- **M&T Bank** · 5630 Connecticut Ave NW
- **Riggs** · 5530 Connecticut Ave NW
- **Wachovia** · 5701 Connecticut Ave NW

Gas Stations

- **Exxon** · 5521 Connecticut Ave NW

o Landmarks

- **Avalon Theatre** · 5612 Connecticut Ave NW

Libraries

- **Chevy Chase Library** · 5625 Connecticut Ave NW

Pharmacies

- **Brookville Pharmacy** · 7025 Brookville Rd
- **Chevy Chase Pharmacy** ·
  3812 Northampton St NW
- **CVS** · 5550 Connecticut Ave NW
- **Safeway** · 5545 Connecticut Ave NW

Police

- **Chevy Chase Village Police** ·
  5906 Connecticut Ave

Post Offices

- **Chevy Chase Branch** · 5910 Connecticut Ave
- **Northwest Station** · 5636 Connecticut Ave NW

Schools

- **Blessed Sacrament** · 5841 Chevy Chase Pkwy NW
- **Chevy Chase Elementary** · 4015 Rosemary St
- **Episcopal Center for Children** ·
  5901 Utah Ave NW
- **Lafayette Elementary** · 5701 Broad Branch Rd NW
- **St John's College High** · 2607 Military Rd NW

Supermarkets

- **Safeway** · 5545 Connecticut Ave NW

Map 28 · **Chevy Chase**

Connecticut Avenue is where the locals go to mingle with riff-raff. Magruder's is one of several pre-Whole Foods gourmet shops with precious produce, and the liquor stores have impressive wine collections. But the family atmosphere here is lighter than Wisconsin Avenue's high-end retail to the west. Here, you can get a bagel in peace or order a milkshake at American City Diner and slurp it down while watching a lousy projection of an old Hitchcock flick.

Coffee
• **Starbucks** • 5500 Connecticut Ave NW

Copy Shops
• **UPS Store** • 5505 Connecticut Ave NW

Farmer's Markets
• **Chevy Chase Farmer's Market** •
Broad Branch Rd & Northampton St NW

Liquor Stores
• **Chevy Chase Wine & Spirits** •
5544 Connecticut Ave NW
• **Circle Liquors of Chevy Chase** •
5501 Connecticut Ave NW
• **Magruder's Produce** • 5626 Connecticut Ave NW

Movie Theaters
• **Avalon Theatre** • 5612 Connecticut Ave NW

Nightlife
• **Chevy Chase Lounge** •
5510 Connecticut Ave NW

Restaurants
• **American City Diner** • 5332 Connecticut Ave NW
• **Arucola** • 5534 Connecticut Ave NW
• **Bread & Chocolate** • 5542 Connecticut Ave NW
• **La Ferme** • 7101 Brookville Rd

Video Rental
• **Potomac Video** • 5536 Connecticut Ave NW

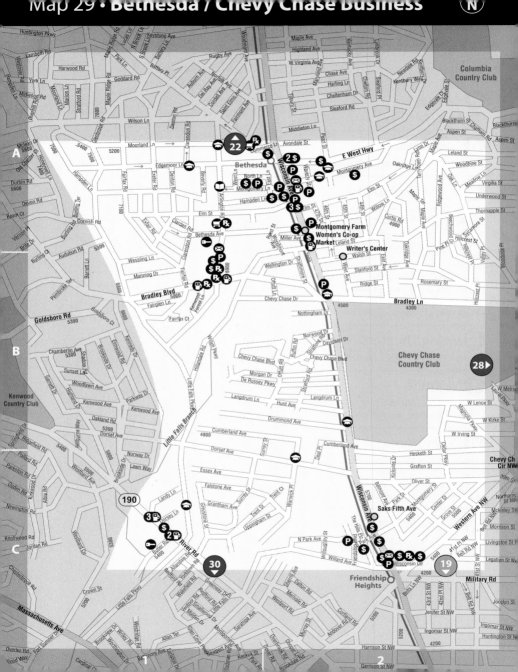

Map 29 • Bethesda / Chevy Chase Business

They may not let you in their country club, but if you have a credit card they'll let you in their stores. Here is what the wealthy around here like to call their very own little Fifth Avenue. Ah yes, same concept as Miami's Little Havana.

$ Banks

- **Bank of America** · 4411 S Park Ave
- **Bank of America** · 5135 River Rd
- **Bank of America** · 7316 Wisconsin Ave
- **BB&T** · 4719 Hampden Ln
- **Chevy Chase** · 4708 Bethesda Ave
- **Chevy Chase** · 5424 Western Ave
- **Chevy Chase** · 5476 Wisconsin Ave
- **Chevy Chase** · 7501 Wisconsin Ave
- **Colombo Savings** · 6917 Arlington Rd
- **Independence Federal Savings** · 5530 Wisconsin Ave
- **M&T Bank** · 4800 Hampden Ln
- **Mellon Bank** · 2 Bethesda Metro Ctr
- **Potomac Valley** · 4424 Montgomery Ave
- **Presidential Savings** · 4520 East West Hwy
- **Provident** · 5416 Wisconsin Ave
- **Riggs** · 7235 Wisconsin Ave
- **Sandy Spring** · 7126 Wisconsin Ave
- **Sun Trust** · 49 Wisconsin Cir
- **Sun Trust** · 7500 Wisconsin Ave
- **United Bank** · 7250 Wisconsin Ave
- **United Bank** · 7535 Old Georgetown Rd
- **Wachovia** · 6921 Arlington Rd

Car Rental

- **Rent-A-Wreck** · 5455 Butler Rd · 301-654-2252
- **Sears Rent A Car** · 4932 Bethesda Ave · 301-816-6050

Gas Stations

- **Amoco** · 5054 River Rd
- **Citgo** · 4972 Bradley Blvd
- **Exxon** · 5001 Bradley Blvd
- **Exxon** · 5143 River Rd
- **Exxon** · 7100 Wisconsin Ave
- **Exxon** · 7340 Wisconsin Ave
- **Getty** · 5151 River Rd
- **Mobil** · 5201 River Rd
- **Shell** · 5110 River Rd

o Landmarks

- **Montgomery Farm Women's Co-op Market** · 7155 Wisconsin Ave
- **Saks Fifth Ave** · 5555 Wisconsin Ave
- **Writer's Center** · 4508 Walsh St

Libraries

- **Bethesda Library** · 7400 Arlington Rd

P Parking

Rx Pharmacies

- **Bradley Care Drugs/Braden's Pharmacy** · 6900 Arlington Rd
- **CVS** · 21 Wisconsin Cir
- **CVS** · 6917 Arlington Rd
- **Giant Food Pharmacy** · 7142 Arlington Rd
- **Safeway** · 5000 Bradley Blvd
- **Safeway** · 7625 Old Georgetown Rd

Post Offices

- **Bethesda** · 7400 Wisconsin Ave
- **Bethesda Chevy Chase** · 7001 Arlington Rd
- **Friendship Heights Station** · 5530 Wisconsin Ave Frnt

Schools

- **Bethesda Elementary** · 7600 Arlington Rd
- **Concord Hill** · 6050 Wisconsin Ave
- **Keller Graduate School of Business Management (Bethesda Campus)** · 4550 Montgomery Ave
- **Oneness Family** · 6701 Wisconsin Ave
- **Our Lady of Lourdes** · 7500 Pearl St
- **Sidwell Friends** · 5100 Edgemoor Ln
- **Somerset Elementary** · 5811 Warwick Pl
- **Washington Episcopal** · 5600 Little Falls Pkwy

Supermarkets

- **Giant Food** · 7142 Arlington Rd
- **Safeway** · 7625 Old Georgetown Rd
- **Safeway** · 5000 Bradley Blvd

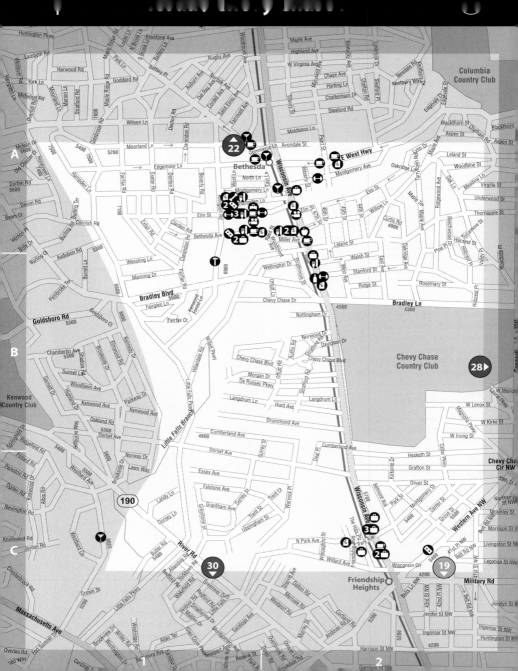

Wisconsin Avenue is a capitalist's dream. But if you're after anything other than high-end mall shopping, it won't be yours. The restaurants tend to be chains and there are plenty of Starbucks to keep you peppy for the next purchase.

Coffee
- **Caffe Appassionato** · 4801 Edgemoor Ln
- **Caribou Coffee** · 7629 Old Georgetown Rd
- **Cosi** · 7251 Woodmont Ave
- **Dunkin' Donuts** · 4810 Bethesda Ave
- **Environomics** · 4405 East West Hwy
- **Starbucks** · 4520 East West Hwy
- **Starbucks** · 5454 Wisconsin Ave
- **Starbucks** · 7140 Wisconsin Ave

Copy Shops
- **ABC Imaging** · 5550 Friendship Blvd
- **ABC Imaging** · 7315 Wisconsin Ave
- **Best Impressions** · 4710 Bethesda Ave
- **Bethesda Chevy Chase Copy** · 4405 East West Hwy
- **Kinko's** · 4809 Bethesda Ave
- **Print 1 Printing & Copying** · 4710 Bethesda Ave
- **Staples** · 6800 Wisconsin Ave
- **UPS Store** · 4938 Hampden Ln

Farmer's Markets
- **Montgomery Farm Women's Co-op Market** · 7155 Wisconsin Ave

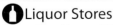 Gyms
- **Curves** · 6831 Wisconsin Ave
- **Fit Inc** · 4963 Elm St
- **Metro Fitness** · 4550 Montgomery Ave
- **Washington Sports Clubs** · 4903 Elm St

Hardware Stores
- **Strosnider's Hardware Stores** · 6930 Arlington Rd

Liquor Stores
- **Chevy Chase Liquors** · 6831 Wisconsin Ave

Movie Theaters
- **Landmark Bethesda Row Cinema** · 7235 Woodmont Ave
- **UA Bethesda 10** · 7272 Wisconsin Ave

Nightlife
- **Flanagan's** · 7637 Old Georgetown Rd
- **Strike Bethesda** · 5353 Westbard Ave
- **Tommy Joe's** · 4714 Montgomery Ln
- **Uncle Jed's Roadhouse** · 7525 Old Georgetown Rd

Pet Shops
- **Tanks for your Business** · 4938 Hampden Ln

Restaurants
- **Green Papaya** · 4922 Elm St
- **Hinode** · 4914 Hampden Ln
- **Pastry Designs** · 4927 Elm St
- **Persimmon** · 7003 Wisconsin Ave
- **Ri-Ra Irish Restaurant Pub** · 4931 Elm St
- **Tara Thai** · 4828 Bethesda Ave
- **Thyme Square Café** · 4735 Bethesda Ave

Shopping
- **Gianni Versace** · 5454 Wisconsin Ave
- **Marvelous Market** · 4832 Bethesda Ave
- **Mustard Seed** · 7349 Wisconsin Ave
- **Parvizian Masterpieces** · 7034 Wisconsin Ave
- **Relish** · 5454 Wisconsin Ave
- **Saks Fifth Avenue** · 5555 Wisconsin Ave
- **Saks Jandel** · 5510 Wisconsin Ave
- **Second Story Books** · 4836 Bethesda Ave
- **Sylene** · 4407 S Park Ave
- **Tickled Pink** · 7259 Woodmont Ave
- **Tiffany & Co** · 5500 Wisconsin Ave

Video Rental
- **Blockbuster Video** · 4860 Bethesda Ave
- **Blockbuster Video** · 5440 Western Ave
- **Hollywood Video** · 4920 Hampden Ln
- **Rocky's Video** · 4920 Hampden Ln

This 'hood is entirely residential and hidden among some of the city's most picturesque parkland. Big names who like their privacy reside here. They are not the types who party with paparazzi. They like the fact that there is really nothing to do here.

$ Banks

- **Bank of America** · 4301 49th St NW
- **Bank of America** · 4815 Massachusetts Ave NW
- **Chevy Chase** · 4860 Massachusetts Ave NW
- **Riggs** · 4835 Massachusetts Ave NW
- **United Bank** · 4900 Massachusetts Ave NW
- **Wachovia** · 4841 Massachusetts Ave NW

Gas Stations

- **Exxon** · 4861 Massachusetts Ave NW
- **Exxon** · 4866 Massachusetts Ave NW

Parking

Rx Pharmacies

- **Center Pharmacy** · 4900 Massachusetts Ave NW
- **CVS** · 4851 Massachusetts Ave NW

Schools

- **Westbrook Elementary** · 5100 Allan Ter

29

Massachusetts Ave NW

Willard Ave

Jordan Rd
Westbard Cr
Butler Rd
Alingdale Rd
5400

Christy Dr
Cromwell Dr
Chesterbrook Rd
Crown St
5500
Redford Rd
Yorktown Rd
Greenway Rd

Augusta Ln
Belvoir Dr
Briley Pl
Little Falls Branch
Westridge Rd
Verior Rd
Redford Rd
Little Falls Dr
Westport Dr
Sherrill Ave
Dalton Rd
Cardins

Martin Dr
Cleves Ln
Nelson St
5700
Namakagan Rd
Brookmont Dr
Brockview Dr
Wiley Rd
Worthington Dr
Allan Ter
Glen Cove Dr
Smallwood Dr
Malden Dr
Montgomery Ave
Saratoga Ave
Murray St
Murray St
Harrison St
Andover
Menvale Rd

A
5700
Overlea Rd
Wood Way
Cardinal Ct
Baltimore Ave
Newport Ave
Montgomery Ave
Keokuk St
Overbrook Rd
Cooksey Ln
Brookdale Rd
River Rd N

Fort Sumter Dr
Fort Sumter Dr
Rockmere Dr
Ontario Cir
Randall Ln
Pioneer Ln
Falmouth Rd
Beauford Ct
5400
Alan Rd
Worthington Dr
Larsson Dr
Flint Dr
Rodman Dr
Park Ave
Westway Dr
Dover Dr
Park Pl
Fort Bayard Park
5000
Fessenden St NW

4800
Cammack Dr
Cove Cod Ct
Jamestown Rd
Beard Blvd
Leroy Pl
Elliott St NW

Portsmouth Rd
Farmington Rd
Falmouth Ct
Jamestown Dr
Crescent St
Belmart St
Ashby Pl NW
48th St NW
47th St NW
Davenport St NW
Chesapeake St NW

Duvall Dr
5400
Elliott Rd
Arnied Rd
Allan Pl
Brandywine St NW

B
Tournay Rd
Albemarle St
Carvel Rd
Blackistone Rd
Carmel Cir
Dalecarlia Dr
Westmoreland Circle NW
Butterworth Pl NW
Murdock Mill Rd NW
4800
Albemarle St
47th St NW
48th St NW
46th St NW
19

Sangamore Ct
Spangler Ave
Boxwood Ct
Wetherill Rd
Abingdon Rd
Yuma St NW
Yuma Pl NW
Alton Pl NW

Chalfont Dr
Boxwood Rd
Torchlight Dr
Westwood Dr
Yuma Ct NW
50th St NW
Yuma St NW

Makakeel Rd
Windward Pl
Chalfont Ct
Leonard Pl
Warren St NW
Windom Pl NW
Warren St NW
Verplanck Pl NW

Dalecarlia Reservoir
52nd St NW
50th St NW
Fordham Rd NW
48th Pl NW
Van Ness St NW

Dalecarlia Reservoir Grounds
Dalecarlia Pkwy NW
Upton St NW
Upton St NW
4700
4800
Massachusetts Ave NW
Wesley Circle NW

C
52nd Ter NW
51st St NW
Tilden St NW
49th St NW
48th St NW

52nd St NW
3800
Sedgwick St NW
Corey Pl NW
University Ave NW

Little Falls Rd NW
5100
Rockwood Pky NW
Rodman St NW
Quebec St NW

MacArthur Blvd NW
Little Falls Rd NW
Overlook Ln NW
Woodway Ln NW
American University

Clara Barton Pkwy
Dalecarlia Pl NW
5000
Overlook Rd NW
Hillbrook Ln NW
Indian Ln NW

Chesapeake and Ohio Canal
Norton St NW
5000
32
5100
Loughboro Rd NW
Overlook Ter NW
Glenbrook Rd NW

5200
Watson St NW

1
2

30 19 20 21 14
32 18 17 16 15
8 9 10 11

Map

Coffee

· **Starbucks** · 4820 Massachusetts Ave NW

Shopping

· **Crate & Barrel** · 4820 Massachusetts Ave NW

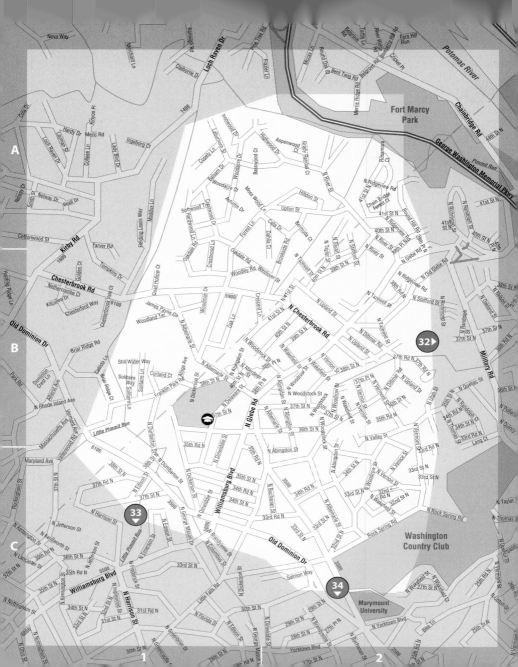

A leafy suburb with a school. Enough said.

33 34 35 36 7
37
38 40

Schools

- **Jamestown Elementary** · 3700 N Delaware St

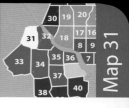

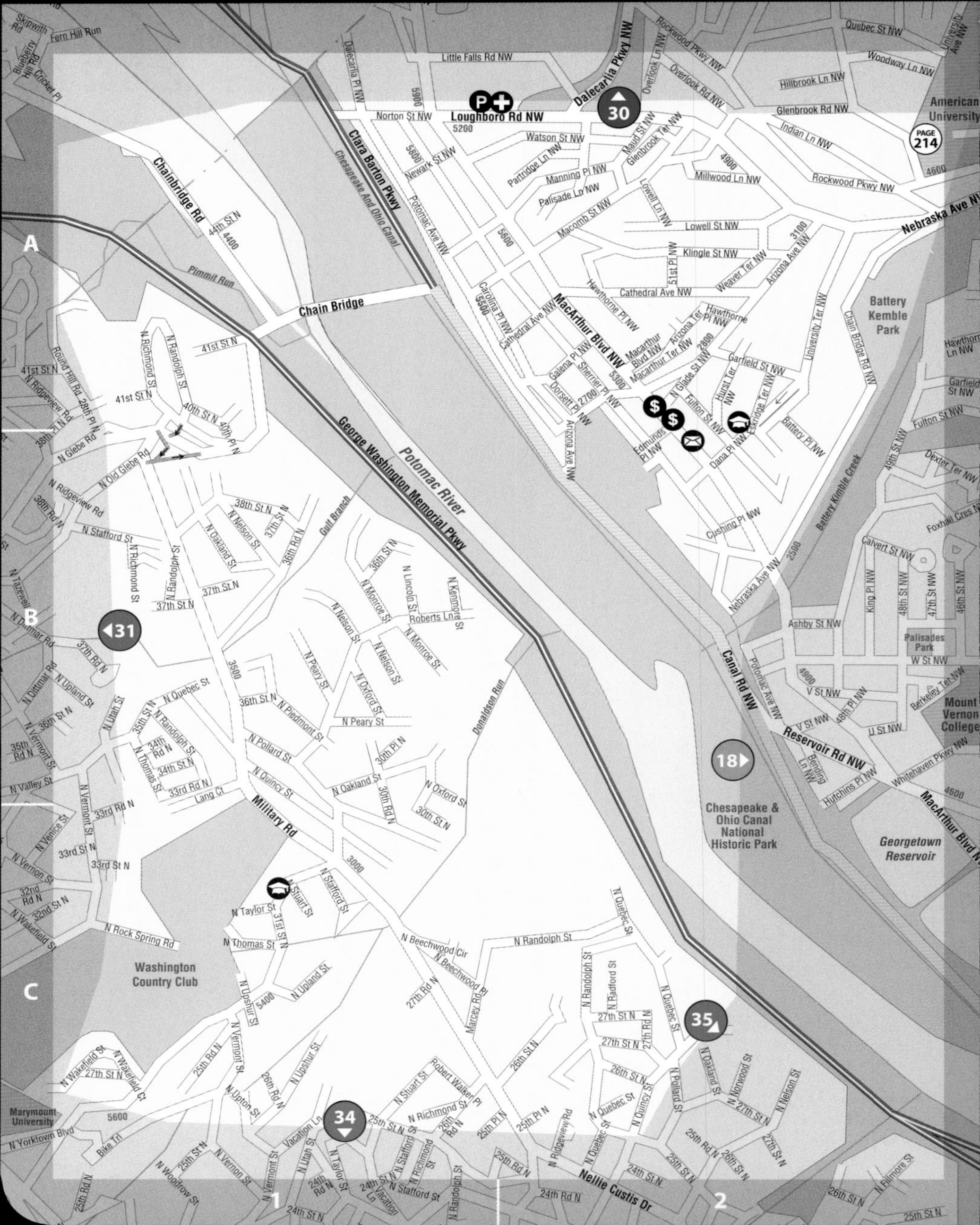

Map 32 · **Cherrydale / Palisades**

N

Fern Hill Run
Sixpenny Rd
Fern Hill Rd
N Culpeper St
Little Falls Rd NW
Dalecarlia Pkwy NW
Rockwood Pkwy NW
Quebec St NW
Woodway Ln NW

Chesterbrook Rd
44th St N
4400
Dalecarlia Pl NW
Norton St NW
Loughboro Rd NW
5200
30
Maud St NW
Overlook Rd NW
Glenbrook Rd NW
Overlook Pkwy NW
Hillbrook Ln NW
Glenbrook Rd NW
Indian Ln NW
American University

Chesapeake And Ohio Canal
Clara Barton Pkwy
Watson St NW
Partidge Ln NW
Manning Pl NW
Palisade Ln NW
Macomb St NW
Glenbrook Rd NW
Lowell Ln NW
4900
Millwood Ln NW
Rockwood Pkwy NW
4600

A
Pimmit Run
Potomac Ave NW
5600
5000
Macomb St NW
Lowell St NW
Klingle St NW
51st Pl NW
Weaver Ter NW
Arcola Ln NW
Nebraska Ave NW
Battery Kemble Park

Chain Bridge
Cathedral Ave NW
Cathedral Ave NW
Hawthorne Pl NW
Hawthorne Pl NW
Cathedral Ave NW
Fulton St NW
Garfield St NW

41st St N
41st St N
41st St N
40th St N
49th Pl N
N Richmond St
Macomb Pl NW
MacArthur Blvd NW
Arcola Pl NW
MacArthur Ter NW
University Ter NW
Garfield St NW
Battery Kemble Rd NW
Garfield St NW

41st St N
N Randolph St
N Glebe Rd
N Old Glebe Rd
N Ridgeview Rd
Glenoa Pl NW
Dorsett Pl NW
Sherrier Pl NW
5200
5300
Hurst Ter
N Glebe Rd
Fulton St NW
$
Edmunds Pl NW
Dana Pl NW
Battery Pl NW
Dexter Ter NW

George Washington Memorial Pkwy
Potomac River
38th St N
N Nelson St
N Lincoln St
N Kenmore St
Roberts Lane
Arizona Ave NW
Nebraska Ave NW
Clyshing Pl NW
Battery Kemble Creek
Calvert St NW
King Pl NW
47th St NW
Foxhall Cres NW

B
N Upton St
N Quantico St
N Taft Rd N
37th St N
N Randolph St
37th St N
◄31
36th St N
N Quebec St
N Peary St
N Nelson St
N Monroe St
N Oxford St
N Peary St
N Oakland St
36th Pl N
N Oakland St
30th St N
Ashby St NW
V St NW
V St NW
U Pl NW
V St NW
4900
Palisades Park
W St NW
Mount Vernon College

N Venice St
36th St N
N Randolph St
34th Rd N
34th St N
33rd Rd N
N Pollard St
N Quincy St
Lang Ct
3900
Canal Rd NW
Reservoir Rd NW
Hutchins Pl NW
Berkley Ter NW
Whitehaven St NW
4600
MacArthur Blvd NW

33rd St N
N Vermont St
33rd Rd N
33rd St N
Military Rd
N Quincy St
N Quebec St
18►
Potomac River NW
Reservoir Rd NW

C
32nd Rd N
32nd St N
N Westfield St
N Rock Spring Rd
N Taylor St
Stuart St
31st St N
N Thomas St
N Stafford St
27th Rd N
N Beechwood Cir
N Beechwood Rd
Marcey Rd
N Randolph St
Chesapeake & Ohio Canal National Historic Park
Georgetown Reservoir

Washington Country Club
N Upton St
5400
N Stuart St
Robert Walker Pl
N Radford St
27th St N
N Randolph St
N Quebec St
N Quincy St
26th Pl N
N Norwood St
N Nelson St
27th St N

Marymount University
5600
27th St N
N Wakefield Ct
N Upton St
N Vacation Ln
25th St N
N Richmond St
N Stuart St
25th Pl N
34 ▼
24th St N
N Quebec St
26th Pl N
25th St N
N Pollard St
N Quincy St
26th St N
35▲
27th St N

N Wakefield St
N Woodrow St
N Vermont St
24th Rd N
N Taylor St
Bike Trl
N Randolph St
24th Rd N
Nellie Custis Dr
25th Rd N
N Filmore St
26th St N
25th St N

1 **2**

Here are two pretty and sleepy residential neighborhoods that line the Potomac and surround the region's favorite baby mill, Sibley Memorial Hospital.

Banks
- **Citibank** · 5250 MacArthur Blvd NW
- **Wachovia** · 5201 MacArthur Blvd NW

Hospitals
- **Sibley Memorial** · 5255 Loughboro Rd NW

Parking

Post Offices
- **Palisades Station** · 5136 MacArthur Blvd NW

Schools
- **Key Elementary** · 5001 Dana Pl NW
- **Taylor Elementary** · 2600 N Stuart St

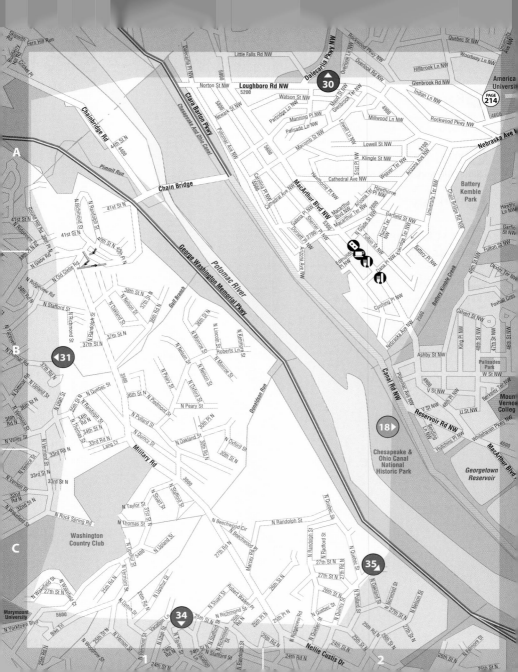

Wait for the delivery at one of the few neighborhood spots along MacArthur Boulevard.

Coffee
- **Starbucks** • 5185 MacArthur Blvd NW

Restaurants
- **Bambu** • 5101 MacArthur Blvd NW
- **Starland Cafe** • 5125 MacArthur Blvd NW

Video Rental
- **Potomac Video** • 5185 MacArthur Blvd NW

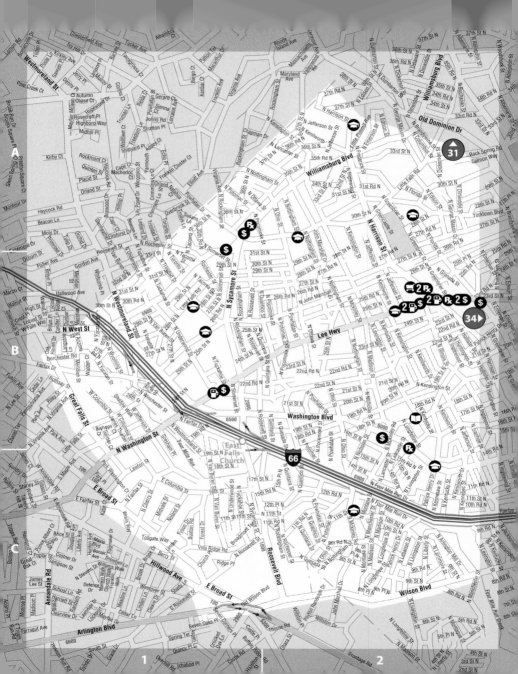

Familyville with a little downtown along Broad Street. When the babysitter's on call, the parents crowd up outside the State Theater for the live music. Otherwise, it's usually a board game and an early bedtime.

$ Banks

- **Bank of America** · 5226 Lee Hwy
- **BB&T** · 5515 Lee Hwy
- **Sun Trust** · 6711 Lee Hwy
- **United Bank** · 5335 Lee Hwy
- **United Bank** · 6402 Williamsburg Blvd
- **Virginia Commerce** · 5350 Lee Hwy
- **Virginia Commerce** · 6500 Williamsburg Blvd
- **Wachovia** · 1701 N McKinley Rd

Gas Stations

- **Amoco** · 5601 Lee Hwy
- **Chevron** · 5618 Lee Hwy
- **Citgo** · 5510 Lee Hwy
- **Exxon** · 6730 Lee Hwy
- **Sunoco** · 5501 Lee Hwy

Libraries

- **Westover Library** · 1800 N Lexington St

Rx Pharmacies

- **CVS** · 5402 Lee Hwy
- **CVS** · 6404 Williamsburg Blvd
- **Harris Teeter Pharmacy** · 2425 N Harrison St
- **Rite Aid** · 5841 N Washington Blvd
- **Safeway** · 2500 Harrison St

Schools

- **Bishop Denis J O'Connell High** ·
  6600 Little Falls Rd
- **McKinley Elementary** · 1030 N McKinley Rd
- **Nottingham Elementary** · 5900 Little Falls Rd
- **Rivendell** · 5700 Lee Hwy
- **Swanson Middle** · 5800 N Washington Blvd
- **Tuckahoe Elementary** · 6550 26 St N
- **Williamsburg Middle** · 3600 N Harrison St
- **Yorktown High** · 5201 28 St N

Supermarkets

- **Safeway** · 2500 N Harrison St

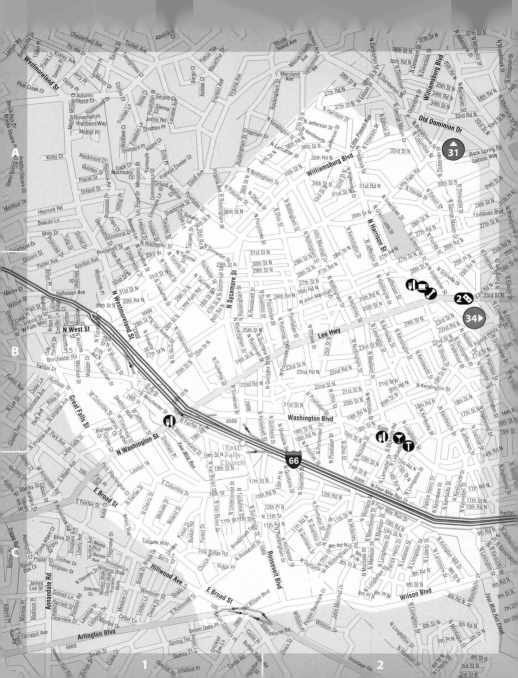

Coffee
• **Starbucks** • 2441 N Harrison St

Hardware Stores
• **Ayer's True Value** • 5853 N Washington Blvd

Nightlife
• **Lost Dog Café** • 5876 Washington Blvd

 Pet Shops
• **Dogma** • 2445 N Harrison St

Restaurants
• **La Cote d'Or Cafe** • 6876 Lee Hwy
• **Lebanese Taverna** • 5900 Washington Blvd
• **Taqueria Poblano** • 2503 N Harrison St

Video Rental
• **Blockbuster Video** • 5400 Lee Hwy
• **Hollywood Video** • 5401 Lee Hwy

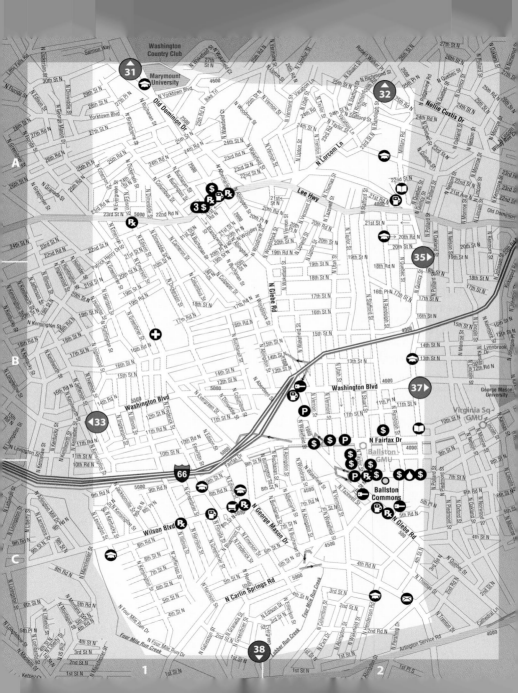

Distinguished as the home to the region's, and possibly America's, worst mall, Ballston Commons. Come only if you're in the market for an overpriced trinket.

33 34 35 36 7
37
38 40

Map

Banks

- **Alliance Bank** · 4501 Fairfax Dr
- **Bank of America** · 4201 Wilson Blvd
- **BB&T** · 4707 Lee Hwy
- **BB&T** · 920 N Taylor St
- **Chevy Chase** · 4100 Wilson Blvd
- **Chevy Chase** · 4700 Lee Hwy
- **Citibank** · 1010 N Glebe Rd
- **Presidential Savings** · 901 N Stuart St
- **Sun Trust** · 4710 Lee Hwy
- **Sun Trust** · 900 N Taylor St
- **United Bank** · 4005 Wilson Blvd
- **Wachovia** · 1011 N Stafford St
- **Wachovia** · 2213 N Glebe Rd

 Car Rental

- **Enterprise** · 1211 N Glebe Rd · 703-248-7180
- **Enterprise** · 601 N Randolph St · 703-312-7900
- **Enterprise** · 700 N Glebe Rd · 703-243-5404

Car Washes

- **Shell Car Wash** · 4030 Wilson Blvd

Gas Stations

- **Exxon** · 4035 Old Dominion Dr
- **Exxon** · 4746 Lee Hwy
- **Exxon** · 660 N Glebe Rd
- **Mobil** · 4601 Washington Blvd
- **Texaco** · 5201 Wilson Blvd

Hospitals

- **Virginia Hospital Center** · 1701 N George Mason Dr

Landmarks

- **Ballston Commons** · 4238 Wilson Blvd

Libraries

- **Arlington Central Library** · 1015 N Quincy St
- **Cherrydale Library** · 2190 Military Rd

Parking

Pharmacies

- **CVS** · 4238 Wilson Blvd
- **CVS** · 4709-A Lee Hwy
- **Harris Teeter Pharmacy** · 600 N Glebe Rd
- **Medicine Shoppe** · 5513 Wilson Blvd
- **Preston's Care Pharmacy** · 5101 Lee Hwy
- **Rite Aid** · 4720 Lee Hwy
- **Safeway** · 5101 Wilson Blvd

Post Offices

- **North Station** · 220 N George Mason Dr

Schools

- **Arlington Traditional** · 855 N Edison St
- **Ashlawn Elementary** · 5950 N 8 Rd
- **Barrett Elementary** · 4401 N Henderson Rd
- **Marymount University** · 2807 N Glebe Rd
- **St Agnes Elementary** · 2024 N Randolph St
- **St Ann Elementary** · 980 N Frederick St
- **Stratford Program** · 4107 N Vacation Ln
- **Washington Lee High** · 1300 N Quincy St

 Supermarkets

- **Safeway** · 5101 Wilson Blvd

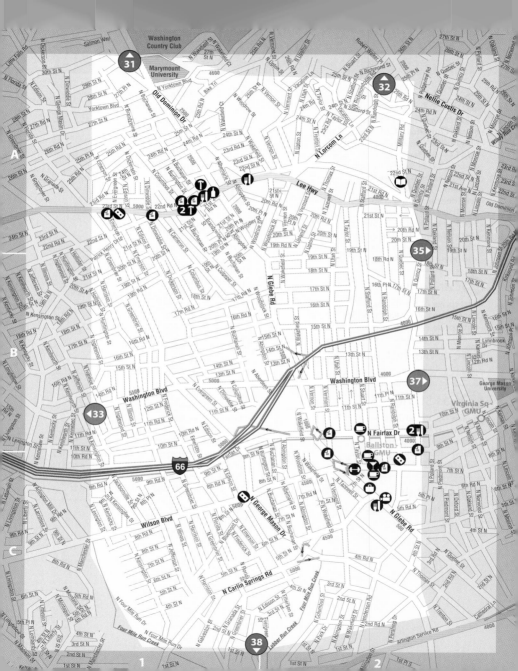

There are a couple of good cheap eats here, like the well-named Crisp & Juicy, and a favorite neighborhood bar in the Rock Bottom Brewery. Oh, and that mall does have one saving grace, there's a first-run movie theater attached.

Coffee

- **Cosi** · 4250 Fairfax Dr
- **Starbucks** · 4238 Wilson Blvd
- **Starbucks** · 901 N Stuart St

Copy Shops

- **Copy & Convenience** · 2219 N Columbus St
- **Insty-Prints** · 5001 Lee Hwy
- **Kinko's** · 4501 N Fairfax Dr
- **Minuteman Press** · 4001 N 9th St
- **Print Time** · 5137 Lee Hwy
- **Quality Graphics** · 4720 Lee Hwy
- **Staples** · 910 N Glebe Rd
- **UPS Store** · 4201 Wilson Blvd

Gyms

- **Sport & Health Clubs** · 4328 Wilson Blvd

Hardware Stores

- **Arlington Bill's Hardware** · 2213 N Buchanan St
- **Bill's True Value Hardware** · 4756 Lee Hwy
- **Caprio & Deutsch** · 4755 Lee Hwy

Liquor Stores

- **Virginia ABC** · 4709 Lee Hwy

Movie Theaters

- **Regal Ballston Common 12** · 671 N Glebe Rd

Nightlife

- **Rock Bottom Brewery** ·
  4238 Wilson Blvd

Restaurants

- **Crisp & Juicy** · 4540 Lee Hwy
- **Metro 29 Diner** · 4711 Lee Hwy
- **Nouveau East** · 671 N Glebe Rd, Ste 1248
- **Rocklands** · 4000 Fairfax Dr
- **Tara Thai** · 4001 Fairfax Dr

Shopping

- **Pottery Barn** · Ballston Commons,
  2700 Clarendon Blvd

Video Rental

- **Dollar Video** · 5133 Lee Hwy
- **Top Video** · 850 N Randolph St
- **Video 95** · 5011 Wilson Blvd

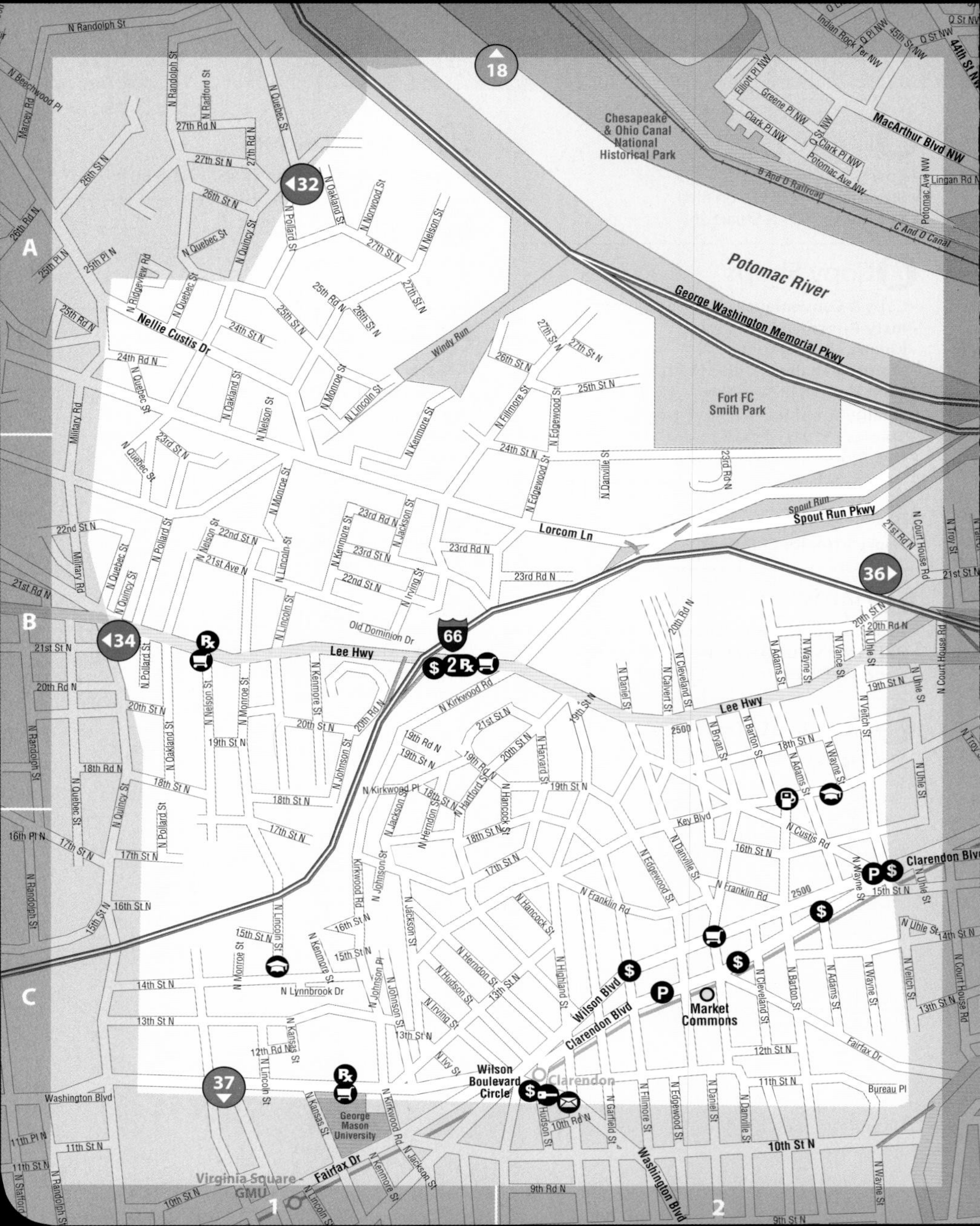

Map 35 · **Clarendon**

N

18

Chesapeake
& Ohio Canal
National
Historical Park

MacArthur Blvd NW

Q St NW

Indian Rock Ter NW

Elliott Pl NW
Greene Pl NW
Clark Pl NW

Potomac Ave NW

B And O Railroad

C And D Canal

◄132

N Randolph St
27th Rd N
27th St N

26th St N

26th Rd N
25th Pl N
25th St N

A

25th Rd N

Nellie Custis Dr

24th St N

24th Rd N

24th St N

Military Rd

N Quebec St

N Quebec St

23rd St N

22nd St N

N Pollard St

21st Rd N

Potomac River

George Washington Memorial Pkwy

Windy Run

27th St N

26th St N

25th St N

24th St N

Fort FC
Smith Park

Spout Run

Spout Run Pkwy

Lorcom Ln

N Edgewood St

23rd Rd N

23rd St N

23rd Rd N

23rd St N

36▶

21st Rd N
21st St N

◄134

B

20th Rd N

Lee Hwy

Old Dominion Dr

66

$ 2 ℞

Lee Hwy

2500

N Quebec St

N Nelson St

N Monroe St

N Kenmore St

N Pollard St

21st Ave N

22nd St N

N Irving St

N Jackson St

20th St N

19th St N

18th St N

17th St N

N Kirkwood Rd

19th Rd N

19th St N

18th St N

18th St N

17th St N

16th St N

16th Pl N

16th St N

N Randolph St

N Quebec St

N Pollard St

N Oakland St

Kirkwood Rd

N Johnson St

N Jackson St

N Herndon St

19th Rd N

19th St N

18th St N

N Hartford St

N Hancock St

N Kirkwood Pl

N Franklin Rd

Key Blvd

16th St N

N Daniel St

N Edgewood St

N Cleveland St

N Danville St

N Barton St

18th St N

N Adams St

N Wayne St

N Vance St

N Uhle St

N Court House Rd

N Court House Rd

N Ode St

Clarendon Blvd

2500

℞

2500

$

$

$

C

15th St N

14th St N

13th St N

N Lynnbrook Dr

N Monroe St

N Kenmore St

15th St N

N Lincoln St

N Johnson St

N Jackson St

N Herndon St

N Hudson St

N Irving St

N Highland St

Wilson Blvd

Clarendon Blvd

$

P

Market
Commons

$

$

N Franklin Rd

N Edgewood St

N Cleveland St

N Danville St

N Barton St

N Adams St

N Wayne St

N Uhle St

N Veitch St

12th St N

Fairfax Dr

Bureau Pl

37

Washington Blvd

11th Pl N

11th St N

N Lincoln St

N Kansas St

George
Mason
University

℞

Wilson
Boulevard
Circle

$

Clarendon

10th Rd N

N Fillmore St

N Edgewood St

N Danville St

N Wayne St

N Veitch St

Washington Blvd

10th St N

9th Rd N

Fairfax Dr

Virginia Square-
GMU

1

2

If you're young and single and insist on living in Virginia, have the decency to at least live here. This is the one suburban neighborhood, actually it used to be part of the city proper before Virginia reclaimed it, which has some spontaneity. That's going to make the Old Town crowd furious, but this is really the most fun of the NoVa options.

33 34 35 36 7
37
38 40

Map

Banks

- **BB&T** · 2200 Wilson Blvd
- **Chevy Chase** · 3141 Lee Hwy
- **Riggs** · 2601 Clarendon Blvd
- **Virginia Commerce** · 2930 Wilson Blvd
- **Wachovia** · 2200 Clarendon Blvd
- **Wachovia** · 3140 Washington Blvd

Car Rental

- **Bargain Buggies Rent A Car** ·
  3140 Washington Blvd · 703-841-0000

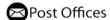 Gas Stations

- **Exxon** · 2410 Lee Hwy

○ Landmarks

- **Market Commons** · 2690 Clarendon Blvd

 Parking

Pharmacies

- **CVS** · 3133 Lee Hwy
- **Eckerd's** · 3130 Lee Hwy
- **Giant Food Pharmacy** · 3450 Washington Blvd
- **Safeway** · 3713 Lee Hwy

Post Offices

- **Arlington Main Office** · 3118 Washington Blvd

Schools

- **Arlington Science Focus** · 1501 N Lincoln St
- **Francis Scott Key Elementary** · 2300 Key Blvd

Supermarkets

- **Giant Food** · 3115 Lee Hwy
- **Giant Food** · 3450 Washington Blvd
- **Safeway** · 3713 Lee Hwy
- **Whole Foods Market** · 2700 Wilson Blvd

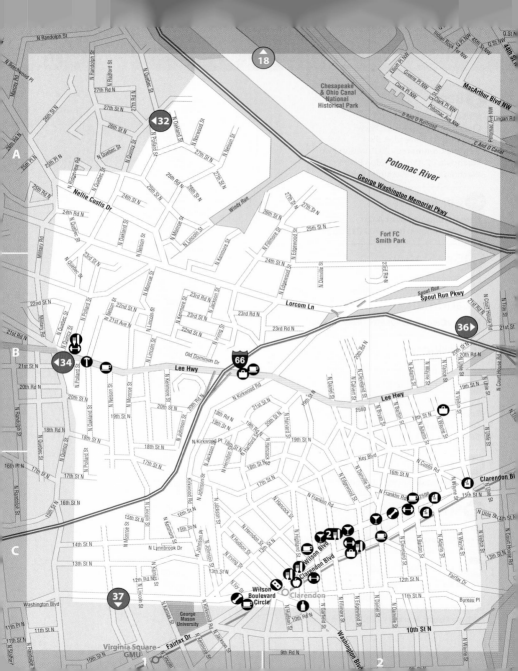

Iota is always worth a trek for the up-close look at the good and great bands passing through. Along with the Birchmere farther a field, this club is one of the destinations for the nation's touring bluegrass and alt-country bands. Common Grounds is a neighborhood gathering place while Wilson Boulevard is split between bars and restaurants that cater to the laid-back locals or the more polished professionals that are beginning to flood the rentals here.

Map

33 | 34 | 35 | 36 | 7
37
38 | 40

Coffee

- **Common Grounds** · 3211 Wilson Blvd
- **Hot Shotz** · 3018 Wilson Blvd
- **Java Shack** · 2507 N Franklin Rd
- **Starbucks** · 2690 Clarendon Blvd
- **Starbucks** · 3125 Lee Hwy
- **Starbucks** · 3713 Lee Hwy

Copy Shops

- **Kinko's** · 2300 Clarendon Blvd
- **Southeastern Printing & Litho** · 2401 Wilson Blvd
- **UPS Store** · 2200 Wilson Blvd

Farmer's Markets

- **Claredon Farmers Market** · Clarendon Blvd & N Highland St

Gyms

- **Curves** · 2105 N Pollard St
- **Curves** · 2529 Wilson Blvd
- **Studio Body Logic** · 3017 Clarendon Blvd
- **Washington Sports Clubs** · 2800 Clarendon Blvd

Hardware Stores

- **Cherrydale Hardware & Garden** · 3805 Lee Hwy
- **Virginia Hardware** · 2915 Wilson Blvd

Liquor Stores

- **Virginia ABC** · 1039 N Highland St

Nightlife

- **Galaxy Hut** · 2711 Wilson Blvd
- **Iota** · 2832 Wilson Blvd

Pet Shops

- **AKA Spot** · 2622 Wilson Blvd
- **Petco** · 3200 Washington Blvd

Restaurants

- **Boulevard Woodgrill** · 2901 Wilson Blvd
- **Faccia Luna Trattoria** · 2909 Wilson Blvd
- **Hard Times Cafe** · 3028 Wilson Blvd
- **Harry's Tap Room** · 2800 Clarendon Blvd
- **Hope Key** · 3131 Wilson Blvd
- **Portabellos** · 2109 N Pollard St

Shopping

- **Brass Knob** · 2311 18th St
- **The Container Store** · 2800 Clarendon Blvd
- **The Italian store** · 3123 Lee Hwy

Video Rental

- **Kat Video** · 3171 Wilson Blvd

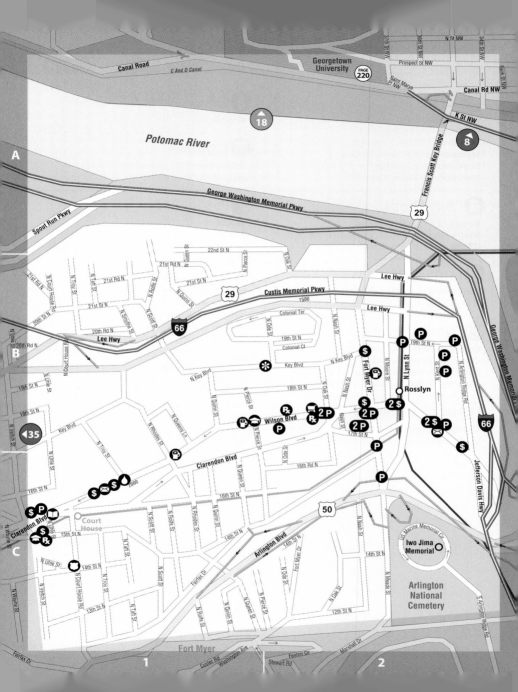

Welcome to the concrete jungle. You should never be at a loss for parking, here in Rosslyn where parking garages outnumber grass blades. This is one of the least life-affirming neighborhoods in the city, with its collection of anonymous office buildings and mean little storefronts. The upshot is that greener and greater neighborhoods are easily accessible. You just have to leave Rosslyn to get there.

Banks

- **Bank of America** · 1700 N Moore St
- **Bank of America** · 2111 Wilson Blvd
- **BB&T** · 1901 Fort Myer Dr
- **Chevy Chase** · 1100 Wilson Blvd
- **Presidential Savings** · 1700 N Moore St
- **Riggs** · 1101 Wilson Blvd
- **Riggs** · 2050 Wilson Blvd
- **Sun Trust** · 1000 Wilson Blvd
- **Sun Trust** · 2121 15th St N
- **Wachovia** · 1300 Wilson Blvd
- **Wachovia** · 2026 Wilson Blvd

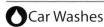 Car Washes

- **Car Cleaning & Restoration** · 2000 Wilson Blvd

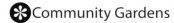 Community Gardens

Gas Stations

- **Amoco** · 1625 Wilson Blvd
- **Chevron** · 1830 Fort Myer Dr
- **Exxon** · 1824 Wilson Blvd

○ Landmarks

- **Iwo Jima Memorial** · Marshall Dr

Libraries

- **Arlington Public Library Information & Referral Office** · 2100 Clarendon Blvd

 Parking

 Pharmacies

- **CVS** · 1555 Wilson Blvd
- **CVS** · 2121 15th St N
- **Safeway** · 1525 Wilson Blvd

Police

- **Arlington County Police Department** · 1425 N Courthouse Rd

 Post Offices

- **Court House Station** · 2043 Wilson Blvd
- **Rosslyn Station** · 1101 Wilson Blvd, Ste 1

Schools

- **Glebe Elementary** · 1601 Wilson Blvd
- **Strayer University (Arlington Campus)** · 2121 15th St

Supermarkets

- **Safeway** · 1525 Wilson Blvd

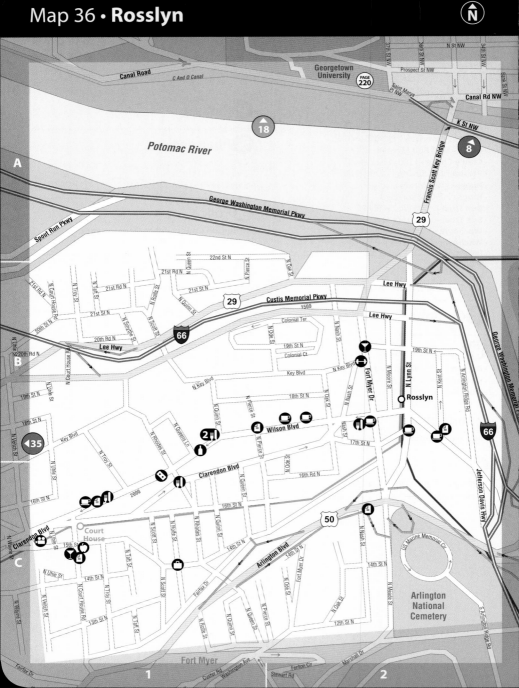

The fast food and lunch joints tend to cater to the working stiffs who head home after 5, but there are markets and dry cleaners and the like to serve those who actually live here. If you're after any real shopping or nightlife, hike a few blocks to Clarendon or across the bridge to Georgetown.

Coffee

- **Atomic Grounds** · 1555 Wilson Blvd
- **Coffee Express** · 1100 Wilson Blvd
- **Coffee Express** · 1300 Wilson Blvd
- **Cosi** · 2050 Wilson Blvd
- **Starbucks** · 1525 Wilson Blvd
- **Starbucks** · 1735 N Lynn St

Copy Shops

- **Minuteman Press** · 1601 N Kent St
- **Office Depot** · 1515 N Courthouse Rd
- **Sir Speedy Printing** · 1600 Wilson Blvd
- **Source One Office Solution** · 1011 Arlington Blvd
- **USA Print & Copy** · 2044 Wilson Blvd

Farmer's Markets

- **Arlington County Farmer's Market** · N 14th St & N Courthouse Rd

Gyms

- **Gold's Gym** · 1400 Key Blvd

Liquor Stores

- **Virginia ABC** · 1731 Wilson Blvd

Movie Theaters

- **AMC Courthouse Plaza 8** · 2150 Clarendon Blvd

Nightlife

- **Continental** · 1911 Fort Myer Dr
- **Summers Grill and Sports Pub** · 1520 N Courthouse Rd

Restaurants

- **Gua-Rapo** · 2039 Wilson Blvd
- **Il Radicchio** · 1801 Clarendon Blvd
- **Mezza9** · 1325 Wilson Blvd
- **Ray's The Steaks** · 1725 Wilson Blvd
- **Village Bistro** · 1723 Wilson Blvd

Shopping

- **Vastu** · 1829 14th St

Video Rental

- **Hollywood Video** · 1900 Wilson Blvd

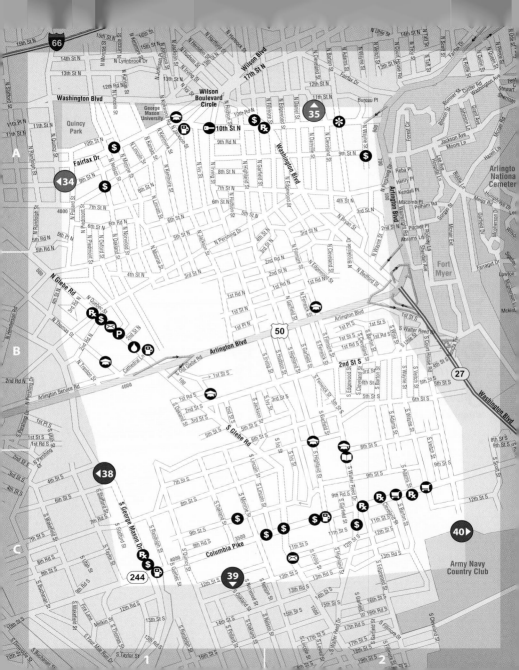

Banks

- **Bank of America** · 3401 Columbia Pike
- **Bank of America** · 3625 Fairfax Dr
- **BB&T** · 1100 S Walter Reed Dr
- **BB&T** · 3001 N Washington Blvd
- **Chevy Chase** · 3532 Columbia Pike
- **Chevy Chase** · 901 N Nelson St
- **Sun Trust** · 249 N Glebe Rd
- **Sun Trust** · 3108 Columbia Pike
- **United Bank** · 2300 S 9th St
- **United Bank** · 3801 Wilson Blvd
- **Wachovia** · 951 S George Mason Dr

Car Rental

- **Avis** · 3206 10th St N · 703-516-4202

Car Washes

- **Mr Wash** · 101 N Glebe Rd

Community Gardens

Gas Stations

- **Chevron** · 67 N Glebe Rd
- **Hess** · 3299 Wilson Blvd
- **Mobil** · 3100 Columbia Pike
- **Shell** · 4211 Columbia Pike

Libraries

- **Columbia Pike Library** · 816 S Walter Reed Dr

Parking

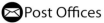Pharmacies

- **CVS** · 256 N Glebe Rd
- **CVS** · 2601 Columbia Pike
- **CVS** · 2900 N 10th St
- **Eckerd's** · 2820 Columbia Pike
- **Giant Food Pharmacy** · 2411 Columbia Pike
- **Rite Aid** · 940 S George Mason Dr

Post Offices

- **Buckingham Station** · 235 N Glebe Rd
- **South Station** · 1210 S Glebe Rd

Schools

- **Henry Elementary** · 701 S Highland St
- **Jefferson Middle** · 125 S Old Gebe Rd
- **Long Branch Elementary** · 33 N Fillmore St
- **St Charles** · 3299 N Fairfax Dr
- **St Thomas More Cathedral** · 105 N Thomas St
- **Technical Education & Career Center** · 816 S Walter Reed Dr

Supermarkets

- **Giant Food** · 2515 Columbia Pike
- **Safeway** · 2303 Columbia Pike

Map 37 • **Fort Myer**

People love Bob & Edith's Diner. Others just come when they're in the market for a crew cut.

Coffee
- **Cafe Laluna** · 2401 Columbia Pike
- **Dunkin' Donuts** · 3100 Columbia Pike
- **Rappahannock Coffee & Roasting** · 2406 Columbia Pike
- **Starbucks** · 901 N Nelson St

Copy Shops
- **Minuteman Press** · 3000 N 10th St

Farmer's Markets
- **Columbia Pike Farmer's Market** · Columbia Pike & S Walter Reed Dr

Gyms
- **Aerobic Workout** · 954 N Monroe St
- **Gold's Gym** · 3910 Wilson Blvd

Movie Theaters
- **Cinema 'n' Draft House** · 2903 Columbia Pike

Nightlife
- **Jay's Saloon** · 3114 N 10th St
- **Royal Lee Bar and Grill** · 2211 N Pershing Dr

Pet Shops
- **Birds 'n' Things** · 2628 Columbia Pike

Restaurants
- **Bob & Edith's Diner** · 2310 Columbia Pike
- **Manee Thai** · 2500 Columbia Pike
- **Matuba** · 2915 Columbia Pike

Video Rental
- **Hollywood Video** · 3263 Columbia Pike
- **Video Warehouse** · 3411 5th St S

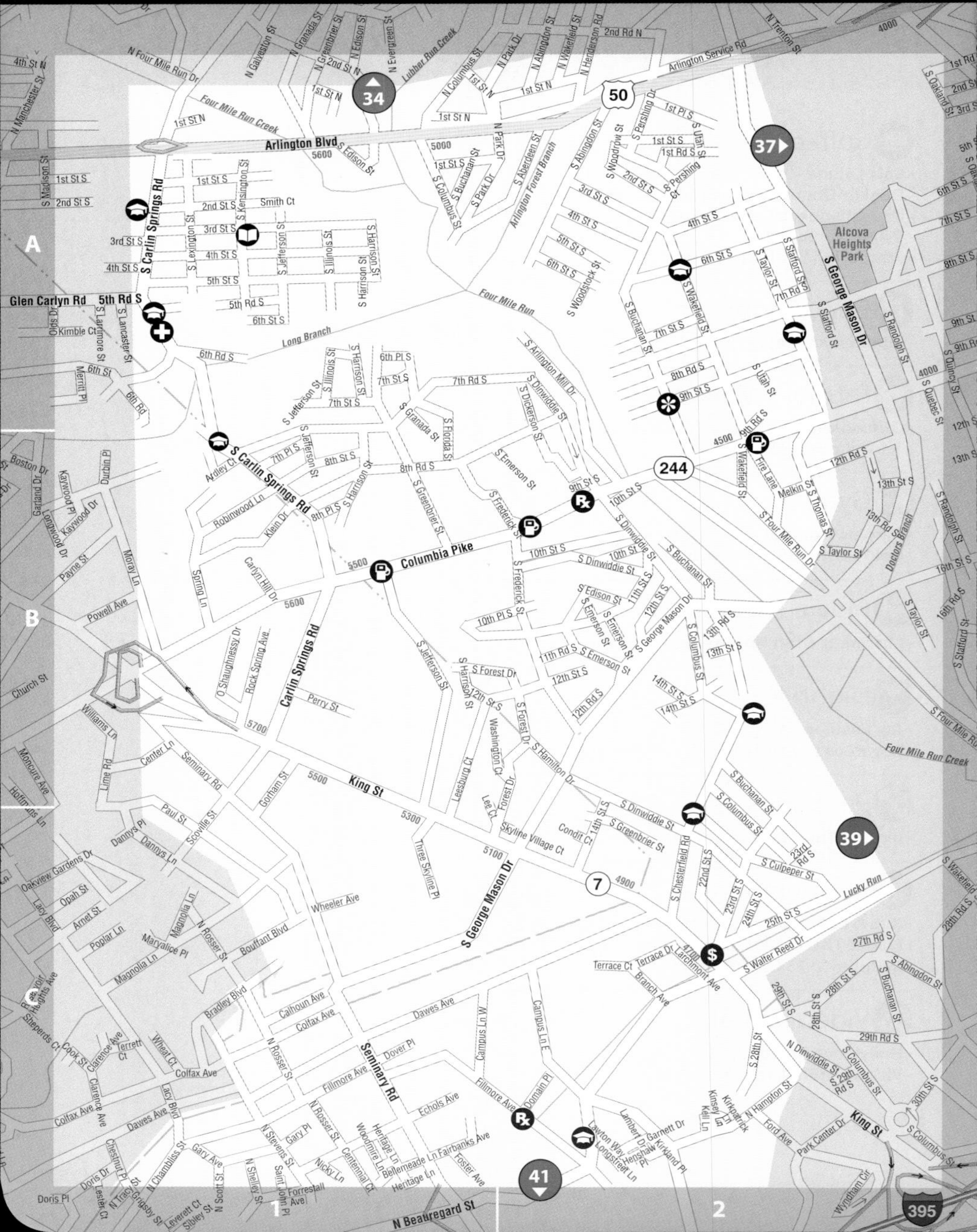

Map 38 · **Columbia Pike**

N

34

50

37▶

Alcova Heights Park

S George Mason Dr

Arlington Blvd

Arlington Service Rd

Four Mile Run Creek

Four Mile Run

Long Branch

Arlington Forest Branch

A

Glen Carlyn Rd   5th Rd S

S Carlin Springs Rd

Columbia Pike

244

S Carlin Springs Rd

Carlin Springs Rd

B

Church St

King St

Powell Ave

39▶

Four Mile Run Creek

Lucky Run

7

S George Mason Dr

Skyline Village Ct

$

C

Seminary Rd

King St

395

41
▼

1   2

N Beauregard St

Ugly high-rises and uglier strip malls await in this northern Virginia traffic oasis!

$ Banks
· **Wachovia** · 4651 King St

✱ Community Gardens

⛽ Gas Stations
· **Amoco** · 4625 Columbia Pike
· **Mobil** · 5200 Columbia Pike
· **Shell** · 5511 Columbia Pike

➕ Hospitals
· **Northern Virginia Community** ·
  601 S Carlin Springs Rd

📖 Libraries
· **Glencarlyn Public Library** · 300 S Kensington St

℞ Pharmacies
· **Allied Pharmacy** · 5100 Fillmore Ave
· **CVS** · 5017 Columbia Pike

🎓 Schools
· **Barcroft Elementary** · 625 S Wakefield St
· **Campbell Elementary** · 737 S Carlin Springs
· **Carlin Springs Elementary** · 5995 5th Rd S
· **Claremont Center** · 4700 S Chesterfield Rd
· **Kenmore Middle** · 200 S Carlin Springs Rd
· **Northern Virgina Community College**
  (Alexandria Campus) · 3001 N Beauregard St
· **Our Savior Lutheran** · 825 S Taylor St
· **Wakefield High** · 4901 S Chesterfield Rd

Map 38 · **Columbia Pike**

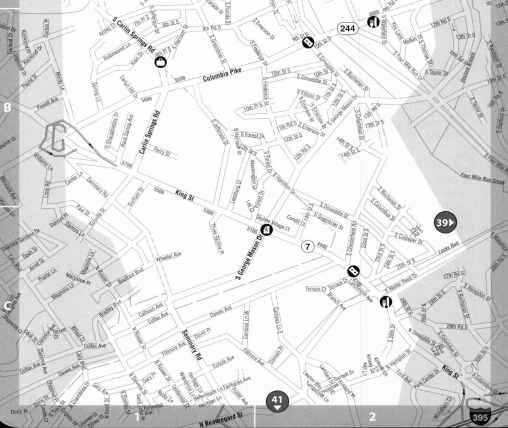

Other than a couple of beloved local chains like Bob & Edith's and Five Guys, there's little of interest.

Copy Shops
· **Kwik Kopy Printing** · 5100 Leesburg Pike

Restaurants
· **Bob & Edith's Diner** · 4707 Columbia Pike
· **Five Guys** · 4626 King St

Shopping
· **REI** · 3509 Carlin Springs Rd

Video Rental
· **Purple Potamus Video** · 4678 King St
· **Tum Videos** · 5001 Columbia Pike

Map 39 · Shirlington

This boring, longtime suburb is quickly becoming a retreat for the gay community that's sick of the high home prices in the city. The newcomers are bringing much needed panache and vibrancy, but have their work cut out for them.

$ Banks

- **BB&T** · 2700 S Quincy St
- **Burke & Herbert** · 1705 Fern St
- **Chevy Chase** · 3690 King St
- **Sun Trust** · 3610 King St
- **Wachovia** · 1711 Fern St
- **Wachovia** · 3624 King St

Car Rental

- **Enterprise** · 2778 S Arlington Mill Dr · 703-820-7100
- **Hertz (Reagan National Airport)** · 3860 Four Mile Run Dr · 703-419-6300

Car Washes

- **David's Car Wash** · 4148 S Four Mile Run Dr

Community Gardens

Gas Stations

- **Exxon** · 2316 S Shirlington Rd
- **Exxon** · 4368 King St
- **Mobil** · 4154 S Four Mile Run Dr
- **Shell** · 1333 N Quaker Ln
- **Shell** · 4060 S Four Mile Run Dr
- **Texaco** · 2817 S Quincy St

Libraries

- **Shirlington Library** · 2786 S Arlington Mill Dr

Pharmacies

- **CVS** · 1521 N Quaker Ln
- **Green Vally** · 2415 S Shirlington Rd
- **Rite Aid** · 3614 King St
- **Safeway** · 3526 King St

Post Offices

- **Park Fairfax Station** · 3682 King St

Schools

- **Abingdon Elementary** · 3035 S Abingdon St
- **Drew Model Elementary** · 3500 S 23 St
- **Randolph Elementary** · 1306 S Quincy St

Supermarkets

- **Giant Food** · 3680 King St
- **Safeway** · 3526 King St

The proliferation of gyms and pet shops speak of more yuppie things to come.

Coffee
- **Starbucks** · 3690 King St

Copy Shops
- **UPS Store** · 2776 S Arlington Mill Dr

Gyms
- **Center Club** · 4300 King St
- **Curves** · 2772 S Arlington Mill Dr
- **Washington Sports Clubs** · 3654 King St

Liquor Stores
- **Virginia ABC** · 3678 King St

Movie Theaters
- **Cineplex Odeon Shirlington 7** ·
  2772 S Randolph St

Nightlife
- **Capitol City Brewing Company** · 2700 S Quincy St

Pet Shops
- **For Pet's Sake** · 1537 N Quaker Ln
- **Happy Hounds** · 1510 S Edgewood St
- **One Good Tern** · 1710 Fern St
- **Pro Feed** · 3690 King St

Shopping
- **Washington Golf Centers** · 2625 Shirlington Rd

Video Rental
- **Blockbuster Video** · 3610 King St

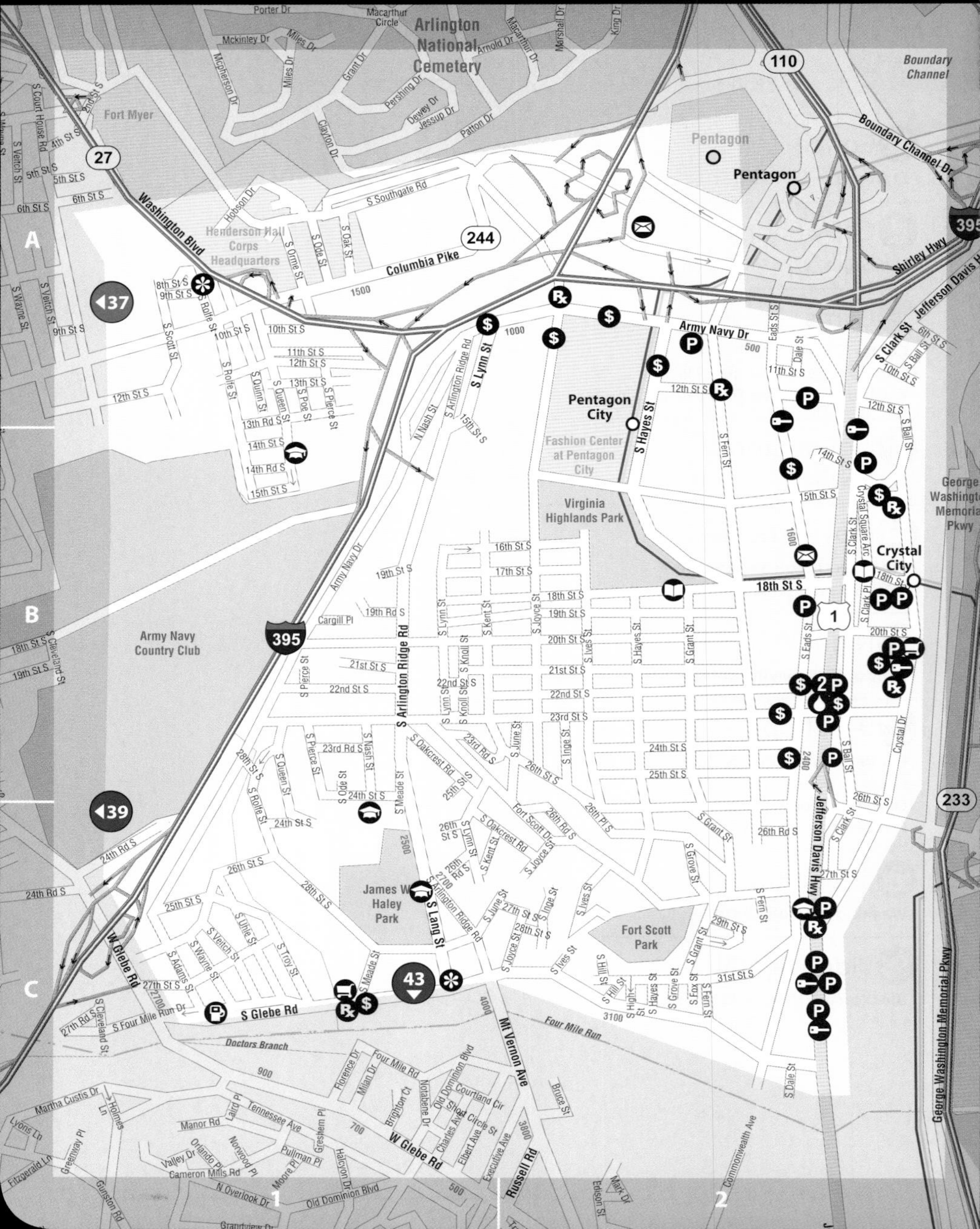

Map 40 · **Pentagon City**

N

Arlington National Cemetery

Boundary Channel

Porter Dr
Macarthur Circle
Mckinley Dr
Miles Dr
Pershing Dr
Arnold Dr
Marshall Dr

Fort Myer

110

Boundary Channel Dr

27

Washington Blvd

S Court House Rd
S Veitch St
4th St S
9th St S
6th St S
6th St S

Hodson Dr
Jessup Dr

S Southgate Rd

Pentagon

Pentagon

395

Shirley Hwy

Henderson Hall Corps Headquarters

S Orme St
S Oak St

244

Columbia Pike
1500

Jefferson Davis Hwy

37

8th St S
9th St S
S Rolfe St

10th St S
11th St S
12th St S
13th St S
13th Rd S
14th St S
14th Rd S
15th St S

S Scott St
S Queen St
S Pierce St
S Quinn St

S Arlington Ridge Rd
N Nash St
S Lynn St

1000

Army Navy Dr
500

Eads St S

S Clark St
S Ball St

George Washington Memorial Pkwy

12th St S
11th St S

Pentagon City

Fashion Center at Pentagon City

S Hayes St
S Fern St

12th St S
13th St S
14th St S

10th St S
12th St S

Virginia Highlands Park

15th St S
1600

Crystal City

George Washington Memorial Pkwy

16th St S
17th St S
18th St S
19th St S

S Lynn St
N Nash St
S Kent St
S Joyce St

S Ives St
S Hayes St
S Grant St

18th St S

1

S Eads St
S Clark St
S Ball St

233

Army Navy Country Club

395

Cargill Pl
19th Rd S

20th St S
21st St S
22nd St S
23rd St S

S Knoll St

20th St S

Crystal Av

21st St S
S Pierce St
S Queen St
22nd St S
23rd Rd S

S Lynn St
S Knoll St
S Meade St

S Oak St

23rd Rd S

24th St S
25th St S

S Ives St
S Grant St

2
2600

39

18th St S
19th St S

24th Rd S

23rd Rd S
24th St S

S Oakcrest Rd
S June St

Fort Scott Park

26th St S

26th Rd S

S Fern St

Jefferson Davis Hwy

25th St S
24th Rd S
25th St S
S Veitch St
S Utah St
S Ode St

S Piedmont
S Lang St
S Meade St
S Oakcrest Rd

27th St S
S Lincoln St

26th St S
27th St S

S Grant St
S George St

27th St S

James W Haley Park

28th St S
S Lang St

28th St S

S Ives St
S Hill St
S Glebe St
S Fox St

31st St S

29th St S
30th St S

S Clark St
S Dale St

W Glebe Rd

S Cleveland St
S Four Mile Run Dr

27th Rd S

S Fillmore St
S Glebe Rd

43

S Meade St
S Lang St

Four Mile Run

S Hill St
S Grove St
3100

Doctors Branch
900

Mt Vernon Ave

S Dale St

Martha Custis Dr
Lyons Ln
Fitzgerald Ln

Florence Dr
Milan Dr
Brighton Ct

Courtland Cir
Shea Circle
3000
Elbert Ave

W Glebe Rd
700
Russell Rd

Manor Rd
Tennessee Ave
Valley Dr
Pullman Pl

Commonwealth Ave

Cameron Mills Rd
Old Dominion Blvd

Imagine *Blade Runner* without Harrison Ford. The Pentagon is a scary version of a possible future, with its vast underground corridors filled with uniformed workers bustling to and from military posts. Weird, and best to avoid.

$ Banks
- **Bank of America** · 1101 S Joyce St
- **Bank of America** · 1425 S Eads St
- **Bank of America** · 900 Army Navy Dr
- **BB&T** · 2113 Crystal Plaza Arcade, S Eads St b/w 24th St S & 25th St S
- **BB&T** · 2221 S Eads St
- **BB&T** · 2947 S Glebe Rd
- **Burke & Herbert** · 500 23rd St S
- **Chevy Chase** · 1100 S Hayes St
- **Chevy Chase** · 1621 Crystal Square Arc
- **Chevy Chase** · 2901 S Glebe Rd
- **Wachovia** · 1755 Jefferson Davis Hwy

Car Rental
- **Alamo** · 2780 Jefferson Davis Hwy · 703-684-0086
- **Budget** · 1200 Eads St · 703-351-7500
- **Dollar** · Reagan National Airport, 2600 Jefferson Davis Hwy · 703-519-8700
- **Enterprise** · 2121 Crystal Dr · 703-553-2930
- **Rent-A-Wreck** · 901 S Clark St · 703-413-7100

Car Washes
- **Crystal Square Car Wash** · 1755 Jefferson Davis Hwy

Community Gardens

Gas Stations
- **Exxon** · 2720 S Glebe Rd

o Landmarks
- **Pentagon** · Boundary Channel Dr

Libraries
- **Arlington County Aurora Hills Library** · 735 18th St S
- **US Patent & Trademark Library** · 2021 S Clark Pl

Parking

Pharmacies
- **Costco Wholesale Pharmacy** · 1200 S Fern St
- **CVS** · 2400 Jefferson Davis Hwy
- **Eckerd's** · 1301 Joyce St
- **Giant Food Pharmacy** · 2901 S Glebe Rd
- **Rite Aid** · 1667 Crystal Square Arc
- **Rite Aid** · 2120 Crystal Plaza Arc

Post Offices
- **Eads Station** · 1720 S Eads St
- **Pentagon Branch** · 9998 The Pentagon

Schools
- **DeVry University (Arlington Campus)** · 2341 Jefferson Davis Hwy
- **Gunston Middle** · 2700 S Lang St
- **Hoffman-Boston Elementary** · 1415 S Queen St
- **Oakridge Elementary** · 1414 24th St

Supermarkets
- **Giant Food** · 2901 S Glebe Rd
- **Safeway** · 2031 Crystal Plz

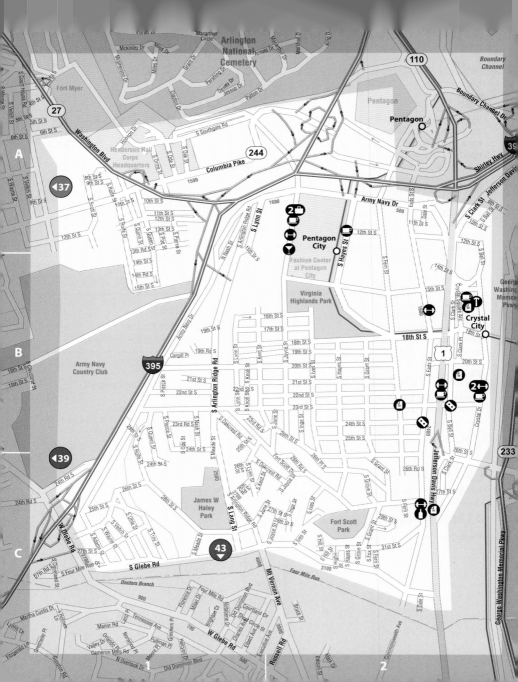

The Fashion Center at Pentagon City is the only traditional mall that's accessible by metro. So if you really miss a good food court meal, take the yellow or blue line straight here.

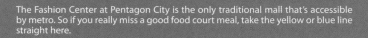Coffee

- **Starbucks** • 1101 S Joyce St
- **Starbucks** • 1201 S Hayes St
- **Starbucks** • 1649 Crystal Sq
- **Starbucks** • 1700 Jefferson Davis Hwy
- **Starbucks** • 2231 Crystal Dr

Copy Shops

- **Crystal City Copy** • 2341 Jefferson Davis Hwy
- **GBS Printers** • 554 23rd St S
- **Kinko's** • 1601 Crystal Sq Arc
- **Minuteman Press** • 2187 Crystal Plz Arc

Gyms

- **Bally Total Fitness** • 1201 S Joyce St
- **Beyond Fitness** • 1600 S Eads St
- **Crystal Park Sport & Health** • 2231 Crystal Dr
- **Gateway Sport & Health** •
  1235 Jefferson Davis Hwy
- **Gold's Gym** • 2900 S Glebe Rd
- **Park Health Club** • 2231 Crystal Dr

Hardware Stores

- **Crystal City Hardware** • 1612 Crystal Square Arc

Liquor Stores

- **Virginia ABC** • 2955 S Glebe Rd

Nightlife

- **Sine Irish Pub** • 1301 S Joyce St

Shopping

- **Elizabeth Arden Red Door Salon & Spa** •
  1101 S Joyce St
- **What's In** • 1101 S Joyce St

Video Rental

- **Review Video Service** • 527 S 24th St
- **Video Warehouse** • 320 S 23rd St

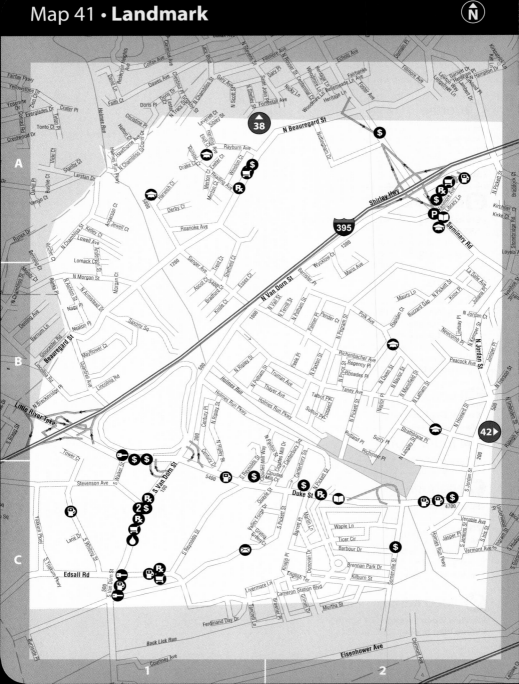

Map 41 • **Landmark**

Essentials

Map 41

Whoever named this neighborhood must have loved irony. There are surprisingly few landmarks in this nondescript residential area. Unless you consider highway entrances and exits noteworthy.

$ Banks

• **Bank of America** · 5801 Duke St
• **BB&T** · 233 S Van Dorn St
• **BB&T** · 4999 Seminary Rd
• **Burke & Herbert** · 155 N Paxton St
• **Provident** · 231 S Van Dorn St
• **Sun Trust** · 1460 N Beauregard St
• **Sun Trust** · 4616 Kenmore Ave
• **Sun Trust** · 5701 Duke St
• **Virginia Commerce** · 185 Somervelle St
• **Virginia Commerce** · 5140 Duke St
• **Wachovia** · 4601 Duke St

Car Rental

• **Avis** · 6001 Duke St · 703-256-4335
• **Enterprise** · 512 S Van Dorn St #C · 703-823-5700
• **Enterprise** · 5800 Edsall Rd · 703-658-0010

Car Washes

• **Mr Wash** · 420 S Van Dorn St

Gas Stations

• **Exxon** · 4550 Kenmore Ave
• **Exxon** · 4657 Duke St
• **Exxon** · 501 S Van Dorn St
• **Mobil** · 190 S Whiting St
• **Mobil** · 5412 Duke St
• **Shell** · 5740 Edsall Rd
• **Texaco** · 4670 Duke St

Libraries

• **Alexandria Charles E Beatley Jr Central Library** ·
  5005 Duke St
• **Ellen Coolidge Burke Branch Library** ·
  4701 Seminary Rd

P Parking

Pharmacies

• **CVS** · 1462 Beauregard St
• **CVS** · 259 S Van Dorn St
• **CVS** · 4606 Kenmore Ave
• **CVS** · 5101 Duke St
• **Giant Food Pharmacy** · 5730 Edsall Rd
• **Safeway** · 299 S Van Dorn

Post Offices

• **Trade Center Station** · 340 S Pickett St

Schools

• **Francis C Hammond Middle** · 4646 Seminary Rd
• **James K Polk Elementary** · 5000 Polk Ave
• **John Adams Elementary** · 5651 Rayburn Ave
• **Patrick Henry Elementary** · 4643 Taney Ave
• **William Ramsey Elementary** · 5700 Sanger Ave

Supermarkets

• **Giant Food** · 1476 N Beauregard St
• **Giant Food** · 5730 Edsall Rd
• **Safeway** · 299 S Van Dorn St
• **Safeway** · 4604 Kenmore Ave

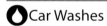

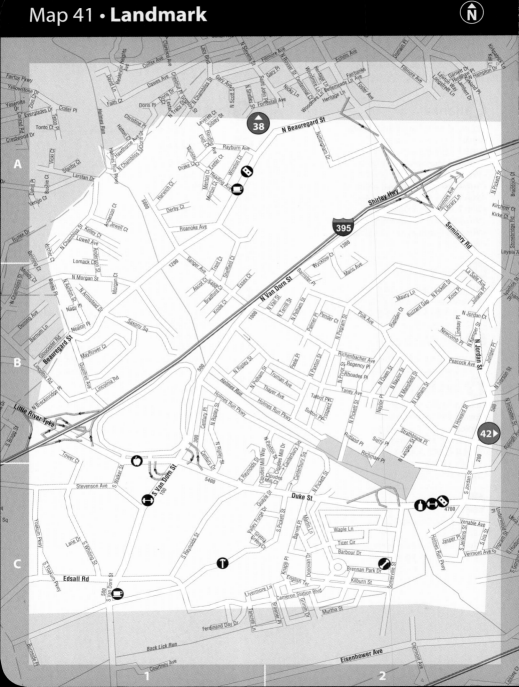

Drive into to Dunkin' Donuts. Get coffee. Drive back onto highway. You've done Landmark.

Map

Coffee
- **Dunkin' Donuts** · 504 S Van Dorn St
- **Starbucks** · 1462 N Beauregard St

Farmer's Markets
- **Northern Neck Vegetable Growers Association Farmer's Market** · 5801 Duke St

Gyms
- **Curves** · 4613 Duke St
- **Fitness First** · 255 S Van Dorn St

Hardware Stores
- **Home Depot** · 400 S Pickett St

Liquor Stores
- **Virginia ABC** · 4647 Duke St

Pet Shops
- **Greenpets** · 4915 Brennan Park Dr

Video Rental
- **Blockbuster Video** · 1480 N Beauregard St
- **Video Palace** · 4607 Duke St

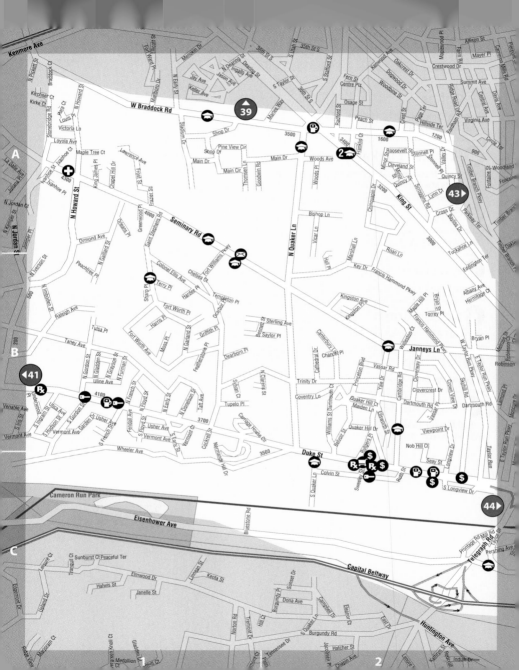

Map

Banks

- **Bank of America** · 2747 Duke St
- **Burke & Herbert** · 2836 Duke St
- **Chevy Chase** · 3131 Duke St
- **Sun Trust** · 3101 Duke St

Car Rental

- **Enterprise** · 4213 Duke St · 703-212-4700
- **Hertz** · 16 Sweeley St · 703-751-1250
- **Rent For Less** · 4105 Duke St · 703-370-5666

 Gas Stations

- **Crown** · 4109 Duke St
- **Mobil** · 2838 Duke St
- **Mobil** · 3500 King St
- **Shell** · 2922 Duke St

Hospitals

- **Inova Alexandria** · 4320 Seminary Rd

 Pharmacies

- **CVS** · 3130 Duke St
- **Giant Food Pharmacy** · 3131 Duke St
- **Rite Aid** · 4515 Duke St

Post Offices

- **Theological Seminary Finance** ·
  3737 Seminary Rd

Schools

- **Bishop Ireton High** · 201 Cambridge Rd
- **Blessed Sacrement** · 1417 W Braddock Rd
- **Douglas MacArthur Elementary** ·
  1101 Janneys Ln
- **Episcopal High** · 1200 N Quaker Ln
- **Foundation School of Alexandria** ·
  25 S Quaker Ln
- **Minnie Howard** · 3801 W Braddock Rd
- **Secondary Training Educational Program** ·
  3330 King St
- **St Stephen & St Agnes** · 1000 St Stephen's Rd
- **Strayer University (Alexandria Campus)** ·
  2730 Eisenhower Ave
- **TC Williams High** · 3330 King St
- **Thornton Friends** · 3830 Seminary Rd
- **Virginia Theological Seminary** ·
  3737 Seminary Rd

Supermarkets

- **Giant Food** · 3131 Duke St

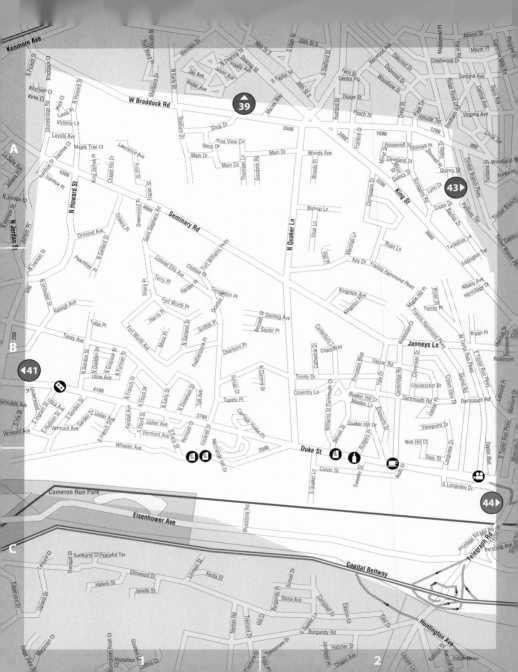

Ho-hum strip mall suburban living.

 ## Coffee
· **Dunkin' Donuts** · 3050 Duke St

 ## Copy Shops
· **Global Printing** · 3670 Wheeler Ave
· **Graphic Images** · 3660 Wheeler Ave
· **UPS Store** · 3213 Duke St

 ## Liquor Stores
· **Virginia ABC** · 3161 Duke St

 ## Movie Theaters
· **Fox Chase** · 2615 Duke St

 ## Video Rental
· **Blockbuster Video** · 4349 Duke St

Map 43 · **Four Mile Run**

N

Army Navy Country Club

40
39
42
44
45
400
1
2

Four Mile Run Park

S Glebe Rd
W Glebe Rd
S Arlington Ridge Rd
Jefferson Davis Hwy
George Washington Mem
Mount Vernon Ave
E Glebe Rd
Russell Rd
Commonwealth Ave
W Braddock Rd
Monroe Ave
King St

Doctors Branch
Four Mile Run

24th Rd S
24th Rd S
25th St S
26th St S
27th St S
S Cleveland St
S Glebe Rd
Martha Custis Dr
Harris Ct
Lyons Ln
Fitzgerald Ln
Mount Eagle Pl
Preston Rd
Corywell St
Ravensworth Pl
Beverly Dr
Farm Rd
Mayer Pl
Crestwood Dr
Summit Ave
Ridge Road Ct
Crescent Dr Dogwood Dr
Woodbine St
Roosevelt St
Stonnell Pl
Cleveland St
Minor St
Quincy St
Lynn Ct
Cross Dr
Roan Ln

Manor Rd
Tennessee Ave
Valley Dr
Cameron Mills Rd
N Overlook Dr
Grandview Dr
S Overlook Dr
Circle Hill Rd
Chalfonte Dr
Eldon St
Cameron Mills Rd
Westminster Pl
Davis Ln
Virginia Ave
Circle Ter
Jackson Pl
Woodland Ter
Fontaine St
Thomas St
Malcolm Pl
Columbia Rd
Oakley Pl
Oakland Ter

25th St S
S Veitch St
S Wayne St
S Utah St
S Troy St
26th St S
S Manor St
27th St S
28th St S
S Kent St
S Oakcrest Dr
Four Scott Dr
S Ives St
S Hill St
S June St
31st St S
3100
3500
3590
3100
2700

Courtland Cir
Circle St
Executive Ave
Mary St
Edison St
Dale St
W Reed Ave
E Reed Ave
Lynnhaven Dr
Evans Ln
Westmond Dr
Montrose Ave
Ashby St
Laverne Ave
E Clifford Ave
Hume Ave
E Raymond Ave
Calvert Ave
Swann Ave
Murray Ave
Oakville St
Forrest St
Groves Ave
E Randolph Ave
Stewart Ave
W Mount Ida Ave
E Mount Ida Ave
W Uhler Ave
E Uhler Ave
W Caton Ave
E Oxford Ave
W Wyatt Ave
E Del Ray Ave
W Del Ray Ave
E Custis Ave
W Custis Ave
E Windsor Ave
W Windsor Ave
E Howell Ave
E Bellefonte Ave
W Bellefonte Ave
E Duncan Ave
Bellaire Rd
E Cliff St
E Mason Ave
E Monroe Ave
E Nelson Ave
44
E Alexandria Ave
E Luray Ave
W Alexandria Ave
E Glendale Ave
W Glendale Ave
Adams Ave
W Spring Ave
E Spring St
W Myrtle St
E Myrtle St
E Masonic View Ave
E Chapman St
W Chapman St

Braddock Road
S Henry St
Janneys Ln

Banks
- **Bank of America** · 600 N Glebe Rd
- **Burke & Herbert** · 306 E Monroe Ave
- **Provident** · 3801 Jefferson Davis Hwy
- **Sun Trust** · 2809 Mount Vernon Ave
- **Wachovia** · 3506 Mount Vernon Ave

Car Rental
- **Enterprise** · 2000 Jefferson Davis Hwy ·
  703-553-7744

Car Washes
- **Mr Wash** · 3407 Mount Vernon Ave
- **Nab Auto Appearance Salon** · 2414 Oakville St

Gas Stations
- **Citgo** · 1015 W Glebe Rd
- **Citgo** · 2312 Mount Vernon Ave
- **Crown** · 3216 Jefferson Davis Hwy
- **Exxon** · 1601 Mount Vernon Ave
- **Exxon** · 2300 Jefferson Davis Hwy
- **Exxon** · 2340 Jefferson Davis Hwy
- **Exxon** · 4001 Mount Vernon Ave
- **Texaco** · 1600 Mount Vernon Ave

Libraries
- **Alexandria James M Duncan Branch Library** ·
  2501 Commonwealth Ave

Parking

Pharmacies
- **CVS** · 3811 Mount Vernon Ave
- **CVS** · 415 Monroe Ave
- **Shopper's Pharmacy** · 3801 Jefferson Davis Hwy
- **Target** · 3601 Jefferson Davis Hwy

Post Offices
- **Potomac Station Finance** · 1908 Mount Vernon Ave

Schools
- **Alexandria Country Day** · 2400 Russell Rd
- **Charles Barrett Elementary** ·
  1115 Martha Custis Dr
- **Cora Kelly Magnet Elementary** ·
  3600 Commonwealth Ave
- **George Mason Elementary** ·
  2601 Cameron Mills Rd
- **Grace Episcopal** · 3601 Russell Rd
- **Immanuel Lutheran** · 109 Belleaire Rd
- **Mount Vernon Elementary** ·
  2601 Commonwealth Ave
- **St Rita** · 3801 Russell Rd

Supermarkets
- **Giant Food** · 425 E Monroe Ave
- **My Organic Market** · 3831 Mount Vernon Ave
- **Shoppers Food Warehouse** ·
  3801 Jefferson Davis Hwy

Map 43 · **Four Mile Run**
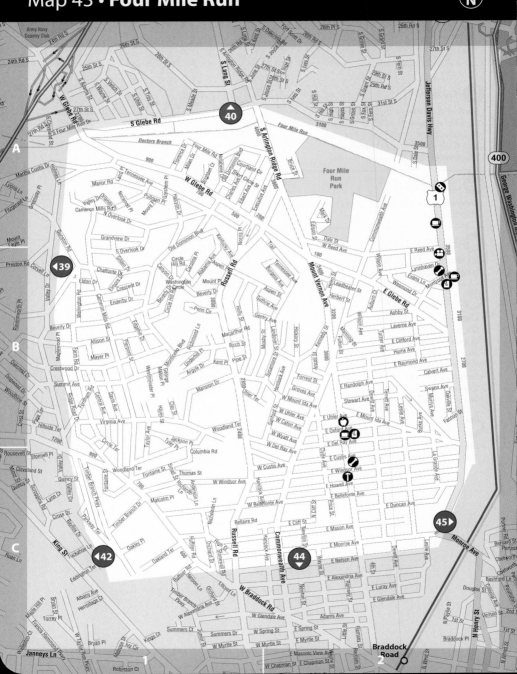

Map 43

See Map 42.

Coffee

- **Dunkin' Donuts** · 3325 Jefferson Davis Hwy
- **St Elmo's Coffee Pub** · 2300 Mount Vernon Ave
- **Starbucks** · 3825 Jefferson Davis Hwy

Copy Shops

- **Staples** · 3301 Jefferson Davis Hwy
- **UPS Store** · 2308 Mount Vernon Ave

Farmer's Markets

- **Del Ray Farmers Market** ·
  Mt Vernon & Oxford Aves

Hardware Stores

- **Executive Lock & Key** ·
  2003 Mount Vernon Ave #B

Movie Theaters

- **Regal Potomac Yards 16** ·
  3575 Jefferson Davis Hwy

Pet Shops

- **Hydrant Dog Bakery** · 2101 Mount Vernon Ave
- **Petsmart** · 3351 Jefferson Davis Hwy

Video Rental

- **Hollywood Video** · 3925 Jefferson Davis Hwy

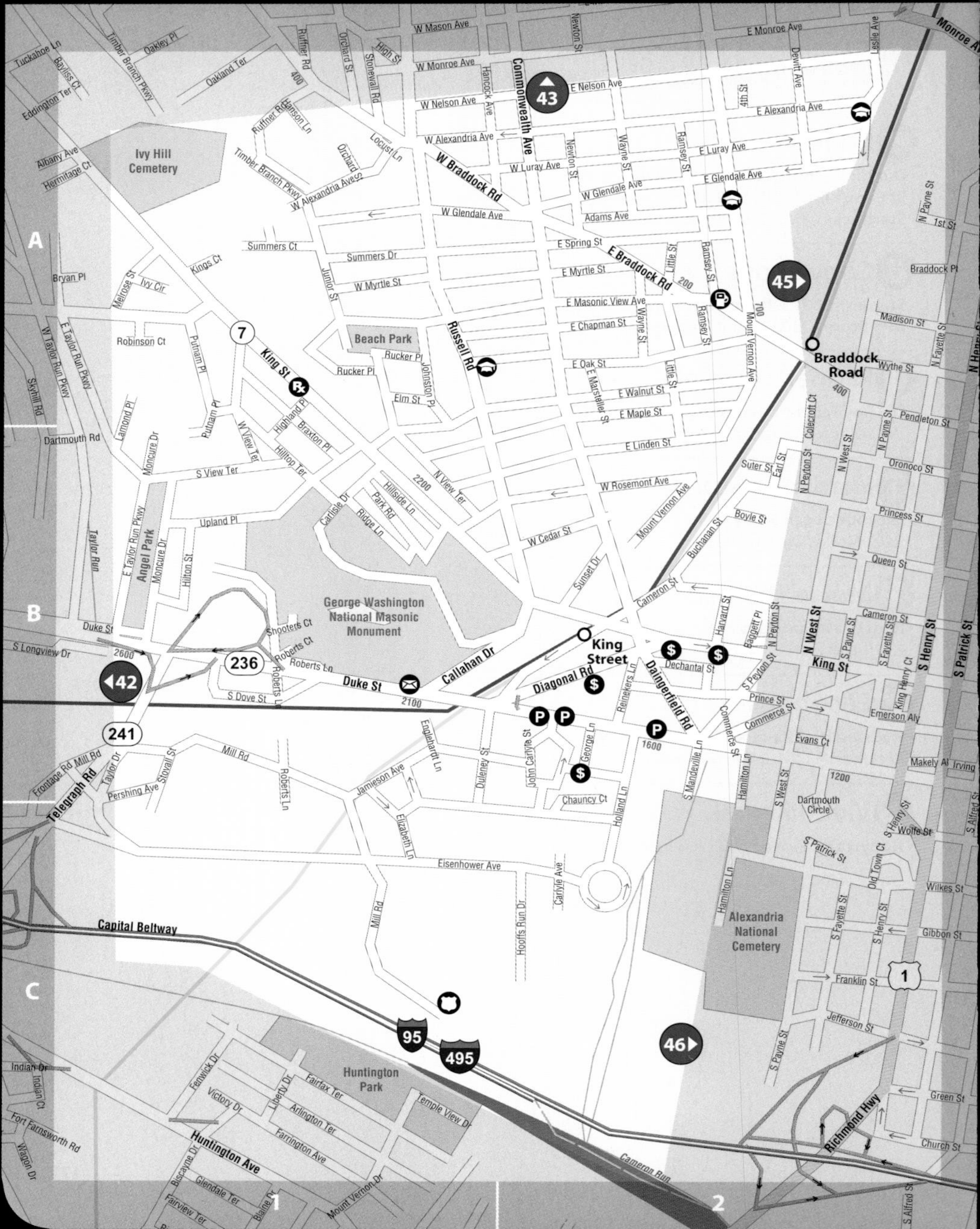

Map 44 · **Alexandria Downtown**

Ⓝ

W Mason Ave

Tuckahoe Ln
Oakley Pl

W Monroe Ave
E Monroe Ave
E Monroe Ave

Timber Branch Pkwy
Oakland Ter

High St
Stonewall Rd
Devott Ave
Leslie Ave

Ruffner Rd
Orchard St
W Nelson Ave
W Nelson Ave
E Nelson Ave

Commonwealth Ave
43

Albany St
Edindton Ter Ct

W Alexandria Ave
W Alexandria Ave
E Alexandria Ave

Locust Ln
Wayne St
Farrell St

Ivy Hill Cemetery

W Braddock Rd
W Luray Ave
W Luray Ave
E Luray Ave

N Payne St

N 1st St

Hermitage Ct
Timber Branch Pkwy
W Alexandria Ave
Orchard Ln

W Glendale Ave
Wayne St
E Glendale Ave

A

Summers Ct
Summers Dr
Adams Ave

E Spring St
E Braddock Rd
Ramsey St
200
Little St

Bryan Pl
King Ct
W Myrtle St
E Myrtle St

Braddock Pl

Melrose St
Ivy Cir
Junior St

E Masonic View Ave
Madison St

Robinson Ct
Putnam Pl
Beach Park
E Chapman St
Wayne St
Mount Vernon Ave

E Taylor Run Pkwy

7
Rucker Pl
Johnston Pl
E Oak St
Little St
Wythe St

Dartmouth Rd
Skyhill Rd
King St
Ⓡ
Rucker Pl
Elm St
E Walnut St

45▶

W View St
Highland Pl
Braxton Pl
Elm St
E Macsonic St
E Maple St
400
Collister St
Pendleton St

S View Ter
Hilltop Ter
E Linden St
Braddock Road
N Peyton St
N West St
Oronoco St

Lamond Pl
Moncure Dr
Hilton St
W Rosemont Ave
Princess St

Carlisle Dr
Ridge Ln
Hillside Ln
Mount Vernon Ave
Suter St
Earl St
Queen St

B

Upland Pl
Park Rd
W Cedar St

George Washington National Masonic Monument
Sunset Dr
Cameron St
Howard St
Daingerfield Rd
Bashford Ln
N Peyton St
N Fayette St
Princess St
Cameron St
S Patrick St

Duke St
Shooters Hill

Sunset Dr
King Street
Dechantal St
S
N West St
King St
N Fayette Ct

S Longview Dr
2600
Roberts Ln
236
Duke St
2100
Diagonal Rd
S
P
P
Reinekers Ln
Prince St
Commerce St
Emerson Aly

◀42
S Dove St

George St
1600
P
Evans Ct
Makely Al
Irving

241
Mill Rd
John Carlyle St
Duleny St
S Mandeville Ln
Hamilton Ln
Commerce St
1200
Dartmouth Circle

Telegraph Rd
Taylor Dr
Pershing Ave
Jamieson Ave
Elizabeth Ln
Chauncy Ct
S
Holland Ln
S Fayette St
S Henry St
Wilkes St

Frontage Rd Mill Rd
Roberts Ln
Eisenhower Ave
Carlyle Ave

Capital Beltway
Hooffs Run Dr
Alexandria National Cemetery
Franklin St
1

C

Indian Dr
Huntington Park
95
495
46▶
Jefferson St
S Payne St

Fort Farnsworth Rd
Wagon Dr
Fairfax Ter
Temple View Dr
Green St
Richmond Hwy
Church St

Huntington Ave
Glendale Ter
Mount Vernon Ave
Cameron Run
S Alfred St

1
2

The Metro entrance to Alexandria is inauspicious, with its anonymous office buildings. Don't turn back. You're a cobblestone's throw away from the action. Point the compass southeast and walk.

Banks

- **BB&T** · 1717 King St
- **Burke & Herbert** · 1775 Jamieson Ave
- **Riggs** · 1700 Diagonal Rd
- **Sun Trust** · 1650 King St

Gas Stations

- **Mobil** · 317 E Braddock Rd

Parking

Pharmacies

- **Safeway** · 2536 King St

Police

- **Alexandria Police Dept** · 2003 Mill Rd

Post Offices

- **Memorial Station** · 2226 Duke St

Schools

- **Commonwealth Academy** · 1321 Leslie Ave
- **George Washington Middle** · 1005 Mt Vernon Ave
- **Maury Elementary** · 600 Russell Rd

Map 44 · Alexandria Downtown

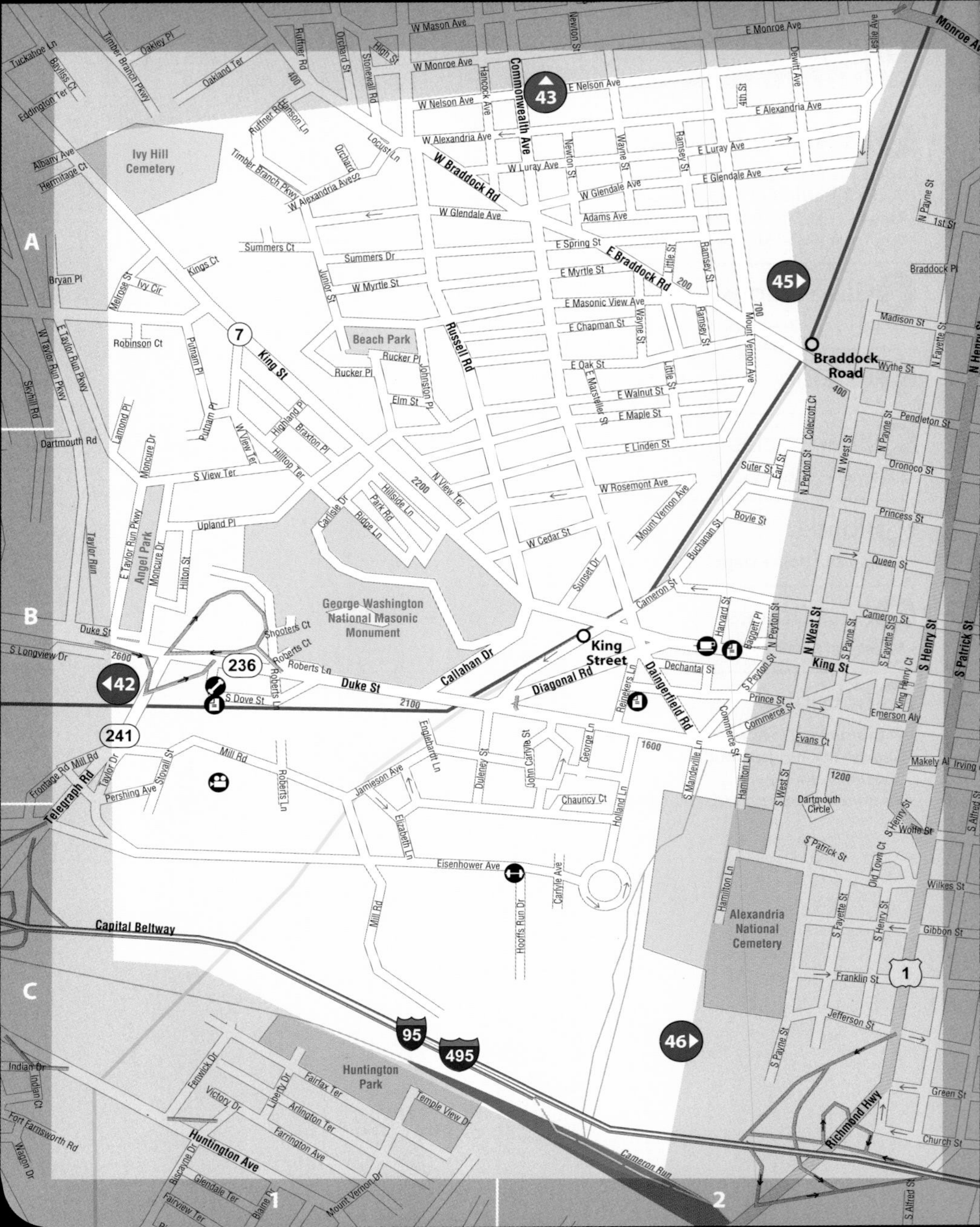

N

Tuckahoe Ln
Oakley Pl
Timber Branch Pkwy
Eddington Ter
Bayliss Ct
Albany Ave
Hermitage Ct
Bryan Pl
E Taylor Run Pkwy
W Taylor Run Pkwy
Dartmouth Rd
S Longview Dr

Ruffner Rd
Oakland Ter
Orchard St
Fern St
Stonewall Rd
W Mason Ave
W Monroe Ave
W Nelson Ave
W Alexandria Ave
W Braddock Rd
W Alexandria Ave
Locust Ln

Hancock Ave
E Nelson Ave
43
E Alexandria Ave
Newton St
15th St
14th St
Depot Pkwy

W Luray Ave
Wayne St
Ramsey St

E Luray Ave
E Glendale Ave

Monroe Ave
Monroe St
Ivy Cir
Kings Ct
Summers Ct
Summers Dr
Junior St
W Myrtle St

Commonwealth Ave
Russell Rd
W Braddock Rd

W Glendale Ave
Adams Ave
E Spring St
E Myrtle St
E Braddock Rd
E Masonic View Ave
E Chapman St

Little St
200
700
Mount Vernon Ave
45
Braddock Road

Madison St
Wythe St
Braddock Pl
N 1st St
N Payne St
N Henry St

King St
7
Robinson Ct
Putnam Pl
Lamond Pl
Putnam St
W View Ter
S View Ter
Highland Pl
Braxton Pl
Hilltop Ter
N View Ter
Hillside Ln
2200
Park Rd
Ridge Ln
Carlisle Dr
Upland Pl
Hilton St
Monroe St

Beach Park
Rucker Pl
Rucker Pl
Johnston Pl
Elm St

E Oak St
E Marshall St
E Walnut St
E Maple St
E Linden St
W Rosemont Ave
W Cedar St
Sunset Dr

Suter St
Earl St
Colecroft Ct
N West St
N Peyton St
N Pitt St
400
Pendleton St
Oronoco St
Princess St
Queen St

Mount Vernon Ave
Boyle St
Buchanan St
Cameron St

Baggett Pl
N Peyton St
Cameron St
N West St
N Payne St
S Fayette St
N Henry St
S Patrick St

George Washington National Masonic Monument

42
236
241
S Dove St
Duke St
2600
Shooters Ct
Roberts Ct
Roberts Ln
Duke St
2100
Callahan Dr
King Street
Diagonal Rd
Dangerfield Rd

Harvard St
Dechantal St
Prince St
Commerce St
King St
S Fayette St
S Henry St
S West St

S Longview Dr
Telegraph Rd
Frontage Rd
Mill Rd
Lucky Dr
Stovall St
Mill Rd
Pershing Ave
Jamieson Ave
Roberts Ln
Engelhardt Ln
Elizabeth Ln
Duleigh St
John Carlyle St
George Ln
Chauncy Ct
Holland Ln
Mandeville Ln
Hamilton Ln
1600
Evans Ct
1200
Makely Al
Irving
S West St
Dartmouth Circle
S Patrick St
Wolfe St
S Fayette St
S Henry St
S St Asaph St
Wilkes St
Gibbon St

Eisenhower Ave
Carlyle Ave
Hooffs Run Dr
Alexandria National Cemetery
Franklin St
Jefferson St
1

Capital Beltway
95
495
46
Huntington Park
Indian Dr
Indian Ct
Fort Farnsworth Rd
Fannick Dr
Victory Dr
Fairfax Dr
Arlington Ter
Farrington Ave
Temple View Dr
Cameron Run
Richmond Hwy
Green St
Church St

Huntington Ave
Fairview Ter
Glendale Ter
Mount Vernon Ave

A

B

C

1

2

The basics of residential life. Head to nearby Old Town for more.

Map

Coffee
• **Cafe Aurora** · 1630 King St

Copy Shops
• **ABC Imaging** · 225 Reinekers Ln
• **Copy Craft** · 2393 S Dove St
• **Olde Towne Print & Copy** · 1604 King St

Gyms
• **Jungle's Gym Fitness** · 305 Hooffs Run Dr

Movie Theaters
• **AMC Hoffman Center 22** · 206 Swamp Fox Rd

Pet Shops
• **Petsage** · 2391 S Dove St

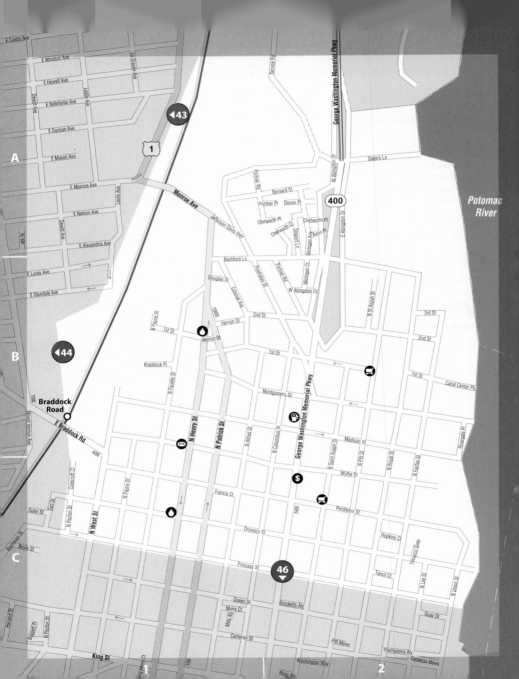

The upper area of Old Town is not much more than offices and homes. It is prime real estate for both, given the proximity to the heart of Old Town. But if you're in for a day or night trip, don't bother.

Map

Banks
- **Chevy Chase** · 697 N Washington St

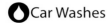Car Washes
- **Andy's Brushless Car Wash** · 1111 Oronoco St
- **Yates's Car Wash** · 1018 N Henry St

Gas Stations
- **Exxon** · 834 N Washington St

Post Offices
- **Alexandria Main Office** · 1100 Wythe St

Supermarkets
- **Giant Food** · 530 1st St
- **Trader Joe's** · 612 N Saint Asaph St

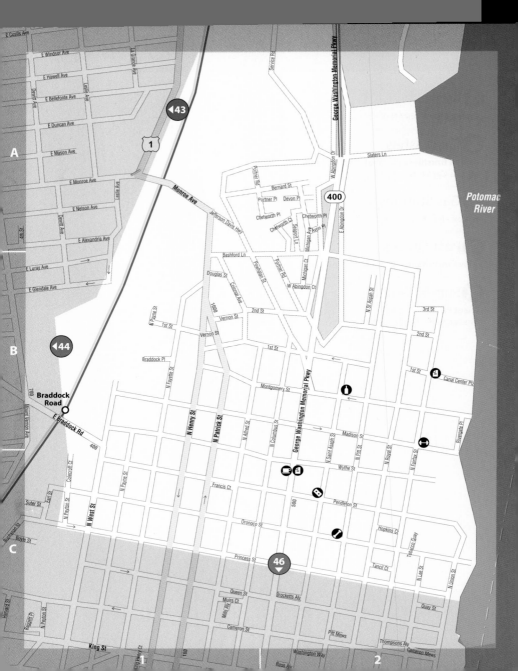

Coffee
- **Starbucks** · 683 N Washington St

Copy Shops
- **Kinko's** · 685 N Washington St
- **Kwik Kopy Printing** · 99 Canal Center Plz

Gyms
- **Old Town Athletic Club** · 209 Madison St

Liquor Stores
- **Virginia ABC** · 901 N Saint Asaph St

Pet Shops
- **Olde Towne School for Dogs** · 529 Oronoco St

Video Rental
- **Blockbuster Video** · 602 N St Asaph St

Go south when you want to mix it up. Walk home and sleep soundly.

Map

Banks

- **Bank of America** · 600 N Washington St
- **BB&T** · 300 S Washington St
- **Burke & Herbert** · 100 S Fairfax St
- **Burke & Herbert** · 621 King St
- **Chevy Chase** · 500 S Washington St
- **Sun Trust** · 515 King St
- **Virginia Commerce** · 1414 Prince St
- **Virginia Commerce** · 506 King St

Car Rental

- **Thrifty** · 1306 Duke St · 703-684-2054

Gas Stations

- **Exxon** · 501 S Washington St
- **Mobil** · 1001 S Washington St

o Landmarks

- **Alexandria Farmers Market** · 301 King St
- **Carlyle House** · 121 N Fairfax St
- **Gadsby's Tavern Museum** · 134 N Royal St
- **Market Square Old Town** · 301 King St
- **Ramsay House** · 221 King St
- **Stabler-Ledbeater Apothecary** · 105 S Fairfax St
- **Torpedo Factory** · 201 N Union St

Libraries

- **Alexandria Kate Waller Barrett Branch Library** · 717 Queen St
- **Alexandria Law Library** · 520 King St, Room L-34

Parking

Pharmacies

- **Alexandria Medical Arts Pharmacy** · 315 S Washington St
- **CVS** · 326 King St
- **CVS** · 433 S Washington St
- **Timberman's Drug Store** · 106 N Washington St

Schools

- **Jefferson-Houston Elementary** · 1501 Cameron St
- **Lyles-Crouch Elementary** · 530 S St Asaph St
- **St Coletta** · 207 S Peyton St
- **St Mary** · 400 Green St

Supermarkets

- **Safeway** · 500 S Royal St

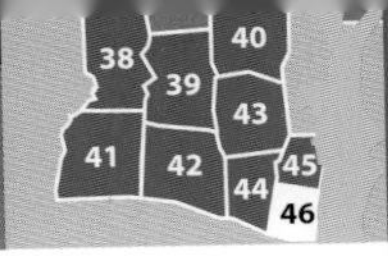

Map 4

This is Georgetown's fiercest rival for preciousness. Its cute-as-a-button downtown and historial architecture are worth occasional visits. If you like it picture perfect and you have the cash, get on the long waiting list to live here.

Coffee

- **Cosi** · 700 King St
- **Et Cetera** · 212 Queen St
- **Firehook Bakery & Coffee House** · 105 S Union St
- **Firehook Bakery & Coffee House** · 214 N Fayette St
- **Starbucks** · 100 S Union St
- **Starbucks** · 510 King St
- **Uptowner Cafe** · 1609 King St

Copy Shops

- **Insty-Prints** · 1421 Prince St
- **Office Depot** · 200 N Washington St
- **UPS Store** · 107 S West St

Farmer's Markets

- **Alexandria City Farmers Market** · 301 King St

Movie Theaters

- **Old Town Theater** · 815 1/2 King St

Nightlife

- **Founders' Brewing Company** · 607 King St
- **Laughing Lizzard Lounge** · 1324 King St
- **Rock It Grill** · 1319 King St
- **State Theatre** · 220 N Washington St
- **Tiffany Tavern** · 1116 King St

Pet Shops

- **Fetch** · 101 S Saint Asaph St

Restaurants

- **Faccia Luna Trattoria** · 823 S Washington St

Shopping

- **Blink** · 1303 King St
- **Comfort One Shoes** · 201 King St
- **Hysteria** · 125 S Fairfax St
- **La Cuisine** · 323 Cameron St
- **My Place in Tuscany** · 1127 King St
- **P&C Art** · 212 King St
- **Tickled Pink** · 103 S St Asaph St
- **The Torpedo Factory** · 105 N Union St

Video Rental

- **Video Unlimited** · 621 S Washington St
- **Video Vault** · 323 S Washington St

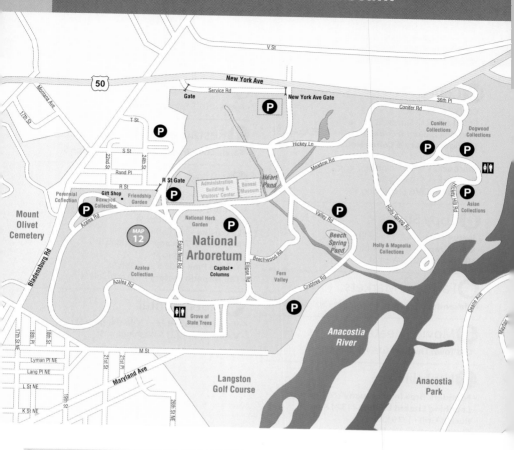

General Information

NFT Map:	12
Address:	3501 New York Ave, NE, Washington, DC 20002
Phone:	202-245-2726
Website:	www.usna.usda.gov
Opening Hours:	8 am-5 pm daily except Dec 25th
Admission:	Free

Overview

Thank Congress for creating one of the most pleasant bike paths and wedding-picture settings in the region. Most of the 600,000 visitors here every year are not taken so much by the research

aspects of this gorgeous gargantuan park, located in northeast DC with entrances on New York Avenue and R Street, as by the swervy paths and greenery that grows smack in the center of the city.

Managed by the US Department of Agriculture, the Arboretum covers 446 acres and includes 9.5 miles of paved roads winding their way through specialized collections like the National Herb Garden, the National Grove of State Trees, Fern Valley, and the National Bonsai Collection. There are also extensive azalea plantings, aquatic plants, holly, peonies, daffodils, daylilies, magnolia, boxwood, dogwood, crabapple, and maple trees scattered throughout the grounds. Not great for

allergy sufferers but, for everyone else, it's an escape from the concrete and grit of urban life.

For those who want to mix education with pleasure, there are plenty of scientific reasons for visiting the National Arboretum. The Economic Botany Herbarium is a collection of over 650,000 dried plant specimens for classification studies of agriculture, medicine, science, and education. The volunteer staff breeds plants for other locales throughout the country in a controlled greenhouse.

There's history too; 22 of the original sandstone Corinthian columns of the National Capitol have been planted on a grassy knoll near the main entrance. But if you just want to stop and smell the roses, you can rest assured that nobody will tap you on the shoulder to lecture you about the scent's Latin name.

The National Bonsai Collection and Penjing Museum is open 10 am-3:30 pm. The Arbor House Gift Shop is open from March 1 through mid-December; weekday hours are 10 am-3:30 pm and weekend hours are 10 am-5 pm.

Activities

Visitors are encouraged to walk, run, and bike on the paved roads. Picnicking is allowed in designated areas. The Arbor Café is located next to the Administration Building and is open on Fridays, Saturdays, and Sundays. Other general restrictions include: no fishing, no fires, no flower picking, and pets must be kept on leashes. The Arboretum also offers public education programs including lectures, workshops, demonstrations, and plant, flower, and art exhibitions.

A 48-passenger open-air Tram runs through the park with a 40-minute, non-stop narrated tour covering the Arboretum's history, mission, and current highlights. Tram services are available on weekends from mid-April to October; $4 adults; $3 seniors; $2 kids 4-16 years old; and free for those aged less than four years.

The Full Moon Hikes involve curators using the moon as a guide to lead participants on a 5-mile trek through the grounds, providing horticultural facts along the way. You'll need to register early as there is limited space and tours fill up quickly. If you're not lucky enough to land one of these coveted spots, Twilight Tours are free, slower-paced, opportunities to check out the Arboretum after closing time. Pre-registration is required for both activities—call 202-245-5898 to make your reservation.

How to Get There – Driving

From northwest Washington, follow New York Avenue east to the intersection of Bladensburg Road. Turn right onto Bladensburg Road and go four blocks to R Street. Make a left on R Street and continue two blocks to the Arboretum gates.

Parking

There is plenty of free parking. Large lots are located near the Grove of State Trees, near the R Street entrance, and near the New York Avenue entrance. Smaller lots are scattered throughout the grounds close to most of the major collections. Several of the parking areas have recently been expanded and a free shuttle through the park is provided during the summer months. The shuttle bus seats up to 24 people and is handicapped-accessible. It runs continuously from the Administration Building, to the National Grove of State Trees, to the National Capitol Columns on weekends from 10 am-5 pm.

How to Get There – Mass Transit

The X6 Metrobus provides a direct shuttle from Union Station on weekends and holidays, except December 25. The bus leaves every 40 minutes from 7:55 am to 4:35 pm and the fare is $1.10 one-way (25¢ with rail transfer). On weekdays, the closest Metro subway stop is Stadium Armory Station on the Blue and Orange lines. Transfer to Metrobus B-2, get off on Bladensburg Road, and walk 2 blocks to R Street. Make a right on R Street and continue 2 blocks to the Arboretum gates.

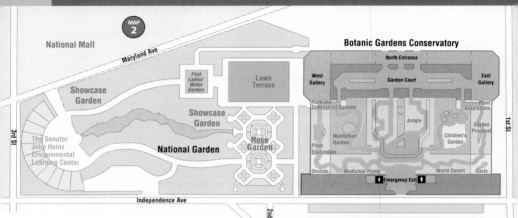

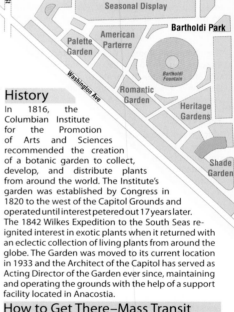

General Information

NFT Map:	2
Address:	100 Maryland Avenue, SW, Washington, DC, 20024
Phone:	202-225-8333
Website:	www.usbg.gov
Hours & Admission:	10 am-5 pm every day, including holidays; free

Overview

In a neighborhood full of marble, the US Botanic Garden offers green respite—and plenty of it. Its conservatory, greenhouse, and garden grow 26,000 kinds of plants. The conservatory recently had a $34 million facelift that left the nation's oldest continually operating botanic garden looking spry. Its distinctive glass façade now houses advanced environmental control systems that allow rain forest buds to bloom in the same building as desert brush and nearly 4,000 other living plant specimens.

The newly developed National Garden, just west of the conservatory, includes an Environmental Learning Center with an outdoor teaching amphitheater, lecture hall, and library. It's also got a water garden, rose garden (a tribute to our national flower), and a showcase garden for local plants that, unlike its human inhabitants, flourish in DC's humidity.

Bartholdi Park, located across Independence Avenue from the conservatory, was created in 1932 and named for sculptor Frederic Auguste Bartholdi. In addition to creating the aptly-named Bartholdi Fountain in the center of the park, he also designed the Statue of Liberty. The park is open daily from dawn until dusk.

History

In 1816, the Columbian Institute for the Promotion of Arts and Sciences recommended the creation of a botanic garden to collect, develop, and distribute plants from around the world. The Institute's garden was established by Congress in 1820 to the west of the Capitol Grounds and operated until interest petered out 17 years later. The 1842 Wilkes Expedition to the South Seas re-ignited interest in exotic plants when it returned with an eclectic collection of living plants from around the globe. The Garden was moved to its current location in 1933 and the Architect of the Capitol has served as Acting Director of the Garden ever since, maintaining and operating the grounds with the help of a support facility located in Anacostia.

How to Get There–Mass Transit

Taking public transportation is highly recommended, as there is limited metered parking near the USBG. By Metro, take the Blue or Orange line to Federal Center SW or Capital South stations. If you're using the Metro Bus, take 30, 32, 34, 35, or 36 to Independence Avenue and First Street SW.

General Information

NFT Map: 5
Location: 225 7th St SE,
             Washington, DC 20003
Telephone: 202-546-2698
Website: www.easternmarket.net
Hours: Tues - Fri 10 am to 6 pm, Sat 8 am to
             6 pm, Sun 8 am to 4 pm.
             Closed Mon.

Overview

Eastern Market is as unpretentious as DC gets. Leave the hill lapel pin and Georgetown classism behind or you'll spill bacon grease on 'em. The 16,500-square-foot indoor market here has barely changed since it opened in 1873. Even now, as it sits at the center of a newly yuppified neighborhood, it's still a work-a-day market.

Join the line at Market Lunch in South Hall to be abused by over-stressed workers doling out pancakes, pork, and killer crabcakes. You need to order quickly because the line is usually long and the staff patience is not—don't even try to pay with plastic.

On weekends, locals and day-trippers jam in to bid for fresh produce, breads, fish, cheeses, and chickens. Outside, the sidewalks give way to artists, farmers, and charlatans hawking their wares. Antique and collectibles vendors fill the playground behind Hines Junior High School with piles of trinkets, textiles, and trash.

Market 5 Gallery

202-543-7293, www.market5gallery.org
A non-profit arts organization dominates the North Hall, hosting an art fair and sponsoring Saturday performances. Artists, musicians, and artisans have always been a part of the traditional "marketplace," and the Saturday festival on the gallery's North Plaza was begun in 1978 to return this tradition to Eastern Market.

Market 5 is also an art gallery that gives classes in the arts for the Capitol Hill community. Open Tuesday through Friday 11 am to 5 pm, Saturday and Sunday from 8 am to 5 pm.

How to Get There—Driving

Parking is scarce, but if you must: from the south, take I-395 across the 14th Street Bridge, bear right over the bridge onto Eisenhower (SW) Expressway; exit at 6th Street SE, the first exit beyond South Capitol Street. At the bottom of the ramp, continue one block and turn left on 7th Street SE. The next major intersection with a traffic light is Pennsylvania Avenue. You'll see Hines School on the opposite corner.

From the west, take I-66 to Rosslyn, Virginia, and Route 110 to I-395 N, then follow the directions above.

From the north, take Baltimore-Washington Parkway and I-295, exiting at Pennsylvania Avenue (East). A U-turn can be made at the second light to head westbound on Pennsylvania to 7th Street SE, where you need to make a right.

From the east, take either Route 50 or I-495 to I-295, and follow the directions above.

Parking

Diagonal parking is available on the Seventh Street and alley sides of the Market and there's some curb parking in the Capitol Hill neighborhood. On weekends, it's best to take Metro.

How to Get There – Mass Transit

Take the Blue or Orange Metro Lines to the Eastern Market station and walk north out of the station along 7th Street SE.

Montrose Park

Oak Hill Cemetery

Dumbarton Oaks

Georgetown University

PAGE 220

MAP 8

Georgetown Recreation Center

The Tombs

Old Stone House

C&O Canal Path

Potomac River

S St
5th St
R St
36th St
Reservoir Rd
Winfield Ln
Dent Pl
Q St
Volta Pl
P St
O St
N St
37th St
36th St
35th St
34th St
33rd St
Potomac St
Bank St
Prospect St
M St
Water St
Canal Rd
29
29
Grace St
Cecil Pl
South St
K St

S St
Caton Pl
32nd St
Wisconsin Ave
Avon Pl
Dem Pl
Avon Ln
Cambridge Pl
Q St
West Ln Kv
P St
O St
Dumbarton St
Congress St
Oak Aly
Blues Aly
Thomas Jefferson St
Pennsylvania
L St
31st St
30th St
29th St
28th St
27th St
26th St
Poplar St
East Pl
K St
26th St
27th St
Queen Annes

Massachusetts
Waterside Dr

Overview

NFT Map: 8

Like a socialite fleeing the masses, Georgetown hides in a metro-inaccessible western corner of northwest Washington. Here it retains its cobblestone charm and snooty superiority despite the mall-ization of its main drags. The tourists and suburbanites may mob its stretch of M Street and Wisconsin Avenue, but those who live here are either current or future (calling all Georgetown students) owners of the city's priciest real estate.

At night, the neighborhood sheds its good breeding to become a mobbed, if not diverse, nightlife scene. The crush of restaurants and bars swing open to welcome college partiers or the better-coiffed see-and-be-seen crowd.

History

Officially created in 1751 and named after King George II, Georgetown's access to the Potomac River catered to a shipping community. Prosperity and desirability followed and the town was annexed to Washington City in 1871.

The area became a haven for freed slaves seeking financial freedom after the Civil War. But a devastating flood in 1890 forced the Canal Company into bankruptcy and triggered an economic depression. By the end of WWI, Georgetown was considered a slum. In the 1930s, New Deal government officials rediscovered the convenience and charm beneath the grime. And with their help, Georgetown began its physical rehab and social climb back to grandeur.

Attractions

Georgetown hosts the city's most compact collection of historic, retail, gastronomic, and nightlife draws. The Old Stone House, built in 1765, is the oldest surviving building on its original lot in the federal city, predating even DC itself. The rumored-to-be-haunted-house and its gardens are both publicly strollable. The C&O Canal Path is a 180-mile leaf-shrouded park that runs alongside a murky but historically interesting canal. The canal was originally a water highway that linked the rapidly growing west to the east and allowed farmers to ship their goods to market. The canal path is now more of a runner and biker highway. Locals use it to work off the one-too-manys they imbibed at bars like Georgetown University's esteemed The Tombs. For a more relaxing respite, Dumbarton Oaks is a Federal-style 19th-century mansion surrounded by sublime gardens.

For a complete list of stores and restaurants in Georgetown, consult the comprehensive Georgetown website: www.georgetowndc.com. For a selection of our favorite Georgetown bars, restaurants, and shopping venues, see Map 8.

How to Get There - Driving

M Street NW can be reached from the Francis Scott Key Bridge, Canal Road NW, and Pennsylvania Avenue.

Parking

Street parking in Georgetown is a pain. A paid garage is your best bet. There are several in the area with reasonable hourly and daily rates:

- Harbor Parking, south side of Water St ($2/hr, $9/day)
- Constitution Parking, 3217 K St, 202-337-1006 ($3/hr, $11/day)
- Georgetown Court Parking, North side of Prospect St b/w Wisconsin Ave & Potomac St, 202-298-6323 ($3.50/hr, $24.50/day)
- Altman's Parking, Bank St & M St, 202-338-8480 ($4/hr, $8.50/day)
- Altman's Parking, East of 29th St & south of M St, 202-298-9139 ($5/hr, $22/day)
- Colonial Parking, 3222 M St, Georgetown Parking Mall, 202-778-1600 ($4/hr, $12/day)
- Diplomat Parking, 30th St & M St, 202-496-4200 ($5/hr, $12/day)
- Parking Services International, south side of M St & Thomas Jefferson St, 202-333-5092 ($5.50/hr, $11/day)
- Jefferson Court Colonial Parking, north side of K St & 30th St, 202-298-7027 ($5/hr, $12/day)

How to Get There - Mass Transit

Metrobus routes 30, 32, 34, 35, or 36 marked "Friendship Heights" run west on Pennsylvania Avenue. It costs $1.20 one-way and, unless you have a pass, you'll need exact change.

There is no dedicated metro stop here, but with a pleasant day and good walking shoes, the Foggy Bottom-GWU stop on the Orange and Blue lines is a ten-minute walk from the east end of the neighborhood and the Rosslyn stop on the same line is a ten-minute walk from the west end.

The Georgetown Metro Connection serves all Metrobus stops in Georgetown and operates express service between Georgetown and Foggy Bottom-GWU, Rosslyn, and Dupont Circle Metro stations. The shuttles run Monday-Thursday 7 am-12 am, Friday until 2 am, Saturday from 8 am-2 am, and Sunday until midnight. The bus leaves the metro stations every ten minutes daily and costs $1 one-way.

The Monuments / Potomac Park / Tidal Basin

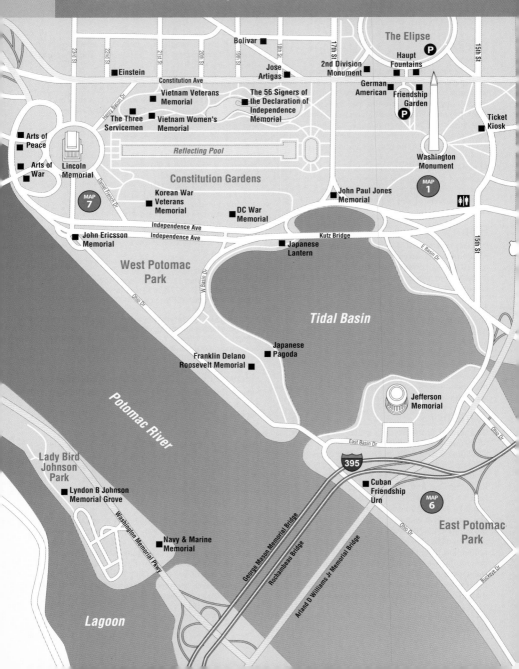

The Elipse

23rd St
22nd St
21st St
20th St
19th St
18th St
17th St
15th St

Bolivar

Einstein

P

Haupt Fountains

Jose Artigas

2nd Division Monument

Constitution Ave

German American

Friendship Garden

Vietnam Veterans Memorial

Harry Bacon Dr

The 56 Signers of the Declaration of Independence Memorial

P

Ticket Kiosk

The Three Servicemen

Vietnam Women's Memorial

Arts of Peace

Arts of War

Reflecting Pool

Lincoln Memorial

Washington Monument

Daniel French Dr

Constitution Gardens

MAP 1

MAP 7

Korean War Veterans Memorial

John Paul Jones Memorial

DC War Memorial

15th St

Independence Ave

John Ericsson Memorial

Independence Ave

Kutz Bridge

W Basin Dr

E Basin Dr

Japanese Lantern

West Potomac Park

Tidal Basin

Ohio Dr

Japanese Pagoda

Franklin Delano Roosevelt Memorial

Potomac River

Jefferson Memorial

Ohio Dr

East Basin Dr

395

Lady Bird Johnson Park

Lyndon B Johnson Memorial Grove

Cuban Friendship Urn

MAP 6

Ohio Dr

East Potomac Park

Washington Memorial Pkwy

Navy & Marine Memorial

George Mason Memorial Bridge

Rochambeau Bridge

Arland D Williams Jr Memorial Bridge

Blckroyr Dr

Lagoon

General Information

NFT Maps: 1, 6, and 7
Website: www.nps.gov/nacc/index.htm
Phone: 202-426-6841

Overview

If there's one thing DC loves, it's a commemorative lawn ornament. The District's grass is covered with monuments, statues, plaques, and fountains. This is especially apparent while strolling through Potomac Park. Here you'll find the Lincoln, FDR, Jefferson, and Washington memorials, as well as the tributes to those who served in WWI, the Korean War, Vietnam, and WWII.

Washington Monument

Fittingly, America's first president has a monument dedicated to him that soars above all others. Although entry to the Washington Monument is free, you will require a timed ticket to get in. Free tickets are distributed each day at the kiosk on the Washington Monument grounds, at 15th Street and Madison Drive, on a first-come, first-served basis. The kiosk is open daily from 8 am until 4:30 pm (closed December 25), but tickets usually run out early in the day. If you plan on visiting the monument, make it your first stop.

If you like to plan in advance, you can make a ticket reservation through the National Park Reservation Service (NPRS) between 10 am and 10 pm by calling 800-967-2283 or online at http://reservations.nps.gov. Unlike the free ticket kiosk, advance reservations will cost you a $1.50 service fee per ticket, plus a 50¢ handling fee per order.

While the view of Washington DC from the top is spectacular, the monument itself is equally impressive, with exterior walls of white marble from Maryland and interior walls lined with Maine granite. The change in stone color a third of the way up is because of the Civil War. Construction began in 1848 and was only one-third done when the war broke out. After the war, construction resumed. But by then, the color of stone in the quarry had changed.

Tidal Basin

The Tidal Basin was constructed in the late 1800s as a swimming hole in the middle of the park. It's no longer a place for a refreshing dip. Besides the questionable cleanliness of this urban pond, the ample federal security forces in the neighborhood are likely the strictest lifeguards in the country. If you must dip a toe in the water, join the tourists and rent a paddle boat. For two weeks every spring, cherry blossoms bloom around the basin and throughout the parks. The original trees were a gift from Japan in 1912 and their bloom inspires an annual Japanese-influenced festival to kick off the city's tourist season.

East Potomac Park

In contrast to the west side, East Potomac Park is a mundane park. Here, you'll find a golf course, tennis courts, swimming pool, basketball court, baseball field, hiking trails, and a playground. The Jefferson Memorial can be found on the basin's edge.

A 5-Piece sculpture titled *The Awakening* can be found on the very southern tip of East Potomac Park at Hains Point (not pictured on the map). This aluminum depiction of a 100-foot giant emerging from the ground is, like the park it's in, more fun, less epic. You'll need to drive or bike out there because there's no public transportation for miles.

How to Get There – Driving

I-66 and I-395 run to the parks from the south. I-495, New York Avenue, Rock Creek Parkway, George Washington Memorial Parkway, and the Cabin John Parkway will get you there from the north. I-66, Route 50, and Route 29 run to the parks from the west. Routes 50, 1, and 4 are the way to go from the east.

Parking

Public parking is available along the Basin, but, depending on the time of day, it's likely to be hard to find a spot. You'll probably end up either driving around and around or walking large distances.

How to Get There – Mass Transit

The Foggy Bottom, Metro Center, Federal Triangle, Smithsonian, and L'Enfant Plaza stops on the Orange and Blue Lines are all within walking distance of various monuments and parks. Metro Center is also a Red Line Stop. L'Enfant Plaza is also on the Green and Yellow Lines.

General Information

NFT Maps:	1 & 2
National Mall Website:	www.nps.gov/nama
National Mall Phone:	202-426-6841
Smithsonian Website:	www.si.edu
Smithsonian Phone:	202-633-1000
U.S. Capitol Website:	www.aoc.gov
House of Reps:	www.house.gov
Senate:	www.senate.gov
Capitol Switchboard:	202-224-2131
Capitol Tour Info:	202-225-6827

National Mall

America's first mall, this sprawling grass lawn pre-dated even Paramus Park. DC's original planner, Pierre L'Enfant, designed it in the late 18th century as an open promenade. Despite the explosive growth of the city surrounding it, the mall remains true to L'Enfant's vision. Its eminent strollability is a magnet to hordes of fanny-packed tourists. It's also got a pretty good collection of marble monuments; the Washington, Jefferson, Lincoln, and FDR monuments are close by, along with the Vietnam and Korean War memorials and the newly unveiled WWII memorial. On any given day, there's also likely to be a kite festival, political rally, or vicious Frisbee game.

Smithsonian Institution

The Smithsonian Institution is really 16 different museums, some of them nowhere near the mall (one is in NYC), and a zoo. The primary museums are mostly clustered here, like the Air and Space Museum, the Natural History Museum, and the Hirshhorn. The Smithsonian Information Center in the Castle is the best orientation point if you plan to become one of the 24 million visitors who check out one of its DC properties this year.

Like the country it caters to, the Smithsonian collection is a hodgepodge—the Hope Diamond here, a Danish experimental work there. A Japanese scroll here, Archie Bunker's chair there. Though there is serious art to be viewed at the Hirshhorn and several of the smaller museums, those are not the most popular. That distinction goes to the Air and Space Museum for its sheer wow-za factor of dangling airplanes and shuttles. Following closely is the National History Museum, known both affectionately and derisively as "America's Attic." Besides Archie's chair, it's got Dorothy's ruby slippers, Muhammad Ali's gloves, George Washington's uniform, Julia Childs' entire kitchen, and Adlai Stevenson's briefcase.

Smithsonian Institution Building (The Castle)

Built in 1855, the Castle was the first Smithsonian building. Originally it housed all aspects of the Smithsonian's operations, including an apartment for the first Secretary of the Smithsonian, Joseph Henry. It now serves as home to the Smithsonian's administrative offices, as well as its Information Center. Its beauty and stature make it a great point of orientation for the mall's visitors. (202-633-1000)

The National Museum of the American Indian

In September, 2004, this new museum opened on the National Mall. Upon entering, visitors are greeted by the Welcome Wall—a projection of hundreds of written and spoken words meaning "welcome" in native languages throughout the Americas. The museum is open from 10:30 am to 5:30 pm daily. Admission is free. (202-633-1000)

National Air and Space Museum

This museum maintains the largest collection of historic aircraft and spacecraft in the world. It has hundreds of artifacts on display, including the original Wright 1903 airplane, the Spirit of St. Louis, Apollo 11 command module, and a lunar rock sample that visitors can touch. The museum is open daily from 10 am to 5:30 pm, and admission is free. (202-357-2700)

Hirshhorn Museum and Sculpture Garden

Conceived as the nation's museum of modern and contemporary art, the Hirshhorn has over 11,500 pieces of internationally significant art. The museum is open from 10 am to 5:30 pm, and the sculpture garden is open from 7:30 am to dusk. Admission for both is always free. (202-357-2700)

Arts and Industries Building

The second-oldest Smithsonian building is not in the best of shape. Things got so bad that "diapers" were installed on the roof to catch falling debris and the building was closed to the public on January 10, 2004 for renovations. The good news is that a new roof is being installed, and the building will be restored to its former glory. In the meantime, visitors can still access the Discovery Theater, a live performance venue for children. It is temporarily located behind the Smithsonian Castle. (202-357-1500)

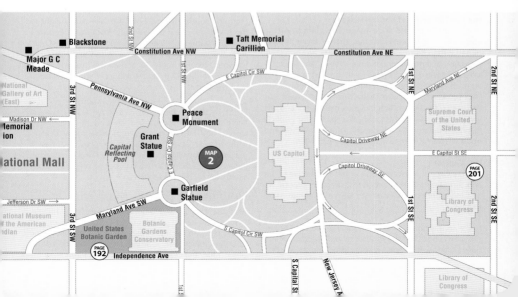

National Museum of African Art

The National Museum of African Art is the only museum in the United States devoted exclusively to the display and study of traditional and contemporary arts of sub-Sahara Africa. The museum displays everything from ceramics, textiles, furniture, and tools to masks, figures, and musical instruments. The museum is open from 10 am to 5:30 pm daily and admission is free. (202-633-4600)

Freer and Sackler Galleries

These twin galleries are connected via an underground passageway and house a world-renowned Asian art collection. The Freer Gallery was the first Smithsonian museum dedicated to the fine arts when it opened in 1923. The Sackler Gallery opened more recently in 1987. The Freer is home to one of the most extensive collections of art by American artist James McNeil Whistler. While the picture of his mom doesn't reside there, you'll find some of his other famous works, including his portraits and the famous Peacock Room. (202-633-4880)

National Museum of American History

This museum's mission is to collect, care for, and study the objects that reflect the experience of the American people. What better place for the Declaration of Independence Desk, Dizzy Gillespie's trumpet, or Eli Whitney's cotton gin? Two of our faves are the original Kermit the Frog puppet and Prince's guitar. This museum is a packrat's dream. (202-633-1000)

National Museum of Natural History

Visitors come far and wide to catch a glimpse of the 45.5-carat Hope Diamond, but there's more to this museum than one rock—it is also home to an impressive collection of dinosaur and mammal fossils, an insect zoo (check out the daily tarantula feeding!), and an amazing array of stuffed animals (courtesy of taxidermy, not FAO Schwartz). If you're really into rocks, check out the gem collection, which includes meteorites and the Logan Sapphire—at 423 carats, it is the largest publicly displayed sapphire in the country. Admission is free, and hours are from 10 am to 5:30 pm. (202-633-1000)

U.S. Capitol

The US Capitol is located on Capitol Hill, between 1st and 3rd Streets and between Constitution Avenue NE and Independence Avenue SE. Big white dome. Hard to miss.

Home to the House of Representatives and the Senate, this icon is both a history museum and an office where Hillary Clinton, Ted Kennedy, and Liddy Dole are working

stiffs. It's also the city's orientation point. Every city address is based on where it lies in relation to the Capitol. After-hours, drunken Hill staffers use it as a compass.

Construction began on the Capitol in 1793 and was more or less finished by 1813. In 1814, the British burned the Capitol during the War of 1812, but rain saved the structure. Restoration and expansion followed, the result being the building that all Americans (at least we hope) recognize today. If you've ever wondered who the lady on top of the dome is, she's no-one in particular. She represents freedom, and was sculpted by Thomas Crawford.

The District of Columbia gets one representative in the House based on population but, like Guam and American Samoa, gets no representation in the Senate because it ain't a state. Hence the local "Taxation without Representation" license plates.

The Capitol is closed New Year's Day, Thanksgiving, and Christmas. Every other day, the public is welcome. Hours are 9:30 am to 8 pm from March to August, and 9 am to 4:30 pm from September to February. Tours are free (unless you count taxes, in which case they're only free if you're a foreigner). The House website says that you don't need tickets, while the Senate site claims tickets are necessary for all Capitol tours. When will the political bickering end? If you can hold off visiting until 2005, they're building a visitors' center.

How to Get There – Driving

From the south, I-66 and I-395 will take you straight to the Mall. I-495, New York Avenue, Rock Creek Parkway, George Washington Memorial Parkway, and the Cabin John Parkway will get you there from the north. From the west, I-66, US Route 50, and 29 will take you to the mall. US Routes 50, 1, and 4 will have you mall-bound from the east.

Parking

There is some handicapped parking at the nearby Lincoln and FDR memorials; otherwise you're dealing with regular street parking, which usually has a maximum time allocation of 3 hours. There are parking garages located close to the mall, but be prepared to pay a hefty fee for the convenience.

How to Get There – Mass Transit

Take the Orange and Blue Lines to Federal Triangle, Smithsonian and Federal Center SW; the Yellow and Green Lines to Archives/Navy Memorial; the Red Line to Union Station and Judiciary Square; and the Yellow, Green, Blue, and Orange Lines to L'Enfant Plaza.

General Information

NFT Maps: 2 & 3
Address: 101 Independence Ave, SE,
Washington, DC 20540
Phone: 202-707-5000
Website: www.loc.gov
Opening Hours: Monday – Saturday, closed Sundays and
federal holidays.

Overview

The Library of Congress doesn't own every book ever published. It is, however, the largest library in the history of the world. The collection includes more than 128 million items packed on 532 miles of bookshelves in a three-building complex; the Thomas Jefferson Building opened in 1897 and is home to the soaring stained glass Great Hall; the John Adams Building was built in 1939; and the James Madison Building was constructed in 1980. All three are clustered together on Capitol Hill. The Declaration of Independence, the Constitution, a Gutenberg Bible, and the Giant Bible of Mainz are permanently on display.

Sounds like a bibliophile's dream, right? Harsh reality: this is no lending library. All resources must remain on the premises and public consumption is limited. The education of Congress remains its primary mission, along with preserving "a universal collection of knowledge and creativity for future generations." If you want to do more than wander through the ornate sections and check out the exhibits, you have to be older than 18 and register with the Reader Registration Station. The Visitors' Center offers information, a short introductory film, and free, guided tours.

The library features two theaters. The Coolidge Auditorium, located in the Thomas Jefferson Building, was built in 1924 and intended to host musical performances. Today the 511-seat auditorium still has remarkable acoustics and, after a recent $2.5 million renovation, the venue continues to host regular concerts. Admission is free, however reservations must be made through TicketMaster (two ticket limit per customer), which charges a $2 handling fee. The 64-seat Mary Pickford Theater, located in the Madison building, shows films ranging from those of Pickford's era to modern films. Admission is free, but reservations are required. Visit the Library's website for movie and show times.

History

The Library of Congress was first established on April 24, 1800 when President John Adams approved legislation that provided $5,000 for the purchase of books for a Congressional law library. The first acquisition consisted

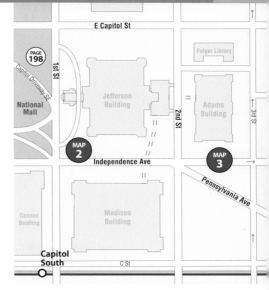

of 740 volumes and three maps from London. Fourteen years later, the British army invaded the city and burned the Capitol building, including the amassed 3,000 volumes that made up the Library of Congress at the time. Thomas Jefferson offered to sell his personal library to Congress to restore its lost collection. Jefferson's 6,487 volumes, which were then the largest and finest collection of books in the country, were purchased for $23,940. Jefferson's collection, which included works on architecture, science, literature, geography, and art, greatly expanded the Library's scope.

A second fire in 1851 decimated about two-thirds of its cumulative 55,000 volumes, including more than half of Jefferson's original library. Congress responded with $168,700 to restore the Library's rooms in the Capitol and replace the ruined books. In 1897, the Library relocated to its roomy new Thomas Jefferson Building across the plaza.

How to Get There – Mass Transit

The two metro stops closest to the Library are Capitol South (Orange/Blue lines) and Union Station (Red line). Capitol South is located a block south of and across Independence Avenue from the Thomas Jefferson building, which is the best public entrance. From Union Station, walk south on 1st Street, NE towards the U.S. Capitol. This path will take you past the U.S. Supreme Court to the Thomas Jefferson building on the left (east) side of 1st Street, in about 15 minutes.

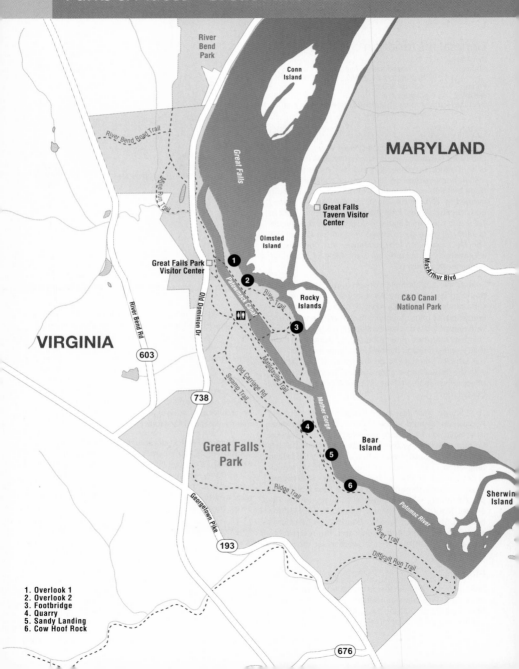

River
Bend
Park

Conn
Island

MARYLAND

Great Falls

River Bend Road Trail

Mine Run Trail

Great Falls
Tavern Visitor
Center

Olmsted
Island

1

Great Falls Park
Visitor Center

2

Potomac Canal

River Trail

Rocky
Islands

MacArthur Blvd

C&O Canal
National Park

VIRGINIA

River Bend Rd

Old Dominion Dr

603

738

Old Carriage Rd

Swamp Trail

Matildaville Trail

3

Mather Gorge

4

**Great Falls
Park**

5

Bear
Island

6

Ridge Trail

Sherwin
Island

Georgetown Pike

193

River Trail

Potomac River

Difficult Run Trail

676

1. Overlook 1
2. Overlook 2
3. Footbridge
4. Quarry
5. Sandy Landing
6. Cow Hoof Rock

General Information

Address: 9200 Old Dominion Dr, McLean, VA 22101
Phone: 703-285-2965
Website: www.nps.gov/gwmp/grfa
Fees: Annual Park Pass - $20
              Vehicle - $5 for 3 days
              Individual - $3 (entering by means other
              than vehicle – e.g. foot, bike)
              All passes valid on both sides of the falls.
Open: Year-round
              Nov to mid-Apr, 10 am–4 pm daily
              Mid-Apr to Oct, Mon-Fri 10 am–5 pm,
              Sat-Sun 10 am–6 pm

Overview

The aptly named Great Falls Park is 14 miles upriver from Washington DC, where the Potomac River cracks into cascading rapids and 20-foot waterfalls. The river drops 76 feet in elevation over a distance of less than a mile and narrows from almost 1,000 feet to 100 feet as it gushes through the narrow Mather Gorge. It's the steepest and most spectacular fall line rapid of any eastern river. You can check out the falls from either Virginia, where the viewing area expands into a massive park, or Maryland, where there are fewer amenities but you can get there with two wheels; the Maryland side of the falls is technically in the C&O Canal National Historical Park.

History

The Great Falls weren't always so admired. In the mid-1700s, they presented a near impossible obstacle for navigating the Potomac. One of the most significant engineering feats of the 18th century in the US was the development of a system of canals to lift and lower riverboats. The remains of the canal can still be seen in the park today.

John McLean and Steven Elkins purchased the land surrounding Great Falls and built an amusement park in the early 1900s that was wildly popular with tourists. Visitors traveled from Georgetown by trolley for the wooden carousel. Time and constant flood damage dampened the thrills until it was eventually closed. Today the land is under the authority and protection of the National Parks Service.

Activities

Picnic areas with tables and grills are available on a first-come, first-served basis. Ground fires are strictly prohibited. Unfortunately, there are no shelters in which to take retreat during inclement weather, so check the forecast before packing your picnic basket. If you forget your picnic, there is a basic concession stand located in the Visitor Center courtyard on the Maryland side.

If it's sweat-breaking activities you're after, a scenic, sometimes rocky bike-riding trail extends between the Maryland side of the falls and downtown Washington. Hiking trails wind along the river, and horseback riding, bird watching, rock climbing, fishing, white water rafting, and kayaking can all be enjoyed at various locations throughout the park.

If you plan on rock climbing, register at the visitor center or lower parking lot on the Virginia side before you climb. If fishing is more your speed, a Virginia or Maryland fishing license is required for anglers over 16 years of age. Whitewater boating is recommended only for experienced boaters and, not surprisingly, you're only allowed to launch your craft *below* the falls.

Stop by the visitor center on the Virginia side of the park or check out the National Park Service website for more information. www.nps.gov/gwmp/grfa/faqs/activities.htm

How to Get There - Driving

From I-495, take Exit 44, Route 193 W (Georgetown Pike). Turn right at Old Dominion Drive (approximately 4 1/2 miles). Drive for 1 mile to the entrance station. Parking, falls overlooks, and the visitor center are all centrally located.

To get to the visitor center on the Maryland side, take I-495 to Exit 41/MacArthur Boulevard E towards Route 189. Follow MacArthur Road all the way to the visitor center.

There is no public transportation available near the park.

General Information

NFT Maps:	20, 21, 23, 24, and 28
Website:	www.nps.gov/rocr
Visitor Information:	202-895-6070

Overview

If tourists get The Mall, locals get Rock Creek Park. This 1,754-acre forest isn't even on many tourist maps, which may be why it's so popular with people who live here year-round. You can bike a full mile without stalling behind waddling fanny-packers. The park stretches from Georgetown to the Maryland state line, is one of the oldest national parks in the National Park Service, and is one of the largest forested urban parks in the US. There are three visitors' centers in the park: the Nature Center and Planetarium, Pierce Mill, and the Old Stone House. A paved bike and running path twists alongside the creek that gives the park its name. Dozens of more secluded rocky paths break off from the path, one of which gained notoriety in 2002 when federal intern/Congressional paramour Chandra Levy was found dead nearby. Despite that, the park actually has some of the lowest crime rates in the city.

History

In 1866, federal officials proposed cordoning off some of the forest area as a presidential retreat. By the time Congress took up the plan in 1890, the vision had been democratized and the forest became a public park. The Rock Creek Park bill was soon followed by authorization of two more national parks, thus making the DC preserve part of the first post-Yellowstone deluge of natural parks established by the federal government.

There are several historical attractions in the park, including the oldest house in Washington, which is appropriately named Old Stone House. Now a colonial museum with an English garden, the house is located on M Street in Georgetown, between 30th and 31st Streets. Pierce Mill, a gristmill where corn and wheat were ground into flour using water power from Rock Creek, was built in the 1820s and is located over the bridge on Tilden Street. (Pierce Mill is closed to the public for repairs until further notice, but the Pierce Barn is open.) There are also remains of several Civil War earthen fortifications in the park, including Fort Stevens, the site of the only battle fought within the District of Columbia during the Civil War.

Activities

Rock Creek Park has more than 30 picnic areas, some that can be reserved in advance for parties of up to 100 (202-673-7646). A large field located at 16th and Kennedy Streets NW has several areas suitable for soccer, football, volleyball, and field hockey. Fields can also be reserved ahead of time (202-767-8363). There are 15 clay and 10 hard-surface tennis courts nearby that must be reserved for a small fee in person through Guest Services, (202-722-5949). The courts are open from April to November with 5 heated indoor courts open during the winter months. Three clay courts located off Park Road east of Pierce Mill can also be reserved in person (202-722-5949) from May to September.

A rather extensive network of hiking trails runs through the whole of Rock Creek Park and the outlying areas, like Clover Archbold Park. Blue-blazed paths maintained by

the Potomac Appalachian Trail Club follow the east side of the creek, and green-blazed trails follow the western ridge of the park. Tan-blazed trails are connectors. The paved path for bikers and rollerbladers runs from the Lincoln Memorial, through the park, and into Maryland. Memorial Bridge connects it to the Mount Vernon Trail in Virginia. Beach Drive between Military and Broad Branch roads is closed to cars from 7 am on Saturdays to 7 pm on Sundays and on all major holidays, giving bikes free range. However, bikes are still not permitted on horse or foot trails at any time. If you're willing to ditch the bike for another kind of ride, horseback riding lessons and guided trail rides are also available at the Rock Creek Park Horse Center (202-362-0117), located next door to the Nature Center.

The Rock Creek Nature Center, 5200 Glover Road NW, is open Wednesday through Sunday 9 am-5 pm, and closed on all national holidays. The Planetarium features after school shows for children on Wednesdays at 4 pm and Saturdays and Sundays at 1 pm and 4 pm. The park also hosts theatrical performances at the Carter Barron Amphitheater (16th St & Colorado Ave, 202-426-0486).

How to Get There – Driving

To get to the Nature Center from downtown DC, take the Rock Creek/Potomac Parkway north to Beach Drive. Exit onto Beach Drive N and take it to Broad Branch Road. Make a left and then a right onto Glover Road, and follow the signs to the Nature Center. Note: the Parkway is one-way going south on weekdays from 6:45 am until 9:45 am. During this time you can take 16th Street to Military Road W, then turn left on Glover Road. The Parkway is one-way going north from 3:45 pm until 6:30 pm; take

Glover Road to Military Road east, then head south on 16th to downtown DC.

Parking

Expansive parking lots are located directly next to the Nature Center and Planetarium. There are parking lots dotted throughout the park, but, depending on your destination, you might need to look for street parking in nearby neighborhoods.

How to Get There – Mass Transit

Take the Red Metro line to either the Friendship Heights or Fort Totten Metro stops to get to the Nature Center. Then transfer to the E2 bus line, which runs along Military/ Missouri/ Riggs Road between the two stations. Get off at the intersection of Glover (also called Oregon) and Military Roads and walk south on the trail up the hill to the Nature Center.

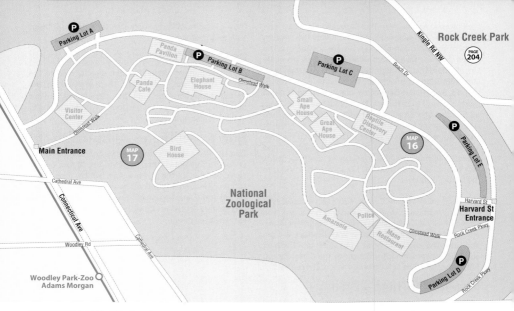

General Information

NFT Maps:	16 & 17
Address:	3001 Connecticut Avenue NW, Washington, DC 20008
Phone:	202-673-4800
Website:	www.natzoo.si.edu
Hours:	6 am–8 pm Apr 6–Oct 25; 6 am–6 pm the rest of the year. (Closed Christmas Day)
Entry:	Free

Overview

Nestled in Rock Creek Park, the National Zoological Park is a branch of the Smithsonian Institute, which means that it takes itself very seriously. The zoo is home to over 2,700 animals of 435 different species, including the unofficial city mascots, giant pandas Tian Tian and Mei Xiang, who are on loan from China. The enclosures mimic natural habitats and most exhibits strive to educate as well as entertain.

The zoo is a favorite jogging route, especially on winter snow days when locals know it to be one of the few regularly plowed paths in the city. In the spring and summer, school buses full of children on field trips usually arrive at the zoo between 10 am and noon daily. For a more peaceful experience, visit early in the day, between 8 am and 10 am, or after 2 pm. The animals tend to be more active at these times, and lines to see the popular exhibits and animals are usually at their shortest.

Parking

Enter the zoo from Connecticut Avenue, Harvard Street, or Rock Creek Parkway. Because parking on zoo grounds and nearby is limited, public transportation is recommended. If you're set on driving, parking at the zoo costs $7 for the first 4 hours, $12 for more than 4 hours, and is free for FONZ (Friends of the National Zoo) members. Lots fill early in the day during the summer, so plan to arrive by 9:30 am at the latest.

How to Get There - Mass Transit

By Metro, take the Red Line to the Woodley Park/Zoo/Adams-Morgan stop or the Cleveland Park stop; the zoo entrance lies halfway between these stops, and both are a short stroll away. It's an uphill walk from Woodley Park, while the walk from Cleveland Park is fairly flat.

From the Woodley Park/Zoo/Adams-Morgan stop, walk north (to your left as you face Connecticut Avenue—away from the McDonalds and the CVS), and the zoo is about three blocks from the stop. From the Cleveland Park stop, walk south toward the greater number of shops and restaurants that line Connecticut Avenue (away from the 7-11 and the Exxon station).

If you prefer above-ground mass transportation, Metrobus lines L1 and L2 stop at the zoo's Connecticut Avenue entrance. L4 and H4 stop at the zoo's Harvard Street entrance.

General Information

Address: 4368 Chantilly Shopping Center
         Chantilly, VA 20153
Phone: 708-378-0910
Website: www.dullesexpo.com

Overview

Don't be fooled by the vast expanse of nothingness on your way to the Dulles Expo and Conference Center; inside, there's bound to be more action. The venue hosts a variety of specialized exhibitions. At any time, it could be full of orchids, motorcycles, caskets, or toy trains. More than 400,000 visitors per year trod its 240,000 square feet. And though it's out of the way for city folks, it's only ten minutes away from Dulles International Airport, so crowds from all over the map find their way to shows.

A cab from Dulles will be about $20. A taxi from Reagan National Airport is approximately $45. If you really want to fly into Baltimore-Washington International Airport, be prepared to cough up $85 for your 1.5-hour schlep.

Hotels

The Expo Center has an on-site Holiday Inn and several hotels within walking distance. Certain hotels have specials for specific conventions, so ask when you book. Or browse hotel-specific websites such as hotels.com and pricerighthotels.com.

- **Comfort Suites Chantilly-Dulles Airport** • 13980 Metrotech Dr, 703-263-2007
- **Fairfield Inn Dulles Chantilly South** • 3960 Corsair Ct, 703-818-8200
- **Hampton Inn-Dulles South** • 4050 Westfax Dr, 703-818-8200
- **Holiday Inn Select** • 4335 Chantilly Shopping Ctr, 703-815-6060
- **Marriott Courtyard** • 3935 Centerview Dr, 703-709-7100
- **Sierra Suites** • 4506 Brookfield Corporate Dr, 703-263-7200
- **TownePlace Suites** • 14036 Thunderbolt Pl, 703-709-0453
- **Westfields** • 14750 Conference Center Dr, 703-818-0300
- **Wingate Inn Chantilly** • 3940 Centerview Dr, 571-203-0999

How to Get There – Driving

From Washington, DC, travel west on Constitution Avenue, and follow the signs to I-66 W to Virginia. Remain on I-66 W for about 25 miles and then take exit 53B, Route 28 N (Dulles Airport). Drive 3 miles north on Route 28, and then turn right onto Willard Road. Take the second left off into the Chantilly Shopping Center. From there, follow the signs to the Expo Center.

From Dulles Airport, follow exit signs for Washington, DC. Stay towards the right, drive for approximately one mile, and take Route 28 S towards Centerville. Drive for 6 miles and pass over Route 50. At the first light past Route 50, make a left on Willard Road. Follow signs to the Expo Center.

Parking

The Dulles Expo and Conference Center has an on-site parking lot for attendees and exhibitors offering over 2,400 free parking spaces. If you brought along your RV, you'll have to find a campsite for the night; campers, RVs, trucks, and oversized vehicles are not allowed to stay overnight.

How to Get There – Mass Transit

There is no public transportation to the Dulles Expo and Conference Center.

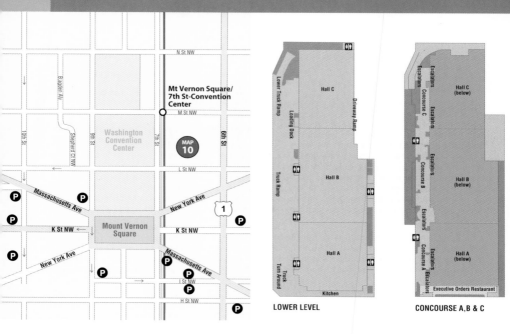

LOWER LEVEL

CONCOURSE A, B & C

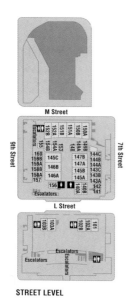

STREET LEVEL

LEVEL TWO

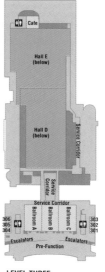

LEVEL THREE

General Information

NFT Map: 10
Address: 801 Mount Vernon Place, NW,
            Washington, DC 20001
Phone: 800-368-9000 or 202-249-3000
Website: www.dcconvention.com

Overview

The new Washington Convention Center is a white and glass 2.3 million-square-foot mammoth covering six city blocks, from 7th Street to 9th Street and N Street to Mt. Vernon Place. The building is the largest in DC, and has the distinction of being the largest excavation site in the Western Hemisphere—2 million tons of earth was removed during construction. Whether exhibiting or attending, you'd be well advised to wear comfy shoes to traverse the 700,000 square feet of exhibit space, 125,000 square feet of meeting space, and 40,000 square feet of retail space. The center hosts everything from small seminars for 80 participants to giant expos that welcome 35,000 attendees.

Along with the MCI Center, the Convention Center is a pillar of revitalization for this previously seedy neighborhood. Thanks to that success, conventioneers have many more nearby amenities. The new City Museum is across the street and a string of shops, restaurants, and nightlife beckon.

If you're flying in for a convention, a cab from BWI or Dulles will cost you more than $70 to downtown DC. From Reagan, it should be no more than $15.

Hotels

If you know which hotel you want to stay at, give them a call and ask if they have any specials for the time you'll be attending. If you're not with any particular rewards program and don't mind which hotel you stay at, try the official Washington tourism website at www.washington.org or hotel-specific websites such as hotels.com and pricerighthotels.com.

- **Renaissance Hotel** • 999 9th St NW, 202-898-9000
- **Henley Park** • 926 Massachusetts Ave NW, 202-638-5200
- **Courtyard Marriott Convention Center** • 900 F Street NW, 202-638-4600
- **Morrison Clark Inn** • 1101 11th St NW, 202-898-1200
- **Marriott Metro Center** • 775 12th St NW, 202-737-2200
- **Four Points by Sheraton** • 1201 K St NW, 202-289-7600
- **Hamilton Crowne Plaza** • 1001 14th St NW (at K St), 202-682-0111
- **Hilton Garden Inn** • 815 14th St NW, 202-783-7800
- **Hotel Sofitel** • 806 15th St NW, 202-737-8800

- **Washington Plaza** • 10 Thomas Circle NW, 202-842-1300
- **Holiday Inn Downtown** • 1155 14th St NW, 202-737-1200
- **Wyndham Washington, DC** • 1400 M St NW, 202-429-1700
- **The Madison** • 15th & M St NW, 202-862-1600
- **Hotel Helix** • 1430 Rhode Island Ave NW, 202-462-9001
- **Homewood Suites by Hilton** • 1475 Massachusetts Ave NW, 202-265-8000
- **Capitol Hilton** • 1001 16th St NW, 202-393-1000
- **Holiday Inn Central** • 1501 Rhode Island Ave NW, 202-483-2000
- **Comfort Inn** • 1201 13th St NW, 202-682-5300
- **Grand Hyatt Washington** • 1000 H Street NW, 202-582-1234

Eating

You'll find a number of restaurants located in the Convention Center and dozens more within easy walking distance. Executive Orders on the L1 Concourse offers selections from Foggy Bottom Grill, Wolfgang Puck, Seafood Cuisine, Subculture, Bello Pronto, My Thai's Fine Asian Cuisine, and Latin American Cuisine. Located on Level Two off the L Street Bridge, the Supreme Court is a retail food court offering Wolfgang Puck Express, Quizno's, and Foggy Bottom Grill.

The Lobby Café, located by the 801 Mt Vernon Place entrance, sells coffee and deluxe pastries to help exhibitors and attendees wake up in the mornings. Within each exhibit hall, there are permanent and portable outlets/carts serving everything from coffee to Tex-Mex.

Parking

The center does not have its own parking facility. There are about 100 metered parking spaces close to the convention center, so you'd be pretty fortunate if you snagged one. Be prepared to pay for one of the many parking lots within a three-block radius of the convention center.

How to Get There – Mass Transit

The closest Metro stop is Mt Vernon Square/7th St-Convention Center on the Yellow or Green Lines.

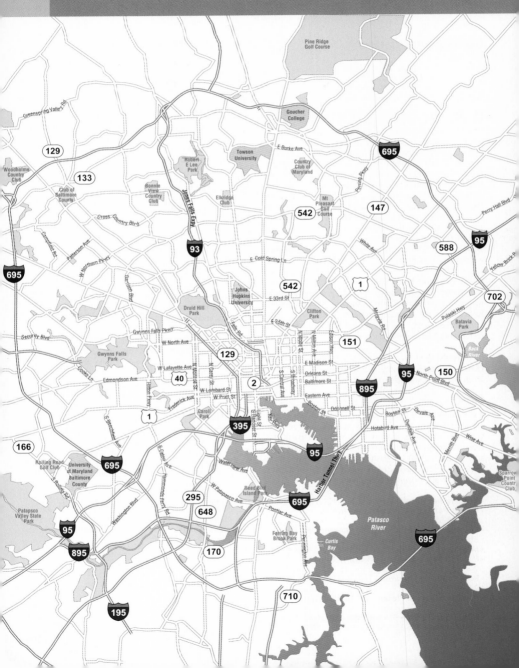

Overview

Baltimore is a city of firsts. The first umbrella in the US was used in Baltimore. The first makers of silverware were in Baltimore. The first commercial ice cream factory was in Baltimore. Without Baltimore, you'd be eating soggy pie with your hands and it wouldn't even be a la mode. Okay, maybe not. Still, Baltimore's got history. It's home to the birthplace of George Washington and site of the first Washington Monument (a bit smaller than that big obelisk in DC). You can take in the whole city by visiting the observation center at the top of the Baltimore World Trade Center, the world's tallest five-sided building.

Getting There

Take I-295 N to Baltimore City past Oriole Park at Camden Yards. 295 will become Russell Street and then Paca Street. Make a right onto Pratt Street. Follow Pratt Street six blocks to the Inner Harbor, which will be on your right. The Visitor Center is located along the Inner Harbor's west wall (near Light Street).

Attractions

HarborPlace
200 East Pratt St; 410-332-4191; www.harborplace.com
One of the biggest draws in Baltimore is HarborPlace, the outdoor mall that circles the harbor. While repellent to many residents, HarborPlace is perpetually mobbed with tourists and day-trippers from DC. Full of retail shops and chain restaurants, the harbor is capitalism run amok. The shops are open from 10 am to 9 pm Monday through Saturday, closing early at 7 pm on Sunday.

National Aquarium in Baltimore
501 Pratt St; 410-576-3800; www.aqua.org
Baltimore's aquarium is certainly the most popular destination in the city. Entry isn't cheap, and you're bound to have to wait in line, but when in Rome, even Atkins would eat pasta. Admission is $17.50 for adults and $9.50 for children between the ages of 3 and 11. The Aquarium is open from 9 am to 7 pm every day, except on Friday when it stays open until 10 pm.

Maryland Science Center
601 Light St; 410-685-5225; www.mdsci.org
Second to the Aquarium, the Maryland Science Center is one of the most popular attractions in Baltimore. The museum is one of the oldest scientific institutions in the country and has six permanent exhibits. The center has just been refurbished and expanded, making more room for the hands-on exhibits that make it so popular. The center is open from 10 am to 6 pm and admission is $14 to $19.50, depending on what exhibits you'd like to visit. Admission for children is $9.50 to $13.50, and admission for members is always free.

Babe Ruth Birthplace and Museum
216 Emory St; 410-727-1539; www.baberuthmuseum.com
Visit the place where Babe was really a babe. The Sultan of Swat was born in this historic building, which has been transformed into a shrine for Babe, as well as Baltimore's Colts and Orioles and Johnny Unitas (famed quarterback for the Colts). Admission is $6.

The Baltimore Zoo
978 Druid Park Lake D; 410-366-LION (5466); www.baltimorezoo.org
Located in Druid Hill Park, the zoo allows you to come face-to-face with over 2,200 exotic mammals, birds, and reptiles amid a wooded 180-acre setting. The kids can enjoy the number-one-rated children's zoo, while the adults can look forward to the zoo's spring beer and wine festival, Brew at the Zoo. Plan on hearing lots of jokes about polar beer, penguinness, and giraffes of wine. Admission to the zoo is $12 for adults, and $8 for the kiddies.

Lexington Market
400 W Lexington St; 410-685-6169; www.lexingtonmarket.com
Baltimore's Lexington Market is the world's largest, continuously running market. Founded in 1782, the market continues to be a rowdy place of commerce, with over 140 vendors selling and displaying foods of all types. The market provides fresh meats, seafood, poultry, groceries, specialty items, and prepared foods for take-out and on-site consumption. The market is also the site for many events, such as the Chocolate Festival and the Preakness Crab Derby (yes, they actually race crabs). Don't miss "Lunch with the Elephants" every spring. A herd of elephants from the Ringling Bros. and Barnum & Bailey Circus marches from the Baltimore Arena to the market, where they are treated to the world's largest stand-up vegetarian buffet.

National Museum of Dentistry
31 S Greene St; 410-706-0600; www.dentalmuseum.org
After munching on goodies at the Lexington Market, swing on by the National Museum of Dentistry to learn about all the cavities you just got. This Smithsonian affiliate offers interactive exhibits and the gift shop sells chocolate toothbrushes—reason enough to check it out. Plaque got you gloomy? Edgar Allan Poe's Grave is just down the street. Admission to the museum is $4.50.

The Power Plant
601 E Pratt St; 410-752-5444
Opened in 1998, the Power Plant has turned a former honest-to-goodness power plant into a mall. Guess retail's just a different kinda community fuel. The Power Plant has a Barnes & Noble, an ESPN Zone, and a Gold's Gym.

Power Plant Live!
Market Pl & Water St; 410-727-LIVE (5483);
www.powerplantlive.com
Located a block away from the Power Plant, Power Plant Live! is an overproduced dining and entertainment district. It's got dinner, dancing, comedy, and stiff drinks. Because of an arena liquor license, you can take your drink from one establishment to the next. During the summer, check out the free outdoor concerts. Past headliners include the Violent Femmes, Better Than Ezra, and the Gin Blossoms.

American Visionary Art Museum
800 Key Highway; 410-244-1900; www.avam.org
Located along the water in Baltimore's inner harbor, the Visionary Art Museum exhibits works from self-taught, intuitive artists whose backgrounds range from housewives to homeless. The museum is also home to Baltimore's newest and already most beloved outdoor sculptural landmark—the Giant Whirligig. Standing at fifty-five feet tall, this multicolored, wind-powered sculpture was created by 76-year-old mechanic, farmer, and artist, Vollis Simpson. Every spring, the museum hosts a race of human-powered works of art designed to travel on land, through mud, and over deep harbor waters. The museum is open from 10 am to 6 pm Tuesdays through Sundays and admission is $9 for adults and $6 for children and seniors.

Pagoda at Patterson Park
One of the most striking structures in Baltimore's Patterson Park is the newly renovated Pagoda. Originally built in 1891, the Pagoda was designed as a people's lookout tower. From the sixty-foot-high octagonal tower, you can see downtown, the suburbs, and the harbor. The Pagoda is open from 12 pm to 6 pm on Sundays from May to October.

Camden Yards
There is more to Camden Yards than just Cal Ripken. At the turn of the century, Camden Yard was a bustling freight and passenger railroad terminal. For decades, Camden Station served as a major facility for the Baltimore and Ohio Railroad (that's the B&O Railroad for Monopoly fans). The Yards were once home to thousands of commuters, and now they're home to thousands of fans who come out to see their beloved Orioles play.

Where to Drink

- **Cross Street Market**, 1065 S Charles St. Indoor market with a raucous, locals-filled happy hour.
- **The Horse You Came In On**, 1626 Thames St, 410-327-8111. Feel like a sailor in this dirty ol' place right on the waterfront.

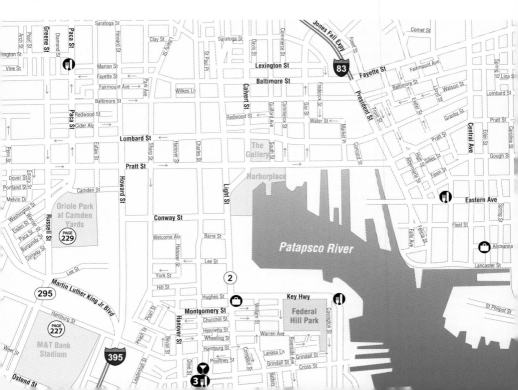

- **Bohager's**, 701 South Eden St, 410-363-7220. Imported sand and palm-trees outside, dance hall and wet t-shirt contests inside.
- **Club Charles**, 1724 N Charles St, 410-727-8815. Dive bar extraordinaire.

Where to Eat

- **Jimmy's**, 801 S Broadway, 410-327-3273. Classic Bawlmer greasy spoon. Check your attitude at the door.
- **Faidley's Seafood**, Lexington Market, 203 N Paca St, 410-727-4898. Seafood. Stand up and rub elbows while chowing down some of the city's best crab cakes.
- **Bertha's**, 734 S Broadway, 410-327-5795. Seafood. Dark, dank and famous for its mussels.
- **Boccaccio**, 925 Eastern Ave, 410-234-1322. Italian. The best, and arguably only, great restaurant in this particularly inauthentic Little Italy.
- **John Steven Ltd**, 1800 Thames St, 410-327-5561. Seafood. Outdoor patio, steamer bar, crab cakes, and stocked bar.
- **Matsuri**, 1105 S Charles St, 410-752-8561. Japanese. Sushi in this blue-collar town is better than you think.
- **Obrycki's Crab House**, 1727 E Pratt St, 410-732-6399. The king of the many local crab houses.
- **Joy America Cafe**, American Visionary Art Museum, 800 Key Highway, 410-244-6500. Latin American. Whacked-out cuisine with a view.
- **Vespa**, 1117-21 S Charles St, 410-675-5999. Italian. If all the blue-collar-ness has got you down, come and find the gold-roped crowd here.
- **So Bo Cafe**, 6 W Cross St, 410-752-1518. Laid-back neighborhood coffeehouse with sandwiches and snacks and Greens literature.
- **Ze Mean Bean**, 1739 Fleet St, 410-675-5999. Eastern European. More than a coffeehouse, with meaty dishes and live music.
- **Helen's Garden**, 2908 Odonnell St, 410-276-2233. Feel like a local at this Canton outpost. Good food, nice owners, wine flows.

Where to Shop

- **A Cook's Table,** 717 Light St, 410-539-8600. For the perfectly-appointed mogul kitchen.
- **Mystery Loves Company**, 1730 Fleet St, 410-276-6708. No mystery to the genre of books here.
- **Sound Garden**, 1616 Thames St, 410-534-9011. Independent music store with impromptu performances.
- **The Antique Man,** 1806 Fleet St, 410-732-0932. The most eclectic of the string of antique/junk shops around Fells Point.

Colleges & Universities • **American University**

Main Campus

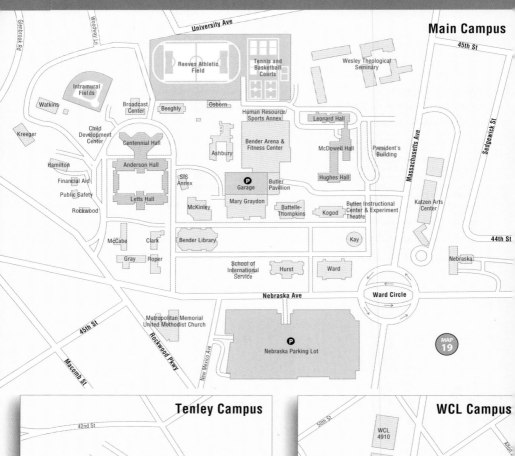

University Ave

45th St

Reeves Athletic Field

Tennis and Basketball Courts

Wesley Theological Seminary

Intramural Fields

Watkins

Broadcast Center

Beeghly

Osborn

Human Resource/ Sports Annex

Leonard Hall

Kreeger

Child Development Center

Centennial Hall

Bender Arena & Fitness Center

McDowell Hall

President's Building

Massachusetts Ave

Sedgewick St

Hamilton

Anderson Hall

Ashbury

Hughes Hall

Financial Aid

SIS Annex

Garage

Butler Pavilion

Public Safety

Letts Hall

McKinley

Mary Graydon

Battelle-Thompkins

Kogod

Butler Instructional Center & Experiment Theatre

Katzen Arts Center

Rockwood

44th St

McCabe

Clark

Bender Library

Kay

Nebraska

Gray

Roper

School of International Service

Hurst

Ward

Nebraska Ave

Ward Circle

MAP 19

Metropolitan Memorial United Methodist Church

45th St

Rockwood Pkwy

New Mexico Ave

Nebraska Parking Lot

Macomb St

Glenbrook Rd

Woodway Ln

Tenley Campus

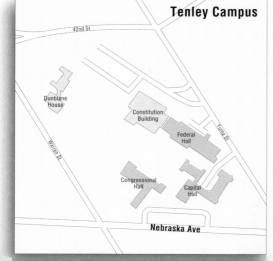

42nd St

Dunblane House

Constitution Building

Federal Hall

Yuma St

Warren St

Congressional Hall

Capital Hall

Nebraska Ave

WCL Campus

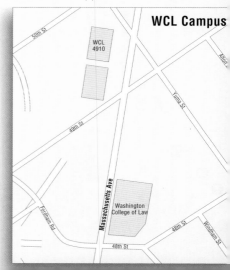

50th St

WCL 4910

Alton

Yuma St

49th St

48th St

Massachusetts Ave

Fordham Rd

Washington College of Law

48th St

48th St

Windham St

General Information

NFT Map: 19
Main Campus: 4400 Massachusetts Ave NW,
               Washington, DC 20016
Phone: 202-885-1000
Website: www.american.edu

Overview

The idea for American University first began in the mind of George Washington himself. His vision of a great "national university" in the nation's capital took more than 100 years to get up and running. But once it did, the big guy would have been proud. Its first class, admitted in 1914, consisted of 28 graduate students, 4 of them women. It was also one of the first colleges in a segregated city to admit black students in 1937.

Today, the school is an independent university with a significantly diverse student body of over 11,000 grads and under-grads from more than 150 countries. This distinction, along with its location, makes the school a good place to focus on public affairs, law, and international studies.

Alas, a less noble side has emerged that the founder may not have expected. AU also has a reputation as a party school, especially among the pampered diplomat brat pack who are less interested in the school's serious-minded pursuits and more in the city that surrounds this leafy residential campus. It was also involved in a scandal in 1990 when obscene phone calls were traced to university president Richard E. Berendzen's office telephone line. He consequently resigned.

Tuition

In the 2004-2005 academic year, undergraduate tuition for students living on campus amounted to $25,920, with room and board at an additional $10,170. Graduate student tuition, fees, and expenses vary by college.

Sports

The AU Eagles do pretty well for themselves in the sports arena. AU has NCAA Division I men's basketball, cross-country, golf, soccer, swimming, tennis, track and field, and wrestling teams. Women's sports include basketball, cross-country, soccer, swimming, tennis, track and field, field

hockey, lacrosse, and volleyball. For tickets to all American University athletic events, including basketball at Bender Arena, call 202-885-TIXX.

Intramural sports, including flag football, indoor and outdoor soccer, tennis, volleyball, basketball, golf, softball, skiing, wiffleball, and football, are also offered.

The American Outdoor Tennis Courts have been the site of several championship wins for the women's and men's tennis teams. And of course there is Reeves Field, which earned the Academy Award of soccer fields when it won "Soccer Field of the Year" from the Sports Turf Managers' Association. Along with other sports played on this illustrious turf, Reeves has also hosted professional practices of the Barcelona and Uruguay national soccer teams.

Culture on Campus

The Watkins Gallery features student exhibitions and several professional rotating shows throughout the school year. The gallery's main collection of over 4,400 works focuses on Washington-area modern art. Bender Arena is a top city venue. Past performers include the Smashing Pumpkins, Bob Dylan, and Archbishop Desmond Tutu. AU also operates its own wildly wonkish and popular FM radio station, WAMU, that broadcasts NPR programs, local news, and traditional, you guessed it, American music.

Phone Numbers

Undergraduate Admissions: 202-885-6000
Graduate Affairs & Admissions: 202-885-6064
College of Arts & Sciences: 202-885-2453
Kogod School of Business: 202-885-1900
School of Communication: 202-885-2060
School of International Service: 202-885-1600
School of Public Affairs: 202-885-2940
Washington College of Law: 202-274-4000
Washington College of Law Library: 202-274-4350
Student Services: 202-885-3310
Athletic Department: 202-885-3000
University Library: 202-885-3232

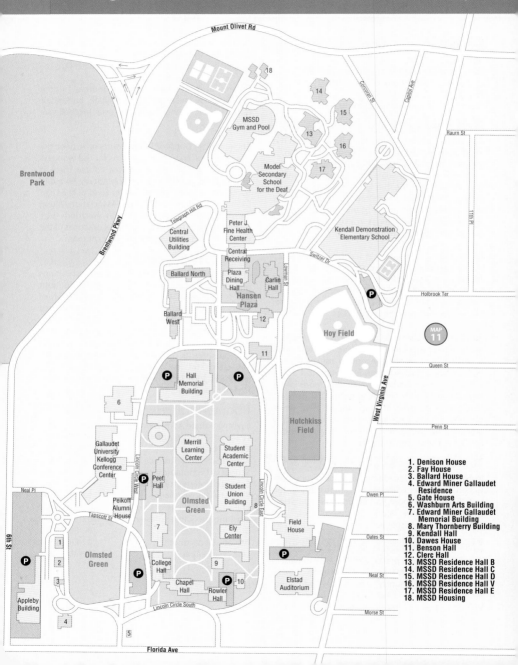

Mount Olivet Rd

Brentwood Park

Brentwood Pkwy

18

14

15

13

16

17

MSSD Gym and Pool

Model Secondary School for the Deaf

Corcoran St

Capitol Ave

Raurn St

11th Pl

Telegraph Hill Rd

Central Utilities Building

Peter J. Fine Health Center

Kendall Demonstration Elementary School

Central Receiving

Switzer Dr

Ballard North

Plaza Dining Hall

Carlin Hall

Lowman St

Holbrook Ter

Hansen Plaza

Ballard West

12

Hoy Field

MAP 11

11

Queen St

Hall Memorial Building

6

West Virginia Ave

Penn St

Gallaudet University Kellogg Conference Center

Lincoln Circle West

Peet Hall

Merrill Learning Center

Student Academic Center

Hotchkiss Field

Neal Pl

Peikoff Alumni House

Olmsted Green

Student Union Building

Lincoln Circle East

8

Owen Pl

Tapscott St

7

Ely Center

Field House

Oates St

6th St

1

2

3

4

Olmsted Green

College Hall

Chapel Hall

9

Rowley Hall

10

Elstad Auditorium

Neal St

5

Lincoln Circle South

Morse St

Florida Ave

1. Denison House
2. Fay House
3. Ballard House
4. Edward Miner Gallaudet Residence
5. Gate House
6. Washburn Arts Building
7. Edward Miner Gallaudet Memorial Building
8. Mary Thornberry Building
9. Kendall Hall
10. Dawes House
11. Benson Hall
12. Clerc Hall
13. MSSD Residence Hall B
14. MSSD Residence Hall C
15. MSSD Residence Hall D
16. MSSD Residence Hall V
17. MSSD Residence Hall E
18. MSSD Housing

Appleby Building

General Information

NFT Map: 11
Address: 800 Florida Avenue, NE,
             Washington, DC 20002
Phone: 202-651-5050
Website: www.gallaudet.edu

Overview

Gallaudet is the premier university for the deaf and hearing-impaired and the only university in the world where deaf students and those without hearing problems mingle. It is a campus where English and American Sign Language coexist. Students can choose from more than 40 majors and all aspects of the school, including classes and workshops, are designed to accommodate deaf students. Even the hearing students, who make up about 5% of each entering class, must always communicate through visual communication.

Thomas Hopkins Gallaudet co-founded the American School for the Deaf in 1817 as the first such school in the country. Forty years later, his youngest son, Dr. Edward Minor Gallaudet, established a school for the deaf in DC. In 1864, that school became the world's first and only liberal arts university for the deaf. In 1988, I. King Jordan, the University's first deaf president was appointed after students, backed by a number of alumni, faculty, and staff, shut down the campus demanding that a deaf president be appointed.

Tuition

In the 2003-2004 academic year, tuition for U.S. residents was $9,000 for undergraduate and $9,910 for graduate programs. For international students tuition was $18,000 and $19,820 respectively. Room and board for both programs was $8,030.

Sports

The birth of the football huddle took place at Gallaudet. Legend has it that prior to the 1890s, football players stood around discussing their plays out of earshot of the other team. This posed a problem for Gallaudet's team; they communicated through signing and opposing teams could see the plays that were being called. Paul Hubbard, a star football player at the university, is credited with coming up with the huddle to prevent prying eyes from discovering plays.

Gallaudet also boasts 14 NCAA Division III teams, and several intramural sports teams.

In the summer, Gallaudet runs popular one-week sports camps, where teens from all over the US, as well as the local area, stay on campus and participate in basketball and volleyball activities. Check the website for details.

Culture on Campus

Gallaudet's Dance Company performs modern, tap, jazz, and other dance styles incorporating ASL. Gallaudet also produces several theatre productions every year, all of which are signed with vocal interpretation. The school is smack in the middle of a neighborhood quickly transitioning from rough to trendy. Check out the nearby theaters, coffeehouses, and farmer's market before gentrification smoothes out the hard edges.

Phone Numbers

Admissions: 800-995-0550
Graduate School and
Professional Programs:. 800-995-0513
College of Liberal Arts, Sciences
and Technologies: 202-651-5470
Center for ASL Literacy: 202-651-5778
Financial Aid:. 202-651-5299
Gallaudet Library: 202-651-5231
Registrar:. 202-651-5393
Visitors Center: 202-651-5050

George Washington University

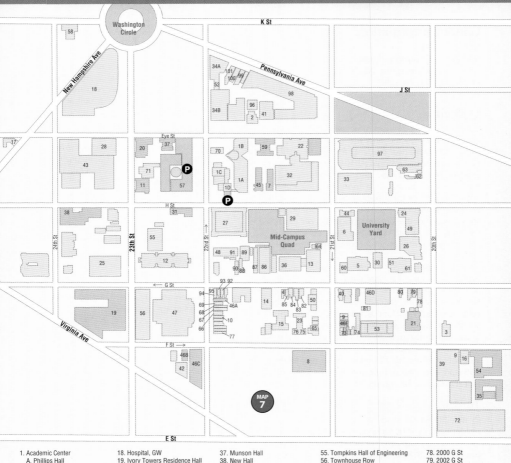

1. Academic Center
 A. Phillips Hall
 B. Rome Hall
 C. Smith Hall of Art
 D. Visitor Center
2. John Quincy Adams House
3. Alumni House
4. Hortense Amsterdam House
5. Bell Hall
6. Corcoran Hall
7. Crawford Hall
8. Dakota
9. Davis-Hodgkins House
10. Abba Eban House
11. Fulbright Hall
12. Funger Hall
13. Hall of Government
14. GSEHD
15. Guthridge Hall
16. The George Washington
 University Club
17. The George Washington
 University Inn

18. Hospital, GW
19. Ivory Towers Residence Hall
20. Kennedy Onassis Hall
21. Key Hall
22. Lafayette Hall
23. Lenthall Houses
24. Lerner Hall
25. Lerner Family Health and
 Wellness Center
26. Jacob Burns Library (Law)
27. Melvin Gelman Library (University)
28. Paul Himmelfarb Health
 Sciences Library (Medical)
29. Lisner Auditorium
30. Lisner Hall
31. Madison Hall
32. Marvin Center
33. Media & Public Affairs
34. Medical Faculty Associates
 A. H. B. Burns Memorial Bldg
 B. Ambulatory Care Center
35. Mitchell Hall
36. Monroe Hall

37. Munson Hall
38. New Hall
39. Old Main
40. Quigley's
41. Rice Hall
42. Riverside Towers Hall
43. Ross Hall
44. Samson Hall
45. Schenley Hall
46. Scholars Village Townhouses
 A. 619 22nd St
 B. 2208 F St
 C. 520-526 22nd St
 D. 2028 G St
 E. 605-607 21st St
47. Smith Center
48. Staughton Hall
49. Stockton Hall
50. Strong Hall
51. Stuart Hall
52. Student Health Service
53. Support Building
54. Thurston Hall

55. Tompkins Hall of Engineering
56. Townhouse Row
57. University Garage
58. Warwick Bldg
59. The West End
60. Woodhull House
61. 700 20th St
62. 812 20th St
63. 814 20th St
64. 714 21st St
65. 600 21st St
66. 609 22nd St
67. 613 22nd St
68. 615 22nd St
69. 617 22nd St
70. 837 22nd St
71. 817 23rd St
72. 1957 E St
73. 2033-37 F St
74. 2031 F St
75. 2101 F St
76. 2109 F St
77. 2147 F St

78. 2000 G St
79. 2002 G St
80. 2008 G St
81. 2030 G St
82. 2106 G St
83. 2108 G St
84. 2112 G St
85. 2114 G St
86. 2125 G St
87. 2127 G St
88. 2129 G St
89. 2129 G St (rear)
90. 2131 G St
91. 2131 G St (rear)
92. 2136 G St
93. 2138 G St
94. 2140 G St
95. 2142 G St
96. 2129-33 Eye St (rear)
97. 2000 Pennsylvania Ave
98. 2100 Pennsylvania Ave
99. 2136 Pennsylvania Ave
100. 2140 Pennsylvania Ave
101. 2142 Pennsylvania Ave

General Information

NFT Map: 7
Address: 2121 Eye Street, NW,
          Washington, DC, 20052
Phone: 202-994-1000
Website: www.gwu.edu

Overview

Located just four blocks from the White House, George Washington University was founded in 1821 by an act of Congress. And like the government that okayed it, this school keeps growing and growing. It is currently the second largest landowner, behind the US government, and the largest private landowner, in the entire city. Don't expect many trees through.

This is mostly an urban campus with a lot of room devoted to luxe student accommodations rather than leafy quads. In the 1970s, the university was known primarily as a night school and graduate school. Since then, it has become a major undergraduate and graduate institution, churning out much of the city's white-collar workforce. Bigshot alums include J. Edgar Hoover, Jackie O, and Kenneth Star.

Tuition

Tuition for the 2004-2005 school year was $34,000, with an additional $10,210 for room and board. With these charges, plus other extraneous expenses, the yearly total is a whopping $46,090.

Athletics

The University's fight song, "Hail to the buff, hail to the blue, hail to the buff and blue," provides hours of double-entendre fun for the students and it seems to work for the athletes too. The university's 22 NCAA Division I teams, known as the fighting Colonials, usually place well in their A-10 conference, especially women's basketball, which won the A-10 division championship in 2003. Women's volleyball won their division in 2004.

Culture on Campus

The Robert H. and Clarice Smith Hall of Art is a modern facility that features five floors dedicated to the study and practice of art. Students participate annually in two major shows, and faculty members also display their art on campus.

The Department of Theatre and Dance produces two dance concerts, three plays, and a musical each year. These productions are performed either in the 435-seat Dorothy Betts Marvin Theatre, or the 1,490-seat Lisner Auditorium. For more information on performances presented by the Theatre and Dance Department call 202-994-6178.

For information on tickets for the Dorothy Betts Marvin Theatre call 202-994-7411 and for information on tickets for the Lisner Auditorium call 202-994-6800.

Phone Numbers

Admissions: 202-994-6040
Athletics: 202-994-6650
Campus Bookstore: 202-994-6870
Financial Aid: 202-994-6620
Gelman Library: .202-994-6558
Registrar: 202-994-4900
Student Activities Center: 202-994-6555
Visitor Center: 202-994-6602

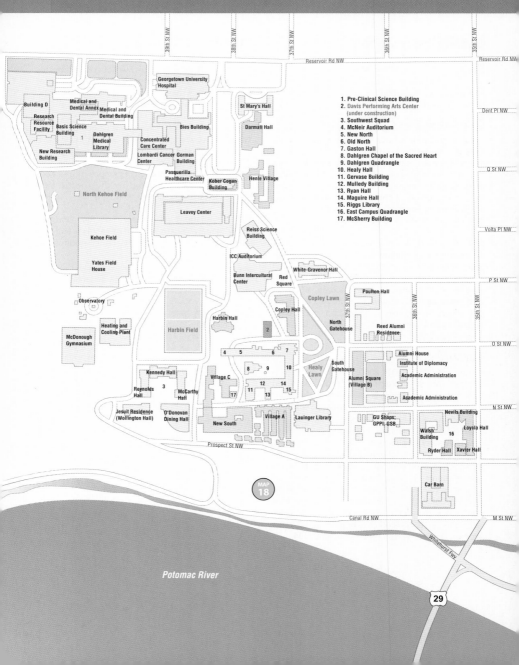

Reservoir Rd NW

38th St NW
38th St NW
37th St NW
36th St NW
35th St NW

Reservoir Rd NW

Georgetown University Hospital

St Mary's Hall

Building D
Medical and Dental Annex
Medical and Dental Building
Research Resource Facility
Basic Science Building
Dahlgren Medical Library
Bies Building
Darnall Hall

Dent Pl NW

New Research Building
Concentrated Care Center
Lombardi Cancer Center
Gorman Building

1. Pre-Clinical Science Building
2. Davis Performing Arts Center (under construction)
3. Southwest Squad
4. McNeir Auditorium
5. New North
6. Old North
7. Gaston Hall
8. Dahlgren Chapel of the Sacred Heart
9. Dahlgren Quadrangle
10. Healy Hall
11. Gervase Building
12. Mulledy Building
13. Ryan Hall
14. Maguire Hall
15. Riggs Library
16. East Campus Quadrangle
17. McSherry Building

Pasquerilla Healthcare Center
Kober Cogan Building
Henle Village

Q St NW

North Kehoe Field

Leavey Center

Volta Pl NW

Kehoe Field

Reiss Science Building

Yates Field House

ICC Auditorium

Bunn Intercultural Center
Red Square
White-Gravenor Hall

P St NW

Observatory

Copley Lawn
Poulton Hall

37th St NW
36th St NW
35th St NW

Heating and Cooling Plant
Harbin Hall
Copley Hall
North Gatehouse
Reed Alumni Residence

O St NW

McDonough Gymnasium
Harbin Field

4   5   6   7

Healy Lawn
South Gatehouse
Alumni House
Institute of Diplomacy
Academic Administration

Kennedy Hall

8   9   10
Village C

Alumni Square (Village B)
Academic Administration

Reynolds Hall
3
McCarthy Hall
12   14
17   11   13   15

N St NW

Jesuit Residence (Wolfington Hall)
O'Donovan Dining Hall
New South
Village A
Lauinger Library

GU Shops; GPPI; GSB
Nevils Building
Loyola Hall

Walsh Building
16

Prospect St NW

Ryder Hall   Xavier Hall

MAP 18

Car Barn

Canal Rd NW
M St NW

Whitehurst Fwy

29

Potomac River

General Information

NFT Map: 18
Main Campus: 37th and O Sts, NW,
               Washington, DC 20057
Phone: 202-287-0100
Website: www.georgetown.edu

Overview

Georgetown University was founded the same year the US Constitution took effect, making Georgetown not just the nation's oldest Catholic and Jesuit university, but also about the same age as the neighborhood's socialites. But seriously, Georgetown is the best collegiate game in town. Alumni include former president Bill Clinton, Supreme Court Justice Antonin Scalia, and broadcast journalist/Kennedy heir/California First Lady Maria Shriver. The campus sets the tone for the neighborhood around it—both are beautiful, old, distinguished, and snooty.

Georgetown's history is long and sometimes spooky. According to campus rumor, the attic of Healy Hall is haunted by the ghost of a priest who died while winding the clock in the building's famous spire. During the Civil War, the university's buildings became bunkers and hospitals for the Yankee troops. Once the war ended, the school adopted blue and gray as its official colors to symbolize the reunification of North and South. More recently, it was part of Hollywood history for providing the setting for *The Exorcist*, a novel by alum William Peter Blatty. The creepy "exorcist stairs" are on campus.

Tuition

In the 2004-2005 academic year, undergraduate tuition for full-time students was $29,808. The average room and board costs were an additional $10,154. With books, travel, and other fees, the average total cost of attendance was $43,340. Tuition fees vary by school and for the graduate division.

Sports

The university's teams are known as the Hoyas because, the story goes, a student well-versed in Greek and Latin started cheering "Hoya Saxa!" which translates to "What Rocks!" The cheer proved popular and the term "Hoyas" was adopted for all Georgetown teams. Since it was difficult to find an animal that represented "what," the mascot became a bulldog.

Georgetown is renowned for its baseball and basketball teams. (This is where Patrick Ewing got his start.) It also offers crew, football, golf, lacrosse, co-ed sailing, soccer, swimming/diving, tennis, and track. Women's sports include basketball, crew, field hockey, golf, lacrosse, sailing, soccer, swimming/diving, tennis, track, and volleyball. For tickets to all Georgetown athletic events, call 202-687-HOYA. Georgetown also offers intramural sports including volleyball, flag football, racquetball, basketball, ultimate Frisbee, arm wrestling, table tennis, softball, and floor hockey.

Culture on Campus

Georgetown has an extensive arts program within its Department of Art, Music, and Theater. Students can major in studio arts, art history, or performing arts. Extracurricular-wise, Georgetown has two theater troupes, an improv group, two a capella singing groups, an orchestra, and a band. There are also six art galleries around campus devoted to the best of student offerings.

Phone Numbers

Undergraduate Admissions: 202-687-3600
Graduate Admissions: 202-687-5568
Georgetown Law Center: 202-662-9000
McDonough School of Business: 202-687-3851
Edmund A. Walsh School
of Foreign Service: 202-687-5696
Georgetown University
Medical Center: .202-687-5100
School of Nursing & Health Studies: . .202-687-2681
Department of Athletics: 202-687-2435

N

Burr Gymnasium

Burr Annex

Howard Manor

Cook Hall

Effingham Apartments

Drew Hall

Greene Memorial Stadium

McMillan Reservoir

Fremont St

School of Business

Minor Hall

Mordecai Johnson Administration Building

Howard Hall

Lindsay Hall (Social Work)

Physical Ed Annex

Crampton Auditorium

Aldridge Theatre

Childers Hall

Blackburn Center

Douglas Hall

Upper Quadrangle

Locke Hall

Economics Mathematics C A R

School of Education

Carnegie Building

Human Ecology Building

Georgia Ave

MAP 15

4th St

4th St

Howard Pl

Mackey Building (Architecture)

Rankin Chapel

Founders Library

Undergraduate Library

Wheatley Hall

Truth Hall

Thirkield Hall

Engineering

Computer Science

Dixon Hall

Health Center

Chemistry Building

Just Hall (Biology)

School of Pharmacy

Baldwin Hall

Crandall Hall

Frazier Hall

McMillan Dr

Barry Pl

College St

ISAS

Bunche Center

Power Plant

Mental Health Center

CB Powell Building (Communications)

Student Resource Building

WHUR-FM

Graduate School

WHUT-TV

Bethune Annex

8th St

6th St

4th St

W St

Book Store

Howard Center

Nursing and Allied Health Center

Louise Stokes Health Science Library

Evolutionary Building

V St

Student Health Center

College of Dentistry

College of Medicine

Adams Building

P Hospital Parking

MAP 10

Sickle Cell Center

Oakdale Pl

HU Hospital

Tower Building

5th St

Elm St

3rd St

V St

General Information

NFT Maps: 10 and 15
Main Campus: 2400 Sixth Street, NW,
                      Washington, DC 20059
Phone: 202-806-6100
Website: www.howard.edu

Overview

Founded in 1867, Howard University is a historically African-American private university that has become a dominant intellectual, cultural, and physical presence. It once occupied a lone single-frame building and now has four campuses, which span more than 260 acres. The library system houses over 2 million books, as well as the largest collection of African-American literature in the nation. Despite its physical size, Howard is a relatively small school with roughly 6,000 undergraduate students.

Its main campus is located on "the hilltop," one of the highest elevation points in the city overlooking downtown DC, and is minutes away from the Capitol and the White House. The campus leads right into one of the premier catwalks of the city; U Street used to be the center of jazz and African-American nightlife before it fell on rough times. Now it's back and considered the hippest of areas, with avant-garde fashion, deluxe condos, and martinis that cost so much 'cause they look so good.

Tuition

In the 2003-2004 school year, undergraduate tuition for students living off-campus was $10,130. Room and board averaged $5,570. Graduate tuition, fees, and expenses vary by school and department.

Sports

Howard is a member of the Mid-Eastern Athletic Conference and participates in the NCAA's Division I. The school mascot is the Bison, of which there are actually two, affectionately known as "Big Blue" and "Lady Blue." Unfortunately, the male basketball team's ranking is less than impressive (319th out of 326 teams in 2004). Losing (a lot) hasn't hurt their popularity on campus though. Games still prove to be a large draw. Intercollegiate men's sports include basketball, cross-country, soccer, tennis, football, swimming, wrestling, and track. Women's sports include basketball, tennis, cross-country, track, volleyball, and swimming.

Culture on Campus

The Howard University Gallery of Art offers rotating exhibitions of national and international artists, as well as a permanent collection of African artifacts, Renaissance and Baroque paintings, European prints, and contemporary art.

The Department of Theatre Arts produces dance and drama performances throughout the school year in the Ira Aldridge Theater. Other fine arts majors are offered through the Department of Art and the Department of Music. The university also has several bands and choirs, which perform regularly.

Howard University Television, WHUT-TV, is the only African-American-owned public television station in the country. It has been operating for 28 years and reaches half a million households in the Washington metropolitan area. Howard University also runs commercial radio station WHUR-FM (96.3).

Phone Numbers

Undergraduate Admissions: 202-806-2763
Graduate Affairs & Admissions:. 202-806-7469
College of Arts & Sciences: 202-806-6700
School of Business: 202-806-1500
School of Communications:. 202-806-7690
College of Dentistry:. 202-806-0100
School of Divinity: 202-806-0500
School of Education:. 202-806-7340
College of Engineering, Architecture,
    and Computer Sciences:. 202-806-6565
Graduate School of Arts & Sciences: 202-806-6800
School of Law:. 202-806-8000
College of Medicine:. 202-806-6270
College of Pharmacy, Nursing, and
    Allied Health Sciences: 202-806-6530
School of Social Work: 202-806-7300
Student Affairs:. .202-806-2100
Athletic Department: 202-806-9090
Founders Library:. 202-806-7234

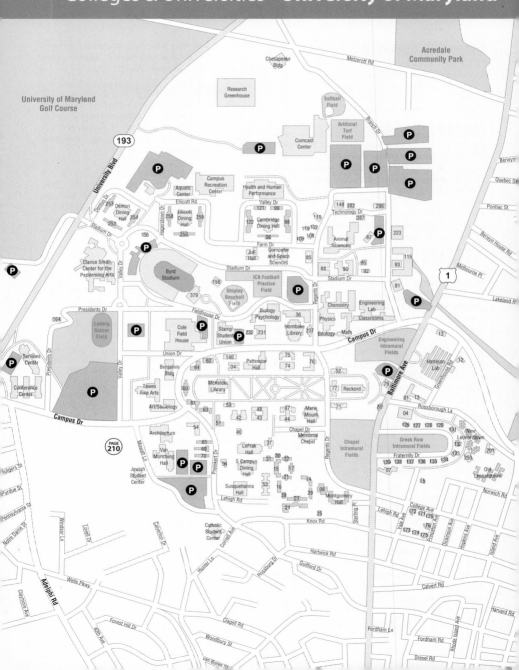

General Information

Address: College Park, MD, 20742
Phone: 301-405-1000
Website: www.umd.edu

Overview

The enormous size of the University of Maryland masks its humble beginnings. First chartered as an agricultural college in March of 1856, the full public university now has more than 34,000 students roaming its 1,500 acres. It's got enough offerings to swallow up the introvert or help them find their hidden passion for organic chemistry, comparative literature, or the mathematical calculations of Dutch painters. If, however, the extroverted student is in need of further stimulation, the school has its own Metro Stop. For a few bucks, the vast city to the south awaits.

Tuition

Undergraduate tuition for the 2004-2005 school year cost $7,410 for in state residents, and $18,710 for non-residents. Room and board averaged around $7,791.

Sports

Terrapin pride has begun to soar in the last several years, following an ACC basketball championship win over the Duke Blue Devils last spring, and a victory at college football's Gator Bowl last winter.

UMD's athletic program is widely recognized as one of the best in the country, for both men and women's sports, and the Terps are one of only 6 schools to have won a national championship in both football and men's basketball.

Culture on Campus

The Clarice Smith Performing Arts Center hosts high profile performers, such as Yo-Yo Ma and the jazz ensemble, The Yellowjackets. Tickets are usually free or, at most, five bucks for students. If you're not enrolled, be prepared to shell out up to $30. 301-405-ARTS; www.claricesmithcenter.umd.edu.

Phone Numbers

Campus Information: 301-405-1000
Undergraduate Admissions: 301-314-8385
Graduate Admissions: 301-405-4198
Bookstore: 301-314-7848
Registrar: 301-314-8249
Bursar: 301-314-9000
Athletic Department: 800-462-TERP
Ticket Office: 301-314-7070
Clark School of Engineering: 301-405-3855
College of Education: 301-405-2344
School of Architecture: 301-405-6284
School of Public Affairs: 301-405-6330
Smith School of Business: 301-405-2286
Art and Humanities: 301-405-2108
Behavioral and Social Sciences: 301-405-1697
Life Sciences: 301-405-2071

1 - Central Heating Plant
4 - Ritchie Coliseum
5 - Service Building Annex
7 - Pocomoke Building
8 - Annapolis Hall
12 - Plant Operations & Maintenance Complex
13 - Shuttle Bus Facility
14 - Harford Hall
15 - Calvert Hall
16 - Baltimore Hall
17 - Cecil Hall
18 - Police Substation
21 - Prince George's Hall
22 - Kent Hall
23 - Washington Hall
24 - Allegany Hall
25 - Charles Hall
28 - Howard Hall
29 - Frederick Hall
30 - Talbot Hall
34 - Jimenez Hall
36 - Plant Science
37 - Shoemaker Building
40 - Morrill Hall
42 - Tydings Hall
43 - Taliaferro Hall
44 - Skinner Building
47 - Woods Hall
48 - Francis Scott Key Hall

51 - Worcester Hall
52 - Mitchell Building Registration Office
53 - Dance Building
54 - Preinkert Field House
59 - Journalism Building
60 - Anne Arundel Hall
61 - Queen Anne's Hall
62 - St. Mary's Hall
63 - Somerset Hall
64 - Dorchester Hall
65 - Carroll Hall
66 - West Education Annex
69 - Wicomico Hall
70 - Caroline Hall
71 - Lee Building
74 - Holzapfel Hall
75 - Shriver Laboratory
76 - Symons Hall
77 - Main Administration
79 - Visitors Center
80 - Rossborough Inn
81 - Wind Tunnel Building
83 - JM Patterson Building
85 - Institute for Physical Science & Technology
87 - Central Animal Resources Facility
90 - Chemical and Nuclear Engineering Building

93 - Engineering Annex
96 - Cambridge Hall
98 - Centreville Hall
99 - Bel Air Hall
102 - Agriculture Shed
108 - Horse Barn
109 - Sheep Barn
110 - Cattle Barn
115 - AV Williams
119 - Blacksmith Shop
121 - Performing Arts Center, Clarice Smith
122 - Cumberland Hall
126 - Kappa Alpha Fraternity
127 - Sigma Alpha Mu Fraternity
128 - Delta Tau Delta Fraternity
129 - Sigma Alpha Epsilon Fraternity
131 - Beta Theta Pi Fraternity
132 - Phi Sigma Kappa Fraternity
133 - Pi Kappa Phi Fraternity
134 - Chi Omega Sorority
135 - Sigma Kappa Sorority
136 - Alpha Epsilon Phi Sorority
137 - Zeta Tau Alpha Sorority
138 - Sigma Phi Epsilon Fraternity
139 - Zeta Beta Tau Fraternity
140 - Health Center

148 - Manufacturing Building
156 - Apiary
158 - Varsity Sports Teamhouse
170 - Alpha Delta Pi Sorority
171 - Phi Kappa Tau Fraternity
172 - Alpha Chi Omega Sorority
173 - Delta Phi Epsilon Sorority
174 - Phi Sigma Sigma Sorority
175 - Delta Gamma Sorority
176 - Alpha Phi Sorority
201 - Leonardtown office building
223 - Energy Research
231 - Microbiology Building
232 - Nyumburu Cultural Center
237 - Geology Building
250 - Leonardtown community center
252 - Denton Hall
253 - Easton Hall
254 - Elkton Hall
256 - Ellicott Hall
258 - Hagerstown Hall
259 - LaPlata Hall
296 - Agriculture/Life Science Surge Building
379 - Football Team Building
382 - Neutral Buoyancy Research Facility
387 - Tap Building

Dream Seats · Concourse · Owner's Club Seats and Press-Box · Joe Gibbs' Club Seats · Suites · Loge

General Information

Address: 1600 FedEx Wy,
Landover, MD 20785
Redskins Website: www.redskins.
com
FedEx Field Website: www.fedex.
com/us/sports/
Stadium Admin: 301-276-6000
Ticket Office: 301-276-6050
Seats: 85,000

Overview

One of the most storied franchises in football, racist nickname notwithstanding, the Washington Redskins no longer actually play in Washington. Much like the New York Jets and Giants, the 'Skins play home games just outside DC, in Prince George's County, Maryland.

FedEx Field was formerly known as the Jack Kent Cooke Stadium, named for the deceased team owner (and ex-L.A. Lakers owner). But in 1999, a corporation dangled a few million carrots in a boardroom and the tribute to the beloved coach, may he rest in peace, became a tribute to overnight shipping.

By 2000, new boy-billionaire owner Daniel Snyder dumped an additional $55 million of improvements into the joint, making it one of the premier facilities of the National Football League. FedEx Field boasts all the amenities you would expect from a modern NFL stadium: luxury boxes, restaurants with a view of the field, and, recently, an unspectacular, overpaid football team. In an attempt to rectify the poor record, Snyder hired former coach/local demigod Joe Gibbs, quarterback Mark Brunell, and running back Clinton Portis. Get your tickets for the Dallas/Parcells Monday night rumble now.

How to Get There – Driving

Take E Capitol Street (Central Ave) to Harry Truman north, then take a right onto Lottsford Road. Follow Lottsford to Arena Drive and you're there. Keep your eyes peeled for the many signs that will direct you to the field.

Parking

FedEx Field provides off-stadium parking that can be as much as $25, with a free shuttle ride to the stadium. The team did their damnedest to prevent fans from parking for free at the nearby Landover Mall and walking to the game, but a Prince George's County judge recently overturned a county policy restricting pedestrian movement in the area. So you can pay up for convenience or exercise your civic rights to park free and schlep.

How to Get There – Mass Transit

Take the Orange Line to the Landover stop or the Blue Line to the Addison Road stop. Five-dollar round-trip shuttle buses depart these stations for FedEx Field every 15 minutes, from 2 hours before the game until 2 hours after.

How to Get Tickets

If you enjoy the prospect of languishing in a years-long line, join the Redskins season ticket waiting list by visiting www.redskinsclub.com/seats/default.aspx. For individual game tickets, call 301-276-6050.

Gate A

PAGE 212

Lower Level   Club Level   Upper Level

General Information

Address:	1101 Russell St, Baltimore, MD 21230
Website:	www.baltimoreravens.com
Phone:	410-261-RAVE
Capacity:	69,084

Overview

M&T Bank Stadium is the modernized home of the Baltimore Ravens, a newer team with an already long, but not entirely illustrious, history. They began as the Cleveland Browns and moved to Baltimore in 1996 to replace the departed Colts. The city christened them the Ravens, based on the famous poem of one-time resident Edgar Allan Poe. The Ravens promptly horrified expansion-phobic NFL fans by winning their first Superbowl in 2001; at the time, MVP Ray Lewis was on probation for his involvement in a double murder. More recently, running back Jamal Lewis set the NFL record for rushing yards in a game in 2003, finished the season with the second highest total yards in NFL history, and was indicted on federal drug charges.

Moving beyond the personal headlines of its players, M&T Bank Stadium is a state-of-the-art facility with a nice view of the Baltimore skyline. Situated next door to the Camden Yards, it's within walking distance of the city's Inner Harbor and a gauntlet of sports bars.

How to Get There – Driving

Take I-95 N towards Baltimore. Take Exit 52 to Russell Street (heading north) and the stadium is on the right.

Parking

M&T Bank provides parking, for which you need to buy a permit ahead of time. There are 15,000 spaces worth of public parking nearby.

How to Get There – Mass Transit

Your only choice on the weekends is the 703 MTA bus that runs from Greenbelt Metro Station to Camden Yards for $9.

How to Get Tickets

To purchase tickets, visit the Ravens' website at www.baltimoreravens.com, or call 410-261-RAVE. Tickets can also be purchased through TicketMaster (www.ticketmaster.com).

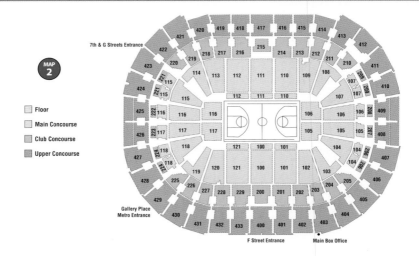

7th & G Streets Entrance

MAP 2

- Floor
- Main Concourse
- Club Concourse
- Upper Concourse

Gallery Place
Metro Entrance

F Street Entrance   Main Box Office

General Information

NFT Map: 2
Address: 601 F Street, NW,
                        Washington, DC 20004
Wizards Website: www.washingtonwizards.com
Capitals Website: www.washingtoncaps.com
Mystics Website: www.washingtonmystics.com
Georgetown Basketball Website: www.guhoyas.com
MCI Center Website: www.MCIcenter.com
Wizards Phone: 202-661-5100
Capitals Phone: 202-266-2200
Mystics Phone: 202-661-5000
Georgetown Basketball Phone:
                        202-687-HOYA
MCI Center Phone: 202-628-3200

Overview

DC's new MCI Center reversed a decades-old trend of arenas planting roots in the suburbs by bringing it all back to the 'hood. The stadium is now a centerpiece to a booming urban revitalization.

In addition to the Caps and the artists-formerly-known-as-the-Bullets, the MCI Center also hosts the Washington Mystics, who yield the largest fan base in the WNBA. Georgetown basketball also calls the center home. Beyond the ballers, MCI Center hosts concerts, circuses, and circus-y concerts like Britney Spears and the traveling American Idol show.

How to Get There – Driving

From downtown, turn left onto 7th Street from either Constitution Avenue or New York Avenue. The MCI Center is on the corner of F and 7th.

Parking

You're on your own. There's a lot of parking around, but, unless you're a season ticket holder, it's not supplied by the MCI Center. Garage prices range from $8 to $12.

How to Get There – Mass Transit

MCI Center is accessible by the Metro's Red, Yellow, and Green Lines, with a stop at Gallery Place/Chinatown.

How to Get Tickets

Tickets for all MCI Center events are available through the Ticketmaster website at www.ticketmaster.com or by calling 202-432-SEAT, 703-573-SEAT, or 410-481-SEAT. Wizards tickets range from $10 to $175 for an individual game, Caps tickets will run you $10-$230, Mystics tickets range from $8 to $50, and Hoyas tickets are between $5 and $35. All teams offer season and multi-game ticket packages. Check out individual team websites for prices.

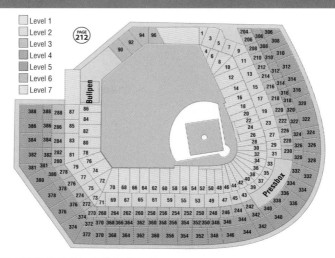

Level 1
Level 2
Level 3
Level 4
Level 5
Level 6
Level 7

General Information

Address: 333 W Camden St, Baltimore, MD 21201
Website: www.theorioles.com
Phone: 410-685-9800
Capacity: 48,876

Overview

Oriole Park at Camden Yards opened in 1992 and launched the old-school-charm trend that continues to this day and, in the face of dozens of corporations eager to smear their names across the park, the Orioles have refused to budge. All brick and history, the Yards stand downtown atop a former railroad center, two blocks from Babe Ruth's birthplace. Center field sits atop the site where the Bambino's father ran a bar. The goods include double-decker bullpens, a sunken, asymmetrical field, and "Boog's BBQ," run by ex-Oriole, Boog Powell, who is known to occasionally man the grill himself.

Sadly, in terms of the actual play at Camden Yards, we've seen little more than Cal Ripken honored for a sterling attendance record (that's our take—don't suggest to Baltimore fans that the reason Cal was so revered was merely for showing up so often). The Birds, unlike their stadium, haven't been much to look at in recent years, although 2004 was a bit of an improvement. New additions, such as shortstop and 2002 American League MVP Miguel Tejada, catcher Javy Lopez, pitcher Sidney Ponson, returning first baseman/Viagra shill Rafael Palmeiro, and manager Lee Mazzilli, have Baltimore looking stronger in the Yanks/Sox dominated American League East.

Meanwhile, DC is trying to lure a team closer to home. The mayor is lobbying hard to bring the Montreal Expos to the city, with suburban Arlington and exurban Loudon County also vying for the, uh, honor. Maybe Mayor Williams could get Boog to come along too. Stay tuned.

How to Get There – Driving

Take MD 295 (B-W Pkwy/Russell St) to downtown Baltimore, which gets very congested on game days. You can also take I-95 North to Exits 53 (I-395), 52 (Russell St), or 52 (Washington Blvd) and follow signs to the park.

Parking

Parking at Camden Yards is reserved, but there are several public garages nearby. Prices range from $3 to $6.

How to Get There – Mass Transit

Take the MARC from Union Station in DC to Camden Station in Baltimore. It takes about an hour and ten minutes and costs $5.75, but the last train leaves at 6:30 pm. To return from a night game, the 701 MTA bus will get you home in 50-minutes for free with your Baltimore-bound MARC ticket.

The weekends are another story. Your only choice here is the 703 MTA bus that runs from Greenbelt Metro Station to Camden Yards for $9.

How to Get Tickets

Orioles tickets can be purchased at their website, www.theorioles.com, or by calling 410-685-9800. Individual game tickets range from $8 to $55. Group and season tickets are also available.

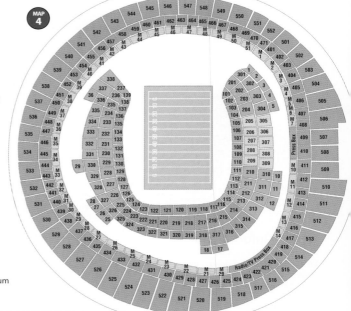

MAP 4

Premium

VIP

Spectator

Mezzanine

Upper Level

General Information

NFT Map: 4
Address: 2400 E Capitol St SE,
Washington, DC 20003
Websites: www.dcunited.com
www.dcsec.com/rfk_stadium
Phone: 202-547-9077
Capacity: 56,000

Overview

Opened in 1961 as DC Stadium, the District's premier sports stadium for three decades was renamed Robert F. Kennedy Stadium in 1969 after Senator Kennedy was killed. RFK Stadium has hosted a wide range of events over the years, from concerts to gigantic religious convocations to sporting events. Most famously, it was home to the Washington Redskins until after the 1996 season, when they moved to FedEx Field.

The stadium is a local favorite for sentimental reasons. From the 1961 to 1996 seasons, football legends like Joe Gibbs, John Riggins, Joe Thiesmann, Vince Lombardi, Art Monk, and George Allen patrolled the RFK gridiron and sidelines. The Redskins played in five Superbowls during that time, with three titles to show for it.

The expansion Washington Senators of Major League Baseball (and "Damn Yankees" fame) also played in RFK stadium from 1962 to 1971, after which they moved to Arlington, Texas and become the Rangers.

RFK Stadium is now home to DC United, participants in the fledgling Major League Soccer competition. United has put together an impressive resume in a short period of time, winning the MLS Cup Championship in 1996, 1997, and 1999, and cementing a promising future by recently signing 14-year-old wunderkind Freddy Adu.

How to Get There – Driving

Follow Constitution Avenue east past the Capitol to Maryland Avenue. Turn left on Maryland and go two blocks to Stanton Square. At Stanton Square, turn right onto Massachusetts Avenue. Go around Lincoln Park to E Capitol Street and turn right.

Parking

RFK Stadium provides parking, but it ain't free. It'll cost you between $3 and $10 to park, depending on the event.

How to Get There – Mass Transit

Take the Metro to the Stadium-Armory Station on the Blue and Orange lines.

How to Get Tickets

For United tickets, call 703-478-6600. All RFK events, including United soccer, can be purchased at www.ticketmaster.com.

General Information

Washington Area Bicyclist Association
  www.waba.org
Bike Washington   www.bikewashington.org
Bike the Sites Bicycle Tours
  www.bikethesites.com
C&O Canal Towpath www.nps.gov/choh
Capitol Crescent Trail www.cctrail.org
Mount Vernon Trail www.nps.gov/gwmp/
  mvt.html

Overview

A bike here is as necessary as a political affiliation. The city caters to mountain and road bikers with plenty of natural trails, a few good urban commuting routes, and one massive citywide bike ride in the fall. The Metrobus and Metrorail have lenient policies that also help when a bike route, or your energy, dead-ends.

Commuting by bike is doable, but may be dicey. What DC offers bikers in the way of amenities, it lacks in bike lanes. State law mandates that cyclists have to follow traffic laws, meaning that you have to mix it up with the cars. Helmets are mandatory and, if you're going to take to the streets, you really should wear one (your mother was right). Even though DC residents are an honest bunch, it's a good idea to keep your bike locked whenever you're out of its sight. For more information regarding bicycle commuting, check out the Washington Area Bicyclist Association website. The site can also tell you about the annual "Bike DC."

Bike Trails

The **Chesapeake and Ohio (C&O) Canal** is probably the most popular biking destination in the city. The trail spans over 184 miles and most of it is unpaved, so it's not a trail for the weak of butt. The trail follows the route of the Potomac River from DC to Cumberland Maryland, mile 0 starting in Georgetown. Know that biking is only permitted on the towpath. If you are interested in doing the full 184 miles, campsites are located from Swains Lock to Seneca. With the first 20 miles being the most heavily used, conditions within the Beltway are significantly better than those outside of it.

The **Capital Crescent Trail** is a "rail trail," a bike trail converted from abandoned or unused railroad tracks. The trail spans 11 miles beginning in Georgetown and ending in Silver Springs, Maryland. The first 7 miles, from Georgetown to Bethesda,

is pretty gentle with its 10 ft-wide asphalt paths. On weekdays, the trail is predominantly used by commuters, but on weekends it's full of recreational cyclists and rollerbladers.

The **Mount Vernon Trail** offers a wide range of scenic views of the Potomac River and national monuments to ensure a stimulating bike ride. The 18.5-mile trail stretches from Roosevelt Island through Old Town Alexandria to George Washington's house in Mount Vernon. To find out more about these and other bike trails, check out the Bike Washington web site.

Bikes and Mass Transit

If you need a break, you can hop off your bike and take it on a bus or on Metrorail for free. All 1,450 Washington, DC buses have recently been equipped with racks to carry up to two bikes per bus. You can also ride the Metrorail with your wheels all day on weekends and most of the day on weekdays. Rush hours are off limits (7 am–10 am and 4 pm–7 pm). Also be sure to use elevators when accessing the Metrorail—blocking the stairs and escalators with your bulky bike makes officials and non-biking commuters testy.

Bike Shops

- **A&A Discount Bicycles** (sales, repair, and rental) • 1034 33rd St NW • 202-337-0254 • Map 18
- **Better Bikes** (rental and delivery) • 202-293-2080 • www.betterbikesinc.com
- **Bicycle Pro Shop** (sales, repair, and rental) • 3403 M St NW • 202-337-0311 www.bicycleproshop.com • Map 18
- **Big Wheel Bikes** (sales, repair, and rental) • 1034 33rd St NW • 202-337-0254 • www.bigwheelbikes.com • Map 18
- **Capitol Hill Bikes** (sales, repair, and rental) • 709 8th St SE • 202-544-4234 • http://capitolhillbikes.com • Map 5
- **City Bikes** (sales, repair, and rental) • 2501 Champlain St NW • 202-265-1564 • http://citybikes.com • Map 16
- **District Hardware/The Bike Shop** (sales and repair) • 2003 P St NW • 202-659-8686 • Map 9
- **Hudson Trail Outfitters** (sales and repair) • 4530 Wisconsin Ave NW • 202-363-9810 • www.hudsontrail.com • Map 19
- **Revolution Cycles** (sales, repair, and rental) • 3411 M St NW • 202-965-3637 • http://revolutioncycles.com • Map 18

General Information

DC Department of Parks and Recreation: http://dc.gov
Roadsters (DC skating club):   www.skatedc.org

Overview

Plenty of marble and asphalt means plenty of room to roll around. The vast expanses of public land and park space here are great for inline skates, boards, and blades.

Inline Skating

DC's Washington Area Roadsters offer free weekly inline skate clinics during spring and summer and group skates several times a week. Rock Creek Park's 3.6-mile Beach Drive is closed to vehicular traffic on weekends and holidays, making it the perfect place to skate unimpeded by traffic lights and vehicles. The 3.2-mile paved loop of Ohio Drive in East Potomac Park is also a good bet. If the weather is grim, the Franconia Roller Rink in Alexandria is open from 7 pm-10 pm Sunday through Thursday, and 7 pm-11pm on Fridays and Saturdays, 703-971-3334.

Commuting by skates can be surprisingly convenient. They're easier to store than a bicycle, but can be more dangerous if you're venturing onto city streets.

Skate Parks

After years of hostile restrictions and citations against the grinding of skaters outside capital buildings, a skate park was finally built in the Shaw neighborhood in the fall of 2003. It's free and located on 11th Street and Rhode Island Avenue. 202-282-0758 – Map10.

Other skate parks in the DC area:

Alexandria Skate Park • 3540 Wheeler Ave, Alexandria, 703-838-4343/4344 • Map 42

The Powhatan Springs Park • 6020 Wilson Blvd, Arlington • 703-228-3337 • Map33
A 15,000-square-foot park, featuring 8'- and 6'-deep bowls and 4' and 6' half-pipes is set to open this year.

Ice-Skating

Finding natural outdoor ice to skate on in DC is difficult. But sometimes, during particularly cold winters, the National Park Service allows ice-skating on the C&O Canal. The ice has to be more than 3" thick, so it has to be *really* cold. The National Park Service hotline provides information on skate-safe areas: 301-767-3707.

Skating at the National Gallery of Art's Sculpture Garden ice-skating rink may not be the same as skating on natural ice, but it's pretty cool to skate in the middle of an art exhibit. Every Thursday night, from December to March, you can skate to live jazz from 5 pm to 8 pm. The rink is open every day from October through March, Monday-Saturday 10 am to 11 pm, Sunday 10 am to 9 pm. Admission for a two-hour session is $6 for adults and $5 for children, students, and seniors. Skate rental is $2.50 and a locker rental is 50¢; 700 Constitution Avenue NW; 202-737-4215 – Map 2.

While the Sculpture Garden rink turns into a fountain once the warm weather arrives, the NHL-sized rink at Mt. Vernon Recreation Center in Alexandria operates year-round. The rink provides ice-hockey lessons, recreational skating lessons, and adult hockey leagues for all levels. On Friday nights, the rink brings in a DJ for teen Rock and Blade skating. Rates and fees vary, so call before you go. 2017 Belle View Boulevard, Alexandria; 703-324-8702.

Other ice-skating rinks are located seasonally at:

Pershing Park Ice Rink • Pennsylvania Ave & 14 St NW • 202-737-6938 • Map 1
$5.50-$6.50 admission + $2.50 rental

Pentagon Row • 1101 S Joyce St, Arlington • 703-418-6666 • Map 40
$6-$7 admission + $3 rental

Bethesda Metro Ice Center • 3 Bethesda Metro Ctr, Bethesda • 301-656-0588 • Map 29

Gear

The Ski Chalet has a comprehensive selection of performance inline skates and offers tune-ups and rentals. Skates can be rented by the hour ($5) or by the day ($15). The Ski Chalet is located at 2704 Columbia Pike, Arlington; 703-521-1700 – Map 37

The Ski Center, located at 4300 Fordham Road, NW, sells reasonably priced ice and inline skates. This shop, which has been serving the DC area since 1959, also rents equipment. 202-966-4474 – Map 30

For skateboarding equipment, check out the Evolve Board Shop at 4856 Bethesda Avenue in Bethesda. While this shop is primarily for snowboarders, it also stocks skateboard equipment and gear. 301-654-1510 – Map 29

Sailing/Boating/Rowing

Boating has a surprisingly passionate following here. As the weather warms, the Potomac River and the Tidal Basin swarm with sailboats, kayaks, and paddleboats.

The Potomac River runs 285 miles, forming part of the boundary between Maryland and West Virginia and separating Virginia from both Maryland and DC. It was also the unofficial boundary between the North and South during the Civil War. Industrialization seriously degraded the water quality, but efforts by the government and citizens have made the water safe for boats. Swimming? Well, we don't suggest it.

The Mariner Sailing School (703-768-0018) gives lessons and rents canoes, kayaks, and sailboats for two to six people.

If you don't mind elbowing out tourists for the thrill of a paddleboat ride, the Tidal Basin is your best bet. It's an artificial inlet, surrounded by cherry trees and flower beds bearing tulips in the spring. Paddleboats can be rented at the boathouse on the east bank (202-484-0206).

Fletcher's Boat House (202-244-0461), a beloved, if gritty, institution since the 1850s, rents rowboats and canoes for $11/hour. They also sell fishing licenses and various baits if you want to attempt to catch dinner.

Sailing/Boating Centers	Address	Phone	Map	URL
Capitol Sailboat Club	James Creek Marina, Washington, DC	202-265-3052	6	www.capitolsbc.com
DC Sail	2000 Half St SW, Washington, DC		6	www.dcsail.org
Tidal Basin Boat House	1501 M Ave SW, Washington, DC	202-484-0206	6	
Fletcher's Boat House	4940 Canal Rd NW, Washington, DC	202-244-0461	18	www.fletchersboathouse.com
Mariner Sailing School	Belle Haven Marina, Alexandria, VA	703-768-0018	N/A	www.saildc.org
Sailing Club of Washington	5945 Norham Dr, Alexandria, VA	202-628-7245	N/A	www.scow.org

Rowing Clubs	Address	Phone	Map	URL
Capitol Rowing Club	1115 O St SE, Washington DC	202-289-6666	5	www.capitalrowing.org
DC Strokes Rowing Club	Anacostia Community Boathouse		5	www.dcstrokes.org
Potomac Boat Club	3530 Water St NW, Washington, DC	202-333-9737	8	www.rowpbc.net
Canoe Cruisers Association	11301 Rockville Pike, Washington, DC	301-251-2978	N/A	www.ccada.org/cca

Golf

In a city obsessed with hierarchy, great importance is placed on where you stroll the greens. Your best bet is to avoid the pricey rat race at the private clubs and reserve a tee time at one of the many, and often more fun, public courses.

East Potomac Park has three different course options (Red, White, and Blue, of course) as well as miniature golf, a driving range, and a store. The Langston Golf Course is close to downtown DC, making it easy to fit in a quick 9-holer. The Rock Creek Golf Course can sometimes suffer from droughts and heavy play, but its location makes it very popular.

Golf Courses	Address	Phone	Map	Type	Fees
East Potomac Golf Courses	972 Ohio Dr SW	202-554-7660	6	Public	9 Holes—WD $8-$14/ WE $11-17
Langston Golf Course	2600 Benning Rd NE	202-397-8638	12	Public	9 Holes—WD $12.50/ WE $15.50
Sligo Creek Golf Course	9701 Sligo Creek Pkwy	301-585-6006	25	Public	9 Holes—WD-$14.50/ WE $24.50
Rock Creek Golf Course	16th & Rittenhouse NW	202-882-7332	27	Public	9 Holes—WD $12.50/ WE $15.50
Washington Golf and Country Club	3017 N Glebe Rd	703-524-4600	31	Private	Membership
Army Navy Country Club	2400 S 18th St	703-521-6800	40	Private	Membership
Belle Haven Country Club	6023 Fort Hunt Rd	703-329-1448	-	Private	Membership
Congressional Country Club	8500 River Rd	301-469-2032	-	Private	Membership
Greendale Golf Course	6700 Telegraph Rd	703-971-6170	-	Public	9 Holes—WD $17/ WE $21
Hilltop Golf Club	7900 Telegraph Rd	703-719-6504	-	Public	9 Holes—WD $24/ WE $28
Leisure World Golf Club	3701 Rossmoor Blvd	301-598-1570	-	Private	Membership
Mount Vernon Country Club	5111 Old Mill Rd	703-780-3565	-	Private	Membership
Pinecrest Golf Course	6600 Little River Turnpike	703-941-1061	-	Public	9 Holes—WD $13/ WE $15

Driving Ranges	Address	Phone	Map	Fees
East Potomac Driving Range	972 Ohio Dr SW	202-554-7660	6	$4.50
Langston Driving Range	2600 Benning Rd NE	202-397-8638	12	$4.50

PENNSYLVANIA

30

16

Catoctin
Mountain
Park

70

81

520

ALT
40

67

15

MARYLAND

WEST VIRGINIA

Harper's
Ferry

70

50

340

Appalachian Trail

270

95

7

522

15

1

50

495

PAGE
204

Rock
Creek
Park

50

81

66

395

Washington DC

522

211

VIRGINIA

95

Shenandoah
National Park

522

29

17

340

33

15

522

Potomac River

29

64

33

6

Overview

One of the best aspects of living in hyper-Type-A DC is how easy it is to get away from it. The ease of leaving behind urbanity for a weekend or just an afternoon is a great amenity. A lush urban park winds its way through the city, and you'll find some of the best hiking routes in the country just outside of town. The National Parks Service website is a valuable resource for planning your hikes (www.nps.gov), and we recommend the gem *60 Hikes Within 60 Miles: Washington, DC* by Paul Elliott (Menasha Ridge Press).

Shenandoah National Park

A short drive out of DC, this is one of the country's most popular national parks, mainly because of the gorgeous Skyline Drive that runs across the top of the ridgeline. Locals know to ditch the wheels, get out, and get dirty. There are 500 miles of trails—enough to lose yourself for a backbreaking week if you get the urge. Otherwise, it's filled with day hikes and overnight backpacking trails that meander through the enormous, well-maintained park.

The Old Rag Trail, with its rock scramble and distinctive profile, is a favorite strenuous day hike. The rangers at the visitor centers will direct you to the toughest climbs, easier routes, the waterfall hikes, or the trails where you'll most likely see bears. The park is 70 miles west of DC. Take Route 66 W to Exit 13 and follow signs to Front Royal. Information is available on the National Parks website at www.nps.gov/shen.

Appalachian Trail

Forget what you've heard about lugging a summer's worth of misery along this Georgia to Maine trail. You don't have to hike the whole thing. Luckily, a good portion of this nationally protected 2,174-mile Appalachian Mountains traverse is accessible near DC. Hook up with it for a few miles at points in Maryland and Virginia and acquire bragging rights with just a day's worth of blister-inducing pain. A good place to start is Harper's Ferry in Maryland, 65 miles from DC—here you can load up on breakfast and some history before you head out. When you return, hoist a well-deserved pint. Information is available on the National Parks website at www.nps.gov/appa.

Catoctin Mountains

While the Catoctin Mountains are home to presidential retreat Camp David, the compound isn't open to the public; you can't even get a peek at it. But you can get a taste of why presidents seem to like it better out here than at the White House. From DC, it's about a two-hour drive. Take the George Washington Memorial Parkway north to the Beltway to I-270 N. Drive 27 miles to Frederick, MD. Take Route 15 N to Route 77 W, to the Catoctin Mountain Park exit. Drive three miles west on 77, turn right onto Park Central Road, and the Visitor Center is on the right.

Rock Creek Park

This is the place for a quick nature fix. The park itself grows between downtown and Maryland in the northwest region of the city. It's laced with several hiking trails, especially in the northern reaches. The major trails follow the western ridge, marked by a green blaze, and the east side, marked by a blue blaze. A tan-blazed trail connects the two. None of the trails are strenuous and all can be tailored to fit a lunch break schedule.

Chandra Levy's murder notwithstanding, the trails tend to be safe and well-trod. But Rock Creek is an urban park, so lugging along a cell phone or a hiking partner ain't a bad idea. Driving from downtown DC, take the Rock Creek and Potomac Parkway north to Beach Drive. Exit and head north to Broad Branch Road. Make a left and then a right onto Glover Road, and follow the signs to the Nature Center, where trail maps are available. See page 204.

The following fees for public pools are based on county residency. Admission is higher for non-residents.

Outdoor pools are open daily from June 23 and close late August or early September. Many of the public pools require you to register as a member at the beginning of the season and, since they have quotas that are reached quickly, it is wise to locate your nearest pool and join at the beginning of the season. Our best advice is to call before you go if you decide to head out for a spontaneous swim and you are not familiar with your proposed pool destination.

Pools

	Address	Phone	Map	Type—Fees
Washington				
William Rumsey Aquatic Center	635 N Carolina Ave SE	202-724-4495	3	Indoor—$4 per day, $130 season pass
Rosedale Pool	17th & Gales St NE	202-727-1502	4	Outdoor—$4 per day, $130 season pass
Barry Farms Pool	1223 Sumner Rd SE	202-645-5041	5	Outdoor—$4 per day, $130 season pass
East Potomac Pool	972 Ohio Dr SW	202-727-6523	6	Opening soon—call for fees
Randall Pool	S Capitol St & I St SW	202-727-1420	6	Outdoor—$4 per day, $130 season pass
Waterside Fitness & Swim Club	901 6th St SW	202-488-3701	6	Indoor and outdoor—$10 per day
Sport & Health Club	2650 Virginia Ave NW	202-298-4460	7	Indoor—$98 per month, $250 joiner fee
The Fitness Company	2401 M St NW	202-457-5070	9	Indoor—$25 per day
YMCA National Capital	1711 Rhode Island Ave NW	202-862-9622	9	Indoor—$15 per day, $55 per month membership, $100 joiner fee
YMCA	1325 W Street NW	202-462-1054	10	Indoor—$70 per year membership
Dunbar Pool	1301 New Jersey Ave NW	202-673-4316	11	Indoor—$4 per day, $130 season pass
Harry Thomas Pool	Lincoln Rd & Seaton Pl NE	202-576-5640	11	Outdoor—$4 per day, $130 season pass
Fort Lincoln Outdoor Pool	31st & Fort Lincoln Dr NE	202-576-6389	13	Outdoor—$4 per day, $130 season pass
Langdon Park Pool	Mills Ave & Hamlin St NE	202-576-8655	13	Outdoor—$4 per day, $130 season pass
Banneker Pool	2500 Georgia Rd SE	202-673-2121	15	Outdoor—free
Marie H Reed Center Pool	2200 Champlain St NW	202-673-7771	16	Indoor—$4 per day, $130 season pass
Georgetown Pool	3400 Volta Pl NW	202-282-2366	18	Outdoor—$4 per day, $130 season pass
Sport & Health Club	4000 Wisconsin Ave NW	202-362-8000	19	Indoor—$100 per month membership
Wilson Pool	3950 Chesapeake St NW	202-282-2216	19	Indoor—$4 per day, $130 season pass
Upshur Outdoor Pool	14th St NW & Arkansas Ave NW	202-727-1503	21	Outdoor—$4 per day, $130 season pass
Takoma Outdoor Pool	4th & Van Buren St NW	202-576-8660	27	Outdoor—$4 per day, $130 season pass
Anacostia Outdoor Pool	Pennsylvania Ave Bridge & 11th	202-724-1441	–	Outdoor—$3 per day, $130 season pass (open weekends)
Benning Park Outdoor Pool	53rd & Fitch St SE	202-645-5044	–	Outdoor—$4 per day, $130 season pass
Douglass Outdoor Pool	19th St & Stanton Ter SE	202-645-5045	–	Outdoor—$4 per day, $130 season pass
Ferebee Hope Community	8th & Yuma St SE	202-645-3916	–	Indoor—$4 per day, $130 season pass
Fort Dupont Outdoor Pool	Ridge Rd SE & Burns St SE	202-645-5046	–	Outdoor—$4 per day, $130 season pass
Fort Stanton Outdoor Pool	1800 Erie St SE	202-645-5047	–	Outdoor—$4 per day, $130 season pass
Francis Outdoor Pool	25th & N St SE	202-727-3285	–	Outdoor—$3 per day, $100 season pass
Kelly Miller Outdoor Pool	49th St NE & Brooks St NE	202-724-5056	–	Outdoor—$4 per day, $130 season pass
Kenilworth-Parkside Pool	4300 Anacostia Ave NE	202-727-0635	–	Outdoor—$4 per day, $130 season pass
Oxon Run Outdoor Pool	6th St & Mississippi Ave	202-645-5042	–	Outdoor—$4 per day, $130 season pass
Arlington				
Upton Hill Regional Park	6060 Wilson Blvd	703-534-3437	33	Outdoor—$5.25 per day, $67 for season pass
Yorktown Swimming Pool	5201 N 28th St	703-532-9739	33	Indoor—$3.50 per day, $220 per year
Washington-Lee Swimming Pool	1300 N Quincy St	703-228-6262	34	Indoor—$3.50 per day, $220 per year
YMCA	3422 N 13th St	703-525-5420	35	Outdoor—$45 per month membership, $100 joiner fee
Wakefield Swimming Pool	4901 S Chesterfield Rd	703-578-3063	38	Indoor—$3.50 per day, $220 per year
YMCA	3440 S 22nd St	703-892-2044	39	Outdoor—$75 per month membership, $100 joiner fee

Pools—*continued*

	Address	Phone	Map	Type—Fees
Alexandria				
Chinquapin Park Rec Center	3210 King St	703-519-2160	42	Indoor—$5 per day, $46 per month
Warwick Pool	3301 Landover St	703-838-4672	43	Outdoor—$2 per day
YMCA	420 E Monroe Ave	703-838-8085	43	Indoor—$15 per day, $67 per month membership, $100 joiner fee
Old Town Pool	1609 Cameron St	703-838-4671	44	Outdoor—$2 per day
George Washington Rec Center	8426 Old Mount Vernon Rd	703-780-8894	–	Indoor—$6.20 per day, $548.50 for year pass
Lee District Rec Center	6601 Telegraph Rd	703-768-9796	–	Indoor—$6.20 per day, $548.50 for year pass
Mount Vernon Rec Center	2017 Belle View Blvd	703-768-3224	–	Indoor—$6.20 per day, $548.50 for year pass
Bethesda				
YMCA	9401 Old Georgetown Rd	301-530-3725	22	Indoor—$62 per month membership, $100 joiner fee
Sport & Health Club	4400 Montgomery Ave	301-656-9570	29	Indoor—$25 per day, $90 per month membership
Bethesda Outdoor Pool	Little Falls Dr	301-652-1598	30	Outdoor—$5.50 per day, $160 for year pass
Mohican Swimming Pool	7117 MacArthur Blvd	301-229-4953	–	By membership—get in quickly, they sell out early in the season
Old Georgetown Swim Pool	9600 Fernwood Rd	301-469-9772	–	Outdoor—$375 for summer pass, $320 per year with $540 joiner fee
Montgomery Aquatic Center	5900 Executive Blvd	301-468-4211	–	Indoor—$5.50 per day, $230 for year pass
Silver Spring				
Long Branch Swimming Pool	8700 Piney Branch Rd	301-431-5700	–	Outdoor—$5.50 per day, $160 for year pass
Wheaton-Glenmont Outdoor Pool	12621 Dalewood Dr	301-929-5460	–	Outdoor—$5.50 per day, $160 for year pass
Martin Luther King Jr Swim Center	1201 Jackson St NE	301-989-1206	14	Indoor/Outdoor—$5.50 per day, $325 for year pass
YMCA	9800 Hastings Dr	301-585-2120	25	Indoor/Outdoor—$62 per month membership, $100 joiner fee
Takoma Park				
Piney Branch Pool	7510 Maple Ave,	301-270-6093	26	Indoor

Kids' pools*

			Map
Lincoln Capper Pool	500 L St SE	202-727-1080	5
Barry Farm Pool	1223 Sumner Rd SE	202-645-5041	5
J O Wilson Pool	7th St NE & K St NE	202-727-1505	11
Trinidad Pool	Childress St &	202-727-1503	12
Parkview Pool	Warder St &	202-576-8658	15
Deanwood Pool	49th & Brooke St	202-727-9583	–
Parkside Pool	711 Anacostia Ave NE	202-727-1100	–
Riggs-La Salle Pool	Riggs Rd & Nicholson St NE	202-576-8659	–
Woodson Junior Pool	42nd & Foote St NE	202-727-1506	–

* Under 6 free, ages 6-17 $3 per day, $46 season pass

Bowling

Bowling alleys in the Washington metro area tend to offer the four B's: Bowling, Beer, Blacklights, and Beyonce. Yup, clubs aren't the only places where you can toss a few back and shake your groove thang. After dark, many of the alleys offer "Cosmic Bowling," "Xtreme Bowling," or whatever the alley's trademark happens to be. The music goes up and the lights and pins go down. Because of the DJ and added atmosphere, bowling fees generally go up a buck or so.

Strike Bethesda offers unlimited bowling on Mondays from 8 pm to 2 am for only $15. Don't forget to have a drink from their two 30-foot long, fully stocked bars. Alcohol improves your game. We swear. If the thought of thumping bass drums and disco lights gives you a headache, try your hand at Duckpin Bowling, a version of the sport using miniature pins and balls. The sport originated in Baltimore and can be found at White Oak Bowling Lanes and AMF College Park, home to the Men's Duckpin Pro Bowlers' Association Master Tournament.

Bowling Alley	Address	Phone	Fees	Map
Bowl America – Silver Spring	8616 Cameron St, Silver Spring, MD	301-585-6990	$2-5 per game, $3.25 for shoes	25
Seminary Lanes	4620 Kenmore Ave, Alexandria, VA	703-823-6200	$1.50-$5.00 per game, $3.40 for shoes	41
Bowl America – Duke	100 S Pickett St, Alexandria, VA	703-751-1900	$2-5 per game, $3.25 for shoes	41
US Bowling	100 S Pickett St, Alexandria, VA	703-370-5910	$3-4.50 per game, $2.87 for shoes	41
Alexandria Bowling Center	6228 N Kings Hwy, Alexandria, VA	703-765-3633	$3.25-5.00 per game, $3.40 for shoes	-
AMF College Park	9021 Baltimore Ave, College Park, MD	301-474-8282	$3.25 per game, $3.25 for shoes	-
AMF Bowl America – Shirley	6450 Edsall Rd, Alexandria, VA	703-354-3300	$2-5 per game, $3.25 for shoes	-
Bowl America – Chantilly	4525 Stonecroft Blvd, Chantilly, VA	703-830-2695	$2-5 per game, $3.25 for shoes	-
Bowl America – Fairfax	9699 Lee Hwy, Fairfax, VA	703-273-7700	$2-5 per game, $3.25 for shoes	-
Bowl America – Falls Church	140 S Maple Ave, Falls Church, VA	703-533-8131	$2-5 per game, $3.25 for shoes	-
Strike Bethesda	5353 Westbard Ave, Bethesda, MD	301-652-0955	$5.45-6.25 per game, $4 for shoes	-
White Oak Bowling Lanes	11207 New Hampshire Ave, Silver Spring, MD	301-593-3000	$2.50-3.25 per game, $2.50 for shoes	-

Tennis

National Park Service • 202-208-6843 • www.nps.gov
Washington, DC Department of Parks and Recreation •
202-673-7665 • http://dpr.dc.gov

Public Courts at Community Recreation Centers

Residents can play tennis at any one of the listed locations throughout the city. All courts are available on a first-come, first-served basis for one-hour intervals, unless a permit has been issued for extended use. Information on regulation, lessons, tournaments, or other special uses can be obtained from the Sports Office of the Department of Parks and Recreation (202-698-2250).

Courts	Address	Phone	Map
Langston	2209 H St NE	202-727-5430	4
Rosedale	17th St & Gale St NE	202-724-5405	4
Barry Farm	1230 Sumner Rd SE	202-645-3896	5
King-Greenleaf	201 N St SW	202-727-5454	6
Randall	S Capitol St & I St SW	202-727-5505	6
Rose Park	26th St & O St NW	202-282-2208	8
Shaw	10th St & Rhode Island Ave NW	202-673-7255	10
Edgewood	Third St & Evart St NE	202-576-6410	11
Arboretum	24th St & Rand Pl NE	202-727-5547	12
Fort Lincoln	3100 Ft Lincoln Dr NE	202-576-6818	13
Taft	18th St & Perry St NE	202-576-7634	13
Banneker	2500 Georgia Ave NW	202-673-6861	15
Raymond	10th St & Spring Rd NW	202-576-6856	15
Hardy	45th & Q Sts NW	202-282-2190	18
Friendship	4500 Van Ness St NW	202-282-2198	19

Courts	Address	Phone	Map
Hearst	37th St & Tilden St NW	202-282-2207	19
Fort Stevens	1327 Van Buren St NW	202-541-3754	27
Takoma	3rd St & Van Buren St NW	202-576-6854	27
Chevy Chase	4101 Livingston St NW	202-282-2200	28
Lafayette	33rd St & Patterson St NW	202-282-2206	28
Palisades	5200 Sherier Pl NW	202-282-2186	32
Bald Eagle	1000 Joliet St SW	202-645-3960	–
Benning Park	53rd St & Fitch St SE	202-645-3953	–
Benning Stoddert	100 Stoddert Pl SE	202-645-3956	–
Congress Heights	Alabama Ave & Randle Pl SE	202-645-3981	–
Douglass Community Center	19th St & Stanton Terr SE	202-698-2342	–
Evans	5600 E Capitol St SE	202-727-5548	–
Fort Davis	1400 41st St SE	202-645-3975	–
Hillcrest	32nd St & Denver St SE	202-645-3988	–

Private Courts	Address	Phone	Map
East Potomac Tennis Center	1090 Ohio Dr SW	202-554-5962	6
Washington Hilton Sport & Health Club	1919 Connecticut Ave NW	202-483-4100	9
Rock Creek Park Tennis Center	16th St & Kennedy St NW	202-722-5949	21
Bethesda Sport & Health Club	4400 Montgomery Ave	301-656-9570	29
Arlington Y Tennis & Squash Club	3400 N 13th St	703-749-8057	35

Airline	Phone	IAD	DCA	BWI
Aer Lingus	800-474-7424			■
Aeroflot	888-686-4949	■		
Air Canada	888-247-2262	■	■	■
Air France	800-237-2747	■		
Air Jamaica	800-523-5585			■
AirTran	800-247-8726	■	■	■
Alaska Airlines	800-252-7522	■	■	
Alitalia	800-223-5730	■		
All Nippon	800-235-9262	■		
American Airlines	800-433-7300	■	■	■
American Trans Air	800-435-9282		■	
America West	800-2FLY-AWA	■	■	■
Austrian Airlines	800-843-0002	■		
BMI	800-788-0555	■		
British Airways	800-247-9297	■		■
BWIA	800-538-2942	■		
Continental	800-523-3273	■	■	■
Delta	800-221-1212	■	■	■
Delta Shuttle	800-933-5935		■	
Ethiopian Airlines	800-445-2733	■		
Frontier	800-432-1359	■	■	■
Ghana Airways	800-404-4262			■
GRUPO TACA	800-400-8222	■		
Hooters Air	888-359-4668			■
Icelandair	800-223-5500			■
Independence Air	800-FLY-FLYI	■		
Jet Blue	800-538-2583	■		
KLM Royal Dutch	800-225-2525	■		
Korean Air	800-438-5000	■		
Lufthansa	800-399-LUFT	■		
Midwest	800-452-2022		■	■
Northwest Airlines	800-225-2525	■	■	■
Pan Am	800-359-7262			■
SAS	800-221-2350	■		
Saudi Arabian Airlines	800-472-8342	■		
Southwest Airlines	800-435-9792			■
Spirit	800-772-7117		■	
TACA	800-535-8780	■		
Ted Airlines	800-225-5833	■		
United Airlines	800-864-8331	■	■	■
United Express	800-864-8331	■		
US Airways	800-428-4322	■	■	■
USA3000	877-872-3000			■
Virgin	800-862-8621	■		

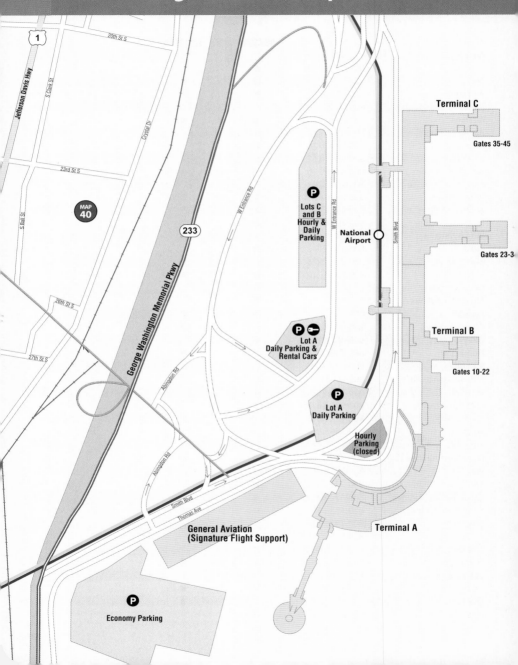

General Information

Phone:	703-417-8000
Lost and Found:	703-417-8560
Parking:	703-417-4311
Website:	www.mwaa.com/national/index.htm

Overview

Reagan National Airport is a small, easy-to-navigate airport that's located practically downtown; perfect for business travelers and politicians. But, for those of us not on expense accounts or the public dole, prices can be prohibitive. If you want a discounted direct flight to Madagascar or enjoy flying on the cattle cars that charge $15 for a roundtrip to Aruba, you'll have to fly from Dulles or BWI. National is too small to host many planes or airlines, making it a short-haul airport with direct connections to cities typically no more than 1250 miles away.

How to Get There—Driving

From DC, take I-395 N to Exit 10. Get on the GW Parkway S and take the Reagan Airport exit.

Parking

Parking at Reagan is not cheap. Garages A, B, C, and Lot A-2 are $2 per half-hour for the first two hours, and $4 per hour thereafter. Garage A and Lot A-2 cost $15 per day. Garages B and C cost $28 per day. If you're heading out for a few days, park in the economy lot, which is only $9 per day. Shuttle buses run between the economy lot and all terminals. Parking in any lot for less than 20 minutes is free.

How to Get There—Mass Transit

The Blue and Yellow Lines have a Metrorail stop adjacent to Terminals B and C. If you're headed to Terminal A, a free shuttle bus will run you there or you can lug your bags on a ten-minute walk. Metro buses are also available from the base of the Metrorail station for areas not served by the rail.

How to Get There— Ground Transportation

Super Shuttle offers door-to-door service to DCA. They also have a shuttle that goes regularly between DCA and Union Station. Call the reservation line on 800-BLUEVAN or go to www.supershuttle.com to book online.

A cab ride to downtown DC will set you back less than $15. DC, Virginia, and Maryland taxis are available at the exits of each terminal. Red Top Arlington: 703-522-3333; Yellow Cab: 202-TAXI-CAB or infor@dcyellowcab.com 703-534-1111; Washington Flyer: 703-276-0002.

Stretch limousine and executive-class sedans start at approximately $42 for downtown Washington. Airport Access: 202-498-8708; Airport Connection: 202-393-2110; Roadmaster: 800-283-5634; Silver Car: 410-788-6100.

Rental Cars—On-Airport (Garage A)

Avis · 800-331-1212   **National** · 800-328-4567
Budget · 800-527-0700   **Dollar** · 800-800-4000
Hertz · 800-654-3131

Off-Airport

Enterprise · 800-736-8222
Alamo · 800-832-7933
Thrifty · 800-367-2277

Hotels—Arlington

Crowne Plaza Washington National · 1489 Jefferson Davis Hwy · 703-416-1600
Crystal City Marriott · 1999 Jefferson Davis Hwy · 703-413-5500
Crystal City Courtyard by Marriott · 2899 Jefferson Davis Hwy · 703-549-3434
Crystal Gateway Marriott · 1700 Jefferson Davis Hwy · 703-920-3230
Days Inn · 2000 Jefferson Davis Hwy · 703-920-8600
Doubletree Crystal City · 300 Army Navy Dr · 703-416-4100
Econo Lodge · 6800 Lee Hwy · 703-538-5300
Embassy Suites · 1300 Jefferson Davis Hwy · 703-979-9799
Hilton · 2399 Jefferson Davis Hwy · 703-418-6800
Holiday Inn National Airport · 2650 Jefferson Davis Hwy · 703-684-7200
Hyatt · 2799 Jefferson Davis Hwy · 703-418-1234
Ritz Carlton · 1250 S Hayes St · 703-415-5000
Residence Inn · 550 Army Navy Dr · 703-413-6630
Sheraton · 1800 Jefferson Davis Hwy · 703-486-1111

Hotels—Washington

Best Western Inn · 724 3rd St NW · 202-842-4466
Crowne Plaza Washington · 14th & K St NW · 202-682-0111
Grand Hyatt Washington · 1000 H St NW · 202-582-1234
Hilton Washington & Towers · 1919 Connecticut Ave NW · 202-483-3000
Hilton Washington Embassy Row · 2015 Massachusetts Ave · 202-265-1600
Holiday Inn · 415 New Jersey Ave NW · 202-638-1616
Homewood Suites Hilton · 1475 Massachusetts Ave NW · 202-265-8000
Hyatt Regency Washington · 400 New Jersey Ave NW · 202-737-1234
Marriott Wardman Park · 2660 Woodley Rd NW · 202-328-2000
Red Roof Inn · 500 H St NW · 202-289-5959
Renaissance Mayflower Hotel · 1127 Connecticut Ave · NW · 202-347-3000
Renaissance Washington DC · 999 9th St NW · 202-898-9000

Airline	Terminal	Airline	Terminal
Air Canada	B	Delta/Shuttle	B
AirTran	A	Frontier	B
Alaska	A	Midwest	A
America West	B	Northwest	A
American/Eagle	B	Spirit	A
ATA	A	United Airlines	B
Continental	B	US Airways/Express	C

Transit · **Dulles International Airport**

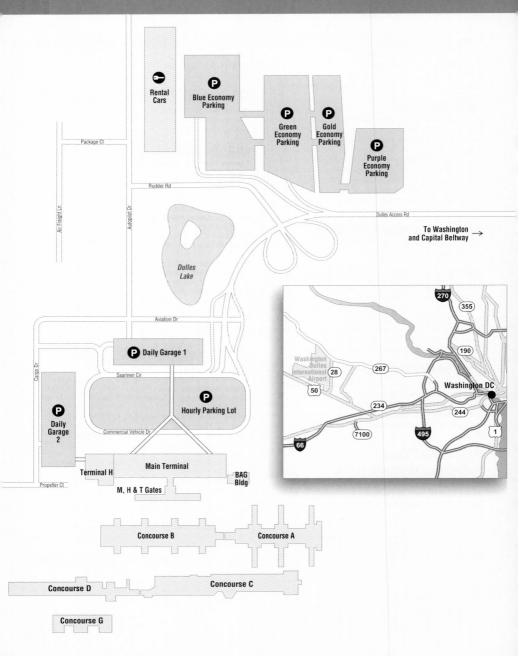

Rental Cars

Blue Economy Parking

Green Economy Parking

Gold Economy Parking

Purple Economy Parking

Package Ct

Rudder Rd

Air Freight Ln

Autopilot Dr

Dulles Access Rd

To Washington and Capital Beltway →

Dulles Lake

Aviation Dr

Daily Garage 1

Saarinen Cir

Cargo Dr

Hourly Parking Lot

Daily Garage 2

Commercial Vehicle Dr

Terminal H

Main Terminal

BAG Bldg

M, H & T Gates

Propeller Ct

Concourse B

Concourse A

Concourse D

Concourse C

Concourse G

Washington Dulles International Airport

Washington DC

270

355

190

28

267

50

234

244

7100

495

1

66

General Information

Address: 45020 Aviation Dr, Sterling, VA 20166
Information: 703-572-2700
Parking: 703-572-4500
Lost and Found: 703-572-2954
Website: www.mwaa.com/dulles/index.htm

Overview

The Mod Squad of airports, Dulles was born in 1958 when architect Eero Saarinen wanted to create something groovy. His design for the terminal building and the control tower was so hip it received a First Honor Award from the American Institute of Architects in 1966. A swoosh roof over a squat building, Dulles still stands out as a modernist stunner. And the oh so suave "mobile lounges" that transport passengers between the terminal building and the aircraft are still in use.

How to Get There—Driving

To get to Washington Dulles Airport from downtown DC, go west on I-66 to Exit 67. Follow signs to the airport.

Parking

Hourly (short-term) parking is located in front of the terminal and is $4 per hour and $36 per day. Daily parking is available in Daily Garages 1 and 2 for $5 per hour and $15 per day. Economy parking (long-term) is available in the four economy parking lots (Blue, Green, Gold, and Purple) located along Rudder Road. Long-term parking is $3 per hour, $9 per day. If you're short on time or energy and long on cash, valet parking is located in front of the terminal and costs $30 for the first 24 hours and $17 per day thereafter. Parking in any lot for less than 20 minutes is free.

How to Get There—Mass Transit

The Metrorail doesn't go all the way to Dulles Airport. You can take the Orange Line to West Falls Church and transfer to the Washington Flyer Coach Service, which leaves every 30 minutes from the station. The coach fare is $8 one-way ($14 round-trip) and the fare for the Metrorail leg will depend on exactly where you're coming from or headed to. A trip from West Falls Church to the Convention Center in downtown DC will cost you $1.70. Check www.washfly.com for Flyer schedules.

How to Get There— Ground Transportation

Super Shuttle is a door-to-door shared van to Washington Dulles Airport. It goes to and from Union Station and anywhere else if you call and book 24 hours in advance. At the airport, you'll find them outside the Main Terminal. Call 800-BLUEVAN or go to www.supershuttle.com to make a reservation. Washington Flyer Taxicabs serve Dulles International Airport exclusively with 24-hour service to and from the airport. Taxis accept American Express, Diners Club, MasterCard, Discover Card, and Visa, and charge metered rates to any destination in metropolitan Washington. If you're heading to downtown DC, it will set you back between $44 and $50. For more information or to book a car call 703-661-6655.

Rental Cars

Alamo • 800-327-9633   **Enterprise** • 800-736-8222
Avis • 800-331-1212   **Hertz** • 800-654-3131
Budget • 800-527-0700   **National** • 800-227-7368
Dollar • 800-800-4000   **Thrifty** • 800-367-2277
                               (off-airport)

Hotels—Herndon, VA

Comfort Inn • 200 Elden St • 703-437-7555
Courtyard by Marriott • 533 Herndon Pkwy • 703-478-9400
Days Hotel & Conference Center • 2200 Centreville Rd • 703-471-6700
Embassy Suites Hotel • 13341 Woodland Park Dr • 703-464-0200
Hilton Washington Dulles • 13869 Park Center Rd • 703-478-2900
Holiday Inn Express Herndon-Reston • 485 Elden St • 703-478-9777
Hyatt Hotels & Resorts • 2300 Dulles Corner Blvd • 703-713-1234
Marriott Hotels & Resorts • 13101 Worldgate Dr • 703-709-0400
Residence Inn • 315 Elden St • 703-435-0044

Hotels—Sterling, VA

Fairfield Inn • 23000 Indian Creek Dr • 703-435-5300
Hampton Inn Dulles Airport • 45440 Holiday Park Dr • 703-471-8300
Holiday Inn Dulles Airport • 1000 Sully Rd • 703-471-7411
Marriott Towne Place Suites • 22744 Holiday Park Dr • 703-707-2017
Washington Dulles Marriott • 45020 Aviation Dr •· 703-471-9500

Airline	Terminal	Airline	Terminal	Airline	Terminal	Airline	Terminal
Aeroflot	B*	America West	D	Frontier	B	TACA	H
Air Canada	C	Austrian Airlines	D*	JetBlue	B	Ted	C
Air France	B*	BMI	C*	KLM	B	United	C & D
AirTran	B	British Airways	D*	Korean Air	B*	United Express	A, C, D
Alaska	D	BWIA	D*	Lufthansa	B*	US Airways/Express	B
Alitalia	H	Continental	B	Northwest	B	Virgin	B*
All Nippon	B*	Delta/Connection	B	SAS	B*		
American/Eagle	D	Ethiopian	H	Saudi Arabian	H		

* Arrives at H

Baltimore-Washington International Airport

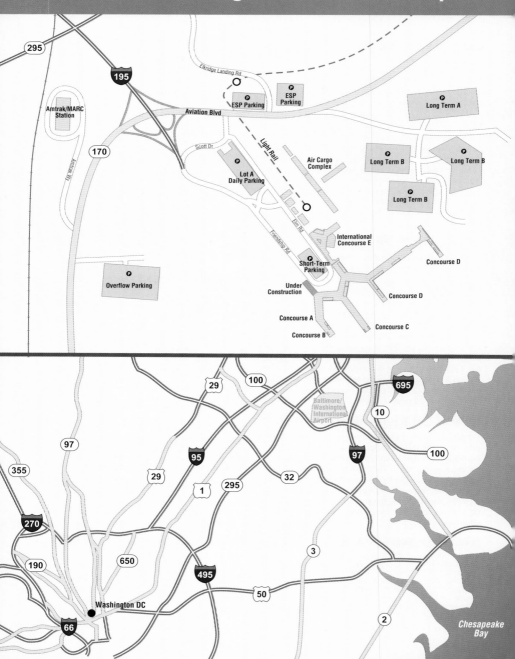

General Information

Information: 800-I-FLY-BWI
Lost and Found: 410-859-7387
Parking: 800-GO-TO-BWI
Police: 410-859-7040
Website: www.bwiairport.com

Overview

Originally named Friendship International Airport when it was built in 1947, Baltimore took control ten years later and creatively renamed it Baltimore International. In 1993, Southwest Airlines moved in, bringing with them their cheap, and wildly popular, cattle cars of the sky. The bargain basement tenant has made BWI a boomtown. Other major carriers joined the dirt-cheap-fares bandwagon, resulting in cheaper flights than you'll find at Dulles or Reagan. It's a helluva haul from the city but, when traveling on your own dime, sometimes price trumps convenience.

How to Get There—Driving

From DC, take New York Avenue to Baltimore/Washington Parkway 295 N to I-195. Take the BWI Exit. From north and west DC, you can take the Washington Beltway (495) E to I-95 N to I-195.

Parking

Hourly parking is located across from the terminal building. The first hour is free. After that, it's $4 per hour and $30 per day. Daily parking is available in the Daily A garage for $2 per hour and $10 per day. ESP parking is located on Aviation Boulevard across from the Air Cargo Complex. It's $3 per hour and $14 per day. If you're going to be gone a while, you might want to try the long-term parking lots, which cost $1 per hour and $8 per day; every seventh day is free.

How to Get There—Mass Transit

Any which way you go, expect to devote a few hours to mimicking a Richard Scarry character. MARC and Amtrak trains service BWI Rail Station from Union Station in DC (Massachusetts Ave & First St NE) for between $5 and $30. A free shuttle runs between the train station and the airport. Or take the Metro Green line to the Greenbelt station and catch the Express Metro Bus/B30 to BWI. The Express bus runs every 40 minutes and costs $2.50.

How to Get There— Ground Transportation

The Airport Shuttle offers door-to-door service within the state of Maryland Call 800-776-0323 for reservations. For door-to-door service to BWI, Super Shuttle (800-BLUE-VAN) services all of the DC airports. The BWI taxi stand is located just outside of baggage claim on the lower level. Average price to DC is $55. 410-859-1100; www.BWIAirportTaxi.com.

Car Rental

Avis · 410-859-1680
Alamo · 410-850-5011
Budget · 410-859-0850
Dollar · 800-800-4000
Enterprise · 800-325-8007
Hertz · 410-850-7400
National · 410-859-8860
Thrifty · 410-859-1136

Hotels

Sheraton International Hotel · 7032 Elm Rd · 800-325-3535
Amerisuites · 940 International Dr · 800-833-1516
Best Western · 6755 Dorsey Rd · 800-528-1234
Candlewood Suites · 1247 Winterson Rd · 888-226-3539
Comfort Inn · 6921 Baltimore-Anapolis Blvd · 800-228-5150
Comfort Suites · 815 Elkridge Landing Rd · 800-228-5150
Courtyard by Marriott · 1671 West Nursery Rd · 800-321-2211
Econo Lodge · 5895 Bonnieview Ln · 800-553-2666
Hampton Inn · 829 Elkridge Landing Rd · 800-426-7866
Hilton Garden Inn · 1516 Aero Dr · 800-774-1500
Holiday Inn · 890 Elkridge Landing Rd · 800-465-4329
Holiday Inn Express · 7481 New Ridge Rd · 800-465-4329
Ramada BWI Hotel · 7253 Parkway Dr · 800-272-6232
Red Roof Inn · 827 Elkridge Landing Rd · 800-843-7663
Residence Inn · 1160 Winterson Rd · 800-331-3131

Airline	Terminal	Airline	Terminal
Aer Lingus	E	Hooters Air	C
Air Canada	E	Icelandair	E
Air Jamaica	E	Midwest	D
AirTran	D	Northwest	D
American	C	Pan Am	E
America West	D	Southwest	B
British Airways	E	United	D
Continental	D	US Airways	D
Delta	C	USA3000	E
Frontier	D		
Ghana Airways	E		

Transit · **Bridges**

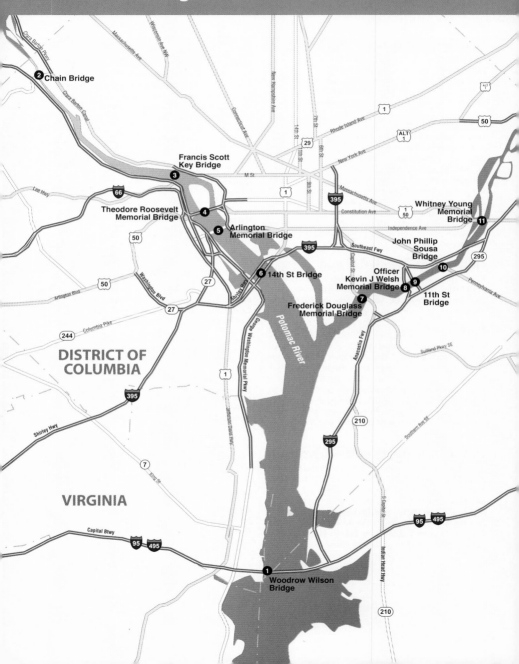

2 Chain Bridge

Francis Scott
Key Bridge

3

Theodore Roosevelt
Memorial Bridge

4

Arlington
Memorial Bridge

5

6 14th St Bridge

Officer
Kevin J Welsh
Memorial Bridge

Frederick Douglass
Memorial Bridge

7

8

9

11th St
Bridge

10

John Phillip
Sousa
Bridge

Whitney Young
Memorial
Bridge

11

**DISTRICT OF
COLUMBIA**

VIRGINIA

1

Woodrow Wilson
Bridge

Potomac River

Chances are if you live in DC and you own a car, you spend a significant amount of your time sitting in traffic on one of DC's bridges. Despite consistent congestion and deteriorating roadways, DC bridges do have one saving grace—no tolls! One of DC's largest is the Woodrow Wilson Bridge, which is unique in two ways: 1) It's one of only 13 drawbridges along the US Interstate highway system. 2) It's the location of one of the worst bottlenecks in the country.

The Woodrow Wilson Bridge was built with only six lanes, but the eastern portion of the beltway was widened to 8 lanes in the '70s, making this spot a continual hassle for DC drivers. In an attempt to alleviate this problem, construction has begun on a new 6,075-foot-long Potomac River Bridge. When this bridge opens, transit officials promise ten lanes and a pedestrian/bicycle facility. Unfortunately, the bridge isn't expected to be completed until 2006. So until then, when it comes to commuting across bridges, be sure to keep the car stocked with ample music and patience.

The outbound span of the 11th Street Bridge was renamed Officer Kevin J Welsh Memorial Bridge, in honor of the police officer who drowned trying to save a woman who jumped into the Anacostia River in an apparent suicide attempt. Unfortunately, the bridge is seldom referred to by its official name, either by traffic reporters or commuters. John Wilkes Booth escaped from Washington via the 11th Street Bridge after he assassinated Abraham Lincoln in 1865.

Websites

Washington Metropolitan Transit Authority (WMATA) • www.wmata.com

Washington Post Commuter Page • www.washingtonpost.com

Wilson Bridge Project • www.wilsonbridge.com

		Lanes	Pedestrians/ Bicyclists?	Vehicles/day (thousands)	Engineer	Main Span / Length	Opened to Traffic
1	Woodrow Wilson Bridge	6	no	195		5,900'	1961
2	Chain Bridge		yes	22		1,350'	1939
3	Francis Scott Key Bridge	4	yes	66	Nathan C Wyeth	1,700'	1923
4	Theodore Roosevelt Bridge	6	yes	100			1964
5	Arlington Memorial Bridge	4	yes	66	McKim, Mead, and White	2,163'	1932
6	14th St Bridge	12	yes	246			1950, 1962, 1972
7	Frederick Douglass Memorial Bridge	5		77		2,501'	1950
8	Kevin J. Welsh Memorial Bridge	3	no				1960*
9	11th Street Bridge	3	no				1960
10	John Phillip Sousa Bridge		yes				
11	Whitney Young Memorial Bridge	4		42.6		1135'	1965

Renamed in 1986

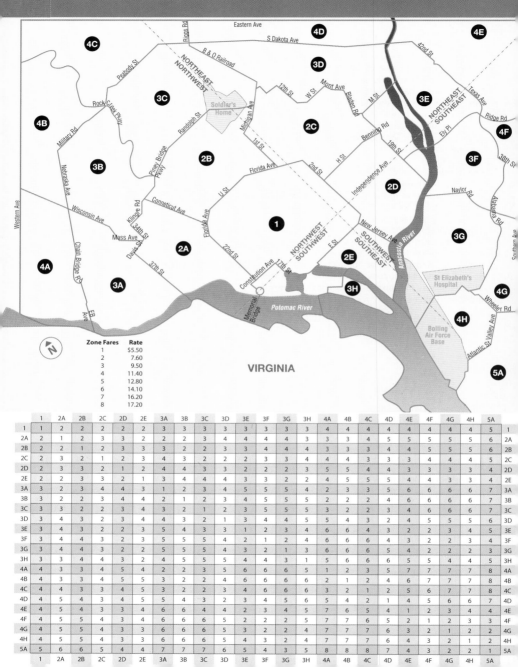

VIRGINIA

Zone Fares	Rate
1	$5.50
2	7.60
3	9.50
4	11.40
5	12.80
6	14.10
7	16.20
8	17.20

	1	2A	2B	2C	2D	2E	3A	3B	3C	3D	3E	3F	3G	3H	4A	4B	4C	4D	4E	4F	4G	4H	5A	
1	1	2	2	2	2	2	3	3	3	3	3	3	3	3	4	4	4	4	4	4	4	4	5	1
2A	2	1	2	3	3	3	2	2	3	4	4	4	4	3	3	3	4	5	5	5	5	5	6	2A
2B	2	2	1	2	3	3	3	2	2	3	3	4	4	3	3	3	3	4	5	5	5	5	6	2B
2C	2	3	2	1	2	3	4	3	2	2	2	3	3	4	4	4	3	3	3	4	4	5	6	2C
2D	2	3	3	2	1	2	4	4	3	3	2	2	2	3	5	5	4	4	3	3	3	4	5	2D
2E	2	3	3	3	2	1	3	4	4	4	3	3	2	2	4	5	5	5	4	4	3	4	4	2E
3A	3	2	3	4	4	3	1	2	3	5	5	5	5	4	2	3	3	5	6	6	6	7	7	3A
3B	3	2	2	3	4	4	2	1	2	3	5	5	5	5	2	2	2	4	6	6	6	6	7	3B
3C	3	3	2	2	3	4	3	2	1	2	3	5	5	5	3	2	2	3	6	6	6	6	7	3C
3D	3	4	3	2	3	4	5	3	2	1	3	4	4	5	5	4	3	2	4	5	5	6	3	3D
3E	3	4	3	2	2	3	5	4	3	3	1	2	2	4	6	6	4	3	2	3	4	5	3	3E
3F	3	4	4	3	2	3	5	5	5	4	2	1	2	4	6	6	6	4	3	2	3	4	4	3F
3G	3	4	4	3	2	2	5	5	5	4	3	2	1	3	6	6	6	5	4	2	2	3	3	3G
3H	3	3	3	4	3	2	4	5	5	5	4	4	3	1	5	6	6	6	5	5	4	4	5	3H
4A	4	3	3	4	5	4	2	2	3	5	6	6	6	5	1	2	3	5	7	7	7	7	8	4A
4B	4	3	3	4	5	5	3	2	2	4	6	6	6	6	2	1	2	4	6	7	7	7	8	4B
4C	4	4	3	3	4	5	3	2	2	3	4	6	6	6	3	2	1	2	5	6	7	7	8	4C
4D	4	5	4	3	4	5	5	4	3	2	3	4	5	6	5	4	2	1	4	6	6	7	4	4D
4E	4	5	5	3	3	4	6	6	6	4	2	3	4	5	7	6	5	4	1	2	3	4	4	4E
4F	4	5	5	4	3	4	6	6	6	5	3	2	2	5	7	7	6	5	2	1	2	3	4	4F
4G	4	5	5	4	3	3	6	6	6	5	4	3	2	4	7	7	7	6	3	2	1	2	4	4G
4H	4	5	5	5	4	4	7	6	6	6	5	4	3	4	7	7	7	6	4	3	2	1	5	4H
5A	5	6	6	6	5	4	7	7	7	6	5	4	3	5	8	8	8	7	4	4	4	5	1	5A
	1	2A	2B	2C	2D	2E	3A	3B	3C	3D	3E	3F	3G	3H	4A	4B	4C	4D	4E	4F	4G	4H	5A	

General Information

Taxicab Commission:
> 2041 Martin Luther King Jr Ave SE, Ste 204
> Washington, DC 20020-7024

Phone: 202-645-6010 (fare calculation)
> 202-645-6018 (complaints)

Website: www.dctaxi.dc.gov

Taxi Fare Calculator:
> http://citizenatlas.dc.gov/atlasapps/taxifare.aspx

Overview

One of the most perplexing aspects of life in DC is the taxi fare system. Unlike the taxis of most major cities, which base their fares on meters, the taxis of our nation's capital charge according to set zones. With 8 zones and 23 subzones, plus extra charges for baggage, rush hour travel, and weather emergencies, even veteran district residents can't decipher their fares. Prices range from $5.50 for a single-zone ride to $17.20 for an eight-zone ride. And forget lowering your fare by sharing a taxi: there is a charge of $1.50 for each additional passenger. Other possible surcharges include a $1 rush-hour fee from 7 am to 9:30 am and 4 pm to 6:30 pm Monday to Friday, 50¢ for every suitcase or shopping bag over your one allotted item, and $2 for radio-dispatched cabs. It's worth taking a few minutes to try hailing one before calling dispatch.

Calculate your Fare

Whenever possible, make sure to calculate your fare first. The zone divisions start from the heart of NW Washington and radiate outward in a semi-circular arrangement. If the zone maps and fare charts are a little too complicated, you can also calculate your fare by calling the DC Taxicab Commission (if you reach voice mail press 0 and an operator should answer during business hours) or by visiting the fare calculator website. If in doubt, verify the fare with the driver before hopping into the cab. Doing your homework will prevent overcharges, preclude confrontations at the end of the trip, and allow you to be confident you have enough cash for the cab ride home.

Ways to Save

One way many district residents avoid extra charges is by getting out just before the zone ends and walking the extra blocks to their destination. Boundary zones that are frequently crossed, and can be avoided by walking just a few extra blocks include: H Street; U Street NW; Florida Ave; and 12th Street NW. Also, always make sure to carry small bills as most cab drivers will not make change for anything over $20.

Still Anxious?

When compared to other US cities, DC taxis are fairly cheap. While one short taxi trip may seem overpriced, remember you're not being charged anything extra while you sit in that 20-minute traffic jam. If you think you are being overcharged or have a complaint, get a receipt, write down the taxi number, and call the DC Taxicab Commission.

Cab Companies

Don't feel like hailing a cab in the rain? All the major cab companies in DC are listed below. Calling a cab will cost you an extra $2.

* All area codes: 202

Company	Phone	Company	Phone
American	398-0529	Georgetown	529-8979
Allied	352-6971	Globe	232-3700
Aspen	554-1200	Gold Star	484-5555
Atlantic	488-0609	Hill Top	529-1212
Autorama	398-6051	Holiday	628-4407
Barwood	526-7555	Imperial	269-0990
Bay	543-1919	Liberty	398-0532
Bell	479-6729	Lincoln	484-2222
Best	265-7834	Lunar	269-1234
Capitol	546-2400	Madison	388-4919
Central	484-7100	Mayflower	783-1111
Checker	398-0528	Meritt Cab	554-7900
City	269-0990	Meteor Cab	441-0404
Classic	399-6815	Mutual Cab	526-1152
Columbia	832-4662	National	269-1234
Constitution	269-1300	Omni	216-0370
Courtesy	269-2600	Orange	832-0436
DC Express	484-8516	Palm Grove	269-2600
DC Flyer	488-4844	Pan Am	526-7215
Dial	269-3602	Presidential	484-5555
Diamond	387-4011	Riteway	832-4662
Diplomat	546-6100	Seasons	484-8119
Dynasty	526-1200	Sun	484-7100
Elite	484-1200	Super	488-4334
Empire	488-7611	World	547-0744
Fairway	832-4662	Yellow	546-7900
Five Star	484-2222	Yourway	488-0609
General	483-3703		

Driving in Washington? Remember this: The numbers go north and south, the alphabet goes east and west and you can't trust the states. Or the traffic circles. Or the streets that end for no reason. Or the constant construction sites. Or the potholes as big as Volkswagens. Or the clueless tourists. Or the cabbies. Never trust the cabbies.

There are four quadrants: Northwest, Northeast, Southeast, and Southwest. The boundaries are North Capitol Street, East Capitol Street, South Capitol Street, and the National Mall. Street addresses start there and climb as you move up the numbers and alphabet. (Note: There is no J Street. After W, they go by names that are in alphabetical order.) Street numbers on alphabet and state-named streets correspond to the numbered cross streets. 1717 K Street NW is between 17th and 18th streets. The letter street addresses correspond to the number of the letter in the alphabet. So 1717 20th Street NW is between R and S because they are the 17 and 18th letters in the alphabet (always leave out "J"). Get it?

Of course, some streets on the grid are more equal than others. North to south, 7th, 14th, and 16th are major thoroughfares, as are K Street, H Street, M Street, and U Street.

The trick to driving in DC like an insider is mastering the avenues named after states and knowing the highway system. If you don't, you will probably find yourself stuck behind a Winnebago with Wisconsin plates, unable to even see all the red lights you're catching. If the force is with you, you'll fly from Adams Morgan to Georgetown in five traffic-free minutes on the Rock Creek and Potomac Parkway.

Young Jedi, study the maps in this book. For every five minutes you spend looking at the maps, you will save five hours over the next year.

Because DC is still a 9-to5 city, many traffic patterns change to accommodate rush hours. Be careful. Some streets, such as 15th Street NW and Rock Creek Parkway go one-way during rush hours. Other routes, including most of downtown, ban parking during rush hours. Also Interstates 395 and 66 have high occupancy vehicle (HOV) lanes that will get you a big ticket unless you follow the rules.

DMV Locations in DC:

301 C St NW
301 C St NW, Rm 1157, Washington, DC 20001
202-727-5000
Tues-Sat: 8:15 am-4 pm
All transactions available.

Penn Branch
3214 Pennsylvania Ave SE, Washington, DC 20020
Mon-Fri: 8:15 am-4 pm, Sat: Closed
Available services: Vehicle registration (first time and renewals) and titles, driver's license issuance and renewal, Fleet transactions (Mon-Fri: 8:30 am-12:15 pm).
Knowledge tests are given Mon-Fri: 8:30 am-3 pm.

Brentwood Square
1233 Brentwood Rd NE, Washington, DC 20018
Mon-Fri: 10 am-6 pm, Sat: Closed
Available services: Vehicle registration (first time on Mon-Fri: 11 am-4 pm, and renewals) and titles, driver's license issuance and renewal.
Knowledge tests are given Mon-Fri: 11 am-4 pm.

Brentwood Road Test Lot
1205 Brentwood Rd NE, Washington, DC 20018
By appointment only, call: 202-727-5000
Available services: Road test (driver's license only).

Shops at Georgetown Park
3222 M St NW, Washington, DC 20007
202-727-5000
Mon-Fri: 10 am-6 pm, Sat: Closed
Available services: Vehicle registration renewal and driver's license renewal.
Knowledge tests are given Mon-Fri: 10 am-3 pm.

65 K St NE
65 K St NE, Washington, DC 20001
202-727-5000
Available services:
Walk-in hearings, Mon-Fri: 8:30 am-4 pm
Permit control/reinstatements, Mon-Fri: 8:30 am-3:30 pm
Certified driver's record, Mon-Fri: 8:15 am-4 pm
Ticket payment, Mon-Fri: 8:15 am-6:45 pm

1001 Half St SW
1001 Half St SW, Washington, DC 20024
202-645-4300
Mon-Fri: 6 am-6 pm, Sat: 7 am-3 pm
Available services: Vehicle inspection.

General Information

Department of Transportation (DDOT):
  202-673-6813 • www.ddot.dc.gov
Department of Public Works: 202-727-1000 •
  http://dpw.dc.gov
Citywide Call Center: 202-727-1000
Department of Motor Vehicles:
  202-727-5000 • http://dmv.washingtondc.gov

Meters

In most areas of DC, parking meters are effective between 7 am and 6:30 pm Monday through Friday. In the more densely populated areas (Georgetown, convention centers, etc.), the hours may extend until 10 pm and reach into Saturday. Metered parking may be prohibited on some streets during morning and rush hours. Vehicles displaying DC-issued handicap license plates or placards are allowed to park for double the amount of time indicated on the meter.

Parking on Weekends and Holidays

Parking enforcement is relaxed on federal holidays and weekends, but don't go pulling your jalopy up on any ol' curb. Public safety parking laws are always in effect, even on weekends. These include the prohibition of blocking emergency entrances or exits, blocking fire hydrants, parking too close to an intersection, obstructing crosswalks, etc. The city officially observes ten holidays, listed below. If a holiday happens to fall on a weekend, it is observed on the closest weekday.

Holiday	Date	Day
New Year's Day	December 31, 2004	Friday
Martin Luther King Jr's Birthday	January 19	Wednesday
President's Day	February 16	Wednesday
Memorial Day	May 31	Tuesday
Independence Day	July 4	Monday
Labor Day	September 6	Tuesday
Columbus Day	October 11	Tuesday
Veterans Day	November 11	Friday
Thanksgiving Day	November 24	Thursday
Christmas Day	December 26	Monday

In some busy, commercial areas, parking may be enforced on Saturdays. It's always a good idea to check all signs and meters to make sure you're legally parked.

Resident Permit Parking

In the 1970s, increasing numbers of out-of-staters parking on residential streets had locals furious—as a result, the Resident Permit Parking Program was initiated. For a $15 fee, residents can buy a permit to park in their neighborhood zone on weekdays from 7 am to 8:30 pm. Commuters have to find a meter.

If you live in a Resident Permit Parking zone and you're planning on hosting out-of-town guests, you can apply for a temporary visitor permit at your local police district headquarters. All you need is your visitor's name, license tag number, length of visit, and a few hours to kill down at the station. Temporary permits are only valid for up to 15 consecutive days—a great excuse to get rid of guests who have overstayed their welcome!

Tow Pound

Didn't pay your parking tickets? If your car was towed, it was taken to the District's Impoundment Lot on 4800 Addison Road in Beaver Heights, MD. The lot is one-half mile from the Deanwood Metrorail station on the Orange Line. It can remain impounded there for up to 14 days. After that time, the car may be transferred to the Blue Plains Storage and Auction facility in Blue Plains at 5001 Shepard Parkway SW. To find out for certain where your car is, call the DMV on 202-727-5000. You can also find out through the Department of Public Works' website at http://dpw.dc.gov.

Top 10 Parking Violations

1. Expired Meter: $25
2. Overtime Parking in Residential Zone: $30
3. No Standing/Rush Hour: $100
4. No Parking Anytime: $30
5. No Parking/Street Cleaning: $30
6. No Standing Anytime: $50
7. Parking in Alley: $30
8. Expired Inspection Sticker: $50
9. Expired Registration/Tags: $100
10. Within 20 Feet of a Bus Stop: $50

Zipcar General Information

www.zipcar.com • 202-737-4976

History

Zipcar is what happens when you cross a taxi with Avis. They rent cars by the hour. Give 'em $8.50/hr, they'll give you a Jetta. It's a good compromise for the car-less urban-bound masses that every once in a while need to go where Metro can't. Be warned, there's a $300 deposit. But it's cheaper and less of a hassle than owning a car.

How It Works

You have to sign up for membership before you go online and reserve one of the hundreds of cars available at zipcar.com. A phone call will get you the same result. Once you reserve an available car, get to the location where it has been parked and use your Zipcard to unlock the car. When you're done, you return it to the same spot where you picked it up.

Don't get any ideas. Your Zipcard will only open your car for the time you've reserved it. During this period, no one else can open the car you've reserved. The car unlocks when the valid card is held to the windshield.

Costs

The cost of Zipcar varies depending on the location, but generally it runs between $8.50-$10.50 an hour. There is a Night Owl Special between the hours of midnight and 6 am, when the cost is only $2 an hour. A 24-hour reservation, which is the maximum amount of time that a car can be reserved, costs about $75-$95, with an additional 18 cents per mile after 125 free miles. At that point, a rental really is a better idea.

Zipcar membership costs are additional. There's a one-time $25 application fee and then an annual or monthly fee, depending on how often you plan on driving. You should think of it in the same way you think about your cell phone bill. If you intend to use Zipcar infrequently, you can pay a $25 annual fee and then pay per usage. If you plan on doing a lot of driving, it works out cheaper to make a monthly payment ($50, $75, $125, and $150 plans are available) and get discounts per usage—they even have rollovers if you don't reach your plan amount each month. Check the Zipcar website for further details.

Car Rental

If traditional car rental is more your style, or you'll need a car for more than 24 hours at a time, try one of the many old-fashioned car rental places in the District.

- **Hertz** • 901 11th St NW • 202-628-6174 • Map **1**
- **Alamo** • 50 Massachusetts Ave NE • 202-842-7454 • Map **2**
- **Budget** • 50 Massachusetts Ave NW • 202-289-5373 • Map **2**
- **Hertz** • 50 Massachusetts Ave NW • 202-842-0819 • Map **2**
- **National** • 50 Massachusetts Ave NE • 202-842-7454 • Map **2**
- **Enterprise** • 970 D St SW • 202-554-8100 • Map **6**
- **Rent-A-Wreck** • 1252 Half St SE • 202-408-9828 • Map **6**
- **Enterprise** • 3307 M St NW • 202-338-0015 • Map **8**
- **Avis** • 1722 M St NW • 202-467-6585 • Map **9**
- **Budget** • 1620 L St NW • 202-466-4544 • Map **9**
- **Enterprise** • 1029 Vermont Ave NW • 202-393-0900 • Map **10**
- **Rent-A-Wreck** • 910 M St NW • 202-408-9828 • Map **10**
- **Thrifty** • 1001 12th St NW • 202-783-0400 • Map **10**
- **A&D Auto Rental** • 2712 Bladensburg Rd NE • 202-832-5300 • Map **13**
- **Enterprise** • 1502 Franklin St NE • 202-269-0300 • Map **13**
- **Thrifty** • 3210 Rhode Island Ave • 202-636-8470 • Map **13**
- **Enterprise** • 2730 Georgia Ave NW • 202-332-1716 • Map **15**
- **Enterprise** • 2601 Calvert St NW • 202-232-4443 • Map **17**
- **Alamoot Rent A Car** • 4123 Wisconsin Ave NW • 202-363-3232 • Map **19**
- **Enterprise** • 5220 44th St NW • 202-364-6564 • Map **19**
- **Avis** • 4400 Connecticut Ave NW • 202-686-5149 • Map **20**
- **Enterprise** • 927 Missouri Ave NW • 202-726-6600 • Map **21**
- **Budget** • 8400 Wisconsin Ave • 301-816-6000 • Map **22**
- **Enterprise** • 7725 Wisconsin Ave • 301-907-7780 • Map **22**
- **Sears Rent A Car & Truck** • 8400 Wisconsin Ave • 301-816-6050 • Map **22**
- **Enterprise** • 9151 Brookville Rd • 301-565-4000 • Map **24**
- **Enterprise** • 8208 Georgia Ave • 301-563-6500 • Map **25**
- **Enterprise** • 8401 Colesville Rd • 301-495-4120 • Map **25**
- **Hertz** • 8203 Georgia Ave • 301-588-0608 • Map **25**
- **Rent-A-Wreck** • 5455 Butler Rd • 301-654-2252 • Map **29**
- **Sears Rent A Car** • 4932 Bethesda Ave • 301-816-6050 • Map **29**
- **Enterprise** • 1211 N Glebe Rd • 703-248-7180 • Map **34**
- **Enterprise** • 601 N Randolph St • 703-312-7900 • Map **34**
- **Enterprise** • 700 N Glebe Rd • 703-243-5404 • Map **34**
- **Bargain Buggies Rent A Car** • 3140 Washington Blvd • 703-841-0000 • Map **35**
- **Avis** • 3206 10th St N • 703-516-4202 • Map **37**
- **Enterprise** • 2778 S Arlington Mill Dr • 703-820-7100 • Map **39**
- **Hertz** • Reagan National Airport 3860 Four Mile Run Dr • 703-419-6300 • Map **39**
- **Alamo** • 2780 Jefferson Davis Hwy • 703-684-0086 • Map **40**
- **Budget** • 1200 Eads St • 703-351-7500 • Map **40**
- **Dollar** • Reagan National Airport 2600 Jefferson Davis Hwy • 703-519-8700 • Map **40**
- **Enterprise** • 2121 Crystal Dr • 703-553-2930 • Map **40**
- **Rent-A-Wreck** • 901 S Clark St • 703-413-7100 • Map **40**
- **Avis** • 6001 Duke St • 703-256-4335 • Map **41**
- **Enterprise** • 512 S Van Dorn St • 703-823-5700 • Map **41**
- **Enterprise** • 5800 Edsall Rd • 703-658-0010 • Map **41**
- **Enterprise** • 4213 Duke St • 703-212-4700 • Map **42**
- **Hertz** • 16 Sweeley St • 703-751-1250 • Map **42**
- **Rent For Less** • 4105 Duke St • 703-370-5666 • Map **42**
- **Enterprise** • 2000 Jefferson Davis Hwy • 703-553-7744 • Map **43**
- **Thrifty** • 1306 Duke St • 703-684-205 • Map **46**

Metrobus

202-962-1234 • www.wmata.com
Fare: $1.25 Regular/ $3 Express
Hours: 24/7

With 12,490 stops around the greater DC area, buses can be a convenient way to get around town once you've figured out the complex system. For a while, the horribly out-of-date maps at the stations and stops offered little to no help. Recently, new maps have been posted that actually give people a clue. There are bike racks on the front of all Metrobus buses. If you don't have a Metro pass, make sure you have exact change for the fare; Metrobus drivers don't carry cash.

Ride On Bus—Montgomery County, MD

240-777-RIDE • http://montgomerycountymd.gov content/dpwt/transit
Fare: $1.25

The Ride On bus system was created to offer residents of Montgomery County a public transit system that complements the Metro system of DC. It accepts exact change, Ride On and Metrobus tokens or passes, and MARC rail passes.

DASH Bus—Alexandria, VA

703-370-3274 • www.dashbus.com
Fares: $1.00/ 25¢ Pentagon Surcharge

For travel within Alexandria, the DASH system offers an affordable alternative to driving. It also connects with Metrobus, Metrorail, Virginia Railway Express, and all local bus systems. DASH honors combined Metrorail/Metrobus Passes, VRE/MARC rail tickets, and Metrobus regular tokens. If you need to pay cash, don't forget to take correct change. If you are traveling to or from the Pentagon Metrorail station, you have to pay the 25¢ Pentagon Surcharge if you don't have a DASH Pass or other valid pass.

ART—Arlington, VA

703-228-RIDE • www.commuterpage.com/art
Fare: $1.25
Ridership: 397,000 passengers per year

Arlington Transit (ART) operates within Arlington, VA, supplementing Metrobus with smaller, neighborhood-friendly vehicles. It also provides access to Metrorail and Virginia Railway Express. The buses run on clean-burning natural gas and have climate control to keep their passengers from sticking to the seats. You can pay a cash fare or use a Metrobus token or pass.

Georgetown Metro Connection

Fares: $1 one-way
Hours: Mon–Thurs: 7 am–12am; Fri: 7 am–2 am;
*   Sat: 8 am–2 am; Sun: 8 am–12 am*

The Georgetown Metro Connection serves all Metrobus stops in Georgetown and operates service between Georgetown and Foggy Bottom-GWU, Rosslyn, and Dupont Circle Metro stations. Buses leave every ten minutes, making it a frequent, convenient commuting option.

Georgetown University Transportation Shuttle (GUTS)

202-687-4372 • http://otm.georgetown.edu/guts.cfm
Fare: Free!
Hours: 5 am-midnight

The GUTS system was created in 1974 to help students and teachers travel to and from the University campus and nearby Metrorail stations. Today, GUTS operates five shuttle routes, connecting the campus to Metro stations at Rosslyn and Dupont Circle and to stops in North Arlington, VA. You need a valid Georgetown University ID card to ride all of the GUTS lines. Visitors can ride free of charge to and from the Metro stations, as long as they show a picture ID when they board.

Greyhound Buses

www.greyhound.com
Locations:
Washington, DC •1005 1st St NE • 202-289-5154 • 24/7
Silver Spring, MD • 8100 Fenton St • 301-585-8700 • 7 am–9 pm
Arlington, VA • 3860 S Four Mile Run Dr • 703-998-6312 •
* 6 am–9 pm*

Greyhound offers service throughout the US and Canada, and at a much more reasonable price than most air and rail services. Keep in mind that you get what you pay for. Booking in advance will save you money, as will buying a round-trip ticket at the time of purchase. For more information about fares and schedules, check out the Greyhound website.

Chinatown Buses to New York

These buses are a poorly-kept secret among the city's frugal travelers. They have odd hours and bargain-basement amenities, but they are far and away the cheapest option to dash outta town. All companies are $20 one-way, $35 round-trip. Most of these buses will drop off/pick up in Baltimore at the request of passengers, with a fare of $9 one-way and $18 return.

Eastern Travel • 715 H St NW •
  www.ivymedia.com/eastern
  8 trips/day • NY Address: 88 E Broadway

Apex Bus • 610 I St NW • www.apexbus.com
  5 trips/day • NY Address: 88 E Broadway

Dragon Coach • 14th St & L St NW •
  www.ivymedia.com/dragoncoach
  7 trips/day • NY Address: 2 Mott St

Washington Deluxe • 1015 15th St NW •
  www.ivymedia.com/washingtondeluxe
  12 trips/day • NY Address: 303 W 34th St

Vamoose Bus • 14th St NW •
  www.ivymedia.com/vamoose/
  2 trips/day • NY Address: W 31st St & 8th Ave

New Century Travel • 513 H St NW • www.2000coach.com
  5 trips/day • NY Address: 88 E Broadway

Today's Bus • 610 I St NW • www.ivymedia.com/todaysbus
  6 trips/day • NY Address: 88 E Broadway

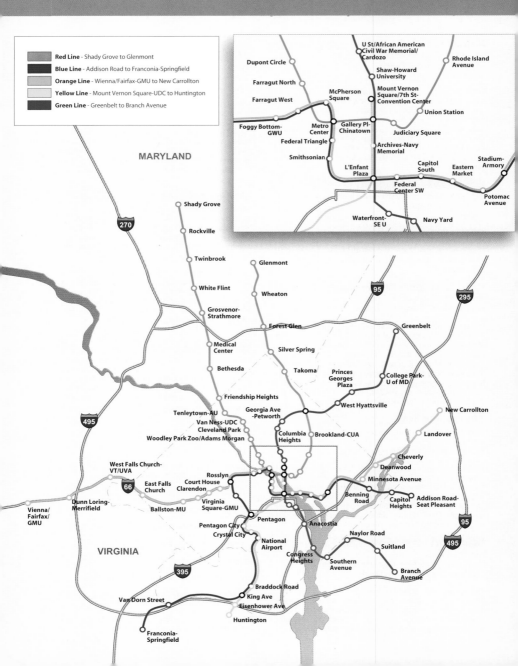

General Information

Address: Washington Metropolitan Transit Authority
600 Fifth St NW,
Washington DC, 20001
Schedules & Fares: 202-637-7000
General Information: 202-962-1234
Website: www.wmata.com

Overview

Don't bother asking where the subway is. Or the underground. Or the T. It'll give away your newbie status. Here, it's called the Metro. Know it because there's really no way to avoid it. Not that you would want to. Metro makes locals proud and it's so simple it seems small. But it isn't; it's the second largest in the country, with 842 rail cars shuttling about 181 million passengers per year between 83 stations—soon to be 86 stations. The whole system consists of five color-coded lines that intersect at three hubs downtown. Trains reach a maximum speed of 59 mph, and average about 33 mph.

The stations are Sixties-futuristic—sterile, quiet, and gaping. Metro cars are carpeted and air-conditioned. Many of them have seen better days, but for the most part they are clean and remarkably clutter- and crime-free. The rules, such as no eating or drinking, are strict and passengers act as citizen police. If the station agents don't stop you from sneaking your Starbucks on with you during your morning commute, a fellow passenger is likely to tag you. Unfortunately, the system shuts down every night, leaving more than a few tipsy out-of-luck riders scraping their pockets for cab fare.

If you're on a Verizon Wireless plan, you're in luck—your phone will still be operational in tunnels. Unlike consuming coffee, there is no rule against using your cell phone whilst on the train.

Believe it or not, the longest escalator in the Western Hemisphere, at a length of 230 ft, is at Wheaton Station. It takes almost five minutes to ride. Just hope that it doesn't break down as you get off the train.

Fares and Schedules

Service begins at 5 am weekdays, and 7 am weekends. Service stops at midnight Sunday–Thursday, and 3 am Friday and Saturday. Fares begin at $1.35 and, depending on the distance traveled, can rise as high as $3.90 during rush hours and $2.35

off-peak. In order to ride the Metro, you'll need a pass or Farecard. Farecards can hold from $1.20 up to $45, and are available for purchase from vending machines within stations or online. Commuters pay $5 for a credit-card-sized SmarTrip that can hold up to $200 and can be used in metro parking lots and on some buses too.

Unlimited one-day passes can be purchased for $6.50 and 7-day unlimited Fast Passes are $32.50. There's a slightly cheaper 7-day Short Trip pass that costs $22, but if you take a trip during rush hour that costs more than $2, you have to pay the difference in fare.

Frequency of Service

Trains come about every 6 minutes on all five lines during rush hour, and every 12 minutes during midday. During the evening the interval between trains on the red line is 15 minutes, and 20 minutes on all other lines.

Parking

Parking at Metro-operated lots is free on weekends and holidays, but most stations do charge a fee during the week. These fees vary, but tend to average $2.75-$3.25 per day. In most suburban Metro stations, parking spaces fill quickly, usually by 8am, so either get dropped off or get to the station early. If your stop is at Twinbrook, White Flint, or Prince George's Plaza, you are in luck, as parking is usually available all day. Multiple-day parking is available at Greenbelt, Huntington, and Franconia-Springfield stations.

Bikes

On weekdays, bikes are permitted on trains free of charge provided there are no more than 2 bikes per car, and provided it is not between commuter hours of 7 am and 10 am or 4 pm and 7 pm. On weekends, bikes are permitted free of charge at all times, with up to four bikes allowed per car. Bicycle lockers are available for $70 for one year, plus a $10 key deposit. Call 202-962-1116 for information on how to rent these lockers. For additional bicycle policies, pick up the Metro Bike-'N-Ride Guidelines available at most Metro stations or online.

Pets

Back to those strict rules: only service animals and small pets in proper carrying containers are permitted.

Transit • **MARC Commuter Trains**

Accurate as of June 2004.
Provided by the Maryland Transit Administration.

LEGEND

- Penn Line
- Camden Line
- Brunswick Line
- ○ Interchange Station or Final terminall
- Amtrak service also available
- Virginia Railway Express service also available
- Ⓜ Metrorail Interchange
- Meet-the-MARC Bus Service From Frederick
- *RIDE ON* Ride On Bus Service
- Ⓛ MTA Light Rail Stop
- Accessible

General Information

Maryland Transit Administration: 410-539-5000
6 St Paul St, Baltimore, MD 21202-1614
www.mtamaryland.com

MARC Train Information: 800-543-9809
MARC Lost and Found:
Camden Line   410-354-1093
Brunswick Line   301-834-6380
Penn Line   410-291-4267
Union Station   202-906-3109
Bike Locker Reservations: 410-767-3440
Certification for people   410-767-3441
with disabilities

Overview

Commuter rail service from DC to surrounding areas in Maryland is called MARC (Maryland Rail Commuter) and has three lines in and out of the city. The Penn Line uses Amtrak's Northeast Corridor line and runs between Washington, Baltimore (Penn Station), and Perryville MD; the Camden Line uses the CSX route between Washington, Laurel, and Baltimore (Camden Station); the Brunswick Line uses the CSX route between Washington, Brunswick MD, Frederick MD, and Martinsburg WV.

With 81 trains carrying more than 20,000 passengers daily, MARC trains can get pretty packed. Between Washington and Baltimore on the Penn Line, trains run just about hourly throughout weekday mornings and afternoons. Service is less frequent on the Camden Line. Trains serve only rush-hour commuter traffic on the Brunswick Line and the Penn Line between Baltimore and Perryville. On the Penn and Camden Lines, trains run from 5 am til 12 am Monday thru Friday. There is no weekend service on any of the lines.

Fares & Schedules

Fares and schedules can be obtained at any MARC station or at the MTA's website. Generally prices fall between $4 and $14, depending on how many zones you're traversing. Tickets are available as single ride, round-trip, ten-trip, or unlimited weekly ($30-$105) and monthly passes ($100–$350). Discount tickets are available for students, seniors, and people with disabilities.

Pets

Only seeing-eye dogs and small pets in carry-on containers are allowed.

Bicycles

Bicycles are not allowed on MARC trains unless they are folded or dismantled, and placed in a carrying case. If you're at Halethorpe or BWI Rail stations, bike lockers are available. If you plan on riding, it's advisable to call ahead and reserve a locker: 410-767-3440.

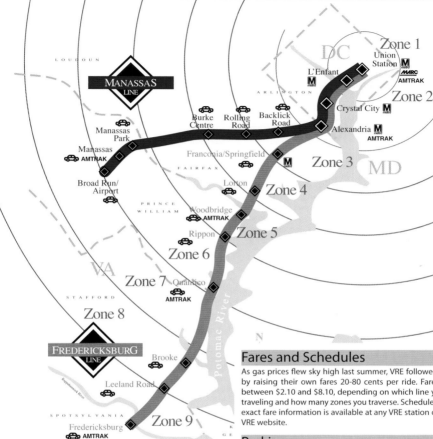

Fares and Schedules

As gas prices flew sky high last summer, VRE followed suit by raising their own fares 20-80 cents per ride. Fares fall between $2.10 and $8.10, depending on which line you're traveling and how many zones you traverse. Schedules and exact fare information is available at any VRE station or the VRE website.

Parking

With the exception of Franconia/Springfield, VRE offers free parking at their outlying stations. (The Manassas station requires a free permit that can be downloaded from the VRE website.) Keep in mind: free does not mean guaranteed. If you're planning to park at the Broad Run station, for example, be sure to get there early. Despite an expansion of the lot two years ago, there is still not enough parking to meet demand.

Pets and Bicycles

Only service animals and small pets in closed carriers are allowed on VRE trains. Full-sized bicycles are not allowed on any VRE train. Collapsible bicycles, however, are permitted on all trains. If you do plan to take a collapsible bicycle on board, you must get on and off the train last and your bike must be clean and free of grease.

General Information

Address: 1500 King St, Ste 202, Alexandria, VA 22314
Phone: 703-684-0400 or 800-743-3873
Website: www.vre.org

Overview

The Virginia Railway Express (VRE) is a commuter train connecting northern Virginia to DC. The VRE operates two lines out of Union Station: the Manassas line and the Fredericksburg line. Service begins weekdays at 5 am and ends at roughly 7 pm; the last train to depart Union Station for Fredericksburg leaves at 7 pm and the last Manassas-bound train leaves Union Station at 7:10 pm. Just the excuse you need to leave work at a reasonable hour! There is no weekend service.

General Information

NFT Map:	2
Address:	50 Massachusetts Ave, NE
Phone:	800-872-7245
Lost and Found:	202-289-8355
Website:	www.unionstationdc.com
Metrorail Line:	Red
Metrobus Lines:	80, 96, D1, D3, D4, D6, D8, N22, X1,X2, X6, X8
Train Lines:	MARC, Amtrak, VRE
Year Opened:	1907

Overview

Union Station opened to the public on October 27, 1907 as the largest train station in the world. In fact, if you were to lay the Washington Monument on its side it would fit within the station's concourse. It was built in a Beaux Arts style by Daniel Burnham (architect who also designed New York's Flatiron Building and quite a bit of Chicago) and remains one of the look-at-me buildings in the city.

Today, Union Station ranks as the most visited destination in Washington, DC, though that's kind of misleading. It's a nice place, but we'll bet many of those 25 million annual visitors are actually just treading the marble floors to get from train to cab and vice-versa.

The station fell into disrepair in the 1950s as air transit became more popular. But, thanks to a $160-million-dollar renovation in the eighties, you'd never know it. It now houses 100 clothing and specialty stores, a movie-theater, an enormous food court and a few upscale restaurants. With so much non-commuting activity taking place, you may forget it's also the hub where the Metrorail, MARC, VRE, and Amtrak all converge.

Parking

The Union Station parking garage is open 24 hours. Rates are as follows:

Up to 1 hour: $5	4–5 hours: $12
1–2 hours: $8	5–12 hours: $14
2–4 hours: $10	12–24 hours: $16

You can have your ticket validated at any Union Station store, restaurant, or the Information Desk and you'll pay only $1 for two hours of parking. For more information on parking, call 202-898-1950.

Stores

Aerosoles
Ann Taylor
Appalachian Spring
Aurea
B Dalton Bookseller
Bath & Body Works
Best Lockers
The Body Shop
Bon Voyage
Chico's
Claire's
Comfort One Shoes
Crabtree & Evelyn
Destination, DC
Discovery Channel Store
Easy Spirit
Express
Faber, Coe, & Gregg
Fire & Ice
Flights of Fancy
Foot Locker
Godiva Chocolatier
Imposters
Incognito
J & A Jewelers
Jos A Bank
Knits, Etc.
Knot Shop
Lids
Lost City Art
Made in America
Moto Photo
Muze
Nine West
Origins
The Paper Trail
Parfumerie Douglas
Pendleton
President Cigars
Sam Goody
Speedo
Sunglass Hut
Swatch
Taxco Sterling Co
Victoria's Secret
Washington Redskins Store
The White House
Wilsons Leather

Dining—Casual

Acropolis
Aditi
Au Bon Pain
Auntie Anne's Pretzels
Ben & Jerry's Ice Cream
Boardwalk Fries
Bucks County Coffee Co
Burrito Brothers
Cajun Grill
Café Renee
Corner Bakery Café
Flamers Charburgers
Frank & Stein Dogs & Drafts
Gourmet Corner
Gourmet Station
Great Steak & Fry Co
Great Wraps
Haagen-Dazs
Johnny Rockets
Kabuki Sushi
King Bar-B-Q
Larry's Cookies
Le Petit Bistro
Mamma Llardo's
Matsutake
McDonald's
New York Deli
Nothing But Donuts
Panda Rice Bowl
Paradise Smoothies
Pasta T Go Go
Primo Cappuccino
Salad Works
Sbarro
Soup Nutsy
Treat Street
Vaccaro
Vittorio's
Wingmaster

Dining— Restaurants

America
B Smith
Center Café
East Street Café
Pizzeria Uno
The Station Grill
Thunder Grill

General Information

Address: Union Station, 50 Massachusetts Ave, NE
Phone: 1-800-USA-RAIL
Website: www.amtrak.com
Connections: Metro Red Line, VRE, MARC

Overview

Blending the words "American" and "track," Amtrak is the United States version of a national train system. Though it's been plagued by budget woes and surly workers that every year threaten its existence, it's been chugging along for more than 30 years. When the federally financed service first began in 1971, it had 25 employees—now it's got more than 22,000 and it stops in more than 500 communities in 46 states.

Fares

Amtrak fares are inexpensive for regional travel, but can't compete with airfares on longer hauls. But, just as airlines deeply discount, so does Amtrak. And like booking an airline ticket, booking in advance will usually save you some dough; call or go online to make a reservation. We recommend the website route, as you could be on hold longer than it takes to ride a train from DC to New York.

Amtrak offers special promotional fares year-round targeting seniors, veterans, students, children under 16, and two or more persons traveling together. The "Rail SALE" page on Amtrak's website lists discounted fares between certain city pairs. Amtrak has hooked its sleeper cars up with plenty of travel partners to create interesting packages. The Air-Rail deals, whereby you rail it one-way and fly back the other, are attractive for long distance destinations. Call 877-937-7245 and surf the "Amtrak Partners" website page for partner promotional fares.

Going to New York

Amtrak runs more than 40 trains daily to New York that vary in service and price. A one-way coach ticket (the cheapest option) varies from $74 to $92 depending on the time, and the trip takes about 3 1/2 hours. If you're in a rush or like the idea of first-class, the Acela express is an option. It shaves about 30 minutes off your travel time and has roomier, cleaner, and generally less-crowded trains. At $126 it's almost double the price—how much is your time worth to you?

Going to Boston

A one-way fare can range from $89 to $111. The trip to downtown Boston's South Station takes eight hours (a stop at a newsstand before boarding to stock up on People and Us is recommended), but impatient travelers can take the Acela express and get there in about seven hours. Convenience doesn't come cheap. The express fare runs from $141 to $165.

Going to Philadelphia

Taking Amtrak to the city of brotherly love takes about two hours and will cost you $47 to $56 for the basic service and $92 to $108 for the nominally faster and significantly luxer Acela.

Going to Atlanta

There are two trips per day between Washington and Atlanta—one there and one back, both leaving in the early evening. You'd better pack your PJs because you'll be traveling through the night; trains get in at around 8 am the following day. The fare is between $185 and $210, depending on when you're going. With airfares being as cheap as they are, the only conceivable reason for taking the train option would be fear of flying.

Baggage Check (Amtrak Passengers)

Each ticketed passenger can check three items not exceeding 50 lbs. For an extra fee, three additional bags may be checked. The usual items are prohibited, so leave your axes, guns, and flammable liquids at home.

Essential Phone Numbers

Emergencies:	911
General Info:	211
Police Non-emergencies:	311
City Website:	www.washingtondc.gov
PEPCO:	202-833-7500
Verizon:	800-275-2355
Washington Gas:	703-750-1000
District Cablevision:	202-635-5100
Public Works, Consumer and Regulatory Affairs, Human Services, and the Mayor's Office	202-727-1000
Fire & Emergency Medical Services Department	202-673-3331

Websites

www.notfortourists.com—The most comprehensive DC website there is.

http://washingtondc.craigslist.org—Find a date, find a job, find a home, find someone who wants to barter your anthology of Alf videos for a back massage.

www.digitalcity.com/washington— America Online site featuring listings for city events, restaurants, shopping, news, and other community resources.

www.dcregistry.com—A comprehensive directory listing of the DC area web sites, plus free classifieds, discussion forums, free home pages, and more.

www.dcpages.com—Another local DC website directory.

www.washingtonpost.com—The Washington Post's website featuring bars, clubs, books, movies, museums, music, restaurants, shopping, sports, and theater listings. Oh, and stuff from the newspaper.

www.embassy.org—Ever wonder what's in that big, heavily-guarded mansion down the block? Check out this online resource of Washington's foreign embassies.

Washington DC Timeline

A timeline of significant events in DC history
(by no means complete)

1608 Capt. John Smith sails from Jamestown up the Potomac. Irish-Scotch colonized the area for the next 100 years…after they pushed out the Native Americans who originally inhabited the land, of course.

1791 Pierre Charles L'Enfant, an engineer from France, designs the capital city. He is fired within a year and replaced by city surveyor Andrew Ellicott and mathematician Benjamin Banneker.

1800 The federal capital is transferred from Philadelphia to an area along the Potomac River now known as Washington DC.

1801 Library of Congress is established.

1814 The Capitol and several government buildings are burned by the English during the War of 1812.

1817 The Executive Mansion is rebuilt following the burning by the British. Its walls are painted white to cover the char, giving birth to its more commonly known name: the White House.

1846 The Smithsonian Institution is established.

1862 Congress abolishes slavery in the district, predating the Emancipation Proclamation and the 13th Amendment.

1865 Lee surrenders to Grant on April 8th.

1865 Lincoln assassinated at Ford's Theatre on April 14th.

1888 The Washington Monument opens.

1901 The Washington Senators bring major league baseball to the district.

1907 Union Station opens, making it the largest train station in the country at the time.

1912 Japan sends 3,000 cherry blossom trees to DC as a gift of friendship. The Cherry Blossom Festival begins.

1922 The Lincoln Memorial is finished.

1937 Washington Redskins arrive in the city.

1943 The Pentagon building and the Jefferson Memorial are completed.

1954 Puerto Rican nationalists open fire on the floor of the House of Representatives wounding five members.

1960 The original Senators baseball team moves to Minnesota and becomes the Twins.

1963 Civil rights march of over 200,000 unites the city. Dr. Martin Luther King, Jr. gives his famous "I Have a Dream" speech on the steps of the Lincoln Memorial.

1968 Urban riots after MLK's assassination devastate whole neighborhoods, some that have yet to fully recover.

1970 The city is granted the right to elect its own representative to Congress.

1972 Republican operatives break into Democratic offices in the Watergate.

1972 The expansion Senators baseball team moves to Texas and becomes the Rangers.

1974 President Nixon resigns under threat of impeachment.

1974 An NBA franchise moves to DC to become the Washington Bullets, and later the Wizards.

1976 The Metrorail opens to the public.

1982 The Vietnam Veterans Memorial is erected.

1992 Mayor Sharon Pratt Dixon takes office. She is the first woman ever elected as the city's mayor.

1992 House of Representatives vote in favor of Washington DC becoming a state. The Senate says "no dice."

1994 Mayor Marion Barry is elected to an unprecedented fourth term as the city's mayor

after being arrested for smoking crack cocaine and serving time in prison for possession.

1995 Korean War Veterans Memorial opens to the public.

1998 The House of Representatives impeaches President Clinton over an intern sex scandal that rocked the White House.

1998 A gunman opens fire in US Capitol killing two policemen.

2001 Thousands protest as President George W. Bush takes office after a hotly contested election. No other president in history has received such a hostile un-welcome on the day of his inauguration.

2001 Terrorist attack destroys part of the Pentagon.

2001 Anthrax mailed to Senate offices causes short-term panic and massive mail disruptions.

2002 Snipers terrorize the region for 3 weeks, killing ten before being caught.

2004 World War II Memorial opens on the National Mall.

2004 Major league baseball negotiates to bring a team to the region.

2004 NFT Washington DC is released.

We're Number One!

- First black woman elected mayor of a major city: Sharon Pratt Dixon, 1991.
- First major US city to have an African-American majority (1957).
- World's largest library: Library of Congress.
- World's largest chair: located on Martin Luther King Jr. Avenue.
- World's largest museum complex: Smithsonian Institution.
- First president to be inaugurated in DC: Thomas Jefferson (who was also the first to grow tomatoes in America).
- World's oldest operating elevator: located inside Old Litwin's Furniture Building at Indiana Avenue, 7th Street, and C Alley.
- World's first prefrontal lobotomy: September 14, 1956.
- World's first all-Black university: Howard University, opened in 1867.
- First live Beatles performance in the US: Washington DC Coliseum, February 11, 1964.
- World's first and only liberal arts college exclusively for deaf people: Gallaudet University, 1864.

6 Essential DC Songs

"The Star-Spangled Banner"—Francis Scott Key
"Yankee Doodle"—Dr. Richard Shuckburgh
"Hail Columbia"—Joseph Hopkinson
"Washington, DC"—Stephen Merritt
"I'm Just a Bill"—School House Rock
"Hail to the Redskins"—Redskins Fight song

Essential Washington DC Books

All the President's Men, Carl Bernstein and Bob Woodward
Primary Colors, Anonymous
Washington, DC: A Novel, Gore Vidal
Coming into the End Zone: A Memoir, Doris Grumbach
The Burning of Washington: The British Invasion of 1814, Anthony S. Pitch
Cadillac Jack, Larry McMurtry
Chilly Scenes of Winter, Ann Beattie
The Congressman Who Loved Flaubert: 21 Stories and Novellas, Ward Just
Cane, Jean Toomer
Man of the House: The Life and Political Memoirs of Speaker Tip O'Neill, Tip O'Neill
Burr, Gore Vidal
Jack Gance, Ward Just
The Confederate Blockade of Washington, DC 1861-1862, Mary Alice Wills
The Armies of the Night : History As a Novel/the Novel As History, Norman Mailer
Personal History, Katharine Graham
One Last Shot: The Story of Michael Jordan's Comeback, Mitchell Krugel

25 Essential DC Movies

Mr. Smith Goes to Washington (1939)
Patton (1970)
The Exorcist (1973)
All the President's Men (1976)
The Man with One Red Shoe (1985)
St. Elmo's Fire (1985)
Broadcast News (1987)
The Hunt for Red October (1990)
JFK (1991)
A Few Good Men (1992)
Patriot Games (1992)
Dave (1993)
In the Line of Fire (1993)
The Pelican Brief (1993)
Clear and Present Danger (1994)
Forrest Gump (1994)
The American President (1995)
Nixon (1995)
Get on the Bus (1996)
Independence Day (1996)
Air Force One (1997)
Wag the Dog (1997)
Primary Colors (1998)
Minority Report (2002)
The Sum of All Fears (2002)

General Information

DC Public Library Website: www.dclibrary.org
Alexandria Library Website: www.alexandria.lib.va.us
Arlington Library Website: www.co.arlington.va.us/lib
Montgomery County Library Website: www.montgomerylibrary.org

Overview

The Washington DC Library system revolves around the massive main Martin Luther King branch downtown. Large in size, scope, and ugliness, this eyesore with dark, scary stairwells is better than it looks. It's divided into rooms by subject area and staffed by an efficient, knowledgeable crew that can find you a 1988 National Geographic faster than you can say "Micronesia." If you don't have particular research needs, some of the other branches, notably Georgetown's, are more pleasant places to spend an afternoon. Then again, if you have time to spare and want both extensive research capabilities and lux quarters, forget the local stuff and head over to the US Library of Congress.

■ = Public   ■ = By Appointment Only   ■ = Other

Type	Library	Address	Phone	Map
■	Charles E Beatley Jr Central Library	5005 Duke St	703-519-5900	41
■	James M Duncan Branch Library	2501 Commonwealth Ave	703-838-4566	43
■	Kate Waller Barrett Branch Library	717 Queen St	703-838-4555	46
■	Alexandria Law Library	520 King St, Room L-34	703-838-4077	46
■	American University Library	4400 Massachusetts Ave NW	202-885-3409	19
■	Anacostia Library	1800 Good Hope Rd SE	202-698-1190	5
■	Arlington Central Library	1015 N Quincy St	703-228-5990	34
■	Aurora Hills Library	735 18th St S	703-228-5715	40
■	Arlington Public Library Information & Referral Office	2100 Clarendon Blvd	703-228-3000	36
■	Arthur R Ashe Jr Foreign Policy Library	1426 21st St NW	202-223-1960	9
■	Bethesda Library	7400 Arlington Rd	240-777-0970	29
■	Bureau of Alcohol & Tobacco Library	650 Massachusetts Ave NW	202-927-7890	10
■	Cherrydale Library	2190 Military Rd	703-228-6330	34
■	Chevy Chase Library	8005 Connecticut Ave	301-986-4313	23
■	Chevy Chase Library	5625 Connecticut Ave NW	202-282-0021	28
■	Cleveland Park Library	3310 Connecticut Ave NW	202-282-3080	17
■	Columbia Pike Library	816 S Walter Reed Dr	703-228-5710	37
■	Comptroller of Currency Library	250 E St SW	202-874-9504	6
■	Dibner Library	12th St & Constitution Ave NW	202-357-1568	1
■	Ellen Coolidge Burke Branch Library	4701 Seminary Rd	703-519-6000	41
■	Federal Aviation Adm Libraries	800 Independence Ave SW #930	202-267-3396	1
■	Federal Reserve Board Research & Law Libraries	20th St & Constitution Ave NW	202-452-3284	7
■	Federal Trade Commission Library	600 Pennsylvania Ave NW #630	202-326-2395	2
■	Foundation Center	1001 Connecticut Ave NW	202-331-1400	9
■	General Services Adm Library	1800 F St NW #1033	202-501-0788	7
■	Georgetown Library	3260 R St NW	202-282-0220	8
■	Glencarlyn Public Library	300 S Kensington St	703-358-6548	38
■	Howard University School of Business Library	2600 6th St NW	202-806-1561	15
■	Information Resources	1300 Pennsylvania Ave NW #7-5	202-927-1350	1
■	International Trade Commission Library	500 E St SW	202-205-2630	6
■	James Melville Gilliss Library	3450 Massachusetts Ave NW	202-762-1463	17
■	Lamond-Riggs Library	5401 South Dakota Ave NE	202-541-6255	14
■	Langston Community Library	2600 Benning Rd NE	202-724-8665	4
■	Martin Luther King Jr Memorial Library	901 G St NW	202-727-1111	1
■	Mt Pleasant Library	3160 16th St NW	202-671-0200	16
■	NASA Headquarters Library	300 E St SW #1J20	202-358-0168	6
■	National Clearinghouse Library	624 9th St NW #600	202-376-8110	1
■	National Endowment for the Humanities Library	1100 Pennsylvania Ave NW #217	202-606-8400	1
■	National Geographic Society Library	1145 17th St NW	202-857-7787	9

■ National Research Council Library	2101 Constitution Ave NW	202-334-2125	7
■ NOAA Central Library	1315 East West Hwy	301-713-2600	25
■ Northeast Library	330 7th St NE	202-698-3320	3
■ Office of Thrift Supervision Library	1700 G St NW	202-906-6470	1
■ Palisades Library	4901 V St NW	202-282-3139	18
■ Petworth Library	4200 Kansas Ave NW	202-541-6300	21
■ Polish Library in Washington	1503 21st St NW	202-466-2665	9
■ RL Christian Community Library	1300 H St NE	202-724-8599	3
■ Shepherd Park Library	7420 Georgia Ave NW	202-541-6100	27
■ Shirlington Library	2786 S Arlington Mill Dr	703-228-6545	39
■ Silver Spring Library	8901 Colesville Rd	301-565-7689	25
■ Southeast Library	403 7th St SE	202-698-3377	5
■ Southwest Library	900 Wesley Pl SW	202-724-4752	6
■ Sursum Corda Community Library	135 New York Ave NW	202-724-4772	11
■ Takoma Park Library	416 Cedar St NW	202-576-7252	27
■ Tenley-Friendship Library	4450 Wisconsin Ave NW	202-282-3090	19
■ Treasury Library	1500 Pennsylvania Ave NW #142	202-622-0990	1
■ US Patent & Trademark Library	2021 S Clark Pl	703-305-4463	40
■ US Department of Commerce Library	1401 Constitution Ave NW	202-482-5511	1
■ US Department of Energy Library	1000 Independence Ave SW	202-586-5000	1
■ US Department of the Interior Library	1849 C St NW	202-208-5815	7
■ US Housing & Urban Development Library	451 7th St SW #8141	202-708-2370	6
■ US Institute of Peace	1200 17th St NW #200	202-457-1700	9
■ US Library of Congress	101 Independence Ave SE	202-707-5000	2
■ US Senate Library	Russell Senate Office Bldg, B15	202-224-7106	2
■ US State Library	2201 C St NW	202-647-2458	7
■ Watha T Daniel Branch Library	1701 8th St NW	202-671-0212	10
■ West End Library	1101 24th St NW	202-724-8707	9
■ Westover Library	1800 N Lexington St	703-228-5260	33
■ Woodridge Library	1801 Hamlin St NE	202-541-6226	13

Hospitals

Depending on where you live in the city, an ambulance ride can mean a quick jaunt to the emergency room that's prepped to treat the president, or it can mean a long stop-and-go-haul through traffic to arrive at the doors of a jammed, overworked emergency room.

The dichotomies of living in the city that is both the nation's capital and one of the nation's most troubled is abundantly obvious in the hospital system. It's only gotten worse since a couple of the major hospitals have closed in recent years. If you have a choice, point the driver toward George Washington University Hospital and ask for the same guy who in 1981 put a just-shot Ronald Reagan back together.

Hospital	Address	Phone	Map
Children's National Medical	111 Michigan Ave NW	202-884-5000	14
George Washington University	901 23rd St NW	202-715-4000	7
Georgetown University	3800 Reservoir Rd NW #2Phc	202-784-2000	18
Howard University	2112 Georgia Ave NW	202-865-4600	10
Inova Alexandria	4320 Seminary Rd	703-504-3000	42
National Naval Medical Center	8901 Wisconsin Ave	301-295-6289	22
Northern Virginia Community	601 S Carlin Springs Rd	703-671-1200	38
Providence Hospital	1150 Varnum St NE	202-269-7000	14
Sibley Memorial	5255 Loughboro Rd NW	202-537-4000	32
Suburban	8600 Old Georgetown Rd	301-896-3100	22
US Veterans Medical Center	50 Irving St NW	202-745-8000	14
Virginia Hospital Center	1701 N George Mason Dr	703-558-5000	34
Walter Reed Army Medical Center	6900 Georgia Ave NW	202-782-1199	27
Washington Adventist	7600 Carroll Ave	301-891-7600	26
Washington Hospital Center	110 Irving St NW	202-877-7000	14

General Information • **Media**

Television

Call letters	Station	Website
50-WBDC	WB	www.wbdc.com
4-WRC	NBC	www.nbc4.com
26-WETA	PBS	www.weta.org
20-WDCA	UPN	www.wdca.com
7-WJLA	ABC	www.wjla.com
9-WUSA	CBS	www.wusatv9.com
30-WMDO	Univision	www.univision.com
5-WTTG	Fox	www.fox5dc.com
32-WHUT	PBS/Howard University	
64 WZDC	Telemundo	www.telemundo.com
43-PXW	Pax	www.pax.com
28-W28BY	Government/NASA	

Radio

AM Call Letters	Dial #	Description	FM Call Letters ctd.		
WMAL	630 AM	News-Talk	WGTS	91.9 FM	Contemporary Christian
WABS	780 AM	Religious	WKYS	93.9 FM	Hip Hop
WCTN	950 AM	Religious	WPGC	95.5 FM	R&B
WTEM	980 AM	Sports	WHUR	96.3 FM	Adult R&B
WUST	1120 AM	International	WASH	97.1 FM	AC
WMET	1150 AM	Talk	WMZQ	98.7 FM	Country
WWRC	1260 AM	Business News	WIHT	99.5 FM	Top 40
WYCB	1340 AM	Gospel	WBIG	100.3 FM	Oldies
WOL	1450 AM	Talk	WWDC	101.1 FM	Rock
WTOP	1500 AM	News	WGMS	103.5 FM	Classical
			WWZZ	104.1 FM	Top 40
FM Call Letters	Dial #	Description	WAVA	105.1 FM	Religious
WAMU	88.5 FM	NPR	WJZW	105.9 FM	Smooth Jazz
WPFW	89.3 FM	Jazz	WJFK	106.7 FM	Talk
WCSP	90.1 FM	Congressional Coverage	WRQX	107.3 FM	Hot AC
WETA	90.9 FM	Classical	WTOP	107.7 FM	News

Print Media

American Free Press	1433 Pennsylvania Ave SE	202-544-5977	"Uncensored" national weekly newspaper.
Roll Call	50 F St NW	202-824-0475	Congressional news publication, Mon-Thurs.
The Common Denominator	650 Rhode Island Ave NE	202-635-6357	Bi-weekly independent newspaper.
The Hill	733 15th St NW	202-628-8500	Non-partisan Congressional newspaper.
Voice of the Hill	Linden Court NE	202-841-9080	Monthly DC neighborhood newspaper.
Washington Business Journal	155 Wilson Blvd, Arlington	703-875-2200	Weekly DC business journal.
Washington City Paper	2390 Champlain St NW	202-332-2100	Free weekly newspaper, focused on local DC.
Washington Post	1150 15th St NW	703-469-2500	Daily, one of the world's most prestigious.
Washington Times	3600 New York Ave NE	202-636-6000	Daily, general interest with conservative bent.
Washington Blade	1408 U St	202-797-7000	Weekly, focused on gay community news.
GW Hatchet	2140 G St NW	202-994-7079	Monthly, independent student newspaper.
Georgetown Hoya	Box 571065, Georgetown U	202-687-3415	Bi-weekly college newspaper.
Georgetown Voice	Box 571066, Georgetown U	202-687-6764	Weekly, college newsmagazine.
Washington Golf	3600 New York Ave NE	202-636-3372	Monthly golf magazine.
Washingtonian Online	1828 L St NW	202-296-3600	Monthly magazine about DC life.

If the proliferation of doggie parks are any clue, this city likes its pooches as much as its donkeys or elephants. All neighborhoods have a least one green spot for Fido to frolic and do his less adorable business. Larger parks, like Rock Creek or Meridian, allow dogs to get some serious roaming done. It's still a hassle to find animal-friendly apartments, but as long as renters are willing to cough up a bit more monthly, there are options.

General Rules for Parks

- Dogs must be under the owner's/handler's control.
- Only three dogs per person are allowed.
- No female dogs in heat allowed.
- Only dogs four months and older are allowed.
- Dogs must be legally licensed, vaccinated, and wearing both current tags.
- Dog owners/handlers must keep their dog(s) in view at all times.
- Dogs must not be allowed to bark incessantly or to the annoyance of the neighborhood.
- Dog owners/handlers must immediately pick up and dispose of all dog feces.
- Aggressive dogs are not allowed at any time. Owners/handlers are legally responsible for their dog(s) and any injury caused by them.
- Dogs must be on leash when entering and exiting parks/fenced areas.

Washington DC	Address	Comments	Map
Mitchell Park	22nd St & S St NW		3
Stanton Park	Maryland Ave & 6th St NE		3
Lincoln Park	Capitol Hill, 11th St SE & N Carolina Ave SE	Busy early mornings and early evenings. Water, benches, and lighting provided.	3
Congressional Cemetery	1801 E St SE	$100 annual fee, plus $20 per dog. Unlimited off-leash roaming of the grass and tombstones.	5
Malcolm X/Meridian Hill	16th St	No off-leash.	16
Glover Park Dog Park	39th & W St NW		18
Battery Kemble Park	Capitol Hill, MacArthur Blvd	Lots of wooded trails. Good parking. No off-leash.	32
Arlington			
Fort Ethan Allen Park	3829 N Stafford St	Dogs not allowed on soccer field. Don't park in the back lot unless you want a ticket.	31
Towers Park	801 S Scott St	Unfenced. Exercise area behind tennis courts.	37
Glencarlyn Park	301 S Harrison St	Unfenced area near creek and woods. Restrooms, fountains, and picnic areas.	38
Barcroft Park	4100 S Four Mile Run Dr	Exercise area between bicycle path and water.	39
Fort Barnard	S Pollard St & S Walter Reed Dr	Fenced park with off-leash area.	39
Shirlington Park	2601 S Arlington Mill Dr	Fenced park with stream, paved trail, and water fountain.	39
Utah Park	3308 S Stafford St	Daytime hours only.	39
Alexandria			
City Property	Chambliss St & Grigsby Ave	Off-leash exercise area.	38
City Property	NW corner of Seminary Rd & Beauregard St	Off-leash exercise area.	38
Fort Ward Park	Area east of entrance. 4401 W Braddock Rd	Off-leash exercise area.	39
City Property	NE corner of N Armistead St & N Beauregard St	Off-leash exercise area.	41
Duke Street Dog Park	5005 Duke St	Fenced dog park.	41
City Property	SE corner of Wheeler Ave & Duke St	Off-leash exercise area.	42
Old Mill Run	Old Mill Run, west of Gordon St	Off-leash exercise area.	43
City Property	SE corner of W Braddock Rd & Commonwealth Ave	Off-leash exercise area.	44
Hooff's Run	E Commonwealth, b/w Oak & Chapman St	Off-leash exercise area.	44
City Property	NE corner of First St & Payne St	Off-leash exercise area.	45
Del Ray Dog Park	Simpson Stadium, Monroe Ave	Fenced dog park.	45
Founders Park, NE corner	Oronoco St & Potomac River	Off-leash exercise area.	45
Montgomery Park	N Fairfax St & First St	Fenced dog park.	45
Powhatan Gateway	Henry St & Powhatan St	Off-leash exercise area.	45
City Property	SW corner of Gibbon St & Union St	Off-leash exercise area.	46

Overview

There's always some mass gathering in Washington DC; from inauguration demonstrations to flower festivals, DC has it all. The best events are free and easily accessible by mass transit.

Event	Approx. Dates	For more info…	Comments
New Year's Eve	Dec 31/Jan 1	www.digitalcity.com/ washington/newyearevents	Celebrate the new year with music, art, and bitter freezing cold.
Martin Luther King's Birthday	Observed January 15	www.whitehouse.gov/kids/ martinlutherkingjrday.html	Music, speakers, and a recital of the "I have a dream" speech on the Lincoln Memorial steps.
Robert E Lee's Birthday	January 19	703-557-0613	Yes, victors write the history books, but some losers' popularity endures.
Presidential Inauguration	January 20, every 4 years	http://memory.loc.gov/ ammem/pihtml/pihome.html	A cold, crowded, tax-payer-funded spectacle.
Chinese New Year	Mid-February		See ya later, Monkey.
Black History Month Celebration	February	www.si.edu	African-American history at the Smithsonian.
Abraham Lincoln's Birthday	Observed February 12	703-619-7222	Reading of Gettysburg Address in front of the city's favorite marble hero.
George Washington's Birthday Parade	February 19	703-838-9350	Parade and party in Alexandria for the city's other favorite guy.
Mt Vernon Open House	February 19	www.mountvernon.org	George & Martha won't trade spaces.
St Patrick's Day Parade	March 17	www.dcstpatsparade.com	Celebration of all things Irish in DC: music, food, oh, and beer too.
Smithsonian Kite Festival	Late March	http://kitefestival.org	Watch adults attack kiddie play like a combat sport.
Washington Flower and Garden Show	March 21	www.flowergardenshow.com	Check out the flora that actually enjoys this climate.
National Cherry Blossom Festival	March 25–April 8	www.nationalcherryblossom festival.org	One of the can't-misses…problem is the tourists think so too.
Filmfest DC opens	Early April	www.filmfestdc.org	For once see a flick before it in NYC.
White House Spring Garden Tours	Mid-April	www.whitehouse.gov	No politics, just flowers.
Shakespeare's Birthday	April 23	703-544-4600	To go or not to go. That is the question.
White House Easter Egg Roll	April 24	www.whitehouse.gov	No politics, just eggs.
Department of Defense/ Joint Services Open House	Mid-May	www.defenselink.mil	The country flexes its muscles with an air show and other military might.
National Symphony Orchestra Memorial Day Weekend Concert	May 27	www.kennedy-center.org/nso	Easy on the ears—and wallet; it's free.
Memorial Day Ceremonies at Arlington Cemetery	May 28	www.arlingtoncemetery.org	Ceremonies at JFK's grave, Tomb of the Unknown Soldier.
Memorial Day Ceremonies at the Vietnam Veterans Memorial	May 28	www.nps.gov/vive	Solemn memorial.
Memorial Day Jazz Festival	May 28	703-838-4844	Jazz in Alexandria.
Virginia Gold Cup	May 4	www.vagoldcup.com	Horse race on the same day as the Kentucky Derby. Someone fire the marketing department.
Dance Africa DC	Early June	703-269-1600	A feat of feet.
Dupont-Kalorama Museum Walk Day	Early June	www.dkmuseums.com/ walk.html	Free admission to the city's smaller, quirkier, pricier exhibits.
Carnival Extravaganza	Early June	703-829-1447	Carribean music, food, and outrageous costumes.

Event	Date	Contact	Description
Capital Pride	June 4-10	www.capitalpride.org	Huge, fun, funky, out, and proud.
Red Cross Waterfront Festival	June 8-10	www.waterfrontfestival.org	If you fall out of the canoe, Clara Barton may rescue you.
National Capital Barbecue Battle	Late June	www.barbecuebattle.com	Hot and sticky BBQ on a hot and sticky day.
Independence Day Celebration	July 4	703-619-7222	July 4th in America-town. The fireworks are a must.
Bastille Day	July 14	703-296-7200	No time to order freedom fries.
Virginia Scottish Games	Late July	www.vascottishgames.org	Kilts and Haggis everywhere!
Hispanic Festival	Late July		Latin American celebration at the Washington Monument.
Latin and Jazz Festival	Late July		Latin food, Latin jazz.
Annual Soap Box Derby	June 11	301-670-1110	The one day parents let their kids fly down city streets in wooden boxes.
Georgia Ave Day	Late August		Parades, music, and food from the southern US and Africa.
National Frisbee Festival	Late August	301-645-5043	Don't fight it, join it.
National Army Band's 1812 Overture Performance	Late August	www.whitehouse.gov	No politics, just patriotic music.
African Cultural Festival	Early Sept		African music, food at Freedom Plaza.
DC Blues Festival	Early Sept	www.dcblues.org	Rock Creek Park gets down and depressed.
Kennedy Center Open House	Early Sept	www.kennedy-center.org	Check out the terrace and the Kennedy sculpture without shelling out for the opera.
Adams Morgan Day	September 9	www.adamsmorganday.org	Neighborhood that gets jammed nightly gets jammed while sun's up.
Oktoberfest	Late Sept	703-787-6601	Beer, sausage, and polka. Two out of three ain't bad.
St. Sophia Greek Festival	Late Sept	202-333-4730	Big, fat, Greek festival.
Taste of DC Festival	Early October	202-724-5347	Nibble at snacks left out in hot sun all day.
White House Fall Garden Tours	Mid-October	www.whitehouse.org	No politics, just leaf peeping.
Reel Affirmations	Mid-October	www.reelaffirmations.org	Like Filmfest DC, except much more gay.
Jewish Film Festival	Late October/ Early Nov	www.wjff.org	Like Filmfest DC, except much more Jewish.
Marine Corps Marathon	Late October	www.marinemarathon.com	26 miles of asphalt and cheers.
Theodore Roosevelt's Birthday	October 27	www.theodoreroosevelt.org	Party for one of the other giant heads in North Dakota.
Civil War Living History Day	November 10	703-838-4848	The culmination of reenactment–stickler bickering.
Veteran's Day Ceremonies	November 11	www.arlingtoncemetery.org	Military ceremony in Arlington Cemetery.
Alexandria Antiques Show	November 10	703-838-4554	Expensive old stuff.
Kennedy Center Holiday Celebration	December	www.kennedy-center.org	X-mas revelry.
Kwanzaa Celebration	December	www.si.edu	Celebration at the Smithsonian.
National Christmas Tree Lighting/ Pageant of Peace	Mid-Dec to January 1	www.whitehouse.gov	Trees, menorahs, yule logs get lit at the White House Ellipse.
Washington National Cathedral Christmas Celebration and Services	Dec 24 - 25	202-537-6247	Humongous tree from Nova Scotia.
White House Christmas Candlelight Tours	December 28	www.whitehouse.gov	Still no politics, just religion.

Yes, it's a great city of history and civics, but sometimes the kids aren't in the mood for another tutorial on the Declaration of Independence. If you check out some of the destinations on this list, you'll discover there's life beyond the mall when it comes to entertaining your mini-yous.

The Best of the Best

★ **Best Kid-Friendly Restaurant:** Café Deluxe (3228 Wisconsin Ave NW, 202-686-2233, and 4910 Elm St, Bethesda, 301-656-3131). You know a restaurant is kid-friendly when the tablecloth is paper and is littered with crayons. At Café Deluxe, your kids can perfect their masterpieces while munching on entrees like buttered noodles, PB&J, cheese quesadillas, or pint-sized pancakes. The prices reflect that your companions are only half-size: Children's menu prices range from $2.50 to $3.95. Runner up: Buca di Beppo in Dupont Circle (1825 Connecticut Ave NW, 202-232-8466). Family-style Italian in a restaurant that will endlessly distract toddlers.

★ **Quaintest Activity:** Canal Boat Rides (1057 Thomas Jefferson St NW, 202-653-5190). Take a boat ride along the historic C&O canal in a boat pulled by mules. Experience rising eight feet in a water lock while park rangers in period clothing describe what life was like for families that lived and worked on the canal during the 1870s. Tours are Wednesday–Friday at 11 am and 3 pm and Saturday and Sunday at 11 am, 1:30 pm, and 3 pm. $8 Adults, $5 Children.

★ **Funnest Park:** Rock Creek Park (5200 Glover Rd NW, 202-895-6070). Rock Creek Park has an area on Beach Drive called Candy Cane City—'nuf said. Leland Street is good for picnicking and has a playground, basketball courts, and tennis courts. In the rest of the park, children's programs include planetarium shows, animal talks, and exploratory hikes.

★ **Coolest Bookstore:** A Likely Story Children's Bookstore (1555 King St, Alexandria, 703-836-2498). It's got weekly story times, writing workshops for kids, and special events almost daily during the summer. Story time for children under 2 is Monday and Wednesday at 11 am, and story time for children 2+ is on Tuesday at 11 am.

★ **Best Rainy Day Activity:** Capital Children's Museum (800 3rd St NE, 202-675-4120). The one museum where they won't whine about being bored. They can drive a bus, get lost in a maze, stand in the middle of a giant bubble, or design their own cartoon. Meanwhile you can duck away to the Mexico exhibit and fix yourself hot chocolate and tortillas. Open daily, 10 am–5 pm. $7 adults and children, $5 seniors, free for children under 2; half-price Sundays before noon.

★ **Sunny Day Best Bet:** National Zoo (3001 Connecticut Ave, 202-673-4717). This free and easily accessible zoo is like a park stroll with benefits. Beyond the pandas and apes, there's also a Kids' Farm with cows, donkeys, goats, chickens, and ducks. Summer camps and classes are available to Friends of the National Zoo Family Members. The $50 membership also includes zoo birthday party reservations, free popcorn for your kids every time they visit, and a 25% discount for activities that cost money. The zoo is open daily and admission is always free. April–November buildings are open 10 am–6 pm, November–April they are open 10 am–4:30 pm.

★ **Neatest Store:** Barston's Child's Play (5536 Connecticut Ave NW, 202-244-3602). It's long, narrow aisles are stocked with games, toys, puzzles, trains, costumes, art supplies, and books. It'll get the kids hooked on shopping early.

Parks for Playing

• **Cleveland Park** (3409 Macomb St NW). Climb a spider web, climb a wall, or catch a train. The park has separate play areas for younger and older children, picnic tables, basketball courts, a baseball field, and a recreation center.

• **East Potomac Park** (Ohio Drive SW). Always a good bet with its miniature golf course, public pool, picnic facilities, and playground at the southern tip. A must while the cherry blossoms are in bloom.

• **Friendship Park** (4500 Van Ness St NW, 202-282-2198). Plenty of slides, tunnels, swings, and climbing structures, as well as basketball and tennis courts, softball/soccer fields, and a recreation center. If you need a break, there's plenty of shade and picnic tables.

- **Kalorama Park** (19th St & Kalorama Rd NW). While the shade is limited here, this is a large playground with a fence dividing big-kid and little-kid playgrounds.

- **Marine Reed Recreation Center** (2200 Champlain St NW, 202-673-7768). Plenty of shady areas to rest your old bones while the kids are devouring the massive jungle gym, slides, tennis courts, and basketball courts.

- **Montrose Park** (R St & 30th St NW, 202-426-6827). For you: lots of open space, a picnicking area, and tennis courts. For your kids: swings, monkey bars, a sandbox, and a maze.

Rainy Day Activities

No problem, this is a city of mostly free museums. And many of them cater to the height—and attention—challenged.

Museums with Kid Appeal

- **National Air and Space Museum** (Independence Ave & 4th St, 202-357-2700). Can you go wrong in museum that sells astronauts' freeze-dried ice cream? Kids can walk through airplanes and spaceships. Check out the Einstein Planetarium and the IMAX Theater. Open daily 10 am – 5:30 pm. Admission is free but does not include special events or activities.

- **National Museum of Natural History** (10th St & Constitution Ave, 202-357-2700). Aside from the dinosaurs, which your kids will of course love, this museum boasts the Discovery Room, complete with animal teeth, a crocodile head, and clothing from different cultures. The best part? Kids can touch absolutely everything! If you're not too squeamish, you must take your kids to see the Orkin Insect Zoo which has a great collection of cockroaches, bees, and ants. Don't miss the tarantula feeding at 10:30 am, 11:30 am, and 1:30 pm! Open daily 10 am–5:30 pm with extended summer hours 10 am–7:30 pm. Free admission.

- **International Spy Museum** (800 F St NW, 202-393-7798). This oh so cool museum may seem a little pricey, but the sleek exhibits filled with high-tech gadgets and fascinating real-life spy stories make the price totally worth it. Special family programs include making and breaking secret codes and disguise creation workshops. Twice a year the museum even offers a Spy Overnight Adventure, which provides kids with a "behind the scenes" look at the life of spy. The museum is open daily but hours vary according to season. Free admission for children under five, $13 adults, $10 kids (ages 5–11).

- **National Museum of American History** (14th St and Constitution Ave, 202-357-2700). While your kids will certainly love a glimpse of Dorothy's ruby red slippers, the hands-on sections of this museum are where they'll really want to be. The Hands-On History Room, open Tuesday through Sunday 12 pm–3 pm for kids 5 and up, allows kids to gin cotton, send a telegraph, or say "hello" in Cherokee. The Hands-On Science Room, also for children over 5, is open from 12 pm–5 pm Tuesday through Friday and 10 am–5 pm weekends. Kids can take intelligence tests, separate food dyes in beverages, or use lasers to see light. Museum admission is free, but tickets (which are also free) are required for the hands-on rooms during weekends and busy hours, so be sure to pick them up at the front desk on your way in.

Other Indoor Distractions

- **Bureau of Engraving and Printing** (14th & C St SW, 202-874-3019). We're all used to seeing money spent. At this museum, you can watch how money is made, although your kids will probably be most interested in watching the destruction of old money. Admission is free, however tickets are required March-August. General tours (the only way to see the museum) are given every 15 minutes from 10 am to 2 pm, Monday through Friday.

- **Discovery Theatre** (900 Jefferson Drive SW, 202-357-3030). Puppet shows, dance performances and storytelling all under one roof. Performances are given daily at 10 am and 11:30 am, Monday through Friday, and Saturday at 11:30 am and 1 pm. Shows are $5 for adults and $4 for children, with special group rates available. Kids ages 4 to 13 can also join the Young Associates Program, where they can learn to animate clay figures or make their own puppets.

- **National Aquarium** (14th and Constitution Ave NW, 202-482-2825). At the nation's oldest aquarium you'll find 50 tanks with over 200 species. Open daily 9 am–5 pm, adults $3.50, kids (2-10) $1.

Outdoor and Educational

If you need some fresh air, you don't have to forgo the teaching opportunity.

- **Fort Ward** (4301 West Braddock Rd, Alexandria, 703-838-4848). The best preserved Union fort in DC. Picnic areas are available and the on-site museum has a Civil War Kids' Camp for ages 8 to 12 during the summer. Open Tuesday through Saturday 9 am–5 pm and Sunday 12 pm–5 pm. Admission is free.

- **National Arboretum** (3501 New York Ave NE, 202-245-2726). Covering 466 acres, the National Arboretum is the ultimate backyard. Picnicking is encouraged in the National Grove of State Trees picnic area. A 40-minute open-air tram ride is available and advised if you want to see everything. The Arboretum is open every day 8 am–5 pm. Admission is free, but the tram will run you $4 for adults and $2 for children 4-16.

- **Sculpture Garden Ice-Skating Rink** (7th St & Constitution Ave NW, 202-737-4215). The Sculpture Garden's rink is specially designed to allow views of the garden's contemporary sculptures while skating. It's like feeding your kids culture subliminally. Admission for a two-hour session is $6 for adults and $5 for children, students, and seniors. Skate rental is $2.50 and a locker rental is 50¢.

Classes

- **Ballet Petite** (Several throughout DC area, 301-229-6882). Fundamental dance instruction mixed with costumes, story telling, props, acting, and music.

- **Budding Yogis** (5615 39th St NW, 202-686-1104). Yoga for kids, teens, and adults. Special summer programs available.

- **Capitol Hill Arts Workshop** (545 7th St SE, 202-547-6839). Classes for children in art disciplines, tumbling, and tae kwon do. If your kids are precociously cool, sign them up for the jazz/hip-hop class and watch them perform a Hip-Hop Nutcracker in December.

- **Dance Place** (3225 8th St NE, 202-269-1600). Creative movement, hip-hop, and African dance instruction for kids.

- **Dancing Heart Center for Yoga** (221 5th St, NE, 202-544-0841). Yoga classes for kids aged 4 to 13. The class for children under 8 is structured around a story.

- **Imagination Stage** (4908 Auburn Ave, Bethesda, 301-960-6060). Classes in music, dance, and theatre for kids and teens. Three-week summer camps also available.

- **Jelleff Boys and Girls Club** (3265 S St NW, 202-462-1317). After-school programs in sports, art, and music at a facility that includes a gym, computer lab, game room, and pool.

- **Joy of Motion** (5207 Wisconsin Ave NW, 202-362-3042). Creative movement and fundamental dance instruction for children.

- **Kids Moving Company** (7475 Wisconsin Ave, Bethesda, 301-656-1543) Creative movement classes for children 9 months to 8 years in a studio with a full-sized trampoline.

- **Kumon Math and Reading Program** (6831 Wisconsin Ave, Bethesda, 703-338-7291). An after-school learning program in math and reading.

- **Music Tots** (4238 Wilson Blvd, Arlington, 703-266-4571). Early instruction in music, rhythm, and sound for children under 5.

- **Musikids** (Bethesda, Chevy Chase, and Silver Spring locations, 301-215-7946) Music and movement classes for newborns to toddlers.

- **Pentagon Row Ice-Skating** (1201 S Joyce St, Arlington, 703-418-6666). Skating lessons and birthday parties are available during winter months at this outdoor skating rink.

- **Power Tech Tae Kwon Do** (2639 Connecticut Ave, 202-364-8244). Martial arts training for kids as young as 3 years.

- **Rock Creek Horse Center** (5100 Glover Rd NW, 202-362-0117). Riding lessons, summer day camp, and equestrian team training. Weekly group lessons $40, private lessons $80/hour, and two-week summer camp $650.

- **Rock Creek Tennis Center** (16th & Kennedy St NW, 202-722-5949). Six-week weekend tennis courses available for children at beginner or intermediate levels.

- **Round House Theatre** (East West Hwy at Waverly St, Bethesda, 240-644-1100). Year-round theatre school and an arts-centered summer day camp program.

- **Sportrock Climbing Center** (5308 Eisenhower Ave, Alexandria, 703-212-7625). Kids learn to climb. 6- to 12-year-olds have the run of the place 6:30 pm–8 pm on Fridays. $20 per participant.

- **Sur La Table** (1101 S Joyce St, Arlington, 703-414-3580). At Sur La Table's junior cooking classes, kids are encouraged to (gasp!) play with food. Classes are for children aged 6-12 and groups are small and well organized.

- **Young Playwrights Theatre** (2437 15th St NW, 202-387-9173). Programs for children from 4th grade and up that encourage literacy, playwrighting, and community engagement.

Shopping Essentials

- **Ambercrombie Kids** (kids' clothes) • 1208 Wisconsin Ave NW • 202-333-1566
- **Barnes and Noble** (books)
  • 3040 M St NW • 202-965-9880
  • 3651 Jefferson Davis Hwy, Alexandria • 703-299-9124
  • 4801 Bethesda Ave, Bethesda • 301-986-1761
- **Barston's Child's Play** (everything kids love) • 5536 Connecticut Ave NW • 202-244-3602
- **Benetton Kids** (kids' clothes) • Wisconsin Ave & M St NW • 202-333-4140
- **Burberry** (kids' coats and clothes) • 1155 Connecticut Ave NW • 202-463-3000
- **Borders** (books)
  • 600 14th St NW • 202-737-1385
  • 1801 K St NW • 202-466-4999
  • 5333 Wisconsin Ave NW • 202-686-8270
  • 1201 Hayes St, Arlington • 703-418-0166
- **Children's Place** (kid's clothes) • 1100 S Hayes St, Arlington • 703-413-4305
- **Discovery Channel Store** (children's gifts) • 50 Massachusetts Ave NE • 202-842-3700
- **Disney Store** (children's gifts) • 1100 S Hayes, Arlington • 703-418-0310

- **Fairy Godmother** (toys and books) • 319 7th St SE • 202-547-5474
- **Fleet Feet** (sneakers for kids and adults) • 1841 Columbia Rd NW • 202-387-3888
- **Full of Beans** (kids' clothes) • 5502 Connecticut Ave NW • 202-362-8566
- **Gap Kids and Baby Gap** (kids' clothes) • 1100 S Hayes St, Arlington • 703-418-4770
- **Gymboree** (kids' clothes) • 1100 S Hayes St, Arlington • 703-415-5009
- **Hecht's** (clothes, furniture, toys, books) • 12th & G St NW • 202-628-6661
- **Imagination Station** (books) • 4524 Lee Highway, Arlington • 703-522-2047
- **Kids Closet** (kids' clothes) • 1226 Connecticut Ave NW • 202-429-9247
- **Kids Shop** (woodworking and crafts) • 6925 Willow St NW • 202-726-0028
- **Kinder Haus Toys** (toys) • 4510 Lee Hwy • 703-522-5929
- **Patagonia** (clothes) • 1048 Wisconsin Ave NW • 202-333-1776
- **Plaza Artist Supplies** (arts and crafts) • 1990 K St NW • 202-331-0126
- **Politics and Prose** (books) • 5015 Connecticut Ave NW • 202-364-1919
- **Ramer's Shoes** (children's shoes) • 3810 Northampton St NW • 202-244-2288
- **Riverby Books** (used books) • 417 E Capitol St SE • 202-543-4342
- **Sullivan's Art Supplies** (arts and crafts) • 3412 Wisconsin Ave NW • 202-362-1343
- **Sunny's Great Outdoors** (sporting goods) • 912 F St NW • 202-737-2032
- **Sur La Table** (pint-sized cooking supplies) • 1101 S Joyce St, Arlington • 703-414-3580
- **Tree Top Toys** (toys, books & clothes!) • 3301 New Mexico Ave NW • 202-244-3500
- **Urban Outfitters** (clothes) • 3111 M St NW • 202-3421012

Where to go for more information

www.gocitykids.com
www.ourkids.com

Dupont Circle is to gay life as Capitol Hill is to politics. And just like politics seeps into most aspects of the city, the gay scene reaches far beyond Lambda Rising. In addition to the world's largest GLBT bookstore (just down the street from another bookstore where the New York Times' first "Weddings" section gay couple met), there are specialized clubs, shops, and media dotted around DC that cater to the GLBT community. But it's more than a special interest here—the city is, for the most part (thanks to the efforts of activists), sexual-orientation-blind.

Websites

Capital Pride · www.capitalpride.org
This website helps to educate the metropolitan area about the GLBT community and celebrates its heritage and history. The organization is also responsible for the planning and development of the annual Capital Pride Parade.

DC GLBT Arts Consortium · www.geocities.com/dcglbtarts
Voluntary collaboration of various arts organizations in the DC area.

DC Dykes · www.dcdykes.com
Guide for lesbians living in DC.

GayDC · www.gaydc.net
In depth and up-to-date network for DC's gay, lesbian, bisexual, and transgendered community.

GayWdc · www.gayWdc.com
Gay and lesbian website for DC restaurant and bar listings, local news and events, classifieds, and personals.

Gay and Lesbian Activists Alliance · www.glaa.org
Local volunteer organization developed to advance the equal rights of gays and lesbians in Washington DC. GLAA is the nation's oldest continuously active gay and lesbian civil rights organization.

Pen DC · www.pendc.org
GLBT business networking group in the DC area.

Slash DC, Gay & Lesbian Guide to DC ·
http://gaybazaar.com/dc
Information on nightlife, media, and news for DC's lesbian and gay community.

Publications

Metro Weekly · 1012 14th St NW · 202-638-6830 ·
www.metroweekly.com
Free weekly gay and lesbian magazine, reliable coverage of community events, nightlife, and reviews of the district's entertainment and art scene.

Washington Blade · 1408 U St, 2nd Floor,
202-797-7000 · www.washingtonblade.com
Respectable weekly news source for Washington's gay community.

Women in the Life · 1623 Connecticut Ave NW,
202-483-9818, www.womeninthelife.com
Glossy quarterly magazine written for and by lesbians of color.

Woman's Monthly · 1718 M St NW · 202-965-5399 ·
www.womo.com.
DC's Monthly Magazine for Lesbians.

Bookstores

Lambda Rising · 1625 Connecticut Ave NW ·
202-462-6969 · www.lambdarising.com
When this bookstore opened in 1974, it carried about 250 titles. Today Lambda Rising operates five stores, including venues in Maryland, Delaware, Virginia, and New York. This bookstore also serves as an information hub for the Washington DC gay community.

Politics and Prose · 5015 Connecticut Ave NW,
202-364-1919, www.politics-prose.com.
Popular bookstore and coffee shop with a small selection of gay and lesbian literature.

Health Center & Support Organizations

Beth Mishpachah: District of Columbia Jewish Center ·
16th St & Q St NW · www.bemishpachah.org
DC's egalitarian synagogue that embraces a diversity of sexual and gender identities.

The Center · 1220 L Street NW, Suite 100-475 ·
202-581-4700 · www.thedccenter.org
A volunteer organization committed to developing a central home for the GLBT community in metro DC.

DC AIDS Hotline · 202-332-2437 or 800-322-7432

DC Black Pride · PO Box 77071, Washington, DC, 20013 ·
202-737-5767 · www.dcblackpride.org
This group aims to build awareness of and pride in the black lesbian, gay, bisexual, and transgendered community. Proceeds from Black Pride events are distributed to HIV/AIDS and other health organizations serving the African-American community in the Washington DC area.

DC Police Department's Gay and Lesbian Liaison Unit ·
300 Indiana Avenue NW, Room 5125 · 202-727-5427·
mpdc.dc.gov/about/units/gllu.shtm
Staffed by openly gay and lesbian members of the police department and their allies. The unit is dedicated to serving the gay, lesbian, bisexual, and transgendered communities in the DC area.

Family Pride · PO Box 65327, Washington, DC, 20035 · 202-331-5015 · www.familypride.org
This group is dedicated to advancing the well-being of lesbian, gay, bisexual, and transgendered parents and their families.

Food and Friends · 58 L St SE · 202-488-8278 ·
www.foodandfriends.org
This wonderful organization packages and delivers meals and groceries to over 1,000 people living with HIV/AIDS and other life-challenging illnesses in the greater DC area.

GLAAD DC · 1700 Kalorama Rd · 202-986-1360 ·
www.glaad.org
Gay and Lesbian Alliance Against Defamation DC chapter.

PFLAG DC · PO Box 66363, Washington, DC, 20035,
202-638-3852 · www.pflagdc.org
Parents and Friend of Lesbians and Gays DC chapter.

Senior Health Resources · Temple Heights Station · PO Box 53453, Washington, DC, 20009 · 202-388-7900 Non-profit organization providing quality health related-services for the aging GLBT community.

Whitman-Walker Clinic · 1407 S Street NW · 202-797-3500 A non-profit organization that provides medical and social services to the GLBT and HIV/AIDS communities of metropolitan DC. Home to one of the oldest substance abuse programs in the US.

Sports and Clubs

Adventuring · PO Box 18118, Washington DC 20036 · 202-462-0535 · www.adventuring.org This group encourages outdoor activities, by organizing GLBT group hikes, bike rides, and more.

Capital Tennis Association · www.capitaltennis.org Casual and organized tennis programs for the metropolitan gay and lesbian community.

Chesapeake and Potomac Softball · PO Box 33394, Washington, DC, 20033 · 202-543-0236 · www.capsoftball.org A friendly place for members of the GLBT community to play softball.

DC Aquatics Club · PO Box 12211, Washington, DC, 20005 · www.swimdcac.org Swimming team and social club for gays, lesbians, and friends of the gay and lesbian community.

DC's Different Drummers · PO Box 57099, Washington, DC 20037 · 202-269-4868 · www.dcdd.org Washington DC's Lesbian and Gay Symphonic Band, Swing Band, Marching Band, and Pep Band.

DC Front Runners · PO Box 65550, Washington, DC, 20035 202-628-3223 · www.dcfrontrunners.org A running club for the gay and lesbian community.

DC Lambda Squares · PO Box 77782, Washington, DC, 20013 · www.dclambdasquares.org Lesbian and gay square dance club.

DC Strokes · PO Box 3789, Washington, DC 20027 · www.dcstrokes.org The first rowing club for gays and lesbians. It rows out of the Thompson Boat Center on the Potomac.

Federal Triangles · 202-986-5363 · www.federaltriangles.org A charitable organization hoping to promote the growth of soccer and foster a sense of community amongst GLBTs.

Gay Men's Chorus of Washington DC: Federal City Performing Arts Association · 2801M Street NW, Washington, DC, 20007 · 202-388-7464 · www.gmcw.org

Lambda Links · www.lambdalinks.org A social forum for golf camaraderie between gays, lesbians, and bisexuals in DC.

Lesbian and Gay Chorus of Washington DC · PO Box 65285, Washington, DC, 20035 · 202-546-1549 · www.lgcw.org

Wetskins Water Polo · www.wetskins.org The first lesbian, gay, and bisexual polo team in the United States.

Renegades Rugby · www.dcrugby.com A Division III club that actively recruits gays and men of color from the DC region.

Annual Events

Capital Pride Festival/Parade · 1407 S St NW · 202-797-3510 · www.capitalpride.org Annual festival and parade honoring the history and heritage of the GLBT community in Washington DC. Usually held the second week in June.

DC Black Pride Festival/Parade · 202-737-5767 · 1-866-94-BLGPD · www.dcblackpride.org. The world's largest Black Pride festival, drawing a crowd of about 30,000 annually. Usually held Memorial Day weekend, end of May.

Reel Affirmations · PO Box 73587, Washington, DC, 20056 · 202-986-1119 · www.reelaffirmations.org Washington DC's Annual Lesbian and Gay Film Festival. Late-October.

Youth Pride Day/Week · PO Box 33161, Washington, DC 20033 · 202-387-4141 · www.youthpridedc.org Usually held in early April. The largest event for gay, lesbian, bisexual, and transgendered youth in the mid-Atlantic region.

Venues

Gay
- **Bachelor's Mill** · 1104 8th St SE · 202-544-1931
- **The Blue Room** · 2321 18th St NW · 202-332-0800
- **Club Ten** · 1824 Half St SW · 202-484-3800
- **Cobalt** · 1639 R St NW · 202-462-6569
- **Crew Club** · 1321 14th, NW · 202-319-1333
- **DC Eagles** (leather) · 639 New York Ave NW · 202-347-6025
- **Deep End** · 1355 H St NE · 202-462-9057
- **Delta Elite** · 3734 10th St NE · 202-529-0626
- **DIK Bar** · 1635 17th St NW · 202-328-0100
- **Fireplace** · 2161 P St NW · 202-293-1293
- **Green Lantern** · 1335 Green Court NW · 202-638-5133
- **JR's** · 1519 17th St NW · 202-328-0090
- **Hamburger Mary's** · 1811 14th St NW · 202-232-7010
- **Remington's** · 639 Pennsylvania Ave SE · 202-543-3113
- **Omega DC** · 2122 P St NW · 202-223-4917
- **Wet** · 52 L St SE · 202-488-1200

Lesbian
- **Between Friends** · 1115-A U St NW · 202-232-2544
- **Edge/Wet** (Wednesday) · 52 L St SE · 202-488-1200
- **Phase 1** · 525 8th St SE · 202-544-6831

Both
- **Apex** · 1413 22nd St NW · 202-296-0505
- **Atlas Lizard Lounge** (Sunday) · 1223 Connecticut Ave NW · 202-331-4422
- **Banana Café** · 500 8th St SE · 202-543-5906
- **Club Chaos** (Wednesday - Ladies night) · 1603 17th St NW · 202-232-4141
- **Ebony II** · 1101-A Kenyon St NW · 202-797-1101
- **Freddy's Beach Bar** · 555 S 3rd St, Arlington · 703-685-0555
- **Larry's Lounge** · 1836 18th St NW · 202-483-1483
- **Playbill Café** · 1409 14th St NW · 202-265-3055
- **Secrets/Ziegfield's** · 1345 Half St SE · 202-554-5141

General Information • **Hotels**

Hanging out at DC hotels is one of the best ways to encounter a "mover and shaker", depending on which hotel you choose to patronize. Go to the Hay Adams for a drink and you won't wait long for the goods to arrive. Hit the Hotel Washington terrace bar and you'll be spending the night with other little people.

For all those with better things to do than people-watch, it's also good to know your neighborhood hotels because quite often they'll have a little-known policy called the neighborhood discount. When booking rooms for friends or family, ask for a neighborhood discount and you may get a few bucks knocked off the rate—which will come in especially handy if they're visiting in late spring when the weather is perfect and prices soar. The neighborhood rate is also beneficial when you're having renovations done or something in your house bursts.

Use the room rates and star ratings below as a guide only. Call or visit the hotel to get accurate room rates for the days you wish to stay. If you're booking in advance, check out sites such as hotels.com, expedia.com, and pricerighthotels.com to see if they offer special discounts for the time of your visit.

Map 1 • National Mall

			Avg rate	
Hay-Adams Hotel	800 16th St NW	202-638-6600	320	★★★★
Hilton Garden Inn	815 14th St NW	202-783-7800	160	★★★
Holiday Inn	115 14th St NW	202-737-1200	160	★★★
Hotel Harrington	436 11th St NW	202-628-8140	100	
Hotel Washington	515 15th St NW	202-638-5900	145	★★★
Hyatt	1000 H St NW	202-582-1234	150	
Marriott	1331 Pennsylvania Ave	202-393-2000	300	★★★
Marriott	775 12th St NW	202-737-2200	310	★★★★
Marriott	900 F St NW	202-638-4600	110	
Marriott	999 9th St NW	202-898-9000	200	★★★
Sofitel Lafayette Sq	806 15th St NW	202-737-8800	210	★★★★
Willard Inter-Continental	1401 Pennsylvania Ave NW	202-628-9100	449	★★★★

Map 2 • Chinatown / Union Station

Best Western	724 3rd St NW	202-842-4466	125	
George Hotel	15 E St NW	202-347-4200	200	★★★★
Holiday Inn	415 New Jersey Ave NW	202-638-1616	150	★★★
Hotel Monaco	700 F St NW	202-628-7177	330	★★★★
Hyatt	400 New Jersey Ave NW	202-737-1234	140	
Phoenix Park	520 N Capitol St NW	202-638-6900	120	★★★
Red Roof Inn	500 H St NW	202-289-5959	90	
Washington Ct Hotel	525 New Jersey Ave NW	202-628-2100	274	★★★★

Map 5 • Southeast

Capitol Hill Suites	200 C St SE	202-543-6000	120	★★

Map 6 • Waterfront

Channel Inn	650 Water St SW	202-554-2400	140	★★★1/2
Holiday Inn	550 C St SW	202-479-4000	110	★★★
Loews L'Enfant Plaza	480 L'Enfant Plz SW	202-484-1000	239	★★★★

Map 7 • Foggy Bottom

Doubletree	801 New Hampshire Ave NW	202-785-2000	190	★★★
George Washington University Inn	824 New Hampshire Ave NW	202-337-6620	200	★★★
Hotel Lombardy	2019 Pennsylvania Ave NW	202-828-2600	120	★★★1/2
River Inn	924 25th St NW	202-337-7600	120	★★★
State Plaza Hotel	2117 E St NW	202-861-8200	120	★★★
Swissotel Watergate	2650 Virginia Ave NW	202-965-2300	170	★★★★

Map 8 • Georgetown

			Avg rate	-
Four Seasons	2800 Pennsylvania Ave NW	202-342-0444	790	★★★★
Georgetown Inn	1310 Wisconsin Ave NW	202-333-8900	110	★★★
Georgetown Suites	1000 29th St NW	202-298-7800	150	★★★
Georgetown Suites	1111 30th St NW	202-298-7800	150	★★★
Holiday Inn	2101 Wisconsin Ave NW	202-338-4600	130	★★★
Hotel Monticello	1075 Thomas Jefferson St	202-337-0900	135	
Latham Hotel	3000 M St NW	202-726-5000	160	★★★
Washington Suites	2500 Pennsylvania Ave NW	202-333-8060	209	★★★

Map 9 • Dupont Circle / Adams Morgan

1 Washington Cir	1 Washington Cir NW	202-872-1680	130	★★★1/2
Best Western	1121 New Hampshire Ave NW	202-457-0565	120	
Carlyle Suites	1731 New Hampshire Ave NW	202-234-3200	160	★★★1/2
Churchill Hotel	1914 Connecticut Ave NW	202-797-2000	160	★★★★
Dupont at the Circle	1604 19th St NW	202-332-5251	200	★★★
Embassy Inn	1627 16th St NW	202-234-7800	110	
Embassy Suites	1250 22nd St NW	202-857-3388	215	★★★
Fairmont	2401 M St NW	202-429-2400	260	★★★★
Four Points	2100 Massachusetts Ave NW	202-293-2100	230	★★★★
Four Points	2350 M St NW	202-429-0100	160	★★★★
Four Points	923 16th St NW	202-638-2626	360	★★★★
Governor's House Hotel	1615 Rhode Island Ave NW	202-296-2100	110	★★★1/2
Hilton	1001 16th St	202-393-1000	105	
Hilton	1919 Connecticut Ave NW	202-483-3000	105	★★★
Hilton	2015 Massachusetts Avenue NW	202-265-1600	130	★★★
Holiday Inn	1501 Rhode Island Ave NW	202-483-2000	160	
Hotel Madera	1310 New Hampshire Ave NW	202-296-7600	170-210	★★★
Hotel Rouge	1315 16th St NW	202-232-8000	180	★★★
Jurys	1500 N Hampshire Ave NW	202-483-6000	125	★★★★
Jurys	1900 Connecticut Ave NW	202-319-1739	125	★★★★
Jurys	2118 Wyoming Ave NW	202-483-1350	125	★★★★
Lincoln Suites	1823 L St NW	202-223-4320	215	★★★
Loews Jefferson	1200 16th St NW	202-347-2200	200	★★★★
Madison	15th & M Sts NW	202-862-1600	200	★★★★
Marriott	1127 Connecticut Ave NW	202-347-3000	250	★★★★★
Marriott	1221 22nd St NW	202-872-1500	180	
Marriott	1600 Rhode Island Ave NW	202-293-8000	180	★★★★
Marriott	1900 Connecticut Ave NW	202-332-9300	120	★★★
Marriott	2120 P St NW	202-466-6800	200	
Melrose Hotel	2430 Pennsylvana Ave NW	202-955-6400	200	★★★1/2
Park Hyatt	24th & M Sts NW	202-789-1234	130	★★★
Radisson Barcelo	2121 P St NW	202-293-3100	200	★★★
Ritz-Carlton	1150 22nd St NW	202-835-0500	445	★★★★★
St Gregory Hotel & Suites	2033 M St NW	202-530-3600	140	★★★★
St Regis	923 16th St NW	202-638-2626	190	★★★★
Topaz Hotel	1733 N St NW	202-393-3000	205	★★★
Washington Terrace	1515 Rhode Island Ave NW	202-232-7000	172	★★★★
Windsor Inn	1842 16th St NW	202-667-0300	109	
Windsor Park	2116 Kalorama Rd NW	202-483-7700	129	★★1/2
Wyndham	1143 New Hampshire Ave NW	202-775-0800	189	★★★

Map 10 • Logan Circle / U Street

DC Guesthouse	1337 10th St NW	202-332-2502	180	
Four Points	1201 K St NW	202-289-7600	215	★★★
Hamilton Crowne Plaza	1001 14th St NW	202-682-0111	160	★★★
Hampton Inn	599 Massachusetts Ave NW	202-842-2500	120	★★★★
Henley Park Hotel	926 Massachusetts Ave NW	202-638-5200	130	★★★1/2

General Information · **Hotels**

Map 10 · Logan Circle / U Street — *continued*

			Avg rate	
Homewood Suites	1475 Massachusetts Ave NW	202-265-8000	180	
Hotel Helix	1430 Rhode Island Ave NW	202-462-9001	150	★★★
Marriott	1199 Vermont Ave NW	202-898-1100	170	★★★
Morrison-Clark Inn	Massachusetts Ave & 11th St NW	202-898-1200	240	★★★
Washington Plaza	10 Thomas Cir NW	202-842-1300	100	★★★
Wyndham	1400 M St NW	202-429-1700	155	★★★★

Map 11 · Near Northeast

Kellogg Conference Hotel	800 Florida Ave NE	202-651-6000	140	★★★

Map 12 · Trinidad

Travelodge	1917 Bladensburg Rd NE	202-832-8600	110	

Map 13 · Brookland / Langdon

Days Inn	2700 New York Ave NE	202-832-5800	90	★★★
Ramada Limited	1600 New York Ave NE	202-832-3200	80	

Map 16 · Adams Morgan (North) / Mt Pleasant

Kalorama Guesthouse	1854 Mintwood Pl NW	202-667-6369	85	

Map 17 · Woodley Park / Cleveland Park

Marriott	2660 Woodley Rd NW	202-328-2000	160	★★★
Omni Shoreham	2500 Calvert St NW	202-234-0700	220	★★★★

Map 18 · Glover Park / Foxhall

Marriott	3800 Reservoir Rd NW	202-687-3200	145	★★★★
Savoy Suites	2505 Wisconsin Ave NW	202-337-9700	170	★★★1/2

Map 19 · Tenleytown / Friendship Heights

Embassy Suites	4300 Military Rd NW	202-362-9300	250	★★★1/2

Map 20 · Cleveland Park / Upper Connecticut

Days Inn	4400 Connecticut Ave NW	202-244-5600	90	★★★

Map 22 · Downtown Bethesda

American Inn	8130 Wisconsin Ave	301-656-9300	115	
Bethesda Court Hotel	7740 Wisconsin Ave	301-656-2100	210	★★★
Four Points	8400 Wisconsin Ave	301-654-1000	145	★★★
Holiday Inn	8120 Wisconsin Ave	301-652-2000	150	
Marriott	5151 Pooks Hill Rd	301-897-9400	110	★★★

Map 25 · Silver Spring

Days Inn	8040 13 th St	301-588-4400	90	★★★
Hilton	8727 Colesville Rd	301-589-5200	105	★★★
Holiday Inn	8777 Georgia Ave	301-589-0800	140	

Map 29 · Bethesda/Chevy Chase

Holiday Inn	5520 Wisconsin Ave	301-656-1500	120	★★★★
Hyatt	1 Bethesda Metro Ctr	301-657-1234	250	
Marriott	7335 Wisconsin Ave	301-718-0200	150	★★★

Map 34 · Ballston

Hilton	950 N Stafford St	703-528-6000	150	★★★
Holiday Inn	4610 N Fairfax Dr	703-243-9800	95	★★★

Map 36 · Rosslyn

			Avg rate	
Best Western	1850 N Fort Myer Dr	703-522-0400	140	★★
Hilton Garden Inn	1333 N Courthouse Rd	703-528-4444	170	
Holiday Inn	1900 N Fort Myer Dr	703-807-2000	170	
Hyatt	1325 Wilson Blvd	703-525-1234	100	
Marriott	1401 Lee Hwy	703-524-6400	230	
Marriott	1533 Clarendon Blvd	703-528-2222	180	★★★
Marriott	1651 N Oak St	703-812-8400	210	★★★

Map 37 · Fort Myer

Days Inn	3030 Columbia Pike	703-521-5570	90	★★★

Map 38 · Columbia Pike

Hampton Inn	4800 Leesburg Pike	703-671-4800	120	★★★★
Homewood Suites	4850 Leesburg Pike	703-671-6500	140	

Map 39 · Shirlington

Best Western	2480 S Glebe Rd	703-979-4400	125	★★

Map 40 · Pentagon City

Days Inn	2020 Jefferson Davis Hwy	703-920-8600	150	★★★
Doubletree	300 Army Navy Dr	703-416-4100	165	★★★
Embassy Suites	1300 Jefferson Davis Hwy	703-979-9799	180	★★★★
Hampton Inn	2000 Jefferson Davis Hwy	703-418-8181	120	★★★★
Hilton	2399 Jefferson Davis Hwy	703-418-6800	140	★★★
Holiday Inn	2650 Jefferson Davis Hwy	703-684-7200	160	
Hyatt	2799 Jefferson Davis Hwy	703-418-1234	120	★★★★
Marriott	1999 Jefferson Davis Hwy	703-413-5500	230	★★★★
Marriott	2899 Jefferson Davis Hwy	703-549-3434	110	★★★
Marriott	550 Army Navy Dr	703-413-6630	110	
Sheraton	1800 Jefferson Davis Hwy	703-486-1111	130	★★★
Sheraton	900 S Orme St	703-521-1900	110	★★★

Map 41 · Landmark

Hilton	5000 Seminary Rd	703-845-1010	125	
Sheraton	4641 Kenmore Ave	703-751-4510	240	★★★
Washington Suites	100 S Reynolds St	703-370-9600	189	★★★1/2

Map 42 · Alexandria (West)

Marriott	2700 Eisenhower Ave	703-329-2323	100	★★★

Map 44 · Alexandria Downtown

Embassy Suites	1900 Diagonal Rd	703-684-5900	200	★★★
Hampton Inn	1616 King St	703-299-9900	120	★★★
Hilton	1767 King St	703-837-0440	115	★★★
Holiday Inn	2460 Eisenhower Ave	703-960-3400	150	★★★

Map 45 · Old Town (North)

Holiday Inn	625 1st St	703-548-6300	180	
Sheraton	801 N St Asaph St	703-836-4700	160	★★★

Map 46 · Old Town (South)

Best Western	1101 N Washington St	703-739-2222	120	
Holiday Inn	480 King St	703-549-6080	220	
Marriott	1456 Duke St	703-548-5474	130	★★★

Between renaming buildings, bridges, and fountains and building new monuments by the garden-full, DC is fast running out of things to convert to memorials. You could spend a month trying to visit every official monument in DC, but you'll have a better time checking out the unofficial local landmarks in the shadow of the White House and Washington Monument.

When in Dupont, hang out by the **Dupont Fountain**. In Silver Springs, head straight to the **AFI Theater**. Need a break from the frenzied Georgetown shopping scene? Walk a few blocks to the city's best garden at **Dumbarton Oaks**. And when you find yourself on New Hampshire Avenue, be proud that DC is one of the few places to properly memorialize **Sonny Bono**.

All Area Codes 202 unless noted

Map 1 · National Mall

Clinton McDonald's	1229 New York Ave NW	347-0047	Taste what Bill couldn't resist.
Decatur House	748 Jackson Place NW	965-0920	Tour worth taking.
Ford's Theater	511 10th St NW	426-6924	Lincoln's finale.
Gatekeeper's House	17th St NW & Constitution Ave NW		Overlooked history.
Hay-Adams Hotel	16th St & H St NW	800-853-6807	The luxury lap where Monica told all.
J Edgar Hoover FBI Building	935 Pennsylvania Ave NW	324-3000	Ask to see Hoover's cross-dressing dossier.
National Press Club	529 14th St NW, 13th Fl	662-7500	Join the ink-stained hacks for a drink.
St John's Church	16th St NW & H St NW	347-8766	Sit in the President's pew.
Smithsonian Institution	1000 Jefferson Dr SW	633-1000	Storm The Castle for information.

Map 2 · Chinatown / Union Station

Chinatown Gate	H St NW & 7th St NW		Ushers you in for cheap eats and cheaper pottery.
Library of Congress	101 Independence Ave SE	707-5000	Lose yourself in letters.
Newseum Front Pages	6th St NW & Pennsylvania Ave NW		Read up on hometown news.
Supreme Court of the United States	1st St NE	479-3211	Bring your favorite protest sign.

Map 3 · The Hill

Folger Shakespeare Library	201 E Capitol St SE	544-4600	To go or not to go?

Map 5 · Southeast

Anacostia Boathouse	1105 O St NE		Take the dirty plunge.
Eastern Market	225 7th St SE	546-2698	Apples and art.
Frederick Douglass House	1411 W St SE	426-5951	A man who showed up his neighborhood and his country.
Washington Navy Yard	805 Kidder Breese SE	433-4882	Haven for men in tighty whites.

Map 6 · Waterfront

Arena Stage	1101 6th St SW	488-3300	Great theater.
Ft Lesley J McNair	4th St and P St		For the Civil War buffs.
Thomas Law House	1252 6th St SW		Impressive house, not open to the public.
Tiber Island	4th St b/w N St & M St		Looking for an apartment?
USS Sequoia	6th St SW & Maine Ave SW	333-0011	Rent it when the VP isn't in the mood to play Mr. Howell.

Map 7 · Foggy Bottom

"Crossfire" Taping	805 21st St NW	994-1000	Lowbrow partisan shoutfest.
Einstein Statue	Constitution Ave NW & 23rd St NW		At his rumpled best.
Kennedy Center	2700 F St NW	416-8000	Highbrow culture.
The Octagon	1799 New York Ave NW	626-7387	Peculiar floor plan.
Watergate Hotel	2650 Virginia Ave NW		Home to scandal; bizarre architecture.

Map 8 · Georgetown

Cooke's Row	3009-3029 Q St NW		Romantic row.
Dumbarton Oaks Museum and Gardens	1703 32nd St NW	339-6401	An absolute treasure.
Exorcist Steps	3600 Prospect St NW		Watch your balance…
Oak Hill Cemetery	3000 R St NW	337-2835	Old and gothic.
Prospect House	3508 Prospect St NW		Spectacular view of the Potomac.
Tudor Place	1644 31st St NW	965-0400	Bring a picnic.
Volta Bureau	3417 Volta Pl NW	337-5220	HQ of the Alexander Graham Bell Association for the Deaf.

Map 9 · Dupont Circle / Adams Morgan

Belmont House (Eastern Star Temple)	1618 New Hampshire Ave NW	667-4737	National Women's party HQ.
Blaine Mansion	2000 Massachusetts Ave NW		Large, red, and brick.
Brickskeller	1523 22nd St NW	293-1885	Get drunk on any beer imaginable.
Chinese Embassy	2300 Connecticut Ave NW	328-2500	Look for the Falun Gong protesters.
Dumbarton Bridge	23rd St NW and Q St NW		It crosses Dupont to Georgetown.
Dupont Fountain	Dupont Cir		Top spot for people-watching.
Freshfarm Market	20th St NW near Q St	331-7300	Where yuppies get their fruit.
Gandhi Statue	Massachusetts Ave & 21st St		Don't peek under the skirt.
Heurich House	1307 New Hampshire Ave NW		It sure feels haunted.
Iraqi Embassy	1801 P St NW	483-7500	Watch the hated old shell come alive.
Lambda Rising	1625 Connecticut Ave NW	462-6969	DC's gay & lesbian gathering place.
Meridian Hill/ Malcolm X Park	15th & 16th St and W St NW		Sunday drum circle and soccer.
The Palm	1225 19th St NW	293-9091	AKA, The Institute For Power Lunching.
Sonny Bono Memorial	20th St NW & New Hampshire Ave NW		Rest In Peace babe.
Temple of the Scottish Rite	1733 16th St NW	232-3579	So that's what that is.
Washington Hilton	1919 Connecticut Ave NW	483-3000	Where Reagan took a bullet.
Woodrow Wilson House	2340 S St NW	387-4062	Another president's crib.

Map 10 • Logan Circle / U Street

African-American Civil War Memorial	1000 U St NW	667-2667	A belated thanks.
Ben's Chili Bowl	1213 U St NW	667-0909	Most beloved joint in the city.
Cato Institute	1000 Massachusetts Ave NW	842-0200	Conservative temple.
Duke Ellington Mural	1200 U St NW		He's watching.
Lincoln Theatre	1215 U St NW	328-6000	Renovated jewel.

Map 12 • Trinidad

Mount Olivet Cemetery	1300 Bladensberg Rd NW		Visit Mary Suratt, hanged for her part in killing Lincoln.

Map 13 • Brookland / Langdon

Franciscan Monastery	1400 Quincy St NE	526-6800	Beautiful gardens and bizarre crypt.

Map 14 • Catholic U

Brooks Mansion	901 Newton St NE		A Greek revival.
Grief in Rock Creek Cemetery	Rock Creek Church Rd NW & Webster St NW		Memorial to Adam's wife is best in the city.
Pope John Paul II Cultural Center	3900 Harewood Road NE	635-5400	When you can't get to the Vatican.
Shrine of the Immaculate Conception	400 Michigan Ave NE	526-8300	Humungo Catholic church.

Map 15 • Columbia Heights

Howard U Blackburn Center	2400 6th St NW	806-5983	Jazz and blues.

Map 16 • Adams Morgan (North) / Mt Pleasant

Marilyn Monroe Mural	Connecticut Ave NW & Calvert St NW		A tiny bit of glamour for DC.
Meridian International Center	1630 Crescent Place NW	667-6800	Look out for the exhibits.
Mexican Cultural Institute	2829 16th St NW	728-1628	Top-notch work by Mexican artists.
White-Meyer House	1624 Crescent Place NW	667-6670	International art exhibitions.

Map 17 • Woodley Park / Cleveland Park

US Naval Observatory	Massachusetts Ave NW	762-1467	VP's disclosed location.

Map 18 • Glover Park / Foxhall

National Cathedral	Massachusetts Ave NW & Wisconsin Ave NW	537-6200	Newly constructed old cathedral. Pure American.

General Information • **Landmarks**

Map 22 • Downtown Bethesda

National Institute of Health	9000 Rockville Pike	301-496-4000	Monkeys and rats beware...

Map 25 • Silver Spring

AFI Theater	8633 Colesville Rd	301-495-6720	Cool theater making the neighborhood cooler.

Map 27 • Walter Reed

Battleground National Military Cemetery	6625 Georgia Ave NW		Check out the entrance.
Walter Reed Medical Center	6900 Georgia Ave NW	782-2200	Giant band-aid dispenser.

Map 28 • Chevy Chase

Avalon Theatre	5612 Connecticut Ave NW	966-6000	Beloved neighborhood movie house.

Map 29 • Bethesda/Chevy Chase

Montgomery Farm Women's Co-op Market	7155 Wisconsin Ave	301-652-2291	Indoor country market.
Saks Fifth Ave	5555 Wisconsin Ave	301-657-9000	The centerpiece of a material girl neighborhood.
Writer's Center	4508 Walsh St	301-654-8664	Take a class, write for NFT.

Map 34 • Ballston

Ballston Commons	4238 Wilson Blvd	703-243-6346	Big box invasion.

Map 35 • Clarendon

Market Commons	2690 Clarendon Blvd		Chain retail disguised as Main Street.

Map 36 • Rosslyn

Iwo Jima Memorial	Marshall Dr	703-289-2500	Visit at night.

Map 40 • Pentagon City

Pentagon	Boundary Channel Dr	703-697-1776	Rummy's playpen.

Map 46 • Old Town (South)

Alexandria Farmers Market	301 King St	703-379-8723	Get yer arugula.
Carlyle House	121 N Fairfax St	703-549-2997	The kids will like it.
Gadsby's Tavern Museum	134 N Royal St	703-838-4242	Many US Presidents slept here.
Market Square Old Town	301 King St		Bring your skateboard.
Ramsay House	221 King St	703-838-4200	Alexandria's visitor center.
Stabler-Ledbeater Apocethary	105 S Fairfax St	703-836-3713	Where GW got his Viagra.
Torpedo Factory	201 N Union St	703-838-4565	Now it churns out art.

3D

2D   BETHESDA   MARYLAND

Capital View Ave

401

Aspen St NW

Eastern Ave NE

Western Ave NW

201

402

Military Rd NW

Missouri Ave NW

Reno Rd NW

403

W Capitol St NE

405

Beach Dr NW

202

203

Decatur St NW

Massachusetts Ave NW

404   **DISTRICT OF**   Taylor St NE   S Dakota Ave NE

COLUMBIA   John McCormick Rd NE

Porter St NW

205

204

301

302

501

502

Bladensburg Rd NE

503

16th St NW

Harvard St NW

15th St NW

303

304

305   S St NW

New York Ave NE

504

Whitehaven Pkwy

206

306

307   308

Rock Creek Pkwy

Florida Ave NE

601   602

44th St NW

23rd St NW

L St NW

New Jersey Ave

Benning Rd NE

Kenilworth Ave

ARLINGTON

Pennsylvania Ave NW

101

102   Maryland Ave

1D

207

17th St NW

Constitution Ave NW   HQ

E Capitol St

66

2nd St NE

9th St

103

2D

104

2nd St SE

E Capitol St SE

603

604

VIRGINIA

105   106   107

S Capitol St SE

6th St SE

13th St SE

Massachusetts Ave SE

3D

4D

605

Good Hope Rd SE

W George Mason Dr

Morris Rd SE

701   606

Arlington Blvd

703

Suitland Pkwy

702

Washington Blvd

707

704

Alexandria

705

Southern Ave

706   295

Potomac River

495

Washington DC is broken up into 44 different Police Service Areas (PSAs). Each PSA has a minimum of 21 MPDC officers, with the exception of PSA 707, which is primarily Bolling Air Force Base, and therefore needs fewer officers. The areas that experience higher crime rates have been assigned more than the minimum number of police. For example, PSA 105 has the minimum 21 officers, while 93 officers patrol PSA 101, which had a higher incidence of homicide (11), other violent crimes (501), property crimes (1,864), and prostitution-related calls for service (199) in 2003.

For a complete listing of crimes committed and officer allocation in each PSA, visit http://mpdc.dc.gov/info/districts/Matrix10_Hearing_022304.pdf. If you're planning on moving to a new neighborhood, this might be an important first port of call. If you can afford it, definitely think about relocating to the 200s; all the PSAs combined witnessed 1 homicide, 299 other violent crimes, and only 4 prostitution-related calls for service.

Metropolitan Police DC

All Emergencies:	911
Non-Emergencies:	311
City Services:	202-727-1000
Crimesolvers Tip Line:	800-673-2777
Child Abuse Hotline:	202-671-SAFE (7233)
Corruption Hotline:	800-298-4006
Gun Tip Hotline:	800-ATF-GUNS (283-4867)
Hate Crimes Hotline:	202-727-0500
Public Information Office:	202-727-4383
Office of Citizen Complaint Review:	202-727-3838
Website:	http://mpdc.dc.gov

Headquarters: 300 Indiana Ave NW • Map 2

District Stations:
• 1st • 415 4th St SW • 202-727-4655 • Map 6
• 1st Substation • 500 E St SE • 202-727-4608 • Map 5
• 2nd • 3320 Idaho Ave NW • 202-282-0070 • Map 18
• 3rd • 1620 V St NW • 202-673-6815 • Map 9
• 3rd Substation • 750 Park Rd NW • 202-576-8222 • Map 15
• 4th • 6001 Georgia Ave NW • 202-576-6745 • Map 27
• 5th • 1805 Bladensburg Rd NE • 202-727-4510 • Map 12

Statistics	2002	2001	2000
Homicide	262	233	242
Forcible Rape	262	181	251
Robbery	3,731	3,777	3,553
Aggravated Assault	4,854	5,003	4,582
Burglary	5,167	4,947	4,745
Larceny/Theft	20,903	22,274	21,637
Stolen Auto	9,168	7,970	6,600

Alexandria Police (VA)

2003 Mill Rd • Map 44

All Emergencies:	911
Non-Emergencies:	703-838-4444
Community Support:	703-838-4763
Crime Prevention:	703-838-4520
Domestic Violence Unit:	703-706-3974
Property-Lost & Found:	703-838-4709
Website:	http://ci.alexandria.va.us/police

Statistics	2003	2002
Homicide	4	2
Rape	26	20
Robbery	179	200
Aggravated Assault	192	186
Burglary	497	486
Auto Theft	640	794
Larceny/Theft	3,754	4,220

Arlington County Police (VA)

1425 N Courthouse Rd • 703-228-4040 • Map 36

All Emergencies:	911
Non-Emergencies:	703-558-2222
Rape Crisis, Victims of Violence	703-228-4848
Child Abuse:	703-228-1500
Domestic Violence Crisis Line	703-228-4848
National Capital Poison Center:	202-625-3333
Gang Hotline:	703-228-GANG (4264)
Website:	www.co.arlington.va.us/police

Statistics	2003	2002	2001
Homicide	3	5	3
Rape	41	33	29
Robbery	212	213	199
Aggravated Assault	183	190	161
Burglary	408	425	490
Larceny/Theft	4,050	4,990	5,395
Auto Theft	662	676	702

Montgomery County Police (MD)

All Emergencies:	911
Montgomery Non-Emergencies:	301-279-8000
Takoma Park Non-Emergencies:	301-891-7102
Chevy Chase Village Police:	301-654-7302
Animal Services:	240-773-5925
Community Services:	301-840-2585
Operation Runaway:	301-251-4545
Party Buster Line:	240-777-1986
Website:	www.montgomerycountymd.gov/poltmpl.asp?url=/Content/POL/index.asp

Chevy Chase Village Police • 5906 Connecticut Ave • Map 28
Takoma Park Police Dept • 7500 Maple Ave • Map 26

Statistics	2003	2002	2001
Homicide	21	32	19
Rape	135	138	120
Robbery	1,004	877	818
Aggravated Assault	954	878	827
Burglary	4,095	3,874	3,539
Larceny	17,875	18,897	18,226
Auto Theft	3,489	3,722	3,150

Post Office	Address	Phone	Zip	Map
Alexandria Main Office	1100 Wythe St	703-684-7168	22314	45
Arlington Main Office	3118 Washington Blvd	703-841-2118	22210	35
Benjamin Franklin	1200 Pennsylvania Ave NW	202-842-1444	20004	1
Bethesda	7400 Wisconsin Ave	301-654-5894	20814	29
Bethesda Chevy Chase	7001 Arlington Rd	301-656-8053	20814	29
Brightwood Station	6323 Georgia Ave NW	202-726-8119	20011	27
Brookland Station	3401 12 St NE	202-842-3374	20017	14
Buckingham Station	235 Glebe Rd	703-525-0459	22203	37
Calvert Station	2336 Wisconsin Ave NW	202-523-2026	20007	18
Catholic University Cardinal Station	620 Michigan Ave NE	202-319-5225	20064	14
Chevy Chase Branch	5910 Connecticut Ave	301-654-7538	20815	28
Cleveland Park Station	3430 Connecticut Ave NW	202-364-0178	20008	17
Columbia Heights Finance	3321 Georgia Ave NW	202-523-2674	20010	15
Court House Station	2043 Wilson Blvd	703-248-9337	22201	36
Eads Station	1720 S Eads St	703-892-0840	22202	40
Farragut Station	1800 M St NW	202-523-2024	20036	9
Fort McNair Station	300 A St NE	800-275-8777	20319	6
Friendship Heights Station	5530 Wisconsin Ave Frnt	301-941-2665	20815	29
Friendship Station	4005 Wisconsin Ave NW	202-842-3332	20016	19
Georgetown Station	1215 31st St NW	202-842-2487	20007	8
Howard University	2400 6th St NW	202-806-2008	20059	15
Kalorama Station	2300 18th St NW	202-523-2906	20009	16
L'Enfant Plaza Station	437 L'Enfant Plz SW	202-842-4526	20024	6
Martin Luther King Jr Station	1400 L St NW	202-523-2001	20005	10
McPherson Station	1750 Pennsylvania Ave NW	202-523-2394	20006	7
Memorial Station	2226 Duke St	703-684-6759	22314	44
Mid City Station	1915 14th St NW	202-842-4628	20009	10
National Capitol Station	2 Massachusetts Ave NE	202-523-2368	20002	2
National Naval Med Center	8901 Rockville Pike	301-941-2786	20889	22
North Station	220 N George Mason Dr	703-536-6269	22207	34
Northeast Station	1563 Maryland Ave NE	202-636-1975	20002	4
Northwest Station	5636 Connecticut Ave NW	202-842-2286	20015	28
Palisades Station	5136 MacArthur Blvd NW	202-842-2291	20016	32
Park Fairfax Station	3682 King St	703-933-2686	22302	39
Pentagon Branch	9998 The Pentagon	800-275-8777	20301	40
Petworth Station	4211 9th St NW	202-842-2112	20011	21
Potomac Station Finance	1908 Mount Vernon Ave	703-684-7821	22301	43
Rosslyn Station	1101 Wilson Blvd, Ste 1	703-527-7029	22209	36
Silver Spring Finance Centre	8455 Colesville Rd	301-608-1305	20910	25
Silver Spring Main Office	8616 2nd Ave	301-608-1305	20910	25
South Station	1210 S Glebe Rd	703-979-2821	22204	37
Southeast Station	600 Pennsylvania Ave SE	202-682-9135	20003	5
Southwest Station	45 L St SW	202-523-2590	20024	6
Takoma Park	6909 Laurel Ave	301-270-4392	20912	26
Techworld Station	800 K St NW	202-842-2309	20001	10
Temple Heights Station	1921 Florida Ave NW	202-234-4253	20009	9
Theological Seminary Finance	3737 Seminary Rd	703-933-2686	22304	42
Trade Center Station	340 S Pickett St	703-823-0968	22304	41
Twentieth St Station	2001 M St NW	202-842-4654	20036	9
Walter Reed Station	6800 Georgia Ave NW	800-275-8777	20012	27
Ward Place Station	2121 Ward Pl NW	202-842-4645	20037	9
Washington Main Office	900 Brentwood Rd NE	800-275-8777	20018	11
Washington Square Station	1050 Connecticut Ave NW	202-842-1211	20036	9
Watergate Station	2512 Virginia Ave NW	202-965-6278	20037	7
Woodridge Station	2211 Rhode Island Ave NE	202-523-2936	20018	13

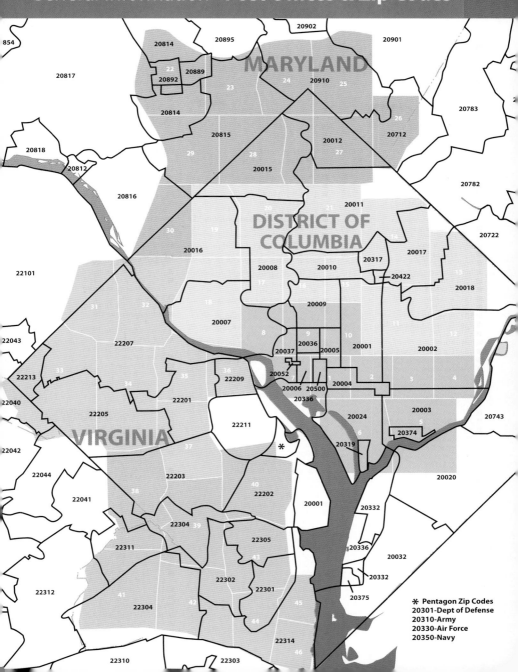

■ = FedEx; ■ = Airborne Express; Times listed are last pick-up time, p.m.; All locations are drop boxes unless otherwise noted.

Map 1 • National Mall

■ 1445 I St NW, FedEx Service Center	8:45
■ 1350 New York Ave NW, FedEx Service Center	8:30
■ 419 11th St NW, FedEx Service Center	8:30
■ 600 13th St NW	7:30
■ 601 13th St NW, Thomas Cook	7:30
■ 1201 New York Ave, Kaemper Bldg	7:30
■ 700 13th St NW	7:15
■ 1200 G St NW	7:15
■ 1300 I St NW	7:15
■ 555 12th St NW, Thurmond Arnold Bldg	7:00
■ 555 13th St NW, Columbia Constitution	7:00
■ 601 13th St NW, Homer Bldg	7:00
■ 734 15th St NW	7:00
■ 888 16th St NW	7:00
■ 750 17th St NW	7:00
■ 900 17th St NW	7:00
■ 800 Connecticut Ave NW	7:00
■ 1201 F St NW	7:00
■ 1201 F St NW	7:00
■ 1317 F St NW	7:00
■ 1310 G St NW	7:00
■ 1325 G St NW	7:00
■ 1341 G St NW, Colorado Bldg	7:00
■ 1250 I St NW	7:00
■ 1350 I St NW	7:00
■ 1300 I St NW, Franklin Square	7:00
■ 1399 New York Ave NW	7:00
■ 1440 New York Ave NW	7:00
■ 1201 Pennsylvania Ave NW	7:00
■ 600 14th St NW, Hamilton Sq	6:45
■ 740 15th St NW	6:45
■ 1700 G St NW	6:45
■ 1701 Pennsylvania Ave NW	6:45
■ 201 14th St SW, USDA Bldg	6:30
■ 805 15th St NW, The Southern Bldg	6:30
■ 624 9th St NW, YWCA	6:30
■ 815 Connecticut Ave NW	6:30
■ 1001 G St NW	6:30
■ 1333 H St NW	6:30
■ 1401 H St NW	6:30
■ 1717 H St NW	6:30
■ 1575 I St NW	6:30
■ 1625 I St NW	6:30
■ 955 L'Enfant Plaza SW	6:30
■ 470 L'Enfant Plz SW, Center Bldg	6:30
■ 400 N Capitol St NW, Hall of the States	6:30
■ 1200 New York Ave NW	6:30
■ 1212 New York Ave NW	6:30
■ 1425 New York Ave NW	6:30
■ 801 Pennsylvania Ave NW	6:30
■ 1331 Pennsylvania Ave NW	6:30
■ 1717 Pennsylvania Ave NW	6:30
■ 655 15th St NW	6:15
■ 17th & G St, Old Executive	6:15
■ 1000 Jefferson Dr SW, Smithonian Institution	6:15
■ 100 Raoul Wallenberg Pl SW, Holocaust Museum	6:15
■ 730 15th St NW, Bank of America	6:00
■ 401 9th St NW, Market Square	6:00
■ 750 9th St NW, Victor Building	6:00
■ 14th & Constitution Ave NW, Dept of Commerce	6:00
■ 1225 I St NW	6:00
■ 1620 I St NW	6:00
■ 1725 I St NW	6:00
■ 1201 New York Ave NW	6:00
■ 1445 New York Ave NW, Suntrust Bank	6:00
■ 1300 Pennsylvania Ave NW	6:00
■ 901 F St NW	5:45
■ 815 14th St NW, Hilton Garden Inn	5:30
■ 910 16th St NW	5:30
■ 733 15th St NW, Woodward Bldg	5:00
■ 701 9th St NW, Pepco	5:00
■ 1455 F St NW, Metropolitan Sq	5:00
■ 1101 Pennsylvania Ave NW	5:00

Map 2 • Chinatown / Union Station

■ 600 Maryland Ave SW	7:00
■ 20 Massachusetts Ave NW	7:00
■ 732 N Capitol St, GPO Building	7:00
■ 732 N Capitol St NW, Government Printing Office	7:00
■ 600 New Jersey Ave NW, Georgetown Law Center	7:00
■ 750 1st St NE	6:30
■ 810 1st St NE	6:30
■ 1 1st St NE, US Supreme Court	6:30
■ Kinko's, 325 7th St NW	6:30
■ 575 7th St NW, Terrell Place	6:30
■ 101 Constitution Ave NW	6:30
■ 200 Independence Ave SW	6:30
■ 600 Maryland Ave SW	6:30
■ 777 N Capitol St NE	6:30
■ 499 S Capitol St SW, Fairchild	6:30
■ 500 1st St NW	6:00
■ 400 1st St NW, Federal Prism Industries	6:00
■ 440 1st St NW, National Association of Countys	6:00
■ 500 5th St NW, National Academy of Science	6:00
■ 122 C St NW, Pan-American Properties	6:00
■ 400 Maryland Ave SW	6:00
■ 50 Massachusetts Ave NW, Union Station	6:00
■ 701 Pennsylvania Ave NW, Market Square	6:00
■ 200 Constitution Ave NW, Dept of Labor	5:45
■ 10 G St NE, Trammell Crowreal	5:30
■ Longworth House Office Building	5:30
■ 600 Pennsylvania Ave NW, FTC	5:30
■ 1 Columbus Cir NE, Federal Judiciary	5:00
■ 401 F St NW, National Building Museum	5:00
■ 601 New Jersey Ave NW	5:00

Map 3 • The Hill

■ 208 2nd St SE, FedEx Service Center	8:00
■ 227 Massachusetts Ave NE	6:15
■ 901 E St NW	6:00

Map 4 • RFK

■ 1400 Independence Ave SW	5:30

Map 5 • Southeast

■ 700 11th St NW	6:30
■ 301 4th St SW	6:30
■ 301 4th St SW	6:30
■ Kinko's, 715 D St SE	6:30
■ 1299 Pennsylvania Ave NW	6:30
■ 409 3rd St SW, Washington Office Center	6:00
■ 600 Pennsylvania Ave SE	5:30
■ 1100 New Jersey Ave SE, Federal Gateway	5:00
■ 3rd St SE & M St SE	5:00

Map 6 • Waterfront

■ 330 C St SW, Sweitzer Bldg	7:00
■ 445 12th St SW, Federal Communication Bldg	6:45
■ 901 D St SW	6:30
■ 7th & D St SW, GSA Bldg	6:30
■ 400 Virginia Ave SW	6:30
■ 600 Water St SW	6:30
■ 600 Water St SW	6:30
■ 400 6th St SW, Child & Family Services	6:00
■ 500 E St SW	6:00
■ 1280 Maryland Ave SW	5:45
■ 550 12th St SW, Potomac Center Plaza	5:30
■ 80 M St SE	5:30
■ 26 N St SE	5:30

Map 7 • Foggy Bottom

■ 431 18th St NW, Red Cross Sq	7:30
■ 2025 E St NW, American Red Cross National Headquarters	7:00
■ 2130 H St NW, George Washington University	7:00
■ 2000 H St NW, Lerner Hall	7:00
■ 1776 I St NW	7:00
■ 1875 I St NW, International Sq	7:00
■ 1735 New York Ave NW	7:00
■ 2100 Pennsylvania Ave NW	7:00
■ 900 19th St NW	6:45
■ 1730 Pennsylvania Ave NW	6:30
■ 2001 Pennsylvania Ave NW	6:30
■ 1747 Pennsylvania Ave NW	6:15
■ 924 25th St NW, River Inn	6:00
■ 900 2nd St NE	6:00
■ 18th & F St NW, GSA Bldg	6:00
■ 2700 F St NW, Kennedy Center for Performing Arts	6:00
■ 1922 F St NW, Old Main	6:00
■ 1750 H St NW	6:00
■ 600 New Hampshire Ave NW	6:00
■ 1801 Pennsylvania Ave NW	6:00
■ 1899 Pennsylvania Ave NW	6:00
■ 2150 Pennsylvania Ave NW	6:00

General Information • FedEx / Shipping

- 2600 Virginia Ave NW, Watergate 6:00
- 1250 24th St NW 5:30
- 1808 I St NW 5:30
- 2401 E St NW, State Department 4:30
- 1750 Pennsylvania Ave NW 4:00

Map 8 • Georgetown

- 1002 30th St NW, FedEx Service Center 8:00
- 3000 K St NW 7:00
- 1055 Thomas Jefferson St NW, Foundry Bldg 7:00
- 1101 30th St NW 6:30
- 2445 M St NW 6:30
- Staples, 3307 M St NW 6:30
- Kinko's, 3329 M St NW 6:30
- 1010 Wisconsin Ave NW 6:30
- 2150 Wisconsin Ave NW 6:30
- 1215 31st St NW 6:00
- 3299 K St NW 6:00
- 3333 K St NW 6:00
- 1000 Potomac St NW 6:00
- 24th St & Massachusetts Ave NW 6:00
- 1055 Thomas Jefferson St NW, Foundry Bldg 6:00
- 1000 Thomas Jefferson St NW 6:00
- 3520 Prospect St NW, Car Barn 5:30
- 2115 Wisconsin Ave NW, Grubbs & Ellis 5:30
- 2121 Wisconsin Ave NW 5:00
- 2445 M St NW, Westend Press 4:00

Map 9 • Dupont Circle / Adams Morgan

- 1029 17th St NW, FedEx Service Center 8:45
- 1 Dupont Cir NW, FedEx Service Center 8:45
- 1825 K St NW, FedEx Service Center 8:45
- 1123 18th St NW, FedEx Service Center 8:30
- 1019 15th St NW, FedEx Service Center 8:00
- 2001 M St, KPMG 8:00
- 1201 15th St NW, National Home Builders 7:30
- 1001 16th St NW, Capitol Hilton Hotel 7:30
- 1730 M St NW, American Express 7:30
- 1400 16th St NW 7:00
- 1150 17th St NW 7:00
- 1145 17th St NW, National Geographic 7:00
- 1015 18th St NW 7:00
- 1200 18th St NW, Ring 7:00
- 1111 19th St NW 7:00
- 1111 19th St NW 7:00
- 1200 19th St NW 7:00
- 1200 19th St NW 7:00
- 1220 19th St NW 7:00
- 1120 20th St NW 7:00
- 1133 20th St NW 7:00
- 1129 20th St NW, Board of Trade Bldg 7:00
- 1155 21 St NW 7:00
- 1101 Connecticut Ave NW 7:00
- 1201 Connecticut Ave NW 7:00
- 1250 Connecticut Ave NW 7:00
- 1330 Connecticut Ave NW 7:00

- 1921 Florida Ave NW 7:00
- 1501 K St NW 7:00
- 1666 K St NW 7:00
- 1900 K St NW 7:00
- 2000 K St NW 7:00
- 1850 K St NW, International Sq 7:00
- 1850 K St NW, International Sq 7:00
- 1828 L St NW 7:00
- 2000 L St NW 7:00
- 2001 L St NW 7:00
- 1620 L St NW, Apsco 7:00
- 1615 M St NW 7:00
- 1850 M St NW 7:00
- 1920 N St NW 7:00
- 1616 P St NW 7:00
- 2401 Pennsylvania Ave NW 7:00
- 1025 Connecticut Ave NW 6:45
- 1625 K St NW 6:45
- 1801 K St NW, Nations Bank 6:45
- 1165 15th St NW 6:30
- 1155 16th St NW 6:30
- 1101 17th St NW 6:30
- 1133 21st St NW 6:30
- 1255 22nd St NW 6:30
- 1150 22nd St NW, Ritz-Carlton Hotel 6:30
- 1255 23rd St NW 6:30
- 1050 Connecticut Ave NW 6:30
- 1133 Connecticut Ave NW 6:30
- 1225 Connecticut Ave NW 6:30
- 1250 Connecticut Ave NW 6:30
- 1725 Desales St NW 6:30
- 11 Dupont Cir NW 6:30
- 1500 K St NW 6:30
- Kinko's, 1612 K St NW 6:30
- Kinko's, 2020 K St NW 6:30
- 2033 K St NW 6:30
- 2001 K St NW, William P Rogers Bldg 6:30
- 1620 L St NW 6:30
- 1801 L St NW, EEOC 6:30
- 2300 M St NW 6:30
- 2440 M St NW 6:30
- 1785 Massachusetts Ave NW, National Trust for History 6:30
- 2030 N St NW 6:30
- 1608 Rhode Island Ave NW 6:30
- 1925 K St NW, Mercury Bldg 6:15
- 1133 15th St NW 6:00
- 1100 17th St NW, Cushman & Wakefield 6:00
- 1150 Connecticut Ave NW 6:00
- 1155 Connecticut Ave NW 6:00
- 1300 Connecticut Ave NW 6:00
- 1350 Connecticut Ave NW 6:00
- 1666 Connecticut Ave NW, Mutual of Omaha Bldg 6:00
- 1825 Connecticut Ave NW, Universal Bldg 6:00
- 2121 K St NW, McGregor Bldg 6:00
- 1909 K St NW, The Millenium Bldg 6:00
- 1660 L St NW 6:00
- 1819 L St NW 6:00
- 1901 L St NW 6:00
- 2001 M St NW 6:00
- 2311 M St NW 6:00
- 1776 Massachusetts Ave NW 6:00
- 1211 Connecticut Ave NW 5:45

- 1733 Connecticut Ave NW 5:45
- 2120 L St NW, Gelman Bldg 5:45
- 1730 M St NW 5:45
- 1529 18th St NW 5:30
- ASL Business and Mailing 1929 18th St NW 5:30
- 1300 19th St NW 5:30
- 1146 19th St NW, Cambridge Asset Advisors 5:30
- 1120 Connecticut Ave NW 5:30
- 1140 Connecticut Ave NW 5:30
- 1225 Connecticut Ave NW 5:30
- 1600 K St NW 5:30
- 1725 K St NW 5:30
- 2175 K St NW 5:30
- 2000 L St 5:30
- 1899 L St NW 5:30
- 1920 L St NW 5:30
- 1717 Massachusetts Ave NW 5:30
- 1250 23rd St NW 5:15
- 2401 Pennsylvania Ave NW 5:15
- 1200 17th St NW, The National Restaurant 5:00
- 2021 K St NW 5:00
- 1875 Connecticut Ave NW, Universal Bldg 4:00
- 2010 Massachusetts Ave NW 3:30

Map 10 • Logan Circle / U Street

- 1090 Vermont Ave NW 7:30
- 1101 14th St NW 7:00
- 1915 14th St NW 7:00
- 1275 K St NW 7:00
- 1275 K St NW 7:00
- 1301 K St NW, Franklin Square 7:00
- 1301 K St NW, Franklin Square 7:00
- 1100 L St NW 7:00
- 1436 U St NW, M A Winter Building 7:00
- 1120 Vermont Ave NW, Riggs National Bank 7:00
- 1200 K St NW 6:30
- 1 Thomas Circle NW, Prudential 6:30
- 1101 Vermont Ave NW 6:30
- 1120 Vermont Ave NW 6:30
- 1425 K St NW 6:15
- 1010 Massachusetts Ave NW, American Road & Transport 6:00
- 800 K St NW 5:45
- 1420 K St NW 5:30
- 1400 K St NW, APA Building 5:30
- 1401 K St NW, Tower Building 5:30
- 1220 L St NW 5:30
- 1201 M St SE, Maritime Plaza 5:30
- 1110 Vermont Ave NW 5:30
- 1400 K St NW, JBG Proper 5:00
- 1400 L St NW 4:30
- 1099 14th St NW 3:45

Map 11 • Near Northeast

- 1501 Eckington Pl NE, FedEx Service Center 8:30
- 416 Florida Ave NW 7:00
- 300 I St NE 6:30
- 900 Brentwood Rd NE 5:30
- 800 Florida Ave NE, Gallaudet University 5:00
- 300 M St SE, Federal Center 5:00

287

General Information • **FedEx / Shipping**

Map 14 • Catholic U

- 3401 12th St NE — 6:30
- 100 Irving St NW, Mid Atlantic Healthcare — 6:30
- 620 Michigan Ave NE — 6:00
- 3211 4th St NE — 5:30
- 216 Michigan Ave NE — 5:30

Map 16 • Adams Morgan (North) / Mt Pleasant

- 2479 18th St NW, Tech Printing — 5:30

Map 17 • Woodley Park / Cleveland Park

- 2500 Calvert St NW, Omni Shoreham Hotel — 7:00
- 3430 Connecticut Ave NW — 6:00
- 3133 Connecticut Ave NW, Kennedy Warren — 6:00
- 3100 Massachusetts Ave NW, Birtish Embassy — 3:00

Map 18 • Glover Park / Foxhall

- 3301 New Mexico Ave NW, Foxhall Square — 7:15
- 3400 Idaho Ave NW — 7:00
- 3970 Reservoir Rd NW, New Research Bldg — 6:45
- 4400 MacArthur Blvd NW — 6:30
- 2233 Wisconsin Ave NW — 6:30
- 4590 MacArthur Blvd NW — 6:00
- 4000 Reservoir Rd NW — 6:00
- 3800 Reservoir Rd NW, Lombardi Cancer Center — 6:00

Map 19 • Tenleytown / Friendship Heights

- 4000 Wisconsin Ave NW, FedEx Service Center — 8:00
- 5335 Wisconsin Ave NW — 7:00
- 5335 Wisconsin Ave NW, Chevy Chase Pavillion — 7:00
- 4005 Wisconsin Ave NW — 6:30
- Kinko's, 5225 Wisconsin Ave NW — 6:30
- 5301 Wisconsin Ave NW, Chevy Chase Plaza — 6:30
- 5301 Wisconsin Ave NW, Chevy Chase Plaza — 6:30
- 4400 Massachusetts Ave NW — 6:00
- 4400 Jenifer St NW, Jenifer Mall — 5:30
- 4620 Wisconsin Ave NW — 5:30

Map 20 • Cleveland Park / Upper Connecticut

- 4201 Connecticut Ave NW — 6:30
- 4301 Connecticut Ave NW — 6:00
- 4455 Connecticut Ave NW — 6:00
- 3509 Connecticut Ave NW, Parcel Plus — 6:00

Map 22 • Downtown Bethesda

- 9030 Old Georgetown Rd — 7:00
- 9650 Rockville Pike — 7:00
- 4833 Rugby Ave — 7:00
- 4849 Rugby Ave, WR Schinnerer Bldg — 7:00
- 7960 Old Georgetown Rd — 6:45
- 2 Center Dr — 6:30
- 1 Cloister Court, Howard Hughes Medical — 6:30
- 8001 Wisconsin Ave — 6:30
- 7900 Wisconsin Ave, Suburban Bank Bldg — 6:30
- 7910 Woodmont Ave, Landow — 6:30
- 7920 Norfolk Ave — 6:00
- 7920 Norfolk Ave, Jhamels Phillips — 6:00
- 7910 Woodmont Ave, Landow Bldg — 6:00
- 7735 Old Georgetown Rd, Fairmont Bldg — 5:30
- 9000 Rockville Pike, NIH — 5:30
- 8901 Wisconsin Ave — 3:00

Map 24 • Upper Rock Creek Park

- 9440 Georgia Ave, Staples — 7:00
- 8750 Brookville Rd — 6:30
- 8639 16th St, Mail Boxes, Etc — 6:00

Map 25 • Silver Spring

- 1025 Bonifant St, FedEx Service Center — 8:00
- 8728 Colesville Rd, Atlis Travel — 7:00
- 8616 2nd Ave — 6:30
- 1407 East West Hwy. Kinko's — 6:30
- 8720 Georgia Ave — 6:30
- 8757 Georgia Ave — 6:30
- Forny Rd, Walter Reed Army Institute, Bldg 503 — 6:30
- 1300 Spring St — 6:30
- 1100 Blair Mill Rd — 6:00
- 8403 Colesville Rd — 6:00
- 8737 Colesville Rd — 6:00
- 8630 Fenton St, Montgomery Ctr — 6:00
- 8601 Georgia Ave, Lee Plaza — 6:00
- 8121 Georgia Ave, World Bldg — 6:00
- 900 Spring St — 6:00
- 1109 Spring St — 6:00
- 1300 Spring St — 5:45
- 8555 16th St — 5:30
- 8403 Colesville Rd, Silver Spring Metro Plaza — 5:30
- 8455 Colesville Rd, Silver Spring Center — 5:30
- 8455 Colesville Rd — 5:00
- 1305 East West Hwy — 5:00
- 1325 East West Hwy — 5:00
- 1335 East West Hwy — 5:00
- 8701 Georgia Ave — 5:00
- 1315 East West Hwy — 4:00

Map 26 • Takoma Park

- 7600 Carroll Ave, Takoma Postal & Business, Washington Adventist — 6:30
- 7304 Carroll Ave — 6:00

Map 27 • Walter Reed

- 6925 Willow St NW — 6:30
- 6930 Carroll Ave, Takoma Park Commerce Bldg — 6:00
- 6900 Georgia Ave NW, Walter Reed Army Medical — 6:00

Map 28 • Chevy Chase

- 5636 Connecticut Ave NW — 5:30

Map 29 • Bethesda / Chevy Chase Business

- 4809 Bethesda Ave, FedEx Service Center — 7:45
- 4800 Montgomery Lane, Empower ABT — 7:00
- 4445 Willard Ave, Ritz Hotel — 7:00
- 7475 Wisconsin Ave, Bethesda Crescent — 7:00
- 7501 Wisconsin Ave, GMAC — 7:00
- 4330 East West Hwy — 6:45
- 5161 River Rd — 6:45
- 7200 Wisconsin Ave, Equity Residential — 6:45
- 2 Wisconsin Cir, Chevy Chase Metro Bldg — 6:45
- 6933 Arlington Rd — 6:30
- 4350 East West Hwy — 6:30
- 4405 East West Hwy — 6:30
- 4416 East West Hwy — 6:30
- 5550 Friendship Blvd — 6:30
- 4550 Montgomery Ave — 6:30
- 4800 Montgomery Ln, Hamden Sq — 6:30
- 4445 Willard Ave, Chase Tower — 6:30
- 5530 Wisconsin Ave — 6:30
- 7101 Wisconsin Ave — 6:30
- 7201 Wisconsin Ave — 6:30
- 7400 Wisconsin Ave — 6:30
- 7475 Wisconsin Ave — 6:30
- 5454 Wisconsin Ave, Barlow Bldg — 6:30
- 7510 Wisconsin Ave, Chevy Chase Bank Hqtr — 6:30
- 4520 East West Hwy — 6:15
- 7200 Wisconsin Ave — 6:15
- 7272 Wisconsin Ave — 6:15
- 7316 Wisconsin Ave, Nations Bank — 6:15
- 4600 East West Hwy — 6:00
- 4630 Montgomery Ave — 6:00
- 7315 Wisconsin Ave — 6:00
- 7315 Wisconsin Ave, Air Rights Center — 6:00
- 2 Wisconsin Cir — 6:00
- 4800 Hamden Lane — 5:15
- 5003 Bethesda Metro Center Metro Printing & Copying —
- 5257 River Rd, Parcel Plus — 5:00
- 6900 Wisconsin Ave, Barclay Building — 5:00
- 7831 Woodmont Ave, Mailboxes of Bethesda — 3:30

Map 30 • Westmoreland Circle

- 4910 Massachusetts Ave NW — 6:00
- 4801 Massachusetts Ave NW, Law Building — 6:00

Map 32 • Cherrydale / Palisades

5125 MacArthur Blvd NW	7:00
5136 MacArthur Blvd NW	6:30

Map 33 • Falls Church

300 N Washington St	7:00
5350 Lee Hwy	7:00
2503 N Harrison St, Parcel Plus	5:30
5877 Washington Blvd	5:15
515 N Washington St	5:00

Map 34 • Ballston

1005 N Glebe Rd, FedEx Service Center	8:00
901 N Stuart St	7:00
4238 Wilson Blvd, Ballston Common	7:00
4301 Fairfax Dr, Ballston Station	6:30
4350 Fairfax Dr, Ellipse	6:30
4001 Fairfax Dr, Quincy St Station	6:30
4301 Wilson Blvd	6:30
1005 N Glebe Rd, Fairgate Building	6:15
4100 Fairfax Dr	6:00
2200 N George Mason Dr	6:00
910 N Glebe Rd, Staples	6:00
1010 N Glebe Rd, Ballston	6:00
4301 Wilson Blvd, NRECA	6:00
850 N Randolph St, Mail Plus	6:00
4201 Wilson Blvd, Mail Boxes Etc	6:00
1100 N Glebe Rd	5:45
1110 N Glebe St. Ballston Plaza	5:45
4501 Fairfax Dr, Kinko's	5:30
1100 N Glebe Rd	5:30
801 N Quincy St	5:30
4245 Fairfax Dr, The Nature Conservancy	5:00

Map 35 • Clarendon

2300 Clarendon Blvd, Kinko's	6:00
2801 Clarendon Blvd	6:00
2200 Clarendon Blvd, Courthouse Plz	6:00
2500 Wilson Blvd	5:30

Map 36 • Rosslyn

1814 N Moore St, FedEx Service Center	8:00
2111 Wilson Blvd, FedEx Service Center	8:00
1560 Wilson Blvd	7:30
1300 17th St N	7:00
1616 N Ft Myer Dr, Red Cross	7:00
1611 N Kent St	7:00
1525 Wilson Blvd	7:00
1600 Wilson Blvd	7:00
1000 Wilson Blvd, USA Today	7:00
1001 19th St N, Potomac Tower	6:30
1616 Ft Myer Dr, Xerox	6:30
1911 N Fort Myer Dr	6:30
1300 Wilson Blvd	6:30
1530 Wilson Blvd	6:30
1916 Wilson Blvd	6:30
1530 Wilson Blvd, Airlines Reporting Corp	6:30
1000 Wilson Blvd, USA Today	6:15

2000 14th St N, Courthouse Plaza	6:00
1911 Ft Myer Dr	6:00
1101 Wilson Blvd	6:00
1840 Wilson Blvd	6:00
1401 Wilson Blvd, Oak Hills Company	6:00
1550 Wilson Blvd	5:45
1560 Wilson Blvd	5:45
1300 Wilson Blvd, Commonwealth Tower	5:45
1333 N Courthouse Rd, Hilton Garden Inn	5:30
1415 N Taft St	5:30
2043 Wilson Blvd	5:30
1655 Ft Myer Dr	5:30
1801 N Lynn St, US Dept of State	5:00
2000 15th St N	4:00

Map 37 • Fort Myer

2300 9th St S	7:00
3138 10th St N	6:45
3259 Columbia Pike	6:30
3601 Wilson Blvd, One Virginia Square	6:30
1632 Crystal Sq	6:00
3701 Fairfax Dr	6:00
1001 N Filmore St, Pak Mail	5:30
200 N Glebe Rd	5:00
1210 S Glebe Rd	5:00
3811 Fairfax Dr	4:00

Map 38 • Columbia Pike

4900 Leesburg Pike	6:00
4900 Leesburg Pike, Atrium Building	6:00
5100 Leesburg Pike	5:30

Map 39 • Shirlington

1707 Osage St	7:00
4212 King St	6:30
4850 31st St S	6:15
3686 King St, Parcel Plus	6:00
2700 S Quincy St	6:00
2800 S Shirlington Rd	5:30
3101 Park Center Dr	5:00
2850 S Quincy St	5:00

Map 40 • Pentagon City

1601 Crystal Sq, FedEx Service Center, Kinko's	8:00
1213 Jefferson Davis Hwy	7:00
1225 Jefferson Davis Hwy	7:00
1201 S Fern St, DHL DCA	7:00
1111 Jefferson Davis Hwy	6:30
1215 Jefferson Davis Hwy	6:30
1101 S Joyce St, Parcel Plus	6:00
775 23rd St S	6:00
2011 Crystal Dr	6:00
1919 S Eads St	6:00
1250 S Hayes St, Ritz-Carlton	6:00
601 12th St S, MCI Bldg	5:30
100 Boundary Channel Dr, Pentagon	5:30
2121 Crystal Dr	5:30
2231 Crystal Dr	5:30
2345 Crystal Dr	5:30
2101 Crystal Plaza, Crystal Plaza Mailboxes	5:00
The Pentagon - Main Concourse	5:00

2341 Jefferson Davis Hwy, Crystal City Copy Center	4:00
1235 Jefferson Davis Hwy, Gateway Mail Boxes	4:00

Map 41 • Landmark

5801 Duke St, Landmark Mall	7:00
1701 N Beauregard St, AB Tech	5:45

Map 42 • Alexandria (West)

2916 Business Center Dr, Otis Elevator	7:00
2900 Eisenhower Ave, Avalon Bay	7:00

Map 43 • Four Mile Run

2320 Fannon St	7:30
907 W Glebe Rd	6:15
3131 Mt Vernon Ave	6:00
1908 Mt Vernon Ave, Henry Knox Field Bldg	6:00
2001 Jefferson Davis Hwy, Crystal Plaza One	5:45
2611 Jefferson Davis Hwy, Airport Plaza	5:30
3301 Jefferson Davis Hwy, Staples	5:00
2341 Jefferson Davis Hwy, Crystal City Copy Center	5:00

Map 44 • Alexandria Downtown

1660 Duke St, American Diabetes Assoc	7:00
1737 King St, Kingstreet Metroplace	5:30

Map 45 • Old Town (North)

1199 N Fairfax St, FedEx Service Center	8:00
820 1st St NE, CNN Bldg	7:00
1029 N Royal St, Direct Impact Bldg	7:00
635 Slaters Ln	7:00
701 N Fairfax St	6:45
1320 Braddock Pl	6:30
601 N Fairfax St, Sheetmetal Fund	6:30
105 Oronoco St	6:30
44 Canal Center Plaza	6:00
1100 Wythe St	6:00
99 Canal Center Plaza	5:45
66 Canal Center Plaza	5:00
400 N Columbus St	5:00
901 N Pitt St	5:00
806 N Fairfax St, Pack n Ship Plus	4:30
806 N Fairfax St, Pack n Ship Plus	4:30

Map 46 • Old Town (South)

1422 Duke St	7:00
127 S Peyton St, IIAA	7:00
320 King St	6:00
615 King St, Old Town Pack & Ship	6:00
201 N Union St	6:00
211 N Union St	6:00
1101 King St	5:30

Computer Services

Action Business Equipment	703-716-4691
On Call 25/8	202-625-2511;
	info@oncall258.com
Saunders Software Duplication	703-893-8294

Copying

		Map
Reliable Copy (202-347-6644)		
	555 12th St NW, Washington DC	1
Kinkos (1-800-254-6547)		
	325 7th St, Washington DC	2
	3329 M St NW, Washington DC	6
	1612 K St NW, Washington DC	9
	2020 K St NW, Washington DC	9
	2300 Clarendon Blvd, Arlington, VA	35

Delivery/Messengers

QMS	202-783-3600
Road Runners	703-321-0100
Washington Courier	202-775-1500

Gas Stations

		Map
Exxon	393 Pennsylvania Ave SE	3
Amoco	1950 Benning Rd NE	4
Texaco	1022 Pennsylvania Ave SE	5
Amoco	1244 S Capital St SE	6
Amoco	2715 Pennsylvania Ave NW	8
Amoco	400 Rhode Island Ave NE	11
Amoco	45 Florid a Ave NE	11
Exxon	1 Florida Ave NE	11
Amoco	1201 Bladensburg Rd NE	12
Amoco	2210 Bladensburg Rd NE	13
Texaco	1765 New York Ave	13
Amoco	3701 12th St NE	14
Amoco	3426 Georgia Ave NW	15
Amoco	4900 Wisconsin Ave NW	19
Amoco	5001 Connecticut Ave NW	20
Amoco	7605 Georgia Ave NW	27
Amoco	6300 Georgia Ave NW	27
Shell	6419 Georgia Ave NW	27

Locksmiths

A 24 Hour Locksmith Service	202-582-0959
AALocksmith	703-521-4990
ADF Automotive	202-546-7877
Advanced Locks & Security	202-491-1058
At Once Locksmith	202-744-2620
Automotive Lockout	202-610-0600
Berry's Locksmith	202-667-3680
District Lock	202-547-8236
DJ's Locksmith Services	202-638-2599
Doors and Devices	800-865-6253
JB's Locksmith	301-567-9283
Lee's Auto Home Locksmith	202-368-2599
Locksmith 24 Hours	202-636-4540
Metro Lock & Security	202-362-1882
Pop-A-Lock	202-331-2929
Safeway Locksmiths	202-986-2552

Pharmacies

		Map
Rite-Aid	1815 Connecticut Ave 202-332-1718	9

Plumbers

All-Magnolia Services	202-829-8510
Brown's Plumbing & Drain Service	202-554-8152
Capitol Area Plumbing & Heating	301-345-7667
James A Wheat & Sons	301-670-1944
John C Flood of DC	202-291-3340
John G Webster	202-783-6100
KC Plumbing Services	800-823-4911
Pipeline Plumbing	703-378-9620
Plumbline Plumbers	202-543-9515
Roto-Rooter	202-726-8888
Smallenbroek Plumbing & Heating	202-237-6400
Vito	800-438-8486

Resume Services

		Map
HBR - 202-842-0869	1411 K St NW, Ste 530	10

Towing

Emergency-1	202-529-2205
Hook Em Up Towing	202-528-8435
Pro-Lift	202-546-7877

Veterinarians

Chevy Chase Veterinarian Clinic ·
8815 Connecticut Ave, Chevy Chase, MD ·
301-656-6655 · Map 23
Friendship Hospital for Animals ·
4105 Brandywine St NW, Washington DC ·
202-363-7300 · Map 19

There is art life beyond the Smithsonian. In fact, the city's smaller galleries tend to be more interesting and spontaneous than the hallowed halls of the national museums.

Dupont Circle is crowded with the best, from impressionism at the **Phillips Gallery** to the shrine of rugs at the **Textile Museum**. The drawback is that, unlike the bigger museums around the mall, these galleries charge entrance fees and sometimes keep quirky hours.

A good time to check out the Dupont art scene is on the first Friday evening of every month, when most of the galleries open their doors briefly for a free peek. Many of the galleries on R Street, which is also known as Gallery Row, are converted row houses with narrow staircases that get jammed up when the art crowd is out on Friday evenings; check out **Alex Gallery** (European and prominent American art), **Burdick Gallery** (sculpture and graphics by Inuit artists), **Elizabeth Roberts Gallery** (local emerging artists), **Gallery K Inc** (Washington-based artists), **Marsha Mateyka Gallery** (European and American living artists), **Robert Brown Gallery** (eclectic, varied exhibitions), and **Studio Gallery** (artist co-op with 30 members).

During the annual Dupont-Kalorama Museum Walk Weekend, held on the first weekend in June, galleries usually allow roaming free of charge (www.dkmuseums.com).

Check out the Post and City Paper listings for shows at some of the other galleries that, ahead of rampant gentrification, are popping up all over the city. A great online resource for gallery information is the entertainment guide at www.eg.washingtonpost.com, which has excellent reviews and editor picks of the art galleries in DC.

All area codes as listed in heading unless otherwise noted

1· National Mall (202)

Arthur M Sackler Gallery	1050 Independence Ave SW	357-1729
Cave	739 15th St NW	639-0505
Coeur du Capitol Gallery	725 Capitol Sq Pl SW	543-6900
Corcoran Gallery of Art	500 17th St NW	639-1700
Henderson Phillips Fine Arts	1627 I St NW	223-5860
National Museum of African Art	950 Independence Ave SW	357-4600
National Museum of Women in the Art	1250 New York Ave NW	783-5000
White House Art Gallery	529 14th St NW	393-6752

2 · Chinatown / Union Station (202)

Artists' Museum	406 7th St NW	638-7001
David Adamson Gallery	406 7th St NW	628-0257
Echo Gallery	50 Massachusetts Ave NE	842-8400
Eklektikos Gallery	406 7th St NW	342-1809
Gallery Place	770 5th St NW	789-8388
Marninart	406 7th St NW	347-3327
Meridian Gallery	450 Massachusetts Ave NW	326-0000
National Gallery of Art	401 Constitution Ave NW	737-4215
Numark Gallery	625 E St NW	628-3810
Szechaun Gallery	617 H St NW	898-1527
Touchstone Gallery	406 7th St NW	347-2787
Zenith Gallery	413 7th St NW	783-2963

3 · The Hill (202)

Market Five Gallery	201 7th St SE	543-7293
Village	705 North Carolina Ave SE	546-3040

4 · Southeast (202)

Alvear Studio Design	705 8th St SE	546-8434
Attitude Exact Gallery	739 8th St SE	546-7186

4 · Waterfront (202)

Art Enables	65 I St SW	554-9455

5 · Foggy Bottom (202)

Dimock Gallery	730 21st St NW	994-7091
Efrom Jean	2440 Virginia Ave NW	223-1626
Foliograph Gallery	919 18th St NW	296-8398
Professional Fine Arts	2450 Virginia Ave NW	861-0638
Watergate Gallery	2552 Virginia Ave NW	338-4488

6 · Georgetown (202)

Addison-Ripley Gallery	1670 Wisconsin Ave NW	338-5180
Alla Rogers Gallery	1054 31st St NW	333-8595
Appalachian Spring	1415 Wisconsin Ave NW	337-5780
Atlantic Gallery	1055 Thomas Jefferson St NW	337-2299
Benetton Mazza Gallerie	3222 M St NW	333-4506
Calvert Gallery	1442 Wisconsin Ave NW	387-8833
Cherub Antiques	2918 M St NW	337-2224
Corcoran Gallery of Art	1801 35th St NW	342-6239
District Fine Arts	1726 Wisconsin Ave NW	387-5657
Fine Art & Artists	2920 M St NW	965-0780
Fraser Gallery	1054 31st St NW	298-6450
G Fine Art	3271 M St NW	233-0300
Gala	1671 Wisconsin Ave NW	333-1337
Georgetown Art Studio	3222 M St NW	625-2225
Georgetown Gallery	3235 P St NW	333-6308
Govinda Gallery	1227 34th St NW	333-1180
Grafix	2904 M St NW	965-4747
Guarisco Gallery	2828 Pennsylvania Ave NW	333-8533
Hemphill Fine Arts	1027 33rd St NW	342-5610
Jackson Art Center	3048 R St NW	342-9778
Ken Frye Art Gallery	3242 Jones Ct NW	333-2505
La Galerie	3222 M St NW	965-2512
Maurine Littleton Gallery	1667 Wisconsin Ave NW	333-9307
Museum of Contemporary Art	1054 31st St NW	342-6230
Old Print Gallery	1220 31st St NW	965-1818
P Street Pictures	2621 P St NW	337-0066
P&C Art	3108 M St NW	965-3833
Parish Gallery	1054 31st St NW	944-2310
Rall's Collection	1516 31st St NW	342-1754
Spectrum Gallery	1132 29th St NW	333-0954
Studio Art 2	3222 M St NW	965-7141

6 • Georgetown — *continued* (202)

Susan Calloway Antique Prints & Fine Art	1643 Wisconsin Ave NW	965-4601
Susan Conway	1214 30th St NW	333-6343
Susquehanna Antiques	3216 O St NW	333-1511
Tomita Arts	1080 Wisconsin Ave NW	338-9029
Ultra Design	3222 M St NW	333-3050

9 • Dupont Circle / Adams Morgan

Aaron Gallery	1717 Connecticut Ave NW	234-3311
Affrica-African Art	2010 R St NW	745-7272
Alex Gallery	2106 R St NW	667-2599
Aluna Gallery	1756 T St NW	234-6400
Burdick Gallery	2114 R St NW	986-5682
Burton Marinkovich	1506 21st St NW	296-6563
Capricorno Gallery	2128 P St NW	223-1166
Chao Phraya Gallery	2009 Columbia Rd NW	745-1111
Conner Contemporary Art	1730 Connecticut Ave NW	588-8750
Diner Gallery	1730 21st St NW	483-5005
Elizabeth Roberts Gallery	2108 R St NW	232-1011
Foundry Gallery	9 Hillyer Ct NW	387-0203
Gallery 10 Limited	1519 Connecticut Ave NW	232-3326
Gallery K	2010 R St NW	234-0339
Gary Edward's Photographs	9 Hillyer Ct NW	232-5926
International Art Gallery	1625 K St NW	466-7979
Irvine Contemporary Art	1710 Connecticut Ave NW	332-8767
Jane Haslem Gallery	2025 Hillyer Pl NW	232-4644
Kathleen Ewing Gallery	1609 Connecticut Ave NW	328-0955
Kelly Nevin Gallery	1517 U St NW	232-3464
Marsha Mateyka Gallery	2012 R St NW	328-0088
Osuna Galleries	1914 16th St NW	296-1963
Pensler Galleries	2029 Q St NW	328-9190
Period Pictures	1801 K St NW	785-1652
Phillips Collection	1600 21st St NW	387-2151
Quadriga Art	1717 K St NW	223-1796
Robert Brown Gallery	2030 R St NW	483-4383
St Luke's Gallery	1715 Q St NW	328-2424
Studio Gallery	2108 R St NW	232-8734
Tartt Gallery	1711 Connecticut Ave NW	332-5652
Textile Museum	2320 S St NW	667-0441
Troyer Gallery	1710 Connecticut Ave NW	328-7189
Washington Very Special Arts	1100 16th St NW	296-9100

10 • Logan Circle / U Street (202)

Art & Culture	504 T St NW	332-7763
Evans-Tibbs Collection	1910 Vermont Ave NW	234-8164
Fusebox	1412 14th St NW	299-9220
International Gallery of African Art	1937 14th St NW	319-1002
Sidney Mickelson	629 New York Ave NW	628-1735
Signal 66	926 N St NW	842-3436
Transformer Gallery	1404 P St NW	483-1102
Wayland House Gallerie	1802 11th St NW	387-8157

11 • Near Northeast (202)

Ella's Coffee & Fine Art	1506 N Capitol St NW	483-3552
NOA Gallery	132 Rhode Island Ave NW	483-7328
Zelano Art Studio	411 New York Ave NE	547-2508

14 • Catholic U (202)

Wohlfarth Galleries	3418 9th St NE	526-8022

15 • Columbia Heights (202)

Cultural Circles	1424 Belmont St NW	667-4324

16 • Adams Morgan (North) / Mt Pleasant (202)

Alexia Gallery	2602 Connecticut Ave NW	667-7773
District of Columbia Arts Center	2438 18th St NW	462-7833
Molinero Gallery	2602 Connecticut Ave NW	464-0311

17 • Woodley Park / Cleveland Park (202)

Adams Davidson Galleries	2727 29th St NW	965-3800
International Visions Gallery	2629 Connecticut Ave NW	234-5112

18 • Glover Park / Foxhall (202)

Browning	3101 New Mexico Ave NW	363-1963
Cathedral Galleries	3301 New Mexico Ave NW	363-6936
Foxhall Gallery	3301 New Mexico Ave NW	966-7144
Kreeger Museum	2401 Foxhall Rd NW	337-3050

19 • Tenleytown / Friendship Heights (202)

Butterfly Alphabet	3871 Rodman St NW	244-5711
CY Katzen Gallery	4624 Wisconsin Ave NW	363-4973

20 • Cleveland Park / Upper Connecticut (301)

Chevy Chase Gallery	5039 Connecticut Ave NW	364-8155
Galleria Internacional	4481 Connecticut Ave NW	244-4481
Japanesque	3060 Davenport St NW	244-3928
Rock Creek Gallery	2401 Tilden St NW	244-2482
Talisman Tribal Arts	2950 Van Ness St NW	686-2151

21 • 16th St. Heights / Petworth (202)

Ramee Art Gallery	5247 14th St NW	291-0067

22 • Downtown Bethesda (301)

Ancient Rhythms	7920 Woodmont Ave	652-2669
Artworks	7847 Old Georgetown Rd	656-0044
Fraser Gallery	7700 Wisconsin Ave	718-9651
Saint Elmo's Fire	4928 Saint Elmo Ave	215-9848
Wee King Art	8100 Norfolk Ave	656-1141

24 • Upper Rock Creek Park (202)

African Hands	1851 Redwood Ter NW	726-2400

25 · Silver Spring

Century Gallery	919 King St	703-684-6967
Colour	1434 Fenwick Ln	301-495-0361
Gallerie La Taj	1010 King St	703-549-0508
House of Safori	1105 Spring St	301-565-0781

26 · Takoma Park *(301)*

Loriola Gallery	7014 Westmoreland Ave	891-0708
Takoma Old Town Gallery	7002 Carroll Ave	270-6566
Two Sisters Gallery	7000 Carroll Ave	270-2670

27 · Walter Reed *(202)*

Willow Street Gallery	6925 Willow St NW	882-0740

28 · Chevy Chase *(202)*

Avant Garde	5520 Connecticut Ave NW	966-1045

29 · Bethesda/Chevy Chase *(301)*

Designers Art Gallery	4618 Leland St	718-0400
Discovery Galleries Limited	4840 Bethesda Ave	913-9199
Glass Gallery	4000 Hampden Ln	657-3478
Margaret Smith Galleries	7249 Woodmont Ave	657-1200
Marin-Price Galleries	7022 Wisconsin Ave	718-0622
Moriah Gallery	7301 Woodmont Ave	657-3001
Osuna Art	7200 Wisconsin Ave	654-4500

30 · Westmoreland Circle *(301)*

Artemis	4715 Crescent St	229-2058

32 · Cherrydale/Palisades *(202)*

Art in Fiber	2821 Arizona Ter NW	364-8404

33 · Falls Church *(703)*

Paul McGhee's Old Town Gallery	109 N Fairfax St	548-7729

34 · Ballston *(703)*

Art Beats	4238 Wilson Blvd	243-8477
Ellipse Art Center	4350 Fairfax Dr	228-7710
Lac Viet Gallery	5179 Lee Hwy	532-4350

35 · Clarendon *(703)*

Metropolitan Gallery	2420 Wilson Blvd	358-0068

38 · Columbia Pike *(703)*

Michael Curtis	110 S Columbus St	836-7736
Miller Fine Art Limited	113 S Columbus St	838-0006

39 · Shirlington *(703)*

Countertop Gallery	1705 Centre Plz	933-3800

40 · Pentagon City *(703)*

Row Gallery	1301 S Joyce St	418-1900
Wentworth Galleries	1100 S Hayes St	415-1166

41 · Landmark *(703*

Gallery Petalouth Limited	4653 Duke St	823-5954

42 · Alexandria (West) *(703)*

Green Door Studio	3211 Colvin St	823-5300
Propeller Studio	3670 Wheeler Ave	370-4800

43 · Four Mile Run *(703)*

African Treasures Gallery	2414 Oakville St	549-8883
Del Ray Artisans	2704 Mount Vernon Ave	838-4827
Fitzgerald Fine Arts	2502 E Randolph Ave	836-1231

44 · Alexandria Downtown *(703)*

Tall Tulips	412 John Carlyle St	549-5017

45 · Old Town (North) *(703)*

First Impressions Gallery	1310 Braddock Pl	684-7525
Green Door Studio	610 Madison St	823-5300
Studio Antiques & Fine Art	524 N Washington St	548-5253

46 · Old Town (South) *(703)*

African Art Gallerie	1203 King St	549-0508
Art League	105 N Union St	683-1780
Artcraft Collection	132 King St	299-6616
Arts Afire Glass Gallery	102 N Fayette St	838-9785
Auburn Fine Arts Gallery	127 S Fairfax St	548-1932
Betsy Anderson	105 N Union St	684-5579
BJ Anderson	105 N Union St	549-5079
Broadway Gallery	1219 King St	549-1162
Citron Ann	105 N Union St	683-0403
Enamelist Gallery	105 N Union St	836-1561
Factory Photoworks	105 N Union St	683-2205
Fibre Workshop	105 N Union St	836-5807
Fire One	105 N Union St	836-2585
Foliograph Gallery	217 King St	683-1501
Fuszion Collaborative	225 N Fairfax St	548-8080
Gallerie Michele	113 King St	683-1521
Gallery Orlov	1307 King St	549-4721
Gallery West	205 S Union St	549-7359
Kennedy Studios	101 N Union St	684-1193
Mindful Hands	211 King St	683-2074
Nuevo Mundo	313 Cameron St	549-0040
P&C Art	212 King St	549-2525
Prince Royal Gallery	204 S Royal St	548-5151
Principle Gallery	208 King St	739-9326

Arts & Entertainment • **Bookstores**

This is a city of policy wonks, lawyers, writers, and activists—frankly, nerds. Bookstores here get as crowded as the beltway at rush hour. Besides the mega-chain stores like Borders and Barnes & Noble, there are several local outlets that have personalities of their own.

Go to **Kramerbooks** to scope out a date with literary interests, **Olsson's** if you like your coffee and ownership independent, and **Politics & Prose** if you want a lefty debate.

Readers of the gay, lesbian, bisexual, and transgendered persuasions should head to **Lambda Rising**, the largest GLBT bookstore in the world.

If you have time to spare, check out the used books stores for cheaper reads and dusty aromas. Try **Riverby Books** on Capitol Hill, **Second Story Books** in Dupont Circle, **Idle Time Books** in Adams Morgan, and **Book Bank** in Alexandria.

Map 1 • National Mall

Barnes & Noble	555 12th St NW	202-347-0176	General.
Borders Books & Music	600 14th St NW	202-737-1385	General.
Chapters Literary Bookstore	445 11th St NW	202-737-5553	Poetry, literary fiction (old and new), children's literature, and natural history.
La Lengua De Cervantes	737 15th St NW	202-347-0759	Books in Spanish.
Olsson's Books	1200 F St NW Metro Center	202-347-3686	General.

Map 2 • Chinatown / Union Station

AMA Management Book Store	440 1st St SW	202-347-3092	Business.
B Dalton Booksellers	50 Massachusetts Ave	202-289-1724	General.
National Academy Press–Bookstore	500 5th St NW	202-334-2812	Science and technology, social/environment issues.
Olsson's Books	418 7th St NW	202-638-7610	General.

Map 3 • The Hill

Riverby Books	417 E Capitol St SE	202-543-4342	Used.
Trover Shop Books & Office	221 Pennsylvania Ave SE	202-547-2665	General.

Map 5 • Southeast

Backstage	545 8th St SE	202-544-5744	Theater and performance.
Bird in Hand Book Store	323 7th St SE	202-543-0744	Art and architecture.
Capitol Hill Books	657 Centre St SE	202-544-1621	Second-hand fiction, mystery, and biography.
Fairy Godmother–Children's Books & Toys	319 7th St SE	202-547-5474	Toddler to young adult fiction and nonfiction.
First Amendment Books	645 Pennsylvania Ave SE	202-547-5585	Current events, political history.

Map 6 • Waterfront

Reprint Book Shop	455 L'Enfant Plz SW	202-554-5070	General.

Map 7 • Foggy Bottom

Bader Fanz Bookstore	1911 I St NW	202-337-5440	Visual arts, fine arts, architecture, and landscape.
Franz Bader Book Store	1911 I St NW	202-337-5440	Art and architecture.
George Washington U Book Store	800 21st St NW	202-994-6870	Academic and college.
Washington Law & Professional Books	1900 G St NW	202-223-5543	Law.
World Bank Info Shop	701 18th St NW	202-458-5454	Development and politics.

Map 8 • Georgetown

Barnes & Noble	3040 M St NW	202-965-9880	General.
Bartleby's Books	3034 M St NW	202-298-0486	Specializes in rare and antiquarian, 18th and 19th-century American history, economics, and law.
Beyond Comics	1419 Wisconsin Ave NW	202-333-8650	Comics.
Big Planet Comics	3145 Dumbarton Ave NW	202-342-1961	Comics.
Bridge St Books	2814 Pennsylvania Ave NW	202-965-5200	General.
Lantern Bryn Mawr Book Shop	3241 P St NW	202-333-3222	Used and rare.
Waldenbooks	3222 M St NW	202-333-8033	General.

Map 9 · Dupont Circle / Adams Morgan

Books-A-Million	11 Dupont Cir	202-319-1374	General.
Borders Books & Music	1801 K St NW	202-466-4999	General.
International Language Ctr	1803 Connecticut Ave NW	202-332-2894	Language.
Kramer Book Stores	1517 Connecticut Ave NW	202-387-1400	General.
Lambda Rising Book Store	1625 Connecticut Ave NW	202-462-6969	Gay and lesbian.
Luna Books & Coffee Shop	1633 P St NW	202-332-2543	General.
News Room	1803 Connecticut Ave NW	202-332-1489	Foreign language and reference.
Olsson's Books	1307 19th St NW	202-785-1133	General.
Reiter's Scientific & Professional Books	2021 K St NW	202-223-3327	Scientific and medical.
Second Story Books & Antiques	2000 P St NW	202-659-8884	Used.
Sisterspace & Books	1515 U St NW	202-332-3433	Afro-centric and women's literature.

Map 10 · Logan Circle / U Street

Brian MacKenzie Infoshop	1426 9th St NW	202-986-0681	Left-wing literature.
Candida's World Of Books	1541 14th St NW	202-667-4811	Language learning and reference, travel, art, cookbooks, current literature, political, science, and children's.

Map 11 · Near Northeast

Bison Shop-Gallaudet University	800 Florida Ave NE	202-651-5271	Academic and sign language.

Map 14 · Catholic U

Newman Book Store of Washington	3329 8th St NE	202-526-1036	Scripture, theology, philosophy, and church history.

Map 15 · Columbia Heights

Blue Nile Book Store	2828 Georgia Ave NW	202-232-2583	Metaphysical.
Howard University Book Store	2225 Georgia Ave NW	202-238-2640	Academic and Afro-centric.
Sankofa Video & Bookstore	2714 Georgia Ave NW	202-234-4755	Afro-centric.

Map 16 · Adams Morgan (North) / Mt Pleasant

Idle Time Books	2467 18th St	202-232-4774	Used.

Map 18 · Glover Park / Foxhall

Georgetown University Book Store	3800 Reservoir Rd NW	202-687-7482	Academic.
Glovers Books & Music	2319 Wisconsin Ave NW	202-338-8100	General.
Tree Top Toys & Books	3301 New Mexico Ave NW	202-244-3500	Children's.

Map 19 · Tenleytown / Friendship Heights

American University Book Store	4400 Massachusetts Ave	202-885-6300	Academic and college.
Borders Books & Music	5333 Wisconsin Ave NW	202-686-8270	General.
Tempo Book Store	4905 Wisconsin Ave NW	202-363-3383	Language.

Map 20 · Cleveland Park / Upper Connecticut

Politics & Prose	5015 Connecticut Ave NW	202-364-1919	American studies and politics.

Map 22 · Downtown Bethesda

Big Planet Comics	4908 Fairmont Ave	301-654-6856	Comics.
Waldenbooks	Montgomery Mall	301-469-8810	General.

Map 23 · Kensington

Audubon Naturalist Bookshop	8940 Jones Mill Rd	301-652-3606	Nature and earth.

Map 25 · Silver Spring

Alliance Comics	8317 Fenton St	301-588-2546	Comics.
Silver Spring Books	938 Bonifant St	301-587-7484	General.

Map 26 • Takoma Park

Takoma Book Exchange	7009 Carroll Ave	301-891-4656	General.

Map 27 • Walter Reed

Literal Books	7705 Georgia Ave NW	202-723-8688	Spanish books.
Sistrum	5920 Georgia Ave NW	202-723-5200	Afro-centric.

Map 29 • Bethesda/Chevy Chase

Barnes & Noble	4801 Bethesda Ave	301-986-1761	General.
Georgetown Book Shop	4770 Bethesda Ave	301-907-6923	History, art, photography, children's, literary fiction, and baseball.
Iranbooks	6831 Wisconsin Ave	301-986-IRAN	Persian books.
Olsson's Books	7647 Old Georgetown Rd	301-652-3336	General.
Second Story Books & Antiques	4836 Bethesda Ave	301-656-0170; 310-770-0477	Used.

Map 34 • Ballston

B Dalton Booksellers	4238 Wilson Blvd	703-522-8822	General.
Bookhouse	805 N Emerson St	703-527-7797	Scholarly history.
Imagination Station	4524 Lee Hwy	703-522-2047	Children's.

Map 35 • Clarendon

Barnes & Noble	2800 Clarendon Blvd	703-248-8244	General.

Map 36 • Rosslyn

Olsson's Books	1735 N Lynn St	703-812-2103	General.
Olsson's Books	2111 Wilson Blvd	703-525-4227	General.

Map 37 • Fort Myer

George Mason University – Arlington Campus Bookstore	3401 N Fairfax Dr	703-993-8170	Law.

Map 38 • Columbia Pike

NVCC - Alexandria Campus Book Store	3101 N Beauregard St	703-671-0043	Academic and college.

Map 40 • Pentagon City

B Dalton Booksellers	2117 Crystal Plaza Arcade	703-415-0333	General.
B Dalton Booksellers	Crystal Square Arcade	703-413-0558	General.
Borders Books & Music	1201 S Hayes St	703-418-0166	General.

Map 41 • Landmark

Waldenbooks	5801 Duke St	703-658-9576	General.

Map 43 • Four Mile Run

Barnes & Noble	3651 Jefferson Davis Hwy	702-299-9124	General.
Book Niche & Capital Comics	2008 Mt Vernon Ave	703-548-3466	General.
Card & Comic Collectorama	2008 Mt Vernon Ave	703-548-3466	Comics and used.

Map 46 • Old Town (South)

A Likely Story	1555 King St	703-836-2498	Children's and parenting.
Aftertime Comics	1304 King St	703-548-5030	Comics.
Bird-In-the-Cage Antiques	110 King St	703-549-5114	General.
Book Bank	110 S West St	703-838-3620	Used.
Books-A-Million	501 King St	703-548-3432	General.
Olsson's Books	106 S Union St	703-684-0077	General.
Why Not	200 King St	703-548-4420	Children's.

Living in a politically aware city means that documentaries play big here, as do opinionated art films. You'll find them in the **Landmark E Street Cinema** downtown or Silver Spring's shrine to film, the **AFI Silver Theater**. If it's an indie flick you want, try the cramped **Loews Dupont Circle 5**.

If you're after a blockbuster, there is always a mainstream theater close to the metro that will oblige. The best of the bunch is Cleveland Park's **Uptown Theater**, where the elaborate elegance of the restored theater is matched by a giant curved screen. It's one of the few places where you'll have to wait in line, but it's also likely the only place the latest Hollywood action flick will seem memorable. The **Loews Georgetown 14** is a massive 14-screen complex—its most redeeming feature is a 175-foot brick smokestack, a remnant from the site's days as the Georgetown Incinerator.

If you want something more obscure and avant-garde, it'll probably be among the borderline freakish offerings at **Visions**, a bar/theater where you can sip wine while you contemplate the bizarre.

Theater	Address	Phone	Map
AFI Silver Theater	8633 Colesville Rd	301-495-6720	25
AFI Theater - Kennedy Center for the Performing Arts	2700 F St NW	202-785-4600	7
AMC City Place 10	8661 Colesville Rd	301-585-3738	25
AMC Courthouse Plaza 8	2150 Clarendon Blvd	703-998-4262	36
AMC Hoffman Center 22	206 Swamp Fox Rd	703-998-4262	44
AMC Mazza Gallerie 7	5300 Wisconsin Ave NW	202-537-9553	19
AMC Union Station 9	50 Massachusetts Ave NE	202-842-3757	2
Avalon Theatre	5612 Connecticut Ave NW	202-966-6000	28
Cinema 'n' Draft House	2903 Columbia Pike	703-486-2345	37
Cineplex Odeon Cinema	5100 Wisconsin Ave NW	202-966-7256	19
Cineplex Odeon Shirlington 7	2772 S Randolph St	703-671-0978	39
Cineplex Odeon Uptown	3426 Connecticut Ave NW	202-966-8805	17
Cineplex Odeon Wisconsin Avenue Cinemas	4000 Wisconsin Ave NW	202-244-0880	19
Fox Chase	2615 Duke St	703-370-5565	42
Johnson IMAX Theater	Constitution Ave NW & 10th St NW	202-633-9049	1
Landmark Bethesda Row Cinema	7235 Woodmont Ave	301-652-7273	29
Landmark E St Cinema	555 11th St NW	202-452-7672	1
Lockheed Martin IMAX Theater	601 Independence Ave SW	202-357-1686	2
Loews Dupont Circle 5	1350 19th St NW	202-872-9555	9
Loews Georgetown 14	3111 K St NW	202-342-6441	8
The Majestic 20	900 Ellsworth Dr	301-681-2266	25
Mary Pickford Theater	Library of Congress, James Madison Memorial Bldg, Independence Ave SE b/w 1st St SE & 2nd St SE	202-707-5677	2
Old Town Theater	815 1/2 King St	703-683-8888	46
Regal Ballston Common 12	671 N Glebe Rd	703-527-9466	34
Regal Potomac Yards 16	3575 Jefferson Davis Hwy	703-739-4054	43
UA Bethesda 10	7272 Wisconsin Ave	301-718-4323	29
Visions Cinema Bistro Lounge	1927 Florida Ave NW	202-232-5689	9

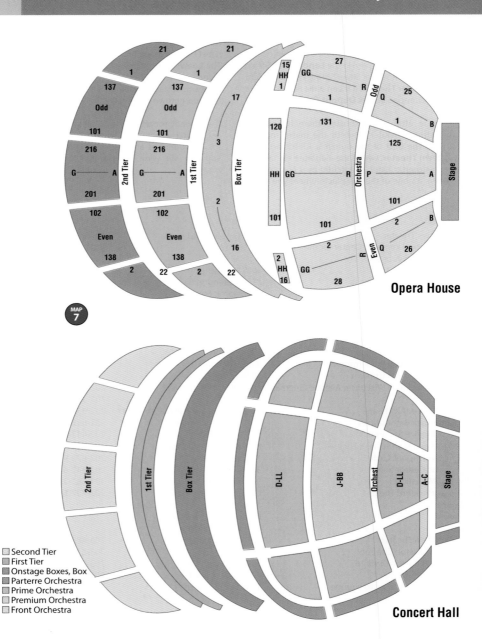

Opera House

MAP
7

Concert Hall

- Second Tier
- First Tier
- Onstage Boxes, Box
- Parterre Orchestra
- Prime Orchestra
- Premium Orchestra
- Front Orchestra

General Information

NFT Map: 7
Address: 2700 F Street NW,
Washington, DC 20566
Website: www.kennedy-center.org
Phone: 202-416-8000
Box Office: 800-444-1324 or 202-467-4600

Overview

The Kennedy Center is best known nationally for its yearly Honors, awards recognizing the nation's most important, accomplished, desperate-for-validation celebrities. Locally, it caters to thick-of-wallet art patrons with highbrow music, theater, opera, and dance. Savvy cultural vultures know that bargains exist, such as the nightly free concerts and choral cheap seats. And there's no charge to show up and check out one of the city's most romantic dusk terrace views or the giant statue of the center's adored namesake.

The Kennedy Center's history began in 1958, when President Dwight D. Eisenhower took a break from the links to sign legislation creating a National Cultural Center for the United States. President John F. Kennedy and First Lady Jackie later did much of the fundraising for what the president called "our contribution to the human spirit." Two months after President Kennedy's assassination, Congress named the center in his memory.

The Kennedy Center houses the Concert Hall, Opera House, Eisenhower Theater, Terrace Theater, Theater Lab, Film Theater, and Jazz Club.

How to Get There – Driving

Heading away from the Capitol on Independence Avenue, get in the left lane as you approach the Potomac. Passing under two bridges, stay in the left lane, and follow signs to the Kennedy Center. After passing the Kennedy Center on your right, make a right onto Virginia Avenue. At the 2nd set of lights, turn right onto 25th Street and follow the Kennedy Center parking signs.

Parking

Kennedy Center garage parking is $15.

How to Get There—Mass Transit

Take the Blue Line or Orange Line to the Foggy Bottom stop, and either walk ten minutes to the center or take a free shuttle that runs every 15 minutes. Metrobus 80 also goes to the Kennedy Center.

How to get Tickets

Prices vary depending on the event. Check the website or call the Box Office for schedules and tickets.

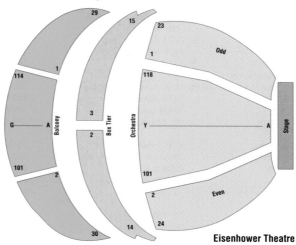

Eisenhower Theatre

The Smithsonian Institute is the national system of museums, which operates mainly around the National Mall. Though some, like the **American History Museum**, are hokey, the art spaces are pretty spectacular. The east and west wings of the **National Gallery** are world-class, the **Freer** and **Sackler** are a rabbit's warren of sublime rooms, and the **Hirshhorn** is, well, avant-garde—what else could you call the collection that includes a giant, bald, naked man?

It would take months to visit all of the Smithsonian museums in DC. They're all free, so consider them friends that need to be checked in on from time to time.

Extending out from the Mall, you'll find pricier private museums. The **Corcoran** usually has a buzz-worthy show and its "veiled nun" piece is worth contemplating. The **National Building Museum's** building and gift shop are interesting, even when the small, offbeat exhibits aren't. When you're in the mood for something more specific, try the targeted collections at places like the **Postal Museum** or the **Museum of Women in the Arts**.

Museum	Address	Phone	Map
Alexandria Archaeology Museum	105 N Union St	703-838-4399	46
Alexandria Black History Resource Ctr	638 N Alfred St	703-838-4356	45
Arlington Historical Museum, Arlington Historical Society	1805 S Arlington Ridge Rd	703-892-4204	40
Art Museum of the Americas	201 18th St NW	202-458-6016	7
Arts & Industries Building	900 Jefferson Dr SW	202-357-1500	1
The Athenaeum	201 Prince St	703-548-0035	46
Bead Museum DC	400 7th St NW	202-624-4500	2
Black Fashion Museum	2007 Vermont Ave NW	202-667-0744	10
Black Heritage Museum of Arlington	951 S George Mason Dr	703-271-8700	37
Capital Children's Museum	800 3rd St NE	202-675-4120	3
City Museum	801 K St NW	202-383-1800	10
The Corcoran	500 17th St NW	202-639-1700	1
DAR Museum	1776 D St NW	202-628-1776	7
DEA Museum & Visitors Ctr	700 Army Navy Dr	703-307-3463	40
Discovery Creek Children's Museum	4954 MacArthur Blvd NW	202-337-5111	18
Einstein Planetarium– National Air & Space Museum	Independence Ave SE & 4th St SW	202-633-4629	6
Folger Shakespeare Library	201 E Capitol St SE	202-544-4600	3
Fort Ward Museum & Historic Site	4301 W Braddock Rd	703-838-4848	42
Frederick Douglass Museum & Hall of Fame for Caring Americans	320 A St NE	202-544-6130	3
Freer Art Gallery and Arthur M Sackler Gallery	1050 Independence Ave SW	202-633-4880	1
Friendship Firehouse Museum	107 S Alfred St	703-838-3891	46
Gadsby's Tavern Museum	134 N Royal St	703-838-4242	46
George Washington Masonic Memorial Museum	101 Callahan Dr	703-683-2007	44
Hillwood Museum & Gardens	4155 Linnean Ave NW	202-686-8500	20
Hirshhorn Museum and Sculpture Garden	7th St SW & Independence Ave	202-357-2700	2
International Spy Museum	800 F St NW	202-393-7798	1
The Kreeger Museum	2401 Foxhall Rd NW	202-337-3050	18
Lillian and Albert Small Jewish Museum/ Jewish Historical Society	701 3rd St NW	202-789-0900	2
The Lyceum	201 S Washington St	703-898-4994	46
Marine Corps Museum	Washington Navy Yard	202-433-3840	5

Museum	Address	Phone	Map
The Mansion on O Street	2020 O St NW	202-496-2070	9
National Air & Space Museum	Independence Ave SE & 4th St SW	202-357-2700	6
National Aquarium	14th St & Constitution Ave NW	202-482-2825	1
National Building Museum	401 F St NW	202-272-2448	2
National Health Museum	1155 15th St NW	202-737-2670	9
National Museum of African Art	950 Independence Ave SW	202-633-4600	1
National Museum of American History	14th St & Constitution Ave NW	202-633-1000	1
National Museum of American Jewish Military History	1811 R St NW	202-265-6280	9
National Museum of Natural History	10th St NW & Constitution Ave NW	202-357-2700	1
National Museum of the American Indian	4th St & Independence Ave SW	202-633-1000	2
National Museum of Women in the Arts	1250 New York Ave NW	202-783-5000	1
National Postal Museum	2 Massachusetts Ave NE	202-633-5555	2
National Zoological Park	3001 Connecticut Ave NW	202-673-4700	17
The Navy Museum	805 Kidder Breese SE	202-433-4882	5
Newseum (opening 2007)	Pennsylvania Ave & 6th St NW	703-284-3544	2
The Octagon Museum	1799 New York Ave NW	202-638-3221	7
The Phillips Collection	1600 21st St NW	202-387-2151	9
Pope John Paul II Cultural Center	3900 Harewood Rd NE	202-635-5400	14
Portrait Gallery (reopening 2006)	8th St & F St NW	202-275-1738	1
Renwick Gallery (Smithsonian American Art Museum)	Pennsylvania Ave NW & 17th St NW	202-633-2850	1
Smithsonian American Art Museum (reopening July 2006)	8th St & G St NW	202-275-1500	1
Smithsonian Institution Building, the Castle	1000 Jefferson Ave SW	202-633-1000	1
The Society of the Cincinnati - Anderson House	2118 Massachusetts Ave NW	202-785-2040	9
Stabler-Leadbeater Apothecary Museum	105-107 S Fairfax St	703-836-3713	46
Stephen Decatur House Museum	1610 H St NW	202-842-0920	1
Textile Museum	2320 S St NW Washington Navy Yard	202-667-0441	9
Torpedo Factory Art Center	105 N Union St	703-838-4565	46
Tudor Place	1641 31st St NW	202-965-0400	8
United States National Arboretum	3501 New York Ave NE	202-245-2726	12
US Holocaust Memorial Museum	100 Raoul Wallenberg Pl SW	202-488-0400	1
Washington's Doll's House & Toy Museum	5236 44th St NW	202-363-6400	19
Woodrow Wilson Center for International Scholars	1300 Pennsylvania Ave NW	202-691-4000	1

Politics and booze make a mean cocktail and you'll find plenty of good drinking establishments splashed all around the city to quench your thirst for both.

Even sleepy neighborhoods have favorite local bars like **Colonel Brooks Tavern** in the Catholic U neighborhood or **State Theater** in Falls Church.

The nightlife districts of Georgetown, Dupont, Adams Morgan, U Street, and some of the livelier suburbs offer a choice of scenes, depending on what kinda mood you're in.

Those looking to hook up should hit **Big Hunt, Stetson's,** and **Hawk and Dove**, where you'll find plenty of others with the same motive. If you're after a good cocktail, try **Spy**

Lounge in Adams Morgan. For a relaxing sip of wine after a long day, head to Cleveland Park's **Aroma**. Sweaty nightclub divas should hit **Dream**, a massive 4-floor complex on Okie Street, where VIP membership will cost you just $500 a year and will save you waiting in line.

The best dive bar in the city is **Pharmacy Bar** in Adams Morgan, which caters more to locals than visitors and has a great jukebox. **Fado Irish Pub** has an excellent selection of imported beers and is a great place to hang out after Caps games. If you like bluegrass music, head over to **Tiffany Tavern** in Alexandria, where you can get a glimpse of what DC's bluegrass heyday must have been like in the 60's and 70's.

Map 1 • National Mall

Capitol City Brewing Company	1100 New York Ave NW	202-628-2222	Great IPA.
Eyebar	1716 I St NW	202-785-0270	Check out the sign.
Gordon Biersch Brewery	900 F St NW	202-783-5454	Five great lagers.
Grand Slam Sports Bar	1000 H St NW	202-637-4789	Sports bar perfection.
Harry's Saloon	436 11th St NW	202-628-8140	Reliable burger 'n' Guinness place.
Home	911 F St NW	202-638-4663	Dress up and wait in line to dance.
Platinum	915 F St NW	202-393-3555	Sleek and swank dance club.
Polly Esther's	605 12th St NW	202-737-1970	Dance to the '80s.
Poste Brasserie Bar	555 8th St NW	202-783-6060	Roomy and comfortable.
Round Robin Bar	1401 Pennsylvania Ave NW	202-628-9100	Old style, old money DC. "Herbal" martinis.
Tequila Beach	1115 F St NW	202-393-5463	Surf-shack tiki bar.

Map 2 • Chinatown / Union Station

Capitol City Brewing Company	2 Massachusetts Ave NE	202-842-2337	Great IPA.
Coyote Ugly	717 6th St NW	202-589-0016	Stripclub lite; sports TV paradise.
Fado Irish Pub	808 7th St NW	202-789-0066	Every beer imaginable.
Insomnia	714 6th St NW	202-737-1003	Spend half the night in line.
Juste Lounge	1015 1/2 7th St NW	202-393-0939	Martinis, martinis, martinis.
RFD Washington	810 7th St NW	202-289-2030	Brickskeller's downtown sibling-- hundreds of beers.

Map 3 • The Hill

Capitol Lounge	231 Pennsylvania Ave SE	202-547-2098	Hill hangout, do-it-yourself Bloody Mary bar.
DC Sanctuary	1355 H St NE	202-339-4033	Music and art intersect.
Hawk and Dove	329 Pennsylvania Ave SE	202-543-3300	Hill staffer hangout.
Lounge 201	201 Massachusetts Ave NE	202-544-5201	Retro martini bar.
Politiki	319 Pennsylvania Ave SE	202-546-1001	1 building=3 bars. This is the tiki bar.
Top of the Hill	319 Pennsylvania Ave SE	202-546-1001	1 building=3 bars. This has pool and red vinyl.

Map 5 • Southeast

Bachelor's Mill	1106 8th St SE	202-544-1931	Gay African-American crowd.
Mr Henry's Capitol Hill	601 Pennsylvania Ave SE	202-546-8412	A spot for jazz lovers.
Phase One	525 8th St SE	202-544-6831	Comfortable lesbian neighborhood bar.
Remington's	639 Pennsylvania Ave SE	202-543-3113	Country & western gay bar.
Tunnicliff's Tavern	222 7th St SE	202-544-5680	Cheers-esque.

Map 6 · Waterfront

Abyss	1824 Half St SW	202-484-1817	Rave-like.
Edge	52 L St SE	202-488-1200	Dance club, part of the gay club scene.
Nation	1015 Half St SE	202-554-1500	Live music venue and gay dance club.
Secrets	1345 Half St SE	202-554-5141	Spectacular views; where the boys are.
Zanzibar on the Waterfront	700 Water St SW	202-554-9100	Hugely popular velvet-rope club.
Ziegfields/Secrets	1345 Half St SE	202-554-5141	Strip club and drag shows.

Map 7 · Foggy Bottom

Potomac Lounge	2650 Virginia Ave NW	202-628-8140	Cocktails at the Watergate.

Map 8 · Georgetown

Blues Alley	1073 Wisconsin Ave NW	202-337-4141	THE place for live jazz.
Degrees	3100 South St NW	202-912-4100	Pretty ritzy.
Martin's Tavern	1264 Wisconsin Ave NW	202-333-7370	Gin and tonic crowd.
Mie N Yu	3125 M St NW	202-333-6122	Exotic, Eastern atmosphere and good food.
Modern	3287 M St NW	202-338-7027	Crowded, go on a weeknight.
Rino-Bar Pump House	3295 M St NW	202-333-3150	Cheap beer, dance music, and pool tables.
Saloun	3239 M St NW	202-965-4900	Dingy drinkin'.
Sequoia	3000 K St NW	202-944-4200	Outdoor people-watch on the Potomac.
The Third Edition - Bar	1218 Wisconsin Ave NW	202-333-3700	One-night stands start here.
The Tombs	1226 36th St NW	202-337-6668	Georgetown institution.

Map 9 · Dupont Circle / Adams Morgan

17th St Bar & Grill	1615 Rhode Island Ave NW	202-872-1126	Tasty food, great outdoor seating.
Acropolis	1337 Connecticut Ave NW	202-912-8444	Line up to get it.
Aroma	2401 Pennsylvania Ave NW	202-296-6383	Good cocktails.
Bar Rouge	1315 16th St NW	202-232-8000	Cool new addition to the neighborhood.
Biddy Mulligan's	1500 New Hampshire Ave NW	202-483-6000	Smoky and Irish in Jury's Hotel.
Big Hunt	1345 Connecticut Ave NW	202-785-2333	Typical bar but Guinness ice cream!
Bravo Bravo	1001 Connecticut Ave NW	202-223-5330	Salsa and Merengue.
Brickskeller	1523 22nd St NW	202-293-1885	Try a beer from Timbuktu.
Buffalo Billiards	1330 19th St NW	202-331-7665	Relaxed poolhall.
Café Japone	2032 P St NW	202-223-1573	Serious sake.
Chaos	1603 17th St NW	202-232-4141	Gay and straight, drag bingo, drag brunch.
Chi-Cha Lounge	1624 U St NW	202-234-8400	Informal (ties forbidden) Ecuadorian hacienda.
Common Share	2003 18th St NW	202-588-7180	Dive; bike courier heaven.
Dragonfly	1215 Connecticut Ave NW	202-331-1775	All-white and all-trendy.
Eighteenth Street Lounge	1212 18th St NW	202-466-3922	Dragonfly's older brother--hip but mature about it.
Firefly	1310 New Hampshire Ave NW	202-861-1310	Sophisticated drinking.
Fireplace	2161 P St NW	202-293-1293	Landmark gay bar.
Gazuza	1629 Connecticut Ave NW	202-667-5500	Upscale tapas lounge--go early for patio seating.
Improv	1140 Connecticut Ave NW	202-296-7008	Don't laugh up your weak rum and coke.
La Frontera Cantina	1633 17th St NW	202-232-0437	Have a Corona and people-watch.
Local 16	1604 U St NW	202-265-2828	Cavernous and cool.
Lucky	1221 Connecticut Ave NW	202-331-3733	Lose your friends on every floor.

Map 9 • Dupont Circle / Adams Morgan — *continued*

Lulu's Club Mardi Gras	1217 22nd St NW	202-861-5858	New Orleans-style meat market.
McClellan's	1919 Connecticut Ave NW	202-483-3000	Hilton Hotel sports bar.
MCCXXIII Spank	1223 Connecticut Ave NW	202-822-1800	Exclusive club--past it's prime?
Omega DC	2122 P St NW	202-223-4917	Mature men gay bar.
Ozio	1813 M St NW	202-822-6000	Sip a cocktail and puff a cigar.
Recessions	1823 L St NW	202-296-6686	Basement bar.
Red	1802 Jefferson Pl NW	202-466-3475	Go after midnight.
Rendezvous Cafe	2226 18th St NW	202-462-4444	Kick back--jazz, soul, hip-hop.
Rumors	1900 M St NW	202-466-7378	After-work drinks downtown.
Russia House Restaurant and Lounge	1800 Connecticut Ave NW	202-234-9433	Caviar and vodka in elegant coziness.
Sign of the Whale	1825 M St NW	202-785-1110	Cozy and cheap.
Soussi	2228 18th St NW	202-299-9314	Outdoor wine bar.
Staccato	2006 18th St NW	202-232-2228	Good music, great burgers.
Stetson's Famous Bar & Restaurant	1610 U St NW	202-667-6295	Drink with Jenna Bush (while you can).
Tabard Inn - Bar	1739 N St NW	202-331-8528	Romantic rendezvous.
The Wave!	1731 New Hampshire Ave NW	202-518-5011	Carlyle Suites club.
Topaz Bar	1733 N St NW	202-393-3000	Go for the drinks.
Townhouse Tavern	1637 R St NW	202-234-5747	Get your Schlitz in a can.
Trio's Fox & Hounds	1537 17th St NW	202-232-6307	Patio drinking.
Zebra Bar and Lounge	1170 22nd St NW	202-974-6600	Hotel cocktail lounge.

Map 10 • Logan Circle / U Street

9:30	815 V St NW	202-393-0930	THE place in DC to see a band.
Bar Nun	1326 U St NW	202-667-6680	Fridays are bound to be interesting.
Between Friends	1115 U St NW	202-232-2544	Gay bar on U Street.
Black Cat	1811 14th St NW	202-667-7960	The OTHER place in DC to see a band.
Bohemian Caverns	2003 11th St NW	202-299-0800	Cool jazz in the basement.
Cafe Saint-Ex	1847 14th St NW	202-265-7839	Outdoor tables on summer nights.
Club 2-K9	2008 8th St NW	202-667-7750	Nightclub.
Club Daedalus	1010 Vermont Ave NW	202-347-9066	Make a reservation.
DC9	1940 9th St NW	202-483-5000	Rock club.
Helix Lounge	1430 Rhode Island Ave NW	202-462-9001	New trendy neighborhood addition.
Kingpin	917 U St NW	202-588-5880	As comfortable as your living room.
Republic Gardens	1355 U St NW	202-232-2710	Famous DC music club.
So Much More	1428 L St NW	202-824-0731	Nightclub.
The Saint	1520 14th St NW	202-234-0886	Worthy tribute to St Exupery.
The Saloon	1205 U St NW	202-462-2640	European appeal--go for the beer.
Titan	1337 14th St NW	202-232-7010	Gay bar at Hamburger Mary's.
Twins Jazz	1344 U St NW	202-234-0072	Intimate bar with Ethiopian food.
Velvet Lounge	915 U St NW	202-462-3213	As comfy as it sounds.

Map 11 • Near Northeast

Bud's	501 Morse St NE	202-543-4419	Off-the-beaten-path restaurant and nightclub.

Map 12 • Trinidad

Dream	1350 Okie St NE	202-347-5255	Huge nightclub.

Map 13 • Brookland / Langdon

Aqua	1818 New York Ave NE	202-832-4878	Asian dance club at a Korean restaurant.
DC Tunnel	2135 Queens Chapel Rd NE	202-526-7960	Go-go and dancehall reggae shows.
Deno's/Breeze Metro	2335 Bladensburg Rd NE	202-526-8880	DC's go-go joint.

Map 14 • Catholic U

Colonel Brooks' Tavern	901 Monroe St NE	202-529-4002	Neighborhood landmark.

Map 16 • Adams Morgan (North) / Mt Pleasant

Adams Mill Bar and Grill	1813 Adams Mill Rd NW	202-332-9577	Pitchers after the softball game.
Angles	2339 18th St NW	202-462-8100	Not just about billiards.
Angry Inch Saloon	2450 18th St NW	202-234-3041	Bare bones drinkin'.
Asylum	2471 18th St NW	202-319-9353	Goth decor and pounding music.
Bedrock Billiards	1841 Columbia Rd NW	202-667-7665	Pool hall with extensive alcohol choices.
Blue Room Lounge	2321 18th St NW	202-332-0800	Great wines, with trip-hop soundtrack.
Bossa	2463 18th St NW	202-667-0088	Cool downstairs, samba upstairs.
Brass Monkey	2317 18th St NW	202-667-7800	Amateur night/Yuppie hangout.
Café Toulouse	2431 18th St NW	202-238-9018	Parisian relaxation.
Chief Ike's Mambo Room	1725 Columbia Rd NW	202-332-2211	Dirty dance 'til dawn.
Columbia Station	2325 18th St NW	202-462-6040	More jazz and blues in an intimate setting.
Cosmo Lounge	1725 Columbia Rd NW	202-332-2233	For the rock-and-roll crowd.
Crush	2323 18th St NW	202-319-1111	Popular and crowded.
Dan's Cafe	2315 18th St NW	202-265-9241	No frills.
Felix Lounge	2406 18th St NW	202-483-3549	Pretentious or sophisticated? Try it out.
Kokopooli's Pool Hall	2305 18th St NW	202-234-2306	Pool and beer.
Madam's Organ	2461 18th St NW	202-667-5370	Redheads get a discount; best blues in DC.
Mantis	1847 Columbia Rd NW	202-667-2400	Mod lounge.
Marx Café	3203 Mt Pleasant St NW	202-518-7600	Was Marx a drinker?
Pharmacy Bar	2337 18th St NW	202-483-1200	Cheap drinks, nasty service.
The Raven	3125 Mt Pleasant Ave NW	202-466-3475	Neighborhood bar.
The Reef	2446 18th St NW	202-518-3800	Jellyfish and drinks.
Rumba Cafe	2443 18th St NW	202-588-5501	Cuban treats.
Saki Asian Grill	2477 18th St NW	202-232-5005	Exclusive Japanese.
Spy Lounge	2406 18th St NW	202-483-3549	Felix's spy dive sibling.
Timehri International	2439 18th St NW	202-518-2626	Reggae, Calypso, R&B.
Tom Tom	2333 18th St	202-588-1300	Play old-school Nintendo upstairs.
Tonic - Bar	3155 Mt Pleasant St NW	202-986-7661	Local tavern.
Zucchabar	1841 Columbia Rd NW	202-332-8642	Friendly bartenders, well-made drinks.

Map 17 • Woodley Park / Cleveland Park

Aroma	3417 Connecticut Ave NW	202-244-7995	Good cocktails.
Ireland's Four Provinces (Four Ps)	3412 Connecticut Ave NW	202-244-0860	Have a pint and name the Ps.
Nanny O'Brien's	3319 Connecticut Ave NW	202-686-9189	Legendary Celtic jam sessions.
Oxford Tavern Zoo Bar	3000 Connecticut Ave NW	202-232-4225	Low-key with live blues bands.

Map 18 • Glover Park / Foxhall

Bourbon	2348 Wisconsin Ave NW	202-625-7770	Great bourbon, of course.
Zebra Lounge	3238 Wisconsin Ave NW	202-237-2202	New and improved.

Map 19 • Tenleytown / Friendship Heights

Chadwick's	5247 Wisconsin Ave NW	202-362-8040	Metro-convenient location--burgers and bar.

Map 21 • 16th St. Heights / Petworth

Twins Lounge	5516 Colorado Ave NW	202-882-2523	Intimate jazz club.

Map 22 • Downtown Bethesda

Rock Bottom Brewery	7900 Norfolk Ave	301-652-1311	Worth the wait.
Saphire Cafe	7940 Wisconsin Ave	301-986-9708	Average bar.
South Beach Restaurants & Bar	7904 Woodmont Ave	301-718-9737	Dirt-cheap happy hour.
Yacht Club of Bethesda	8111 Woodmont Ave	301-654-2396	Best known for cheezy TV commericals.

Map 25 • Silver Spring

Mayorga	8040 Georgia Ave	301-562-9090	Coffee by day, microbrew by night.
Quarry House Tavern	8401 Georgia Ave	301-587-9406	Simply great.

Map 26 • Takoma Park

Taliano's	7001 Carroll Ave	301-270-5515	Open mic nights are a must.

Map 27 • Walter Reed

Charlie's Bar & Grill	7307 Georgia Ave NW	202-726-3567	Soul food and contemporary jazz.
Takoma Station Tavern	6914 4th St NW	202-829-1999	Jazz haven.

Map 28 • Chevy Chase

Chevy Chase Lounge	5510 Connecticut Ave NW	202-966-7600	Parthenon Restaurant's wood-panelled lounge.

Map 29 • Bethesda/Chevy Chase

Flanagan's	7637 Old Georgetown Rd	301-986-1007	Authentic Irish bartenders.
Strike Bethesda	5353 Westbard Ave	301-652-0955	Not your average bowling alley.
Tommy Joe's	4714 Montgomery Ln	301-654-3801	Frat boy central.
Uncle Jed's Roadhouse	7525 Old Georgetown Rd	301-913-0026	Southern-style roadhouse.

Map 33 • Falls Church

Lost Dog Café	5876 Washington Blvd	703-237-1552	Buy a beer, adopt a pet.

Map 34 • Ballston

Rock Bottom Brewery	4238 Wilson Blvd	703-516-7688	Go for happy hour.

Map 35 • Clarendon

Galaxy Hut	2711 Wilson Blvd	703-525-8646	Cute bartender.
Iota	2832 Wilson Blvd	703-522-8340	Great place to see a twangy band.

Map 36 • Rosslyn

Continental	1911 Fort Myer Dr	703-465-7675	Pool with a modern spin.
Summers Grill and Sports Pub	1520 N Courthouse Rd	703-528-8278	Soccer-watching bar.

Map 37 • Fort Myer

Jay's Saloon	3114 N 10th St	703-527-3093	Down-home and friendly.
Royal Lee Bar and Grill	2211 N Pershing Dr	703-524-5493	All American.

Map 39 • Shirlington

Capitol City Brewing Company	2700 S Quincy St	703-578-3888	Great IPA.

Map 40 • Pentagon City

Sine Irish Pub	1301 S Joyce St	703-415-4420	Generic Irish pub.

Map 46 • Old Town (South)

Founders' Brewing Company	607 King St	703-684-5397	German-style beers.
Laughing Lizzard Lounge	1324 King St	703-548-2582	Go for the pool and a cold beer.
Rock It Grill	1319 King St	703-739-2274	Lowbrow and proud.
State Theatre	220 N Washington St	703-237-0300	Grab a table, a beer, and listen.
Tiffany Tavern	1116 King St	703-836-8844	Bluegrass central.

Besides the range of good eating that all of America's biggest cities boast, DC also has a choice buffet of American regional and international cuisines.

You can get a mouthful of Northern California and a touch of romance at **Nora** or a bite of Southern hospitality at **Colorado Kitchen**. Good Tex-Mex can be found at **Lauriol Plaza**, while chunky gumbo is served hot at **Johnny's On The Half Shell**.

Some of the best international cuisine can be had at **Zaytinya** (Spanish), **Ten Penh** (Asian fusion), **Jaleo** (Spanish in Chinatown), **Café Sofia** (Bulgarian), **Bistro Lepic** (French), **Sushi-Ko** (Japanese), **Grill From Ipanema** (Brazilian), and **Indique** (Indian)… This ain't the Epcot Center either—the clientele's authentic and so is the cooking.

*Key: $: Under $10 / $$: $10-$20 / $$$: $20-$30 / $$$$: $30+   * : Does not accept credit cards. / † : Accepts only American Express.*

Map 1 · National Mall

Bistro D'Oc	518 10th St NW	202-393-5444	$$	Tasteful French.
Cafe Atlantico	405 8th St NW	202-393-0812	$$$	Elegante nuevo Latino.
Caucus Room	401 9th St NW	202-393-1300	$$$$$	The taste of power. A favorite for DC's elite.
Ceiba	701 14th St NW	202-393-3983	$$$	Latin American from the Tenpenh and DC Coast restauranteurs.
Occidental	1475 Pennsylvania Ave NW	202-783-1475	$$$*	Opulent White House classic.
Ortanique	730 11th St NW	202-393-0975	$$$*	Caribbean fare and Miami flavor.
Ten Penh	1001 Pennsylvania Ave NW	202-393-4500	$$$$	DC's hottest Asian fusion.
Willard Room	1401 Pennsylvania Ave NW	202-637-7440	$$$$	If not the richest breakfast in town, definitely the most expensive.
Zaytinya	701 9th St NW	202-638-0800	$$$	Classy, polished atmosphere and wonderful Middle Eastern.

Map 2 · Chinatown / Union Station

701	701 Pennsylvania Ave NW	202-393-0701	$$$$	Posh food and soft jazz.
B Smith's	50 Massachusetts Ave NE	202-289 -6188	$$$	Creole elegance, jarring in Union Station.
Bistro Bis	15 E St NW	202-661-2700	$$$$	French cuisine for the lobbyist crowd.
Burma	740 6th St NW	202-638-1280	$$	Bare-bones Burmese joint.
Capital Q	707 H St NW	202-347-8396	$*	BBQ for homesick Texans. Closes early.
Capitol City Brewing Company	2 Massachusetts Ave NE	202-842-2337	$$*	Great microbrewery.
Fado Irish Pub	808 7th St NW	202-789-0066	$$	Home of the famous Monday night Pub Quiz.
Flying Scotsman	233 2nd St NW	202-783-3848	$$	Pub favored by young Hill elites.
Jaleo	480 7th St NW	202-628-7949	$$$	Flashy tapas.
Matchbox	713 H St NW	202-289-4441	$$*	A pizza tavern with martinis.
Rosa Mexicano	575 7th St NW	202-783-5522	$$	MCI Center destination. Try the pomegranate margarita.
Tortilla Coast	400 1st St SE	202-546-6768	$	Favorite Hill non-power lunch spot.

Arts & Entertainment • **Restaurants**

Key: $: Under $10 / $$: $10-$20 / $$$: $20-$30 / $$$$: $30+   * : Does not accept credit cards. / † : Accepts only American Express.

Map 3 • The Hill

Café Berlin	322 Massachusetts Ave NE	202-543-7656	$$	For all your Oktoberfest needs.
Il Radicchio	223 Pennsylvania Ave SE	202-547-5114	$$	Same as Galileo but more relaxed.
Kenny's Smokehouse	732 Maryland Ave NE	202-547-4553	$	BBQ with oodles of sides.
La Brasserie	239 Massachusetts Ave NE	202-546-9154	$$	Cozy French fare at very reasonable prices.
Two Quail	320 Massachusetts Ave NE	202-543-8030	$$$	Romantic little Hill spot.
White Tiger	301 Massachusetts Ave NE	202-546-5900	$$	Best Capitol Hill Indian food.

Map 4 • RFK

| Phish Tea Café | 1335 H St NE | 202-396-2345 | $$ | Casual island food, from Caribbean to West Indian. |

Map 5 • Southeast

Banana Cafe & Piano Bar	500 8th St SE	202-543-5906	$$	Democrat-friendly Hill cabana.
Bread & Chocolate	666 Pennsylvania Ave SE	202-547-2875	$	Here it's dessert before dinner. Go with the chocolate truffle cake.
Meyhane	633 Pennsylvania Ave SE	202-544-4753	$$	Exotic Turkish tapas.
Montmartre	327 7th St SE	202-544-1244	$$	Comfortable French bistro.
Starfish	539 8th St SE	202-546-5006	$$	Seafood from the people behind Banana Cafe.

Map 6 • Waterfront

Cantina Marina	600 Water St SW	202-554-8396	$$	Corny Cajun "dock" with a nice view.
H2O at Hogate's	800 Water St SW	202-484-6300	$$$	Waterfront home of the rum bun.
Pier 7	650 Water St SW	202-554-2500	$$$	Showy waterfront seafood.

Map 7 • Foggy Bottom

Aquarelle	2650 Virginia Ave NW	202-298-4455	$$$	Revived Clinton-era Mediterranean restaurant at the Watergate.
Brasserie at the Watergate	600 New Hampshire Ave NW	202-337-5890	$$$	Formerly Dominique's; the pre-Kennedy Center locale.
Dish	924 25th St NW	202-383-8707	$$	New takes on traditional American and Southern food.
Karma	1919 I St NW	202-331-5800	$$	Mediterranean restaurant and art gallery.
Kinkead's	2000 Pennsylvania Ave NW	202-296-7700	$$$$	Elegant seafood, extravagent raw bar.
Nectar	824 New Hampshire Ave NW	202-298-8085	$$$	Nice wine and cheese lists.
Primi Piatti	2013 I St NW	202-223-3600	$$$	Dressed-up Italian.

Map 8 · Georgetown

1789	1226 36th St NW	202-965-1789	$$$$$	The epitome of Georgetown haute.
Cafe Bonaparte	1522 Wisconsin Ave NW	202-333-8830	$	Fine French-onion soup.
Citronelle	3000 M St NW	202-625-2150	$$$$	A preferred destination of Mayor Anthony Williams.
Clyde's	3236 M St NW	202-333-9180	$$	Famous Georgetown saloon, made less notable through suburban franchising.
Fahrenheit Restaurant	3100 South St NW	202-912-4110	$$$	Italian-American in the deco Ritz-Carlton hotel.
The Landmark	2430 Pennsylvania Ave NW	202-955-3863	$$$	Melrose Hotel continental restaurant.
Nathan's	3150 M St NW	202-338-2000	$	Take a shopping break and grab a burger and beer.
Old Glory All-American BBQ	3139 M St NW	202-337-3406	$	Southeast-style BBQ, with hoppin' john on the side.
Pizzeria Paradiso	3282 M St NW	202-337-1245	$	Perfect after a day spent strolling.
Sequoia	3000 K St NW	202-944-4200	$$$	A Georgetown see-and-be-seen hotspot.
The Tombs	1226 36th St NW	202-337-6668	$$	An underground GU favorite.

Map 9 · Dupont Circle / Adams Morgan

Chi-Cha Lounge	1624 U St NW	202-234-8400	$$	Kick off an evening on U with tapas, sangria, and a hookah.
Galileo	1110 21st St NW	202-293-7191/ 202-331-0880	$$$$	DC's finest Italian.
Kramerbooks & Afterwards Cafe	1517 Connecticut Ave NW	202387-1462	$$	Fine bookstore and all-night diner known by all.
Lauriol Plaza	1835 18th St NW	202-387-0035	$$$	Ritzy architecture and none-too-bad Tex-Mex.
Local 16	1602 U St NW	202-265-2828	$$	The classiest place on U.
Love Cafe	1501 U St NW	202-265-9800	$*	Achingly tasty fresh-baked sweets and cakes.
Luna Grill & Diner	1301 Connecticut Ave NW	202-835-2280	$	Great brunch.
Marcel's	2401 Pennsylvania Ave NW	202-296-1166	$$$$$	Extraordinary pre-Kennedy Center spot. French cuisine.
Olives	1600 K St NW	202-452-1866	$$$	Quaint but pricey Mediterranean.
Pizzeria Paradiso	2029 P St NW	202-223-1245	$	For the Italian pizza purist.
Tabard Inn	1739 N St NW	202-331-8528	$$$	Jazzy, romantic lounge. A unique spot.
Thaiphoon	2011 S St NW	202-667-3505	$$	Colorful Thai.
Vidalia	1990 M St NW	202-659-1990	$$$$$	A brilliant experience.

Key: $: Under $10 / $$: $10-$20 / $$$: $20-$30 / $$$$: $30+   * : Does not accept credit cards. / † : Accepts only American Express.

Map 10 · Logan Circle / U Street

Ben's Chili Bowl	1213 U St NW	202-667-0909	$*	A District chili institution.
Coppi's	1414 U St NW	202-319-7773	$$$	Organic fun for the true foodie.
DC Coast	1401 K St NW	202-216-5988	$$$$	Innovative contemporary seafood.
Dukem	1114 U St NW	202-667-8735	$	Authentic Ethiopian. Special weekend outdoor grill menu.
Georgia Brown's	950 15th St NW	202-393-4499	$$	Upscale Southern featuring a beloved brunch.
Logan Tavern	1423 P St NW	202-332-3710	$$	Pleasant spot featuring comfort food and a bit of everything.
Oohhs and Aahhs	1005 U St NW	202-667-7142	$*	The District's best soul food.
Rice	1608 14th St NW	202-234-2400	$$	Swanky minimalist Thai. Try the green tea dishes.
U-topia	1418 U St NW	202-483-7669	$$	Reasonably priced eclectic international cuisine.

Map 13 · Brookland / Langdon

Bamboo Joint Café	2062 Rhode Island Ave NE	202-526-7410	$	Cheap and tasty Brookland Jamaican diner.

Map 14 · Catholic U

Colonel Brooks' Tavern	901 Monroe St NE	202-529-4002	$	Typical pub grub, good beer selection.
Java Head Café	3629 12th St NE	202-997-5282	$*	Northeast destination for caffeine, sandwiches, and spoken word.
Kelly's Ellis Island	3908 12th St NE	202-832-6117	$	Anchor pub for the growing 12th St corridor.

Map 15 · Columbia Heights

Five Guys	2301 Georgia Ave NW	202-986-2235	$	Juicy, actually fresh burgers for fast-food prices.
Florida Ave Grill	1100 Florida Ave NW	202-265-1586	$*	Greasy spoon from the dirty south.
Negril	2301 Georgia Ave NW	202-332-3737	$*	Local Caribbean quick-eats chain.
Soul Vegetarian and Exodus Café	2606 Georgia Ave NW	202-328-7685	$*	Eclectic African vegan take-out.

Map 16 · Adams Morgan (North) / Mt Pleasant

Bardia's New Orleans Café	2412 18th St NW	202-234-0420	$	Perfect brunch with great Cajun takes on poached egg classics.
The Diner	2453 18th St NW	202-232-8800	$	As the name suggests. Open 24 hours.
Dos Gringos	3116 Mt Pleasant St NW	202-462-1159	$*	Great for late-night Salvadorean and classy breakfasts.
La Fourchette	2429 18th St NW	202-332-3077	$$	Casual creperie.

Map 16 • Adams Morgan (North) / Mt Pleasant — *continued*

Leftbank	2424 18th St NW	202-464-2100	$$	Americana diner, sushi bar, cafeteria aesthetic, hipster chic.
Little Fountain Café	2339 18th St NW	202-462-8100	$$	Continental food in a charming Adams Morgan nook.
Meskerem	2434 18th St NW	202-462-4100	$$	Authentic Ethiopian meets DC posh.
Pasta Mia	1790 Columbia Rd NW	202-328-9114	$*	Opens at night and worth the long queue.
Rumba Café	2443 18th St NW	202-588-5501	$$	Perfectly seasoned steak.
Tonic	3155 Mt Pleasant St NW	202-986-7661	$$	Comfort food and a can't-be-beat happy hour.
Tryst	2459 18th St NW	202-232-5500	$	Excellent Wi-Fi cafe. A central DC spot.

Map 17 • Woodley Park / Cleveland Park

Café Paradiso	2649 Connecticut Ave NW	202-265-8955	$$	Three stories of contemporary Italian.
Lavandou	3321 Connecticut Ave NW	202-966-3002	$$	Casual French sidewalk-style bistro.
Lebanese Taverna	2641 Connecticut Ave NW	202-265-8681	$$	Family-style Lebanese. Nice after the zoo.
Petits Plats	2653 Connecticut Ave NW	202-518-0018	$$	A French connection outside downtown.
Sake Club	2635 Connecticut Ave NW	202-332-2711	$$	Sake and Japanese, with prices ranging from low to quite high.
Sorriso	3518 Connecticut Ave NW	202-357-4800	$$	Brick-oven pizza to complement nearby Cafe Paradiso.
Spices	3333A Connecticut Ave NW	202-686-3833	$$*	Casual Asian fusion from the people behind Yanyu.
Yanyu	3433 Connecticut Ave NW	202-686-6968	$$$	Upscale neighborhood Asian fusion.

Map 18 • Glover Park / Foxhall

2 Amys	3715 Macomb St NW	202-885-5700	$$	Real Neopolitan pizza. Romantic or just for kicks.
Cactus Cantina	3300 Wisconsin Ave NW	202-686-7222	$$	Same as Lauriol Plaza, minus the genteel architecture.
Cafe Deluxe	3228 Wisconsin Ave NW	202-686-2233	$$	American fare, but with an accent.
Faccia Luna Trattoria	2400 Wisconsin Ave NW	202-337-3132	$	Good pizza for a low-key night out or in.
Heritage India	2400 Wisconsin Ave NW	202-333-3120	$$	Great neighborhood Indian hideaway.
Rocklands	2418 Wisconsin Ave NW	202-333-2558	$	Take a window seat for ribs and people watching.
Saveur	2218 Wisconsin Ave NW	202-333-5885	$$$	Off-beat Provencal.
Sushi Sushi	3714 Macomb St NW	202-686-2015	$	Sushi for your budget.
Sushi-Ko	2309 Wisconsin Ave NW	202-333-4187	$$	Washington's first sushi bar, since 1976.

Key: $: Under $10 / $$: $10-$20 / $$$: $20-$30 / $$$$: $30+   * : Does not accept credit cards. / † : Accepts only American Express.

Map 19 · Tenleytown / Friendship Heights

Cafe Ole	4000 Wisconsin Ave NW	202-244-1330	$$	Fun neighborhood Spanish-style tapas.
Krupin's	4620 Wisconsin Ave NW	202-686-1989	$	One of DC's few Jewish delis.
Maggiano's Little Italy	5333 Wisconsin Ave NW	202-966-5500	$	Good for a quick, solid Italian meal.
Matisse	4934 Wisconsin Ave NW	202-244-5222	$$$	French and Mediterranean with all the details.
Murasaki	4620 Wisconsin Ave NW	202-966-0023	$$	Wide range of Japanese cuisines.
Steak 'n Egg Kitchen	4700 Wisconsin Ave NW	202-686-1201	$	This greasy spoon hasn't changed a thing in over 60 years.

Map 20 · Cleveland Park / Upper Connecticut

Buck's Fishing & Camping	5031 Connecticut Ave NW	202-364-0777	$$$	Game. More sophisticated than the name suggests.
Delhi Dhaba	4455 Connecticut Ave NW	202-537-1008	$	Quick, passable Indian take-out.
Indique	3512 Connecticut Ave NW	202-244-6600	$$	Consistent DC Indian franchise.
Palena	3529 Connecticut Ave NW	202-537-9250	$$$	Continental food and an engrossing dessert menu.
Sala Thai	3507 Connecticut Ave NW	202-237-2777	$	No-frills Thai.

Map 21 · 16th St. Heights / Petworth

Colorado Kitchen	5515 Colorado Ave NW	202-545-8280	$	Homey, friendly American with a Southern accent.

Map 22 · Downtown Bethesda

Bacchus	7945 Norfolk Ave	301-657-1722	$$	Lebanese with a lengthy meze menu.
Faryab	4917 Cordell Ave	301-951-3484	$$	Premier DC metro area Afghan stop.
Grapeseed	4865 Cordell Ave	301-986-9592	$$$	Spanish cuisine to go with a massive wine list.
Haandi	4904 Fairmont Ave	301-718-0121	$$	One of suburban Maryland's oldest Indian joints.
Matuba	4918 Cordell Ave	301-652-7449	$	Basic sushi and buffet.
Olazzo	7921 Norfolk Ave	301-654-9496	$$	Italian with a brick oven (and yet no pizza!).
Tako Grill	7756 Wisconsin Ave	301-652-7030	$$	Traditional and nontraditional Japanese for the enthusiast.
Tragara	4935 Cordell Ave	301-951-4935	$$$	Elegant surroundings and traditional Italian.

Map 24 · Upper Rock Creek Park

Parkway Deli	8317 Grubb Rd	301-587-1427	$	Another rare high-quality Jewish deli.
Red Dog Cafe	8301A Grubb Rd	301-588-6300	$$	Constantly changing decor.

Map 25 • Silver Spring

Cubano's	1201 Fidler Ln	301-563-4020	$$	Extremely cheesey decor, complete with fountain and foliage.
Eggspectation	923 Ellsworth Dr	301-585-1700	$$	Pretty ridiculous number of egg dishes.
El Aguila	8649 16th St	301-588-9063	$$	Better than its location would have you believe.
Mi Rancho	8701 Ramsey Ave	301-588-4872	$	Quite cheap Mexican/Salvadorean.
Roger Miller Restaurant	941 Bonifant St	301-650-2495	$	Unique Cameroon fare, named after a soccer star.

Map 26 • Takoma Park

Mark's Kitchen	7006 Carroll Ave	301-270-1884	$	Green-friendly American and Korean fare.
Savory	7071 Carroll Ave	301-270-2233	$$*	Veggie/vegan and a basement café.

Map 28 • Chevy Chase

American City Diner	5332 Connecticut Ave NW	202-244-2949	$	1950s drive-in themed diner, complete with movies.
Arucola	5534 Connecticut Ave NW	202-244-1555	$	Straightforward Italian.
Bread & Chocolate	5542 Connecticut Ave NW	202-966-7413	$	Can't go wrong with this combination.
La Ferme	7101 Brookville Rd	301-986-5255	$$$$	Charming (if bizarre) French bistro in a residential area.

Map 29 • Bethesda / Chevy Chase

Green Papaya	4922 Elm St	301-654-8986	$$	Tasty but ridiculously inauthentic Vietnamese.
Hinode	4914 Hampden Ln	301-654-0908	$	No surprises Japanese.
Pastry Designs	4927 Elm St	301-656-0536	$	Get anything with the fig honey.
Persimmon	7003 Wisconsin Ave	301-654-9860	$$$	Superlative Bethesda continental experience.
Ri-Ra Irish Restaurant Pub	4931 Elm St	301-657-1122	$$	Irish pub...inexplicably American food.
Tara Thai	4828 Bethesda Ave	301-657-0488	$$	Well-known for bold Thai.
Thyme Square Café	4735 Bethesda Ave	301-657-9077	$$*	Boasts a healthy menu; no red meat.

Map 32 • Cherrydale / Palisades

Bambu	5101 MacArthur Blvd NW	202-364-3088	$$	Reliable Asian fusion.
Starland Cafe	5125 MacArthur Blvd NW	202-244-9396	$$	Starland Vocal Band's Bill Danoff's joint, if you miss the '70s.

Key: $: Under $10 / $$: $10-$20 / $$$: $20-$30 / $$$$: $30+   * : Does not accept credit cards. / † : Accepts only American Express.

Map 33 • Falls Church

La Cote d'Or Cafe	6876 Lee Hwy	703-538-3033	$$$	High romance for a reasonable price.
Lebanese Taverna	5900 Washington Blvd	703-241-8681	$$	Family-style Lebanese. Everyone shares.
Taqueria Poblano	2503 N Harrison St	703-237-8250	$	Generic, but nice and cheap.

Map 34 • Ballston

Crisp & Juicy	4540 Lee Hwy	703-243-4222	$	Latino-barbecued chicken.
Metro 29 Diner	4711 Lee Hwy	703-528-2464	$	Diner breakfast with some Greek touches.
Nouveau East	671 N Glebe Rd, Ste 1248	703-807-4088	$$	Thai plus sushi.
Rocklands	4000 Fairfax Dr	703-528-9663	$	DC BBQ in NoVA.
Tara Thai	4001 Fairfax Dr	703-908-4999	$$	A tasty Thai chain.

Map 35 • Clarendon

Boulevard Woodgrill	2901 Wilson Blvd	703-875-9663	$$	Exceptionally plain.
Faccia Luna Trattoria	2909 Wilson Blvd	703-276-3099	$	Good pizza for a low-key night out or in.
Hard Times Cafe	3028 Wilson Blvd	703-528-2233	$	Great chili lowers the brow of posh Clarendon.
Harry's Tap Room	2800 Clarendon Blvd	703-778-7788	$$$	Nearly a dozen filet mignon options.
Hope Key	3131 Wilson Blvd	703-243-8388	$	Exotic Hong Kong Chinese food.
Portabellos	2109 N Pollard St	703-528-1557	$$	Contemporary American.

Map 36 • Rosslyn

Gua-Rapo	2039 Wilson Blvd	703-528-6500	$$*	Chi-Cha Lounge flavor in NoVA.
Il Radicchio	1801 Clarendon Blvd	703-276-2627	$$	Traditional Italian from chef Roberto Donna.
Mezza9	1325 Wilson Blvd	703-276-8999	$$	The Rosslyn Hyatt's take on Turkish.
Ray's The Steaks	1725 Wilson Blvd	703-841-7297	$$	Meat. No frills about it.
Village Bistro	1723 Wilson Blvd	703-522-0284	$$	Quaint bistro for a shopping strip.

Map 37 • Fort Myer

Bob & Edith's Diner	2310 Columbia Pike	703-920-6103	$*	Probably the most charming all-night diner in Virginia.
Manee Thai	2500 Columbia Pike	703-920-2033	$$	True Thai treasure.
Matuba	2915 Columbia Pike	703-521-2811	$	Unlike the Bethesda location, no buffet.

Map 38 • Columbia Pike

Bob & Edith's Diner	4707 Columbia Pike	703-920-4700	$*	Probably the most charming all-night diner in Virginia.
Five Guys	4626 King St	703-671-1606	$	Actually fresh burgers, yet fast-food prices.

Map 46 • Old Town (South)

Faccia Luna Trattoria	823 S Washington St	703-838-5998	$	Good pizza for a low-key night out or in.

Arts & Entertainment • **Shopping**

Washington takes much abuse for its lack of sartorial flair. We hate to say it, but it's deserved. This is a city that accepts hose with white pumps and considers seersucker a staple.

A few intrepid shopkeepers are trying to change our dowdy ways. For their efforts, they deserve to be patronized. **All About Jane** and **Plaid** are going after the women while **Thomas Pink** and **Pop** have us all in their sights.

If the raging interior design districts along 14th Street and M Street in Georgetown are any indication, our interior lives must be a little more daring.

Map 1 • National Mall

ADC Map & Travel Center	1636 I St NW	202-628-2209	Fantasize about your next trip.
Blink	1776 I St NW	202-776-0999	Wear your sunglasses at night.
Café Mozart	1331 H St NW	202-347-5732	Germanic treats.
Celadon Spa	1180 F St NW	202-347-3333	Great haircuts.
Chanel Boutique	1455 Pennsylvania Ave NW	202-638-5055	Dress like Jackie O.
Fahrney's	1317 F St NW	202-628-9525	Fussy pens.
International Spy Musuem Gift Shop	800 F St NW	202-654-0950	James Bond would be jealous.
Penn Camera	840 E St NW	202-347-5777	Say cheese.
Political Americana	1331 Pennsylvania Ave NW	202-737-7730	Souvenirs for back home.
Utrecht Art & Drafting Supplies	1250 I St NW	202-898-0555	Channel Picasso.
Weschler's	909 E St NW	202-628-1281	Furniture auctions.

Map 2 • Chinatown / Union Station

Alamo Flags	Union Station shops	202-842-3524	Don't bring matches.
Apartment Zero	406 7th St NW	202-6284067	Too cool for your living room.
Comfort One Shoes	50 Massachusetts Ave NE	202-408-4947	Beyond Birkenstocks.
Godiva Chocolatier	50 Massachusetts Ave NE	202-289-3662	Indulge.
Marvelous Market	730 7th St NW	202-628-0824	Takeout treats.
Olsson's Books	418 7th St NW	202-638-4882	Independent books and coffee.
Political Americana-Memorabilia	Union Station shops	202-289-7090	Stock up on Nixon '72 buttons.
Washington Redskins Official Store	50 Massachusetts Ave NE	202-842-8043	Hog central.

Map 5 • Southeast

American Rescue Workers' Thrift Store	745 8th St SE	202-547-9701	Cheap, cheap, cheap.
Backstage	545 8th St SE	202-544-5744	A store with theatrics.
Capitol Hill Bikes	709 8th St SE	202-544-4234	Pedal away from politics.
Capitol Hill Books	657 Centre St SE	202-544-1621	Plenty of page-turners.
Eastern Market	225 7th St SE	202-547-6480	Open-air stalls and weekend flea market.
Plaid	715 8th St SE	202-675-6900	Party dresses, etc.
Wooven History & Silk Road	315 7th St SE	202-543-1705	Visit Afghanistan without the war hassle.

Map 6 • Waterfront

Maine Avenue Fish Market	Maine Ave & Potomac River		Fresh off the boat.

Map 7 • Foggy Bottom

Motophoto	1819 H St NW	202-822-9001	Develop cheese.
Saks Jandel	2522 Virginia Ave NW	202-337-4200	For the well-dressed socialite.
Tower Records	2000 Pennsylvania Ave NW	202-331-2400	Music superstore.

Map 8 • Georgetown

Ann Saks	3328 M St NW	202-339-0840	Bury yourself in tile.
The Art Store	3019 M St NW	202-342-7030	For experts and amateurs.
Baker Georgetown	3330 M ST NW	202-342-7080	Traditional furnishings.
BCBG	3210 M St NW	202-333-2224	B well-dressed.

Map 8 • Georgetown — *continued*

Betsey Johnson	1319 Wisconsin Ave NW	202-338-4090	Mix girlie and insane.
Beyond Comics 2	1419-B Wisconsin Ave NW	202-333-8651	Never grow up.
Blink	3029 M St NW	202-525-5351	Wear your sunglasses at night.
Blue Mercury	3059 M St NW	202-965-1300	Spa on premises.
Bo Concepts	3342 M St	202-333-5656	Modern décor.
Commander Salamander	1420 Wisconsin Ave NW	202-337-2265	Teenage funk.
Dean and DeLuca	3276 M St NW	202-342-2500	Dean and delicious.
Deja Blue	3005 M St NW	202-337-7100	Stacks and stacks of jeans.
Design Within Reach	3307 Cady's Alley NW	202-339-9480	Furniture showroom.
Georgetown Running Company	3401 M St NW	202-337-8626	Gear up for a race.
Georgetown Tobacco	3144 M St NW	202-338-5100	Celebrate smoke.
Illuminations	3323 Cady's Alley NW	202-965-4888	Hot flashes.
Jaryam	1631 Wisconsin Ave NW	202-333-6886	Lacy lingerie.
Kate Spade	3061 M St NW	202-333-8302	Preppy polish.
Kenneth Cole	1259 Wisconsin Ave NW	202-298-0007	Stylish shoes.
Ligne Roset	3306 M St NW	202-333-6390	Check out the caterpillar couch.
Marvelous Market	3217 P St NW	202-464-0322	Try their blueberry muffins.
Movie Madness	1083 Thomas Jefferson St NW	202-337-7064	Movie posters.
Old Print Gallery	1220 31st St NW	202-965-1818	The name says it all.
Pottery Barn	3077 M St NW	202-337-8900	Yuppie interior style.
Proper Topper	3213 P St NW	202-333-6200	Cutesy hats and gifts.
Relish	3312 Cady's Alley NW	202-333-5343	For your bod, not your hot dog.
Revolution Cycles	3411 M St NW	202-965-3601	Replace stolen bikes here!
Sassanova	1641 Wisconsin Ave NW	202-223-4050	The latest and greatest in shoes.
Sherman Pickey	1647 Wisconsin Ave NW	202-333-4212	Pet-friendly attire.
Smith & Hawken	3077 M St NW	202-965-2680	Pricey graden gloves.
Sugar	1633 Wisconsin Ave NW	202-333-5331	Overly sweet concoctions.
Toka Salon	3251 Prospect St NW	202-333-5133	Relax.
Urban Outfitters	3111 M St NW	202-342-1012	More like dorm outfitters.
Zara	1234 Wisconsin Ave NW	202-944-9797	European cheap chic.

Map 9 • Dupont Circle / Adams Morgan

Andre Chreky, the Salon Spa	1604 K St NW	202-293-9393	Fancy trims.
Bang Salon	1612 U St NW	202-299-0925	Cool trims.
Bedazzled	1507 Connecticut Ave NW	202-265-2323	Make your own jewelry.
Best Cellars	1643 Connecticut Ave NW	202-387-3146	Non-snobby wines.
Betsy Fisher	1224 Connecticut Ave NW	202-785-1975	Expensive casual Fridays.
Blue Mercury	1745 Connecticut Ave NW	202-462-1300	Pricey make-up and lotions.
Brooks Brothers	1201 Connecticut Ave NW	202-659-4650	DC's uniform supply shop.
Burberry	1155 Connecticut Ave NW	202-463-3000	Fashionistas & foreign correspondents.
Cake Love	1506 U St NW	202-588-7100	Lust-worthy cupcakes.
Chapters Literary Bookstore	1512 K St NW	202-347-5495	Lunch-hour reads.
Comfort One Shoes	1621 Connecticut Ave NW	202-232-2480	Beyond Birkenstocks.
Comfort One Shoes	1630 Connecticut Ave NW	202-328-3141	Beyond Birkenstocks.
Custom Shop Clothiers	1033 Connecticut Ave NW	202-659-8250	Design your own button-down.
Doggie Style	1825 18th St NW	202-667-0595	Irreverant pet gifts.
Downs Engravers & Stationers	1746 L St NW	202-223-7776	When the occasion calls for uptight.
Drilling Tennis & Golf	1040 17th St NW	202-737-1100	Big Bertha lives here.
Fufua	1642 R St NW	202-332-5131	Previously owned Prada.
Ginza	1721 Connecticut Ave NW	202-331-7991	Japanica.
Godiva Chocolatier	1143 Connecticut Ave NW	202-638-7421	Indulge.
The Guitar Shop	1216 Connecticut Ave NW	202-331-7333	Self-explanatory.
Human Rights Campaign	1629 Connecticut Ave NW	202-232-8621	Gifts and cards for a cause.
J Press	1801 L St NW	202-857-0120	Conservative conservative.
The Kid's Closet	1226 Connecticut Ave NW	202-429-9247	Buy your niece an Easter dress.
Kramerbooks	1517 Connecticut Ave NW	202-387-1462	Scope for books and dates.
Kulturas	1706 Connecticut Ave NW	202-462-5015	Used books galore.

Map 9 • Dupont Circle / Adams Morgan — *continued*

Lambda Rising Bookstore	1625 Connecticut Ave NW	202-462-6969	Center of gay culture.
Marvelous Market	1511 Connecticut Ave NW	202-332-3690	Bread and brownies.
Meeps and Aunt Neensy's	1520 U St NW	202-265-6546	Vintage clothes.
Melody Records	1623 Connecticut Ave NW	202-232-4002	Best record store in town.
Millenium Decorative Arts	1528 U St NW	202-483-1218	Cool stuff for your crib.
Nana	1534 U St NW	202-667-6955	Chic boutique.
National Geographic Shop	17 & M St NW	202-857-7000	Travel the world in a shop.
Newsroom	1754 Connecticut Ave NW	202-332-1489	Café with foreign papers.
Pasargad Antique and Fine Persian	1217 Connecticut Ave NW	202-659-3888	Beautiful rugs.
Pleasure Palace	1710 Connecticut Ave NW	202-483-3297	Sex toys and gear.
Proper Topper	1350 Connecticut Ave NW	202-842-3055	Cutesy hats and gifts.
Rizik's	1100 Connecticut Ave NW	202-223-4050	Designer department store.
Rock Creek	2029 P St NW	202-429-6940	Great men's clothes.
Second Story	2000 P St NW	202-659-8884	Second-hand women's clothes.
Secondi	1702 Connecticut Ave NW	202-667-1122	Slightly used and funky.
Skynear and Co	2122 18th St NW	202-797-7160	Funky décor.
Sticky Fingers Bakery	1904 18th St NW	202-299-9700	Vegan bakery.
Tabletop	1608 20th St NW	202-387-7117	Dress-up your dinner table.
Taxation Without Representation	1500 U Street NW	202-462-6000	T-shirts for a cause.
The Third Day	2001 P St NW	202-785-0107	Plants on P.
Thomas Pink	1127 Connecticut Ave NW	202-223-5390	The perfect dress shirt.
Tiny Jewel Box	1147 Connecticut Ave NW	202-393-2747	Ready to pop?
Wild Women Wear Red	1512 U St NW	202-387-5700	Pay dearly for shoe art.
Wine Specialists	2115 M St NW	202-833-0707	Bone up on your grapes.
The Written Word	1365 Connecticut Ave NW	202-223-1400	Invites and cards.

Map 10 • Logan Circle / U Street

Blink	1431 P ST NW	202-234-1051	Wear your sunglasses at night.
Capitol Records	1020 U St NW	202-518-2444	Record fiends.
Garden District	1801 14th St NW	202-797-9005	Urban gardeners dig it here.
Go Mama Go!	1809 14th St NW	202-299-0850	Whacked-out décor.
Good Wood	1428 U St NW	202-986-3640	Furniture with history.
Home Rule	1807 14th St NW	202-797-5544	Kitchen treasures.
Maison 14	1325 14th St NW	202-588-5800	Pricey décor.
Muleh	1831 14th St NW	202-667-3440	Javanese furniture.
Pop	1803 14th St NW	202-939-0507	Trendy Wendys.
Pulp	1803 14th St NW	202-462-7857	Dirty birthday cards.
Reincarnation Furnishings	1401 14th St NW	202-319-1606	Furnishings for your inner movie star.
Ruff and Ready	1908 14th St NW	202-667-7833	Find a diamond in the ruff.
Urban Essentials	1330 U St NW	202-299-0640	Lust-worthy decor.

Map 16 • Adams Morgan (North) / Mt Pleasant

All About Jane	2438 1/2 18th St NW	202-797-9710	All about pricey casual.
Betty	2439 18th St NW	202-234-2389	Little shop of local designers.
City Bikes	2501 Champlain St NW	202-265-1564	Where the couriers shop.
Daisy	1814 Adams Mill Rd	202-797-1777	Boutique of trends.
Fleet Feet	1841 Columbia Rd NW	202-387-3888	Sneaks and mo.'
Idle Times Books	2467 18th St NW	202-232-4774	Disorganized lit.
Kobos African Clothiers	2444 18th St NW	202-332-9580	Traditional African.
Little Shop of Flowers	1812 Adams Mill Rd NW	202-387-7255	Great name, good flowers.
Miss Pixie's Furnishing and What-Not	1810 Adams Mill Rd NW	202-232-8171	Second-chance finds.
Shake Your Booty	2439 18th St NW	202-518-8205	Watch for their kick-ass sales.
So's Your Mom	1831 Columbia Road NW	202-462-3666	Imported NY bagels.
Trim	2700 Ontario Rd NW 2nd Flr	202-462-6080	If you need hip bangs.
Yes! Natural Gourmet	1825 Columbia Rd NW	202-462-5150	Yes! Wheat germ!

Map 17 • Woodley Park / Cleveland Park

Vace	3315 Connecticut Ave NW	202-363-1999	Best pizza in town.

Map 18 • Glover Park / Foxhall

Inga's Once Is Not Enough	4830 MacArthur Blvd NW	202-337-3072	Chanel, Valentino, and Prada, for example.
Skynear and Co	3301 New Mexico Ave NW	202-362-5523	Retro, modern furniture.
Theodore's	2233 Wisconsin Ave NW	202-333-2300	Funky décor.
Treetop Toys	3301 New Mexico Ave NW	202-244-3500	Independent and fun.

Map 19 • Tenleytown / Friendship Heights

The Container Store	4500 Wisconsin Ave	202-478-4000	Buckets, shelves, hangers…
Elizabeth Arden Red Door Salon & Spa	5225 Wisconsin Ave NW	202-362-9890	Serious pampering.
Georgette Klinger	5345 Wisconsin Ave NW	202-686-8880	It's all about extraction.
Hudson Trail Outfitters	4530 Wisconsin Ave NW	202-363-9810	Tents and Tevas.
Johnson's Florist & Garden Centers	4200 Wisconsin Ave NW	202-244-6100	For those of you with a yard.
Neiman Marcus	5300 Wisconsin Ave NW	202-966-9700	Ultra upscale department store.
Pottery Barn	5335 Wisconsin Ave NW	202-244-9330	Yuppie interior style.
Roche Bobois	5301 Wisconsin Ave NW	202-686-5667	African traditions.
Serenity Day Spa	4000 Wisconsin Ave NW	202-362-2560	Name says it all.

Map 20 • Cleveland Park / Upper Connecticut

Marvelous Market	5035 Connecticut Ave NW	202-686-4040	Try their blueberry muffins.
Politics & Prose	5015 Connecticut Ave NW	202-364-1919	Politics with your coffee.

Map 22 • Downtown Bethesda

Crate & Barrel	Montgomery Mall, Benton Ave & Fresno Rd	301-365-2600	Wedding registry HQ.
Daisy Too	4940 Saint Elmo Ave	301-656-2280	Unique and girly.
Mystery Bookshop	7700 Old Georgetown Rd	301-657-2665	Guess what genre?
Zelaya	4940 Saint Elmo Ave	301-656-2280	Shoes for the fashion forward.

Map 25 • Silver Spring

Kingsbury Chocolates	1017 King St	703-548-2800	Mmmmmm.

Map 26 • Takoma Park

Chuck & Dave's Books	7001 Carroll Ave	301-891-2665	Chuck & Dave want you to read.
Dan the Music Man	6855 Eastern Ave	301-270-0246	Forget records, the oldies here are on CDs.
Polly Sue's	6915 Laurel Ave	301-270-5511	Vintage heaven.
Takoma Underground	7030 Carroll Ave	301-270-0874	Outfits fit for Marilyn Monroe.

Map 27 • Walter Reed

KB News Emporium	7898 Georgia Ave	301-565-4248	Catch up on the headlines.

Map 29 • Bethesda/Chevy Chase

Gianni Versace	5454 Wisconsin Ave	301-907-9400	Pay homage to the God of Gaudy.
Marvelous Market	4832 Bethesda Ave	301-986-0555	Try their blueberry muffins.
Mustard Seed	7349 Wisconsin Ave	301-907-4699	Not your typical resale store.
Parvizian Masterpieces	7034 Wisconsin Ave	301-656-8989	Serious rugs.
Relish	5454 Wisconsin Ave	301-654-9899	For your bod, not your hot dog.
Saks Fifth Avenue	5555 Wisconsin Ave	301-657-9000	Where rich people shop.
Saks Jandel	5510 Wisconsin Ave	301-652-2250	For the well-dressed socialite.
Second Story Books	4836 Bethesda Ave	301-656-0170	Best known antiquarian book operation.
Sylene	4407 S Park Ave	301-654-4200	Fine lingerie.
Tickled Pink	7259 Woodmont Ave	301-913-9191	Palm Beach chic.
Tiffany & Co	5500 Wisconsin Ave	301-657-8777	Pop the question.

Map 30 • Westmoreland Circle

Crate & Barrel	4820 Massachusetts Ave NW	202-364-6100	Wedding registry HQ.

Map 34 • Ballston

Pottery Barn	Ballston Commons, 2700 Clarendon Blvd	703-465-9525	Yuppie interior style.

Map 35 • Clarendon

Brass Knob	2311 18th St	202-332-3370	Historical doorknobs!
The Container Store	2800 Clarendon Blvd	703-469-1530	Buckets, shelves, hangers…
The Italian store	3123 Lee Hwy	703-528-6266	The best Italian heros.

Map 36 • Rosslyn

Vastu	1829 14th St	202-234-8344	Upscale contemporary furnishings.

Map 38 • Columbia Pike

REI	3509 Carlin Springs Rd	703-379-9400	Sports emporium.

Map 39 • Shirlington

Washington Golf Centers	2625 Shirlington Rd	703-979-7888	Gear up for the links.

Map 40 • Pentagon City

Elizabeth Arden Red Door Salon & Spa	1101 S Joyce St	703-373-5888	Pampered facials.
What's In	1101 S Joyce St	703-414-3353	New York style.

Map 46 • Old Town (South)

Blink	1303 King St	703-518-5007	Wear your sunglasses at night.
Comfort One Shoes	201 King St	703-549-4441	Beyond Birkenstocks.
Hysteria	125 S Fairfax St	703-548-1615	Wearable art at museum prices.
La Cuisine	323 Cameron St	703-836-4435	Upscale cookware.
My Place in Tuscany	1127 King St	703-683-8882	Hand-painted ceramics.
P&C Art	212 King St	703-549-2525	Original art.
Tickled Pink	103 S St Asaph St	703-518-5459	Palm Beach chic.
The Torpedo Factory	105 N Union St	703-838-4565	Local artists' workshops.

The theater scene here ain't New York. You have to accept that up front, otherwise Washington will always pale in comparison. It's not worth it to try to chase down the traveling Broadway shows that charge exorbitant prices and offer second-string productions. Forget the spectacles at the **Kennedy Center** and the **National Theatre** unless you really want to see a lousy version of *The Producers*.

Though the big venues sometimes stage innovative works, the way to appreciate theater here is to peruse the smaller stages. The **Arena Stage** complex in the Southwest houses three theaters: the larger 816-seat

Fichandler Stage; the 514-seat fan-shaped **Kreeger Theater;** and the **Old Vat Room**, which has flexible seating for up to 120. Arena Stage produces eight plays per year and hosts visiting productions; www.arena-stage.com.

Studio Theatre has two theaters and an experimental performing space. The **Mead Theater** downstairs and **Milton Theater** upstairs both hold 200 people. The Studio is renowned for its development of some of Washington's best actors and directors and it also has an acting school.

Theater	Address	Phone	Map
Arena Stage	1101 6th St SW	202-488-3300	6
Blair Mansion Inn/Murder Mystery Dinner Theatre	7711 Eastern Ave	301-588-6646	27
Carter Barron Amphitheatre	16th & Colorado Ave NW	202-426-0486	21
Casa de la Luna	4020 Georgia Ave	202-882-6227	21
Dance Place	3225 8th St NE	202-269-1600	14
Discovery Theater	900 Jefferson Dr SW	202-357-1500	1
District of Columbia Arts Center	2438 18th St NW	202-462-7833	16
Fichandler Stage	1101 6th St SW	202-488-3300	6
Flashpoint	916 G St NW	202-315-1305	1
Folger Elizabethan Theatre	201 E Capitol St SE	202-544-7077	3
Follies Theatre	24 O St SE	202-484-0323	6
Ford's Theatre	511 10th St NW	202-347-4833	1
Gunston Arts Center	2700 S Lang St	703-553-7782	40
H Street Playhouse	1365 H St NE	202-396-2125	3
Hartke Theatre	3801 Harewood Rd NE	202-319-5358	14
Kennedy Center	2700 F St NW	202-467-4600	7
Kreeger Theater	1101 6th St SW	202-488-3300	6
Lincoln Theatre	1215 U St NW	202-328-6000	10
Little Theatre of Alexandria	600 Wolfe St	703-683-0496	46
Mead Theater	1333 P St NW	202-332-3300	10
Metro Stage	1201 N Royal St	703-548-9044	45
Milton Theater	1333 P St NW	202-332-3300	10
Mount Vernon Players	900 Massachusetts Ave NW	202-783-7600	10
Nannie J Lee Center	1108 Jefferson St	703-838-2880	46
National Theatre	1321 Pennsylvania Ave NW	202-628-6161	1
Old Vat Room	1101 6th St SW	202-488-3300	6
Round House Theatre	8641 Colesville Rd	240-644-1100	25
Round House Theatre	7501 Wisconsin Ave	240-644-1100	29
Shakespeare Theatre	450 7th St NW	202-547-1122	2
Source Theatre	1835 14th St NW	202-462-1073	10
St Mark's Players	118 3rd St SE	202-546-9670	3
Stanislavsky Theater Studio	1742 Church St NW	800-494-8497	9
Studio Theatre	1333 P St NW	202-332-3300	10
Takoma Theatre	6833 4th St NW	202-291-8060	27
Theatre on the Run	3700 S Four Mile Run Dr	703-228-1850	39
Thomas Jefferson Community Center	3501 2nd St S	703-228-5920	37
Warehouse Theater	1021 7th St NW	202-234-7174	10
Warner Theatre	513 13th St NW	202-783-4000	1
West End Dinner Theatre	4615 Duke St	703-370-2500 x3	41
Woolly Mammoth Theatre	917 M St NW	202-289-2443	10

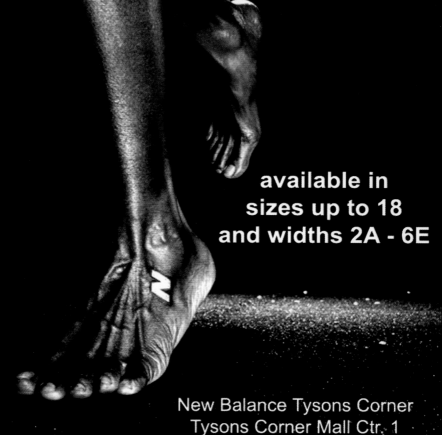

Eating well in D.C.

Restaurant Finder is an online restaurant database with more than 2000 entries.

Ratings and comments made by D.C. locals give you the real dish on District food.

Search for your perfect-fit restaurant by cuisine, location,
price, and almost anything else you can think of.

Restaurant Finder

washingtoncitypaper.com

D.C. readers count on the *Washington City Paper* to let them know what's going on in the District.
Now that includes restaurants: restaurants.washingtoncitypaper.com.

News. Talk. Culture.

News. Local stories that captivate the greater Washington community, distinguished international and national coverage that brings the world to you. **Talk.** Engaging conversations with today's newsmakers on the issues that matter; community, politics, health, science and the arts. **Culture.** Championing the local arts community through stories, features, previews and reviews; revealing the latest trends in the world of arts and the best in traditional American music.

WAMU 88.5 FM AMERICAN UNIVERSITY RADIO

WAMU 88.5 FM is your listener-supported NPR station in the nation's capital, delivering intelligent radio for busy people. Every day we offer international, national and locally produced news, talk and cultural programs from our own studios as well as National Public Radio, British Broadcasting Corporation and Public Radio International. Listen, learn and enjoy.

www.wamu.org

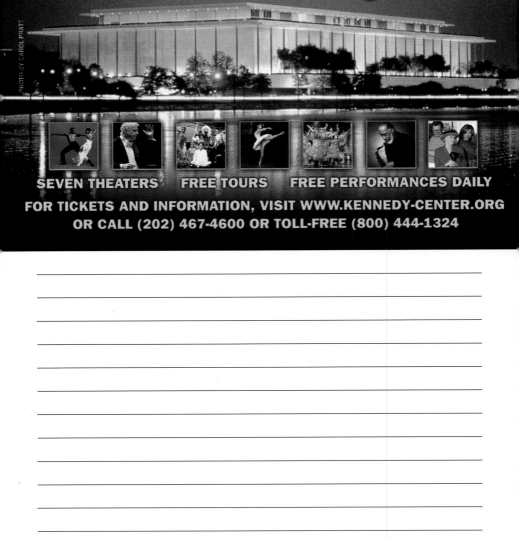

The John F. Kennedy Center for the Performing Arts

SEVEN THEATERS   FREE TOURS   FREE PERFORMANCES DAILY

FOR TICKETS AND INFORMATION, VISIT WWW.KENNEDY-CENTER.ORG

OR CALL (202) 467-4600 OR TOLL-FREE (800) 444-1324

Street Index

Washington

Street	Page	Grid
1st Ave	6	B2/C2
1st Ave SW	2	C2
1st Pl NE		
(2100-2121)	11	B1
(4400-5924)	14	A1/B1
1st Pl NW		
(1100-1199)	11	C1
(5400-5649)	14	A1
1st St NE		
(1-5510)	14	A1/B1
(51-832)	2	A2/B2
(833-1999)	11	B1/C1
1st St NW		
(100-849)	2	A2/B2
(850-2812)	11	A1/B1/C1
(2813-5549)	14	A1/C1
(5758-6699)	26	C1
1st St SE		
(1-249)	2	C2
(250-599)	5	A1
(900-4550)	6	A2/B2
1st St SW	6	A2/B2/C2
1st Ter NW	11	C1
20th St NE		
(200-849)	4	A2/B2
(850-4499)	13	A1/B1/C1
20th St NW		
(100-949)	7	A2/B2
(950-2349)	9	A1/B1/C1
(2350-2499)	16	C1
21st Pl NE	13	C2
21st St NE		
(200-898)	4	A2/B2
(890-1149)	12	C2
(1150-4399)	13	A2
21st St NW		
(100-986)	7	A2/B2
(987-1749)	9	B1/C1
22nd St NE	4	B2
(900-1899)	12	A2/C2
(2400-4399)	13	A2/B2/C2
22nd St NW		
(100-899)	7	A2/B2
(490-1760)	9	B1/C1
22nd St SE	4	C2
23rd Pl NE	4	B2
23rd St NW		
(100-949)	7	A1/B1
(950-2099)	9	A1/B1/C1
24th Pl NE	13	C2
24th St NE		
(400-2399)	4	A2/B2
(1700-1899)	12	A2
(2501-4099)	13	A2/B2/C2
24th St NW		
(500-5074)	7	A1
(1001-9228)	9	C1
(1700-2099)	8	A2
(2500-2558)	16	C1
25th Pl NE	13	A2/C2
25th St NE	13	B2
25th St NW		
(650-964)	7	A1
(965-1299)	8	C2
26th St NE	13	A2/B2/C2
26th St NW		
(800-949)	7	A1
(950-5749)	8	B2/C2
27th St NE	13	B2
27th St NW		
(1200-1599)	8	B2/C2
(2700-5299)	17	A2/B2
(5300-5749)	28	C2
28th Pl NW		
(4000-4099)	20	C2
(6300-6399)	28	B2
28th St	13	A2
28th St NE	13	B2/C2
28th St NW		
(1200-1699)	8	B2/C2
(2500-2999)	17	B2/C2
(4500-5349)	20	B2
(5350-6099)	28	B2/C2
29th Pl NW		
(2800-2899)	17	B2
(4600-4799)	20	B1
(6300-6399)	28	B2
29th St NW		
(1001-1699)	8	B2/C2
(2601-3499)	17	A2/B2/C2
(4000-5399)	20	A2/B2/C2
(5500-6299)	28	B2/C2
2nd Ave	6	C2
2nd Ave SW		
(100-257)	2	C1
(258-499)	6	A2
2nd Pl NW	27	C2
2nd Pl SE	5	A1/B1
2nd St NE		
(1-849)	3	A1/B1/C1
(850-2599)	11	A1/B1/C1
(4200-5649)	14	B1
2nd St NW		
(200-2341)	11	A1/B1/C1
(550-849)	2	A1/B2
(4200-5549)	14	A1/B1
(5650-6399)	27	C2
(6600-6754)	26	C1
2nd St SE		
(200-1199)	3	C1
(200-1199)	5	A1/B1
2nd St SW	6	B2/C2
30th Pl NE	13	A2/C2
30th Pl NW		
(4900-5449)	20	A1
(5450-5599)	28	C2
30th St NE	13	B2/C2
30th St NW		
(1000-2249)	8	B2/C2
(2250-3549)	17	A2/C2
(3550-5425)	20	A1/B1
(5426-6399)	28	B2/C2
31st Pl NE	13	A2
31st Pl NW		
(2700-5908)	17	B1
(5909-6699)	28	B2
31st St	13	A2
31st St NE	13	C2
31st St NW		
(900-2649)	8	B1/B2/C2
(2850-5425)	20	B1
(5426-7099)	28	A2/B2/C2
32nd Pl NW	28	B2
32nd St NW		
(1500-1749)	8	B1
(2750-3099)	17	B1
(4500-5360)	20	A1/B1
(5361-6999)	28	A2/B2/C2
33rd Pl NW		
(2900-3499)	17	A1/B1
(3700-3799)	20	C1
33rd St NW		
(1000-1699)	8	B1/C1
(5100-5199)	20	A1
(5400-6999)	28	A2/B1/C1
34th Pl NW		
(2700-3449)	17	B1
(3450-6099)	28	B1
34th St NW		
(1020-1799)	8	B1/C1
(2750-3457)	17	A1/B1
(3458-5199)	20	A1/C1
35th Pl NW		
(1900-1999)	8	A1
(2700-2799)	17	B1
35th St NW		
(1200-2099)	8	A1/B1/C1
(2700-3399)	17	A1/B1
(3500-4499)	20	B1/C1
36th Pl NW	18	A2/B2
36th St NW		
(1200-1499)	8	B1/C1
(1600-3460)	18	A2/B2/C2
(3461-3599)	19	C2
(4301-5299)	20	A1/B1
37th St NW		
(1200-2547)	18	B2/C2
(3500-4399)	19	B2/C2
38th St NW		
(1600-3449)	18	A2/B2/C2
(3450-5255)	19	A2/B2/C2
(5256-5399)	20	A1
39th Pl NW	18	B2
39th St NW		
(1600-5410)	19	A2/B2/C2
(1691-3550)	18	A2/B2
(5411-5711)	28	C1
3rd Ave	6	B2/C2
3rd Ave SW		
(100-249)	2	C1
(250-399)	6	A2
3rd Pl NW	14	A1
3rd St NE		
(1-849)	3	A1/B1/C1
(850-2699)	11	A2/B2/C2
(5200-5635)	14	A2
3rd St NW		
(1-849)	2	A1/B1
(850-2099)	11	B1/C1
(3900-5506)	14	A1/B1
(5850-6799)	27	B2/C2
3rd St SE		
(1-249)	3	C1
(250-1199)	5	A1/B1
3rd St SW		
(400-1499)	6	A2/B2
40th Pl NW	18	A2/B2
40th St NW		
(2200-2499)	18	B2
(4200-4699)	19	B2
41st Pl NW	29	C2
41st St NW		
(2300-2699)	18	B2
(4200-5411)	19	A2/B2/C2
(5412-5609)	28	C1
42nd Pl NW	19	A1
42nd St NW		
(2200-2749)	18	B2
(2750-5415)	19	A1/B1/C1
(5416-5499)	29	C2
43rd Pl NW	19	A1/B1
43rd St NW		
(2900-3099)	18	A2
(4200-5399)	19	A1/B1/C1
44th Pl NW	18	A1
44th St NW		
(1400-3299)	18	A1/B1/C2
(3900-5399)	19	A1/B1/C1
45th St NW		
(1607-3449)	18	A1/C1/C2
(3800-5299)	19	A1/B1/C1
46th St NW		
(2200-2299)	18	B1
(4100-5099)	19	A1/B1/C1
47th Pl NW	18	C1
47th St NW		
(1900-2299)	18	B1
(3800-5099)	30	A2/B2/C2
48th Pl NW	18	B1
48th St NW		
(2000-2399)	18	B1
(3700-4999)	30	A2/B2/C2
49th St NW		
(2100-3613)	18	A1/B1
(3614-4799)	30	B2/C2
4th Ave	6	B2/C2
4th Pl SW	6	A2
4th St NE		
(1-849)	3	A1/B1/C1
(850-2849)	11	A2/B2/C2
(2850-5522)	14	A2/C2
4th St NW		
(1-849)	2	A1/B1
(850-2149)	11	B1/C1
(2213-2499)	15	C2
(3800-5049)	14	A1/B1
(5550-5661)	21	A2
(5850-6999)	27	B2/C2
4th St SE		
(1-261)	3	C1
(262-3955)	5	A1/B1
4th St SW	2	C1
4th St SW		
(200-1499)	6	A2/B2
50th Pl NW	30	B2
50th St NW	30	B2
51st Pl NW	32	A2
51st St NW	30	C2
52nd Ct NW	30	B2
52nd St NW	30	B2/C2
52nd Ter NW	30	C2
5th Ave	6	B2/C2
5th St NE		
(1-849)	3	A1/B1/C1
(850-2849)	11	A2/B2/C2

Silver Spring

Street Index

Street Index

Street	Page	Grid
N Quaker Ln		
(1-1317)	42	A2/B2
(1318-1911)	39	B2/C2
S Quaker Ln		
(1-198)	42	C2
(1913-1999)	39	B2/C2
Quantrell Ave	41	B1
Quay St	46	A2
Queen St	46	A1/A2
Quincy St	41	C2
Radford St	39	C2
(1300-1648)	42	A2
Raleigh Ave		
(4100-4444)	42	B1
(4445-4699)	41	C2
Ramsey Aly	46	A2
Ramsey St	44	A2
E Randolph Ave	43	B2
Rapidan Ct	41	B1
Ravens Worth Pl	39	C2
Rayburn Ave	41	A1
E Raymond Ave	43	B2
Reading Ave	41	A1
Reed Ave	43	B2
Regency Pl	41	B2
Reinekers Ln	44	B2
S Reynolds St	41	C1
Rhoades Pl	41	B2
Richards Ln	43	C1
Richenbacher Ave	41	B2
Richmarr Pl	41	B2
Richmond Hwy	46	C1
Richmond Ln	43	B1
Ricketts Walk	41	B1
Riddle Walk	41	B1
Ridge Ln	44	B1
Ridge Road Dr	43	B1/C1
N Ripley St	41	B1
Ripon Pl	39	C2
Rivergate Pl	45	B2
Roan Ln	42	A2
Roberts Ct	44	B1
Roberts Ln	44	B1
Robinson Ct	44	A1
Rolfe Pl	45	A1
Roosevelt St	42	A2
E Rosemont Ave	44	B2
W Rosemont Ave	44	B1/B2
Ross Aly	46	A2
N Rosser St	38	C1
Roth St	42	C2
Roundhouse Ln	46	B1
N Royal St		
(100-349)	46	A2
(350-1299)	45	B2/C2
S Royal St	46	B2/C2
Rucker Pl	44	A1
Ruffner Rd	43	C1
Russell Rd		
(1-1549)	44	A1/B2
(1550-3999)	43	A2/B1/C1
Rutland Pl	41	B2
N Saint Asaph St		
(100-356)	46	A2
(357-999)	45	B2/C2
S Saint Asaph St	46	B2/C2
Sanborn Pl	43	B2
Sanford St	43	B2
Sanger Ave	41	A1/B1
Saxony Sq	41	B1
Saylor Pl	42	B1
N Scott St	38	C1
Scroggins Rd	42	A2
Seminary Rd		
(2554-4449)	42	A1
(4550-5099)	41	A2
Sharp Pl	42	B1
N Shelley St	38	C1
Shooters Ct	44	B1
Shop Dr	42	A1
Shorter Ln	43	A1
Sibley St	41	A1
Skyhill Rd	42	B2
Skyline Village Ct	38	C2
Slaters Ln	45	A1/A2
Small St	43	C1
Somervelle St	41	C2
South St	46	C1
South View Ter	44	B1
E Spring St	44	A2
St John Pl	38	C1
St Stephens Rd	42	A1/B1
Stadium Dr	42	A1
Stanton Ln	41	C1
Stanton Pl	41	C1
Sterling Ave	42	B2
Stevens St	38	C1
Stevenson Ave	41	C1
Stewart Ave	43	B2
Stonebridge Rd	41	A2
Stonewall Rd	43	C1
Stonnell Pl	42	A2
Stovall St	44	C1
Strathblane Pl	41	B2
Strutfield Ln	38	C2
Summers Ct	44	A1
Summers Dr	44	A1
Summit Ave		
(700-1149)	43	B1
(1150-2799)	39	C2
Sunset Dr	44	B2
Surry Pl	41	B2
Suter St	44	B2
Sutton Pl	41	B2
Swann Ave	43	B2
Sweeley St	42	C2
Swift Aly	46	A2
Sycamore St	43	B2
Sylvan Ct	42	B1
Taft Ave	42	B1
Talbot Pl	41	B2
Tancil Ct	45	C2
Taney Ave		
(3900-4449)	42	B1
(4450-5499)	41	B1/B2
Taylor Ave	43	B1
Taylor Dr	42	C2
Taylor Run Pky E		
(1-150)	44	B1
(401-1199)	42	B2
Taylor Run Pky W	42	B2/C2
Telegraph Rd		
(122-129)	44	B1
(130-7323)	42	C2
Templeton Pl	42	B1
Tennessee Ave	43	A1/B2
Terrace Ct	38	C2
Terrace Dr	38	C2
Terrett Ave	43	B2
N Terrill St	41	B2
Terry Pl	42	B1
The Strand	46	B2
Thomas St	43	C1
Thompsons Aly	46	A2
Thomsen Ln	42	A1
Timber Branch Dr	43	C1
E Timber Branch Pky		
(401-498)	44	A1
(601-999)	43	C1
W Timber Branch Pky		
(899-998)	42	A2
(432-898)	43	C1
Tivoli Passage	45	C2
Tobacco Quay	45	C2
Torrey Pl	42	B2
N Tracy St	38	C1
Trinity Dr	42	B1/B2
Truesdale Dr	44	C2
Truman Ave	41	B2
Tuckahoe Ln	42	A2
Tull Pl	41	C2
Tulsa Pl	42	B1
Tupelo Pl	42	B1
Turner Ave	43	B2
Tyler Pl	43	B1
Uhler Ave	43	B2
W Uhler Ter	43	B1
Uline Ave	42	B1
Underhill Pl	43	B1
Underwood Pl	42	B1
N Union St		
(100-374)	46	A2
(375-499)	45	C2
S Union St	46	B2/C2
Upland Pl	44	B1
Usher Ave	42	B1
Usher Ct	42	B1
Utica Ave	42	B1
N Vail St	41	B2
Valley Cir	42	A2
Valley Dr		
(1098-2454)	43	A1
(2300-3760)	42	A2
(2423-3726)	39	B2/C2
Valley Forge Dr	41	C2
N Van Dorn St		
(300-4798)	41	A2/B1/B2
(2569-2699)	39	C1
S Van Dorn St	41	C1
Vassar Pl	42	B2
Vassar Rd	42	B2
Venable Ave	41	C2
Vermont Ave		
(3901-4412)	42	B1
(4413-6129)	41	C2
Vermont Ct	42	B1
Vernon St	45	B1
Victoria Ln	42	A1
N View Ter	44	A1/B1
W View Ter	44	A1
Viewpoint Rd	42	B2
Virginia Ave	43	B1
Wales Aly	46	B2
S Walker St	41	C1
Walleston Ct	42	B2
E Walnut St	44	A2
W Walnut St	44	B1
Waple Ln	41	C2
Washington Cir	43	B1
Washington Ct	38	B2
Washington St	46	
Washington Way	46	A2
Water Pl	45	B2
Waterford Pl	46	B2
Watkins Mill Dr	42	C1
Wayne St	44	A2
Wellington Rd	43	B1
Wesmond Dr	43	B2
N West St		
(100-349)	46	A1
(350-899)	45	B1/C1
S West St	46	A1/B1
Westminster Pl	43	B1
Wharf St	46	C2
Wheeler Ave		
(3500-3599)	38	C1
(3600-4099)	42	C1
Whiskey Ln	42	C1
White Post Ct	42	C1
S Whiting St	41	C1
Wild Turkey Ln	42	C2
Wilkes St	46	B1/B2
Williamsburg St	42	C2
Wilson Ave	43	B2
E Windsor Ave	43	C2
W Windsor Ave	43	C1/C2
Winston Ct	41	A1
Witter St	42	C2
Wolfe St	46	B1/B2
Woodbine St	39	C2
Woodland Ter	43	B1/C1
Woodlawn Ct	42	C1
Woodmire Ln	38	C1
Woods Ave	42	A2
Woods Pl	42	A2
Wyatt Ave	43	B2
Wycklow Ct	41	B2
Wyndham Cir	39	C1
Wythe St	45	B1/C2
Yale Dr	42	B2
Yoakum Pky	41	C1

Arlington

Street	Page	Grid
1st Pl N		
(3150-3299)	37	B1
(5300-5399)	34	C1
1st Pl S		
(2500-2899)	37	B2
(4400-4499)	38	A2
1st Rd N	37	B1/B2
1st Rd S		
(2400-3799)	37	B1/B2
(4400-4499)	38	A2
1st St N		
(2900-3399)	37	B1/B2
(4700-4849)	38	A1/A2

Street Index